Nouvelle Théolo

Nouvelle Théologie – New Theology

Inheritor of Modernism, Precursor of Vatican II

Jürgen Mettepenningen

t&t clark

Published by T&T Clark International
A Continuum Imprint
The Tower Building, 11 York Road, London SE1 7NX
80 Maiden Lane, Suite 704, New York, NY 10038

www.continuumbooks.com

British Library Cataloguing-in-Publication Data
A catalogue record for this book is available from the British Library

ISBN :   978–0–567–03409–0 (Hardback)
           978–0–567–03410–6 (Paperback)

Typeset by Pindar NZ, Auckland, New Zealand
Printed and bound in Great Britain by CPI Antony Rowe Ltd, Chippenham, Wiltshire

To my wife Els and our daughter Gloria

CONTENTS

PART II: PHASES/FACES OF THE *NOUVELLE THÉOLOGIE* PRIOR
TO VATICAN II

ACKNOWLEDGEMENTS

This book is the result of a great deal of work, a multitude of contacts, and above all an abundance of grace and opportunity.

I learned about the *nouvelle théologie* and its themes while preparing my doctoral dissertation on the debate that raged in the 1930s and 1940s in the French-speaking part of Western Europe on the nature and methods of theology. More particularly, in my dissertation I presented and commented on the contribution of the Dutch Jesuit Piet Schoonenberg and his own understanding and approach to the question. But my thirst for knowledge relating to the *nouvelle théologie* remained unsated and finally resulted in the present book, a work that moves beyond my dissertation yet continues to recognize its roots therein. For this reason, an initial word of gratitude is due to the promoter of my dissertation, Leo Kenis, who became an intellectual sparring partner in the process of guiding my dissertation, not in the least because he did not always share my vision with respect to the *nouvelle théologie*.

An academic is enriched by reading and sparring partners. The privilege of having an office in the Maurits Sabbe Library, the renowned library of the Faculty of Theology of the K.U.Leuven, ensured access to an almost endless supply of literature. My thanks are due, therefore, to the librarian Étienne D'hondt and the staff of the library for the countless treasures they preserve with enormous care. Thanks go as well to a number of archivists who were kind enough to permit me access to many different archives in France, Belgium and the Netherlands. In addition to being granted access to literature and archives, I was also granted access to the thoughts of a number of historians and theologians in many enriching conversations that provided the opportunity to put my own insights to the test: Hans Boersma (Vancouver), Erik Borgman (Tilburg), Leo Declerck (Louvain), Ward De Pril (Louvain), Anthony Dupont (Louvain), Étienne Fouilloux (Lyon), Wim François (Louvain), Lieve Gevers (Louvain), Marcel Gielis (Utrecht/Tilburg), Anthony Godzieba (Villanova), Gerd-Rainer Horn (Warwick), Leo Kenis (Louvain), Mathijs Lamberigts (Louvain), William L. Portier (Dayton), Michael Quisinsky (Geneva), Herwi Rikhof (Utrecht/Tilburg) and Karim Schelkens (Louvain).

It is only possible to work efficiently in an agreeable and professional context. In addition to the members of the research unit of History of Church and Theology of the Louvain theological faculty, I would like to thank the group of scholars who participated in the research project 'Orthodoxy: Process and Product' and its successor 'The Normativity of History'. A special word of gratitude is due to the three professors who continue to give leadership to this interdisciplinary group: Lieven Boeve, Mathijs Lamberigts and Terrence

Merrigan. Besides my Louvain colleagues, I would like to offer a special word of thanks to Jos Aelvoet, the director of the 'Belgian House' at the Cité Internationale Universitaire de Paris in Paris, where I had the pleasure of staying from March to October 2009 while conducting research in a variety of archives.

Outside my professional framework, a great deal of thanks is due to my wife Els Vermeiren for the love, support and freedom she gave me to work on this book. She and our daughter Gloria are my most precious treasures. They know that their love is reciprocated.

Last but not least: this book would not have been possible were it not for the support of the 'Research Foundation – Flanders' (my research framework), Brian Doyle (the translator), John Dick (the copy editor) and Thomas Kraft of Continuum/T&T Clark (the publisher). Many thanks!

Jürgen Mettepenningen
Louvain – Paris
2009

INTRODUCTION

What can possibly be new about theology? Such is the question that comes to mind when one reads the expression *nouvelle théologie* ('new theology'): the theological movement from the 1930s, 40s and 50s that was to set the tone for the Catholic theology of the Second Vatican Council, although it took a council to give the movement a positive connotation after three decades of magisterial rejection. Surprisingly enough, an age-old and venerable religious order stands at the basis of this *nouvelle théologie*. The contribution of several Dominicans was indeed innovative: before, during and after the Second World War, they called for a theology that was oriented towards the sources of the Christian faith and not (exclusively) towards a system based on scholasticism. In short, theology needed to restore its contact with the living reality of faith, and Dominicans such as Marie-Dominique Chenu, Yves Congar and Henri-Marie Féret were at the forefront of this appeal. In order to achieve this goal, theologians had to become aware of the urgent need to refresh theology's bonds with history, more specifically with the thought of Thomas Aquinas himself and not (only) with what others had made of it. To draw from the well of history is to return to the true sources of the faith and thereby transform the faith into the living object of theology.

In addition to the French Dominicans, the French Jesuits were also renowned representatives of the *nouvelle théologie*, particularly in the 1940s when they pioneered a *ressourcement* that was to lead to a 'source theology'. Figures such as Henri Bouillard, Jean Daniélou and especially Henri de Lubac did a great deal to lead theology beyond the meta-historical. In spite of rejection by their superiors and by the magisterium, the core of their aspirations was to be assimilated during Vatican II at which the sources of the faith served as the primary basis for Catholic theology and neo-scholasticism was dethroned.

The goal of the present volume is to chart the development of the *nouvelle théologie*. It thus hopes to offer a contribution to the history of twentieth-century theology, especially of the generation of theologians who formed the bridge between the crisis of Modernism and the Second Vatican Council. It was this generation's endeavour to renew Catholic theology – and thus the prevailing neo-scholasticism – from within and that makes it so unique, having inherited Modernism and then laying some of the foundations for Vatican II. Its uniqueness is reflected in the enormous present-day interest in the life, work and significance of the said theologians.

The time is not yet ripe for an exhaustive account. When research into the building blocks is still underway, one should not cherish the pretention of being able to offer a synthesis or full story. It is for this reason that we must insist that the research results offered in these pages represent an interim report of the work that is still being done on the *nouvelle théologie*. The goal of the present volume is thus to introduce the reader into the most important building blocks, into the specificity and development of this intellectual movement. In short, we want to present the most important aspects of the *nouvelle théologie*. The fact that the book requires supplementation and remains open to nuancing and critique goes without saying.

We present the reader a theological-historical reconstruction of the genesis and evolution of the *nouvelle théologie*, whereby the first part of the book serves as a detailed introduction to the second.

In Part I, we explore the origins of the concept of *nouvelle théologie* and of its content. We then offer some insights into the theological background and context of the theological reform movement in the period from 1935 to 1965. We conclude Part I with an overview of the four phases in the evolution of the *nouvelle théologie*, an overview that serves as framework for what will be treated in Part II of the book.

In Part II, we explore the first three phases of the *nouvelle théologie* on the basis of its most important representatives. For the first phase we examine contributions from the French Dominicans Chenu, Congar and Féret, the Belgian Dominican Louis Charlier and the Belgian academic René Draguet. It will become clear at this juncture that the first phase of the *nouvelle théologie* is dominated by the Dominicans. The first chapter of Part II is concluded with a survey of a number of additional contributions to the debate on the specificity and method of theology (Jean-François Bonnefoy, Marie-Rosaire Gagnebet, Yves Congar [revisited], Dominicus De Petter and Charles Boyer). In the second chapter, the Jesuits take pride of place. Here we focus on the work of Bouillard, Daniélou and de Lubac. Based on our discussion of Henri de Lubac and his work, we examine the course of the debate on the *nouvelle théologie* both inside and outside the Jesuit order, an account that reaches its conclusion in 1950 with de Lubac's enforced move to Paris, the promulgation of *Humani generis* by Pope Pius XII and the circular letter despatched by the Jesuit general exhorting the society's members to caution in their thought, teaching and publication. While French *nouvelle théologie* was gagged around 1950, the movement expanded into new territories. In the third chapter we explore the case study of the Low Countries, focusing our attention on the Dominican Edward Schillebeeckx and the Jesuit Piet Schoonenberg, both influenced by the French developments of the *nouvelle théologie* and promoters thereof.

Given that the goal of the present volume is to offer a portrait of the *nouvelle théologie* as the inheritor of Modernism and one of the precursors of Vatican II, the fourth phase of the *nouvelle théologie* (which took place during the Council and has to do with its assimilation by the Council Fathers) is only dealt with in brief in the third chapter of Part I and in the closing considerations.

Our historical survey is based on a large number of sources. In addition to a considerable amount of secondary literature, we have drawn in the first instance on the publications of the authors under discussion as well as on archive material. We have chosen to base ourselves in the present study on original texts, i.e. documents in French, English, German, Dutch, Italian and Latin. The bibliography makes reference to English translations where these are available. Personal discussions have also been a source of insight, although complete agreement with our dialogue partners was not always attained.

It is our hope that the results of our research will be of service to the ongoing study of the *nouvelle théologie*.

In the process of writing this book, the words written in 1954 by the renowned French historian Henri-Irénée Marrou were never far from our thoughts: 'History and the historian are inseparable' (from *De la connaissance historique*, Paris: Seuil). The considerations and reconstruction found in the present book are indeed the 'work of human hands', the result of personal study and personal choices (including the subdivision of the *nouvelle théologie* into four phases). But the words of Étienne Fouilloux, entrusted to me on 18 December 2008, have also remained by my side: 'A theologian should never lose sight of history', words with which I completely agree.

PART I

CONCEPT, CONTENT, CONTEXT, CONTOURS

Chapter 1

NOUVELLE THÉOLOGIE: CONCEPT AND CONTENT

Our exploration of the *nouvelle théologie* begins with the concept itself: how did a theological movement situated in the 1930s, 40s and 50s come to acquire the designation *nouvelle théologie*? Our first chapter goes on to discuss the content behind the concept: what does the banner '*nouvelle théologie*' ultimately represent? The answer to both questions is intended to introduce the reader to the theme of the present volume and to its preliminary chapters.

1.1 *The Origins of a Concept and Its Evolution into a Proper Name*

Nouvelle théologie, an expression that can be translated into every language, has a long and often complex history, but one in which its representative function is not always clear. The French translation of Jan Sperna Weiland's Dutch book *Oriëntatie* (1966), for example, is entitled *La nouvelle théologie*, although it does not deal with any of the individuals who have a prominent role to play in the present volume.[1] Much earlier, in 1919, Étienne Gilson described the thought of Thomas Aquinas as 'nouvelle théologie'.[2] Twelve years earlier, in 1907, George Tyrrell distinguished in his turn between old theology and new theology,[3] while Reginald John Campbell published a book entitled *The New Theology* in precisely the same year, stating that a number of people considered him its 'exponent' and indeed the inventor of 'both the name and the thing'.[4]

Evidence of new theology as a theological movement, however, is not confined to the twentieth century. The letters of Paul, for example, already affirm a 'new theology' based on Jesus' 'new teaching – with authority' (Mk 1.27), to which the 'New Testament' ultimately bears witness. The predicate 'new theology' can also be employed for the theological vision of Martin Luther. Indeed, every paradigm shift in the history of theology would appear to go hand in hand, almost by definition, with the emergence of a new theology. The latter implies a metamorphosis – a process of shedding skin, of engaging in self-correction and self-rediscovery – whereby a new definitive and broadly supported profile in theology comes to the fore.[5] The uniqueness and methodology of such theological profiles tend to be central: what is theology and how should it be practised?

The expression *nouvelle théologie* is used today almost exclusively as a technical designation for the theological movement associated with the period between c. 1935 and 1960. The expression tends to be left untranslated, bearing in mind that the movement's core is to be located in France and Belgium. While designations such as the German *Neue Theologie* or the English *New Theology* obviously have a right to exist, theological historiography would appear nevertheless to prefer the French *nouvelle théologie*, an expression maintained in the majority of theological dictionaries and encyclopaedias.

The first to employ the expression *nouvelle théologie* to describe the theological movement was not a Frenchman, however, but an Italian by the name of Pietro Parente, Secretary to the Holy Office in 1965 – although already from 1959 onwards the right hand of Alfredo Ottaviani at the head of the Holy Office – and future cardinal (1967). In *L'Osservatore Romano*, the Church's daily newspaper, Parente published an article in 1942 in which he critically assessed and ultimately condemned the 'nouvelle théologie'.[6] The article was occasioned by Rome's condemnation of two works on the nature of theology and in particular its method, and their relegation to the *Index Librorum Prohibitorum*, i.e. the Church's list of forbidden books.[7] Two years prior to the publication of Parente's article, Mariano Cordovani, Pius XII's personal theologian, spoke about 'modern theology' during a conference for candidate priests at the Angelicum, the Dominican order's house of studies in Rome, in which he warned against the dangers of these 'nuove tendenze teologiche' or 'new theological tendencies'. Symbolically enough, the Feast of Saint Thomas – in those days March 7 – served as the context for Cordovani's presentation, which was published later in article form in *L'Osservatore Romano* and in *Angelicum*, the journal of the Roman Dominicans.[8] It is hardly accidental that the title of Parente's contribution to *L'Osservatore* echoed Cordovani's opinion.

Four years after the appearance of Parente's article, the most important voice of the magisterium itself adopted the expression 'new theology'. On 17 September 1946, Pope Pius XII condemned the 'nova theologia' in an address given to the authorities of the Jesuit order.[9] He observed in his – Latin – address that enough had been said about the *nouvelle théologie* and that it was time to draw the discussion to a close. A few days later, he addressed the superiors of the Dominican order, urging them along similar lines to focus more attention on the *nouvelle théologie*'s antidote, namely Thomism.[10]

In the same year as the two papal addresses, Réginald Garrigou-Lagrange, an authoritative and influential Roman Dominican, penned an article on the *nouvelle théologie*, which did not appear in print until February 1947 in *Angelicum*. The French expression *nouvelle théologie* had now entered the public forum and became definitive. Garrigou-Lagrange posed a question in the title of his article: 'La nouvelle théologie où va-t-elle?' (Where is the *nouvelle théologie* leading us?).[11] His answer was unequivocal: 'The *nouvelle théologie* will lead us back to Modernism.'[12] His claim could not have been more pejorative as far as *nouvelle théologie* was concerned. After all, a resurgence of Modernism implied the revival of 'the collection of all heresies', as Pope Pius X had described Modernism in the encyclical *Pascendi dominici gregis* (1907).[13] In 1950, a little more than 40 years later, Pius XII made similar use of the vigour of an encyclical in an effort to banish the movement to theological wastebasket, albeit without referring to it by name. Promulgated on 12 August 1950, *Humani generis* gave expression to the Pope's concern, among other things, for the authenticity of theology and firmly rejected the new tendencies referred to by Cordovani and Parente as betraying and violating the truth of the faith.[14] Both Pius IX's and Pius X's anti-modern(ist) thinking are clearly hovering in the background at this juncture, enough to make one wonder whether the date on the official text of *Humani generis* in the *Acta Apostolicae Sedis* – 1850 instead of 1950 – was an accident or not . . . [15]

The unrest brought about by French theological developments in the second half of the 1940s led to a number of developments endeavouring to establish a clear picture of the problem as well as the polemic to which it had given rise.

Against the background of an internal investigation into the Jesuit order and the vigorous reactions in Lyon to the article of Garrigou-Lagrange (see Part II, Chapter 2 in this volume), the Secretariat of the French Bishops put together a triptych of articles in an effort to clarify matters. In the first half of 1947, these three extended notas were published, providing a *status questionis* on the various positions[16] and using the expression *nouvelle théologie* as a key concept. The French bishops and nuntius – Giuseppe Roncalli, later to be Pope John XXIII – now had access to the problem, its diversity and its various representatives.

In addition to the French episcopate, the academic world also let itself be heard. In 1947, the German Hugo Rahner – brother of Karl Rahner – published an article in the Swiss periodical *Orientierung* entitled 'Wege zu einer "neuen" Theologie?', which served as the first 'foreign' overview of the *nouvelle théologie*.[17] The article was immediately summarized by a Dutch periodical and published under the French title '*La nouvelle théologie*'.[18] In line with Rahner's article, many other attempts were made to chart the controversial developments associated with the *nouvelle théologie*, thus granting the concept increasing acceptance. The editors of numerous periodicals and journals were confronted with the need to inform their readership about the *nouvelle théologie*, with or without critical commentary. In 1947, for example, Philip J. Donnelly introduced the expression 'new theology' as the equivalent of *nouvelle théologie* in the first English language survey of the French theological developments,[19] but the English expression never caught on, not even after the publication of James M. Connolly's *The Voices of France* (1961) and John Auricchio's *The Future of Theology* (1970).[20] In 1948, Aloïs van Rijen published an article which introduced the Dutch translation of the expression *nouvelle théologie*: 'nieuwe theologie'.[21] In 1949, the Spanish periodical *Revista Española di teologia* published a virtual catalogue of no less than 353 works, which its author Avelino Esteban Romero considered to be contributions to the 'teología nueva'. The Spanish translation of *nouvelle théologie* thus made its entrance.[22]

In spite of the Latin, German, Dutch, Spanish and English equivalents, the French expression continued to prevail and international authors continued to prefer it to proposed local variants.

On the eve of the Second Vatican Council, the expression *nouvelle théologie* was thus quite familiar. The implicit 'rehabilitation' of the *nouvelle théologie* during Vatican II was ultimately to attract increased attention to the concept, ascribing to it a different set of connotations and appraising it in a different way. A significant example in this regard is the differing description of the lemma '*nouvelle théologie*' to be found in the second and third editions of the authoritative German theological dictionary *Lexikon für Theologie und Kirche*. In its second edition (1962) the lexicon described '*nouvelle théologie*' as a problematic expression since it referred to disparate phenomena related to tendencies in French Catholic theology.[23] Almost 40 years later, however, the third edition (1998) alludes to the originally negative connotation – its rejection by Rome – and its positive reception after Vatican II.[24] Indeed, the Council does appear to represent a moment of transformation in the reception of the *nouvelle théologie*. Not only were several representatives of the movement granted the opportunity to participate in the Council itself, but their influence, as we can see from the *acta* of the Council and different Council diaries, turned out to be quite considerable.

The expression *nouvelle théologie* may have been the invention of the doctrinal authorities designed to collectively describe and condemn a variety of theological aspirations but it finally became an apposite expression in the history of theology that transcended Rome's interpretation thereof. The explanation of the French lemma '*nouvelle théologie*' in a plethora of international theological dictionaries and encyclopaedias bears witness to this fact.[25]

In spite of its newly acquired positive connotation, the collective expression *nouvelle théologie* continued to be treated with caution and discussion on its use carried on unabated. In 2001, for example, Étienne Fouilloux argued from the historical perspective that the use of the expression *nouvelle théologie* could only be justified when used to describe the magisterium's endeavour to counter the ideas it represented in defence of its own position.[26] He further qualifies this usage by placing the expression between inverted commas. In so doing, he seems to uphold the negative or preconciliar connotation of the *nouvelle théologie*, reserving the expression for the Roman interpretation thereof. This cautious and, in my opinion, wise perspective, deserves additional comment. Indeed, the desire to do justice to each of the representatives of the *nouvelle théologie* should not lead to a denial of its existence. The magisterium's systematization of a movement is also a historical datum that ought to be accepted as a component of theological historiography. Fouilloux prefers not to use this systematization as a guiding principle in itself because it does not do justice to every representative of the *nouvelle théologie* (hence he employs the expression *théologie nouvelle* side by side with *nouvelle théologie*, the latter representing the Roman interpretation, the former representing the *nouvelle théologie* that transcends the Roman interpretation).[27] In addition to this justifiable concern, we must also account for the fact that the magisterium is the most important actor in the domain of Catholic theology, that doctrinal authority had pride of place therein at that time, and that *nouvelle théologie* has since become the dedicated expression for the movement in theological historiography. The fact that such a movement once existed will become evident in the remainder of the present volume and can be confirmed on the basis of a number of works, including those of Fouilloux.

While the use of the expression *nouvelle théologie* is inescapable today, it continues to require further qualification on every occasion. This is true for the interpretation thereof by the authorities of the Church prior to Vatican II as well as the postconciliar, positive interpretation thereof. Indeed, this latter approach already anticipated the concern to do justice to every representative of the *nouvelle théologie*. Right of access to archives and the availability of diaries kept by theologians, moreover, oblige us to differentiate where necessary and to avoid labels.

It should be noted that a distinction can be made between the expression *nouvelle théologie* and other so-called new theologies. Although both expressions are used in the present book as synonyms, '*nouvelle théologie*' has become a dedicated proper name while 'new theology' is a generic expression: the *nouvelle théologie* may be a new theology, but there are more 'new theologies' than the *nouvelle théologie*.

In what follows, I refer to the representatives of the *nouvelle théologie* as *new theologians*, translating the French 'nouveaux théologiens'.[28] In line with the overview presented above, however, I maintain the use of the French expression *nouvelle théologie* as a designation of the movement itself.

1.2 *The Content: What Does* Nouvelle Théologie *Stand For?*

While *nouvelle théologie* is to be understood as a cluster concept and the dedicated expression for a theological movement, the originally negative connotations surrounding it and the fact that its representatives were not always eager to identify themselves with the movement, make it difficult to provide an unambiguous description of the *nouvelle théologie*. This is likewise the case for the post Vatican II period. It seems appropriate at this juncture, therefore, that we examine the use of the expression by some of its own representatives.

In his *Situation et tâches présentes de la théologie*, published in 1967, Yves Congar states that he was frequently confronted with the impossibility of defining the *nouvelle théologie* in the period between 1946 and 1950.[29] For Congar, such a definition would have been as much a fancy as the *nouvelle théologie* itself. In 1975, Congar repeats a comparison he made in 1950: the *nouvelle théologie* is like a monster that does not exist, although its traces can be found wherever we look.[30] In 1985, Henri de Lubac likewise described the *nouvelle théologie* as a 'myth', as something that never existed.[31] Indeed, his conviction in this regard dates back as far as 1947, when he wrote in an 'examination of conscience' on his theological endeavours that he lacked the temperament to be a reformer, that he was even less inclined to the task of a renewer, and that he had never promoted the *nouvelle théologie*.[32] Likewise in 1947, de Lubac's confrere Henri Bouillard argued along similar lines that 'the creation of a *théologie nouvelle* was not something to which he pretended', a conviction he was to repeat with vehemence some three years later.[33] Here we see that *théologie nouvelle* and *nouvelle théologie* are used as synonyms.

We thus have statements from three prominent protagonists in which it is made clear that the *nouvelle théologie* is difficult to delineate or define, and that its very existence can even be called into question.

Do the opinions of Congar, de Lubac and Bouillard imply that theologians and theological dictionaries are labouring under a misapprehension when they suggest that the *nouvelle théologie* once existed? In my opinion, such a perspective would be far from accurate. Congar, de Lubac and Bouillard endeavoured to do justice to the uniqueness of their own contribution at a time in which the emphasis was on umbrella terms. In 1967, for example, Congar does not deny the existence of the *nouvelle théologie*, but he is unable, nevertheless, to find an appropriate and unequivocal definition thereof that might enjoy unanimous acceptance. While de Lubac may have denied the existence of the *nouvelle théologie* 20 years later, his denial should be seen against the background of the transformation he underwent during Vatican II and the 1960s: in the second half of the 1960s, a so-called conservative theology became authoritative for the Church (Joseph Ratzinger also experienced such a transformation[34]). While reference was being made to the *nouvelle théologie* as early as the 1940s, Bouillard, de Lubac and Congar clearly deny any involvement therein. In my opinion, however, it would be correct to ask whether such denials had not more to do with the desire to avoid the slurs and insinuations – and in the last analysis condemnation – associated with the *nouvelle théologie* at the time.

If we set the content of the vision of Bouillard, de Lubac and Congar to one side – we will discuss their visions in Part II – it remains evident that the individuals in question were reacting to something or endeavouring to correct something. In their opinion, the image they had acquired as representatives of the *nouvelle théologie* was in need of revision. According to Congar, the problem was related to the use of the definite article 'the': 'the' *nouvelle théologie*, he maintains, never existed. The expression cannot be described in generalizing terms and he denies any association with it. For Bouillard and de Lubac, on the other hand, the problem appears to be associated with the expression '*nouvelle théologie*' with the accent on the inverted commas, an expression that had acquired such a life of its own on the basis of ecclesial condemnation that it no longer corresponded to the historical reality of the 1940s. It is not insignificant, therefore, that a number of theologians experienced difficulties with the conceptualization and mythologization of the *nouvelle théologie* as a theological movement.

Bearing in mind the reservations expressed by Bouillard, de Lubac and Congar, it would be unwise for the present volume to take a strict definition of the *nouvelle théologie* as its point of departure. At the same time, however, it also makes little sense to deny that the *nouvelle théologie* ever existed. I opt therefore for a more moderate middle path, taking the historically well-founded hypothesis as our point of departure that this important theological movement did exist and that it acquired its name from its adversaries. My use of the expression *nouvelle théologie* will also endeavour to avoid value judgements. I presuppose *that* the movement once existed and focus my research on *the way it manifested itself.* I locate myself, therefore, on the same wavelength as present-day theology, accepting that *nouvelle théologie* is a theological move- ment to be located in the 1930s, 40s and 50s. The 'what' of this movement represents the research object of our theological-historical approach.

No research project of this kind can begin with a tabula rasa. A considerable amount of research has already been done on the theological history of the twentieth century, including the period from c. 1935 to 1960. The contributions of Étienne Fouilloux, Christoph Frey, Rosino Gibellini, Jean-Claude Petit, Mark Schoof, Tarcisus Tshibangu, Evangelista Vilanova, Raymond Winling and others bear witness to this fact.[35] Combining their research and my own, I plan to begin the present study with a number of generally accepted characteristic features associated with the *nouvelle théologie*, without, of course, reducing the movement to one or more of these features. I am convinced, nevertheless, that without the four characteristics I will presently sketch little if anything can be said about the *nouvelle théologie*. I consider these features to be central to the content of the '*nouvelle théologie*' concept. If our goal is to be able to see the wood for the trees, then it makes sense to begin by establishing the predominant colour of the leaves. We will devote ourselves in Part II of this book to doing justice to the different trees.

The first essential characteristic of the *nouvelle théologie* is the French language. While the movement may have spread into other language regions in the 1940s, its origins remain French. This does not need to imply, however, that the *nouvelle théologie* of the 1930s and 1940s was exclusive to France, since the first centre of the *nouvelle théologie* was located in the – French- speaking – southern part of Belgium. French as the language of the *nouvelle théologie* also seems to imply a reaction to Latin, the Church's universal language (the liturgy, papal documents, etc.). Future priests were formed in seminaries where their professors still used Latin handbooks. Of course, the theological endeavour was not exclusively conducted in the Latin language, as the abundance of vernacular journals established at the end of the nineteenth century and the beginning of the twentieth clearly testifies, like, for example, *Jahrbuch für Philosophie und spekulative Theologie* (1887), *Philosophisches Jahrbuch* (1888), *Revue thomiste* (1893), *La revue néo-scolastique* (1894, later *Revue philosophique de Louvain*), *Revue des sciences philosophiques et théologiques* (1907), *Rivista Italiana di filosofia neoscolastica* (1909),

Recherches de science religieuse (1910) and *Ciencia Tomista* (1910).

The embeddedness of the *nouvelle théologie* in the French-speaking area should not come as much of a surprise, however, if one bears in mind that the Modernist crisis likewise had its major roots in the French language. As such, the linguistic origins of the two major crises in Catholic theology between Vatican I and Vatican II were French. This reality, together with the precarious political situation in which French Catholicism found itself at the time, saw to it that (theological) developments in France were observed from Rome with considerable vigilance. In short, Rome could have suspected the potential revival of Modernism in the French-speaking world, in spite of its flat condemnation by the magisterium. Against this background, it should also come as no surprise that the *nouvelle théologie* was ultimately seen as just such a revival. While Modernism quite quickly became an international phenomenon, however, the *nouvelle théologie* remained French for a considerable number of years.

In addition to the original embeddedness of the *nouvelle théologie* in the French language, three additional characteristic features of the movement can be discerned at the level of content, thus forming a triptych of aspirations, the third of which being the logical consequence of the first two.

The endeavour to ascribe a worthy place to history within the theological endeavour is a characteristic feature of the *nouvelle théologie*. Up to this juncture, history had tended to take second place to theology's abstractions, theories and speculations. The word sequence employed in the expression 'Catholic theology', moreover, also had a role to play: first Catholic, then theology. The 'Catholic way of thinking' constituted the conceptual horizon and determined the degree of openness with respect to history. In other words, history was only given a place when it suited accepted Catholic theology. In practice, this implied that theologians took dogmas and other Roman texts as their point of departure, arriving at new faith insights by way of deduction that were completely compatible with existing and familiar tenets of the faith. The representatives of the *nouvelle théologie*, however, considered the time to be more than ripe to abandon such closed thinking and to resist an unworldly conceptual system that was determined to preserve itself whatever the cost. All things considered, the system in question did not take revelation seriously as a historical event: God made Himself known through human beings and as a human being (the incarnation). According to the *new theologians*, historical-critical research deserved to be recognized if one wanted to engage in theology in an authentic manner. Those who refused to integrate history into the practice of theology were ultimately adherents of a meta-historical system rather than an incarnated faith. This was in fact the primary critique addressed by the representatives of the *nouvelle théologie* to the prevailing Catholic theological establishment: it severed, or at least distorted the natural relationship between the Church and the world, between faith and life, between the sources of faith and theology.

A further characteristic feature can be added at this juncture, namely the appeal of a positive theology. Positive theology can be described as the search for the building blocks of theology in an exploration of the sources of faith, namely the Bible, liturgy and patristics. The representatives of the *nouvelle théologie* attached the same importance to this positive theological method as to the speculative method. In their opinion, all-embracing speculative theology had lost contact with (the) reality (of faith) to such a degree that a corrective manoeuvre had become necessary. The practice of speculative theology had deduction at its core, while positive theology arrived at its insights by way of induction. While the magisterium opted for the former rather than the latter, the representatives of the *nouvelle théologie* supported the complementarity of both theological approaches, i.e. a positive-speculative theology. The word order is similarly important at this juncture: valid contributions to Catholic theology can only be made thorough critical source analysis. One first has to search for building blocks before one can build. The *new theologians* thus devoted themselves to a *ressourcement*: a return to the sources of the faith. In addition to the Bible, liturgy and patristics, this also implied a return to the historical Thomas Aquinas, Catholic theology's authority par excellence. The *new theologians* lamented that the common practice of making reference to commentaries on Thomas from the sixteenth and seventeenth centuries had become sufficient in theology, while reference to the work of Thomas himself was often treated as secondary and rarely if ever considered more important. If theologians were to take the Doctor Angelicus seriously, the exponents of the *nouvelle théologie* argued, they would have to refer in the first instance to the man himself and to his own writings. This return to the thirteenth-century Thomas Aquinas served as the preparatory step and permanent support in a return to the sources of the faith. The paradox, of course, will already be clear: the *new theologians* were 'new' because they insisted on the return to the oldest sources of the faith.[36]

The fourth and final characteristic feature of the *nouvelle théologie* is its critical attitude towards neo-scholasticism, the specific and preferred form of speculative theology supported by the magisterium. The reduction of speculative theology to neo-scholastic theology had its roots in the understanding of neo-scholasticism as the exclusive antidote to modern thought. Against the background of a handbook tradition, the re-publication of many prominent commentaries on Thomas, and the magisterium's assertive reaction to the Modernists – a reaction that transformed neo-scholasticism into a conceptual framework that defined the norms of orthodoxy – such critique on the part of the *nouvelle théologie* was daring and far from evident. The *new theologians* did not want to hem themselves and their aspirations in with neo-scholastic boundaries. In their opinion, neo-scholasticism was a form of philosophical metaphysics in which the conceptual system took pride of place to the relationship between theology, faith and life. Neo-scholasticism's tightly fitting straightjacket was not open to reality and history and was thus closed to the fully fledged contribution of positive theology.

The three latter characteristics seem to represent more than a casual allusion to the work of Melchior Cano, one of the fathers of positive theology. In the sixteenth century, Cano had referred to the seven *loci proprii* of theology – the primary sources of theology: Scripture, Tradition, the Catholic Church, the Councils, the Fathers, the Magisterium, Scholastic theologians and canonists – and the three *loci alieni* or secondary sources of theology. These latter *loci alieni* – history, reason and philosophy – would appear to be important to the exponents of the *nouvelle théologie*. History had been ignored for centuries, philosophy had been reduced to neo-scholastic philosophy, and reason had been forced to adapt itself to the boundaries established by the scholastic theology supported by the magisterium.

Of greater importance than the reference to Cano, however, is the *nouvelle théologie*'s reaction to the so-called *Denzingertheologie*. The latter term refers to Heinrich Denzinger, a professor at Würzburg (Germany) who in 1854 published the first collection of Roman texts, including conciliar documents and papal texts. The term *Denzingertheologie* thus referred to an approach to theology that limited itself to magisterial texts and sought its legitimation therein.[37] It was a theology that followed the course set out by the magisterium to the letter. Against the background of the magisterium's reaction to various schools of thought that appeared to run counter to the Roman system, the said magisterium evolved in the nineteenth century into an executive and regulatory authority in the domain of theology, a domain it considered its own, and in which it ultimately made the decisions. The magisterium was no longer one player among others in the theological playing field, but also – and primarily – the key player and the referee, the one charged with the authority to hand out yellow and red cards.[38] This became particularly clear at the time of the Modernist crisis and likewise with the emergence of the *nouvelle théologie*.

We conclude the present chapter with some observations on an important aspect of the concept '*nouvelle théologie*' and its content. With reference to the practice of theology between the First and the Second Vatican Councils, the emphasis is often placed on the so-called *conclusion theology*, a concept on which Johannes Beumer offered some interesting reflections in 1939, particularly with respect to its shifting meaning through time.[39] During the first half of the twentieth century, conclusion theology referred to a system of reasoning, the conclusions of which had to be compatible with neo-scholasticism. Theology was thus reduced to a technique of reasoning within neo-scholasticism, its goal being to reinforce the system and arrive at interesting conclusions (hence the name). The status of the premises and the value of the conclusion were central. This description of Catholic theology between Vatican I and Vatican II, however, does not do justice to the valuable contributions made by numerous philosophers and theologians in the given period. While the tendency to make a caricature of neo-scholasticism was perhaps all too prevalent, neo-scholasticism itself was not entirely innocent of blame in this regard.

What then were the primary themes that preoccupied the *new theologians*? The question might appear simple, but there is no simple answer available, primarily because the *nouvelle théologie* shared points of contact with virtually every domain of Catholic theology. The crisis surrounding the *nouvelle théologie* was also related to the discussion concerning the foundations of theology: its nature, its methodology and its sources. This explains why we have been left with the expression *nouvelle théologie* rather than *nouvelle dogmatique* ('new dogmatics') or *nouvelle exégèse* ('new exegesis').

Chapter 2

THEOLOGICAL BACKGROUND AND CONTEXT

Having examined the concept and central components of the *nouvelle théologie* in the preceding chapter, we now turn to its historical setting. As with every crisis, the *nouvelle théologie* also had its background and context, which together form the theological-historical horizon necessary for obtaining an adequate understanding of the movement. In the first part of the present chapter, we examine the wider background, and in particular a number of important moments in the theological history of the century between the 1810s and the 1910s. In the second part we turn our attention to the historical embeddings of the *nouvelle théologie* focusing, in particular, on the most important developments therein during the years between the wars, the Second World War and the years immediately following (c. 1920–50).

2.1 *A Century of Background*

In this section we turn our attention to the century between 1819 and 1914, i.e. from the year that saw the birth of the *Tübinger theologische Quartalschrift*, a German periodical, to the year in which Pope Pius X passed away and the First World War began. In so doing, we ascribe a symbolic significance to the said events. Since it is not our intention to present an exhaustive or detailed picture of the century, we will limit ourselves to the *Tübinger Schule*, the contribution of John Henry Newman, the events leading up to the First Vatican Council and the Council itself, and the crisis of Modernism.

The Tübinger Schule

The *Tübinger theologische Quartalschrift* symbolizes the importance of the so-called *Tübinger Schule*. The journal was established in 1819 by Johann Sebastian Drey, the school's most prominent representative.[1] Together with Johann Adam Möhler, Drey was the primary figure in nineteenth-century German theology for the period prior to the First Vatican Council. Möhler also belonged to the *Tübinger Schule*, although he only served ten years as a professor in Tübingen (1826–35).[2]

One of Drey's most important merits was the emphasis he placed on the value of history in Catholic theology. Influenced by Schelling's romantic philosophy of history, he wanted to rethink the task of the historian in order to guarantee the systematic character of theology. While revelation was central to this endeavour, Drey also understood Christianity to include development and discovery of new perspectives as well as new insights about earlier events. For him, Christianity was a living event and dogmas could only be understood, judged and employed in the context of such a dynamic. His vision had obvious repercussions for theological methodology. Speculative theology was clearly obliged to account for the organic and dynamic character of revelation. It should come as no surprise to the reader that Drey was the first Catholic theologian to organize a course in the history of dogma.[3]

Möhler likewise sided with history and historians. Based on a study of the Church Fathers, he arrived at an ecclesiology centred around Christ: the Church as the community of the incarnate Word kept alive and united by the Holy Spirit. The Church was thus seen as the historical continuation of the life of Jesus and his work of redemption. Möhler's interest in patristics, however, is not accidental. In contrast to the Protestants' *sola Scriptura*, he wanted to draw more attention to the tradition, which he described as the activity of the Holy Spirit through the generations. In like fashion to Drey, Romanticism clearly sets the tone at this juncture: the Church is the *communio sanctorum*, the community of the Spirit. In his *Die Einheit der Kirche* (1825), he abandons a solely juridical understanding of the Church (conceived in terms of hierarchy and power) and explores the world of pneumatology and mysticism.[4] It would be historically correct to argue that Möhler was responsible for the rediscovery of patristics and that his ecclesiology was more in tune with the Second Vatican Council rather than with the First.

One of the primary tasks of the *Tübinger Schule* was to explore the tradition, particularly the Bible and patristics. In so doing, they entered into debate with Schelling and Schleiermacher – but also with Kant and Hegel – in an atmosphere of ecumenical openness (encouraged by their Protestant colleagues at Tübingen).

John Henry Newman

John Henry Newman, who converted to Roman Catholicism in 1845 after contributing to the peak years of the Anglican Oxford Movement, was similarly influenced by changing attitudes towards the doctrine of the faith, patristics and the revaluation of history.[5] In the same year as his 'conversion', he published *An Essay on the Development of Christian Doctrine*, a revised edition of which appeared in 1878.[6] His essay distinguished seven criteria any development of a facet of the Christian tradition had to fulfil if it was to be considered an authentic development of the Church's doctrine: the preservation of type or idea, the continuity in principles, the power of assimilation, the early anticipation, the logical sequence, preservative additions and the chronic vigour. Newman's conviction that the magisterium should play the important role of guarantor when it comes to recognizing such authentic development contributed, together with other factors, to his conversion to Roman Catholicism.

Newman was warmly welcomed as a gifted individual into the Church and was ordained priest in 1847. He was made cardinal 32 years later, in 1879. He kept his distance from the discussions of Vatican I, just as he had always kept his distance from Ultramontanism. In 1870, the year of the Council, he published *An Essay in Aid of a Grammar of Assent*, an exploration of the actual thought processes that lead to assent with respect to the doctrine of the Church, paths that are likewise used by God's Providence to bring people to certainty in this regard.[7]

A study of both the aforementioned essays reveals that Newman's thought can be characterized by the following two terms: 'development' and 'assent'.

Using the term 'development' Newman accounts for history, insisting that neither the Church's doctrine nor the Church itself are static entities, but rather living realities. Christianity is not a theory or a closed system. Catholicism, rather, is an *idea*, a spiritual principle that permeates reality to function at the level of the individual and the community, and in a transcendent and immanent manner. Newman's concept of development is not unconditional, however, as we can see from the seven criteria he proposed for determining whether we can speak of a legitimate development of (a facet of) a doctrine of the faith.

Newman's concept of *assent* refers to the 'why?' of our faith. What gives us certitude when we say we believe? Newman's response to this question is both classical and innovative. He approaches the faith in the first instance as something real rather than something purely non-rational, not simply to be imposed from above (the magisterium), but requiring consultation and an awareness of the faith of the laity. As such, he ascribes a role to human intuition as well as human conscience (cf. the 'illative sense').

Ultramontanism, Neo-Scholasticism and Vatican I

While Newman's various publications betray evidence of a degree of intellectual openness within the Roman Catholic Church, papal leadership turned in on itself with every increasing intensity. Five elements related to the history of the Church and of theology in the third quarter of the nineteenth century deserve further attention in this regard.

The first of these elements was liberalism, which Pius IX supported on his election to the papacy in 1846, but fervently opposed from 1848 – the Year of Revolutions – onwards. He then aligned himself with the position of his predecessor Gregory XVI, author of the encyclical *Mirari Vos*.[8] Pius countered liberalism with an increasing centralism within the Church, egged on by the threats posed to the Papal States by the *risorgimento*, the Italian pursuit of unification, a goal achieved in 1870 with the creation of Italy at the cost of the Papal States.

A second and escalating element to be considered in relation to this period is Ultramontanism. The latter can be characterized on the basis of the six features employed in *Mirari Vos*: (1) the Church is free, separate from state, and the state cannot impose restrictions upon it; (2) the Church is above the state and enjoys more authority than the state on account of its divine origins; (3) the state must be obedient to this higher authority in order to obey the will of God; (4) the intellectual disciplines – in particular philosophy and theology – were to align themselves with the thought of the Church; (5) the thought of the Church is centred around neo-scholasticism; (6) the Church should be free to proclaim its message through every possible channel. Ultramontanism bears an inherent aversion to modern thought, which the authorities of the Church considered (too) liberal and anti-ecclesial. An effective twofold reaction was required: a list was to be made of every form of thinking considered reprehensible and a powerful antidote was to be developed.

The idea of creating a list of objectionable propositions was first suggested by Gioacchino Pecci in 1849 during a synod of the bishops of Umbria in Spoleto. The further elaboration of the idea of a list was given over to a number of bishops and institutions, as is evident from the reports of Bishop Louis Désiré Édouard Pie (Poitiers), Prosper Guéranguer (abbot of the Benedictine Abbey of Solesmes), and the Catholic University of Louvain (under rector Pierre François Xavier De Ram). Each of the reports contained a list of propositions to be condemned. Pius IX finally published the encyclical *Quanta Cura* on 8 December 1864 together with an appended *Syllabus errorum*.[9] At least four factors occasioned the encyclical: (1) the political situation in which a unified Italy presented a threat to the Church States, (2) the aforementioned reports, (3) the status of the pastoral letter of Philippe Gerbet, the bishop of Perpignan, published in 1860 and containing 85 propositions, and (4) the speech given by Charles-René de Montalembert during a Catholic congress in Malines in 1863[10] together with that given in the same year by Ignaz von Döllinger in Munich on the role of theology in the Church.[11] The *Syllabus* is a list of 80 propositions, which include (semi-)rationalism, indifferentism, socialism, the separation of Church and state, etc. Pointed reactions were thus to be expected. The governments of Russia, France and Italy prohibited the list's publication. Gioacchino Pecci, who had been made cardinal in 1853, was elected nevertheless to succeed Pius IX in 1878 as Pope Leo XIII.

The rejection of modern thought via the *Syllabus* necessitated the creation of a counterweight: an anti-modern intellectual framework.[12] Around the middle of the nineteenth century, Thomism became the focus of attention in this regard, although it had been confined to centres of priestly formation for more than a century.[13] In the same period, Johann Baptist Franzelin and – especially – Joseph Kleutgen set themselves up in Rome as the defenders and promoters of neo-scholasticism. There were three contributing causes for the relatively swift formation of their movement. First were the various ecclesial condemnations of non-scholastic 'modern' visions, whereby the unfulfilled idealistic expectations had transformed themselves, in the opinion of the Church authorities, into pantheism, relativism and subjectivism. The condemnations in question included the traditionalism of Augustin Bonnetty in 1855, the publications of

Anton Günther in 1857, the vision of Jacob Frohschammer in 1862, and the ontologism of the Louvain professor Gerard Casimir Ubaghs in 1866. Secondly, there was a variety of publications supporting a complete return to scholasticism in the period 1850–70. The periodical *Civiltà cattolica*, for example, which emerged as the mouthpiece of 're-scholasticization', was established in 1850. In addition, Matteo Liberatore and – once again – Joseph Kleutgen were the two most important authors of the period.[14] Thirdly, the rise of neo-scholasticism was influenced by papal elections. After the pontificate of Pius IX – with the dogma of the Immaculate Conception (1854), the *Syllabus errorum* (1864) and the proclamation of papal infallibility (1870) as its ultramontane 'high points' – Leo XIII was in complete agreement with Liberatore and Kleutgen.[15] Indeed, the latter was considered the 'spiritual father' of *Aeterni Patris*, the encyclical promulgated in 1879 in which Thomism was disseminated as the Church's intellectual framework.[16]

The aforementioned developments culminated in the First Vatican Council, which commenced on 8 December 1869. On 18 July 1870, the constitution *Pastor Aeternus* had proclaimed the infallibility of the Pope.[17] The day after, on 19 July, the Franco-German war started. Due to the latter, the Council was cut short and was never to be resumed. In addition to *Pastor Aeternus*, Vatican I also produced the constitution *Dei Filius*[18] in which the relationship between faith and reason enjoyed a central place. Let us have a closer look at *Dei Filius*.

In its chapter on revelation, *Dei Filius* admits that God can be known with certainty from creation in the natural light of reason, but insists in addition that there is another, supernatural way to know God, namely through God's revelation, primarily as it was made manifest in Christ. This revelation is necessary because human beings ultimately have a supernatural goal. It is insisted that the magisterium is the only authentic interpreter of the Bible. The chapter on faith reacts against the autonomy of reason. Given the fact that humanity is totally dependent on its Creator, and bearing in mind that created reason is subordinate to uncreated Truth, our reason and our will are thus subordinate to God, who, by virtue of revelation, is the guarantee par excellence of the primacy of faith. Faith and reason are also interrelated, however, since God's revelation went hand in hand with signs that our reason is capable of grasping miracles and prophecies. While the Council reacted thereby to fideism, agnosticism and mythologism, faith continued in the first instance to be a gift of God and the magisterium saw itself as the guardian of the doctrine of faith and a helper of the faith side by side with the grace of God. The constitution's following chapter discusses the relationship between faith and reason at greater depth, focusing immediately on two orders of knowledge: the order of natural reason, which can only grasp truths that can be obtained by natural reason, and the order of faith, whereby divinely revealed truths can also be grasped with the help of faith. According to the Council Fathers, reason is called to come to a degree of insight into the secrets of the divine, enlightened by faith and with 'care, piety and respect'.[19]

While faith is necessary, it does not contradict reason, nor does it set itself up as reason's opposite. After all, the God who reveals the secrets of the divine and grants faith is the same God who dispenses the light of reason on humankind. Reason thus points to the foundations of the faith, enlightened by the same faith. Faith for its part protects reason from error and misapprehension, and provides it with various sorts of knowledge. It is for this reason that the magisterium, which forbids the support of opinions and so-called truths that run counter to the faith, is not against science as such. At the same time, however, the magisterium does not want science to invade the domain of faith heavy-handedly. From this perspective, the Council Fathers state that the Church wishes to be faithful to the *depositum fidei*, which implies that the meaning of the Church's dogmas is that given once and for all by the Church. The Council Fathers made use of the constitution *Dei Filius* primarily to react against rationalism, the leading figures of which were Georg Hermes and Anton Günther. In the years that followed the Council, Vatican I's neo-scholastic operating framework quickly became the only intellectual space in which Catholic theologians were permitted to function.

The Modernist Crisis

In the period from the promulgation of *Aeterni Patris* to the 1920s, neo-scholasticism gradually established itself as exclusive and all-pervading. The vicious circle created by the magisterium on the one hand, which granted scholasticism the highest authority, and neo-scholasticism on the other, which constituted the Church's only intellectual conceptual framework, was reinforced by an ambitious handbook tradition and the republication of prominent scholastic thinkers. The circle provided little room for creativity and renewal within Catholic theology. Against such a background, little if any innovation and spirit can be detected in Catholic theology, with the exception of the dynamism radiated by Modernism.

It would be impossible to understand the Modernist crisis without returning to its background and context, namely the last decades of the nineteenth century. While the period was characterized by the resurgence of Thomistic ideas, it was also a time when the growing independence and secularization of science became an important factor, especially the independence of the religious sciences. This evolution could be observed in particular in France, where the work of historians such as Louis Duchesne, Pierre Batiffol and Alfred Loisy served to illustrate the emancipation of science from ecclesial norms and guidelines. A third component of the context in which the Modernist crisis emerged has to do with the influence and attraction of scholarly activities within liberal Protestantism. Lucien Laberthonnière, a disciple of Maurice Blondel, articulated the difference as follows: 'Liberal Protestants opt for faith without tradition, while Catholics of today opt for tradition without faith.'[20] With the *Syllabus* and the First Vatican Council still prominent in people's minds, the authority of the magisterium came to be seen as an impediment to science's struggle for independence. The Modernists, it should be noted, were not interested in attacking the magisterium's claim to authority, in spite of the fact that the ecclesial hierarchy perceived, described and condemned their efforts as such.

Since the first decade of the twentieth century, Modernism has tended to be described in the terms used by Rome to condemn it, namely as a philosophical-theological conceptual system that represented 'the sum of all heresies'.[21] Such a description clearly does not do justice to the ideas of the Modernists (academically justifiable positions rather that heresies), their intentions (not infrequently at the service of the Church) and the relationships between them (absence of a uniform character and certainly not a system). The so-called Modernists were in reality intellectuals who had tried to integrate the historical-critical method into their scientific research. This methodology, however, together with many of their insights, ran counter to the vision of the magisterium, albeit as a consequence of their research and not so much of their aims. The individuals in question did not see themselves as representatives of Modernism. They did not constitute a group or school as such, although they exchanged much information, critique and thoughts on one another's publications and hypotheses, often in the context of a lively personal correspondence. Bearing this in mind, we can still designate a number of common components of the Modernist inheritance, accepting that they were not adhered to by all with the same degree of permanence or measure. In the first instance, the Modernists understood revelation as a reality that did not stop with the death of the last apostle. Revelation continued up to and including the present day. Secondly, they presupposed that dogmas were not immutable. Ecclesial dogmatic formulas could change, not only in terms of interpretation, but also in terms of content. Thirdly, the Modernists did not insist on making a sharp distinction between nature and reason, on the one hand, and revelation and the supernatural on the other: in their vision of things it was equally important to respect the perspective of the transcendent as the perspective of the immanent. Fourthly, they insisted that it was permitted to use inductive reasoning side by side with deductive reasoning. Fifthly, they favoured the application of the historical-critical method in biblical exegesis. These five positions can be categorized further under two main headings: the introduction of history into theology (cf. the *historical*-critical method, the *development* of dogma) and the – partial – abandonment of neo-scholasticism as an exclusive conceptual framework (cf. induction, immanence). Both these points were to become central in the period between c. 1935 and Vatican II.

While the list of Modernism's core points may appear small, the importance of the Modernist vision is clearly significant as can be seen from, among other things, the various ecclesial condemnations thereof. One might be inclined to describe the situation at this juncture as a clash of good intentions: the Modernists set out to bring Catholic thought up to date, while the magisterium considered it its duty to condemn any mindset that posed a threat to the continued existence of the doctrine of the faith. The magisterium, however, did not give the ideas of the Modernists the chance to develop. Put bluntly, the Modernist movement was robbed of any chance of survival before it could reach maturity and the Church's authorities used everything at its disposal to achieve this end: the decree *Lamentabili sane exitu* with its 65 objectionable propositions, also known as the 'small syllabus' (July 1907); the encyclical *Pascendi dominici gregis* (September 1907); the motu proprio *Praestantia Scripturae* (1908) on the occasion of the fifteenth anniversary of the encyclical *Providentissimus Deus*; the condemnation of publications to the Index; and dismissal from teaching positions and excommunications.[22] The anti-Modernist oath of 1910 appeared to have averted further crisis once and for all.[23] According to Pierre Colin, the 'document storm' should be associated more with the pontificates of Gregory XVI and Pius IX than that of Leo XIII.[24] Along similar lines, and against the background of the anti-modern climate, Thomas Loome refers to Modernism as 'yet another episode in the perennial conflict between two mutually antagonistic intellectual traditions within Roman Catholicism'.[25]

Modernism had its roots in France,[26] with figures such as Maurice Blondel, Lucien Laberthonnière, Édouard Le Roy who published the book *Dogme et critique* in the year *Pascendi* was promulgated,[27] Albert Houtin who questioned the Bible on historical grounds[28], Henri Bremond, father of the history of spirituality in France,[29] Alfred Loisy, 'father of Catholic Modernism'[30] and Joseph Turmel 'unmasked' by Rome as late as 1930 and immediately excommunicated.[31] At the same time, however, Modernism was an international movement with several protagonists in Great Britain, such as Friedrich von Hügel,[32] Maude Petre[33] and George Tyrrell,[34] and in Italy, including Salvatore Minocchi, Giovanni Semeria, Antonio Fogazzaro and Ernesto Buonaiuti.[35] While Germany, Belgium and the Netherlands could not boast prominent representatives,[36] there were – as in France (like, among others, Marie-Joseph Lagrange) – a number of 'suspects', among them Hermann Schell in Germany and Albin Van Hoonacker and Paulin Ladeuze in Belgium. The Belgian suspects were forced to depend on the diplomatic skills of Cardinal Désiré-Joseph Mercier in order to avoid a Roman intervention. In the Netherlands, Henri Andreas Poels, who defended his doctorate in theology in Louvain in 1897 under A. Van Hoonacker[37], encountered resistance from his local bishop, forcing him to leave for Washington, where he later taught at its recently established Catholic University.[38] In the meantime, a US variant of Modernism – 'Americanism' – had already been condemned by Rome (cf. the apostolic letter *Testem benevolentiae* of Pope Leo XIII).[39] Pierre Colin considers the latter condemnation to be the interpretative key and matrix for the condemnation of the European variant, although the latter clearly had to deal with much more than an apostolic letter.

It would be impossible to examine the ideas of each of the so-called Modernists in the present chapter or the condemnations emanating from Rome in their regard. For our purposes, it is important that we endeavour to describe Modernism as a theological movement. As such, the Modernist crisis gave significant impetus to the 'golden age of biblical research'[40] and generated a crisis within fundamental theology. Developments in both domains represent an important horizon for discussing the practice of theology during the first half of the twentieth century. Within the scope of our brief sketch of the theological-historical background of the *nouvelle théologie*, therefore, a succinct summary of the influence of the Modernists on biblical studies and fundamental theology should suffice for the time being.[41]

On 17 November 1893, the day before Leo XIII's encyclical *Providentissimus Deus* was to establish guidelines for biblical research within Catholic theology, Alfred Loisy was relieved of his teaching duties at the Institut Catholique de Paris on account of his deviant opinions and the aftermath of an unfortunate article penned by the Institute's rector Maurice d'Hulst.[42] For Loisy, however, the encyclical was nothing more than an echo of the Council of Trent and Vatican I. The publication a decade later of his two 'red books' – named after the colour of the dust-jacket – stand as clear evidence to his refusal to remain silent. *L'Évangile et l'Église* and *Autour d'un petit livre* were unsurprisingly banished to the Church's Index.[43] Together with *Le quatrième Évangile* (1903),[44] both works did indeed serve as an important source of inspiration for the propositions condemned in the decree *Lamentabili*. Loisy supported a historical-critical reading of the Bible, whereby its various books were ascribed to human authors who put the story of God's relationship with humanity into writing using human language. Loisy's vision, which clearly ascribed a relative character to the Bible and its inspiration, was condemned by the magisterium and he was excommunicated on 7 March 1908, the then feast day of Saint Thomas Aquinas. Others who shared his vision, albeit less explicitly, were also sanctioned (cf. Édouard Le Roy) or only just managed to escape sanction (cf. Marie-Joseph Lagrange[45]). The fact that Loisy had taken the lead in the matter explains, moreover, why Modernist ideas prior to 1907 tended to be referred to as '*Loisysme*'.

In order to respond to and counter Modernist tendencies in the domain of biblical research, Leo XIII established the Pontifical Biblical Commission in 1902.[46] Using the question and answer procedure, the commission determined the 'truth' of the Bible with the help of a number of biblical books and passages. Five years later, from the publication of the aforementioned *Praestantia Scripturae* onwards, it was insisted that the statements of the commission be recognized by all on pain of censure. With as much concern as his predecessor about the influence of biblical 'innovators' in the seminaries (cf. *Providentissimus Deus*), Pius X addressed a document to those responsible for priestly formation with guidelines for the study of the Bible. Ten years after the obligation to take the anti-modernist oath, Benedict XV promulgated the encyclical *Spiritus Paraclitus* (1920) on the occasion of the 1,500th anniversary of the death of Saint Jerome (343–420), the translator of the Vulgate – the only authorized translation of the Bible.[47] In the spirit of Jerome, Benedict insisted on the divine inspiration of the Bible, in spite of the fact that human beings were its physical authors (a *quantité négligeable*, as it were). It was only in 1943, with the promulgation of Pius XII's encyclical *Divino afflante Spiritu*, that the door was opened to a historical-critical approach to the Bible.[48]

An assault on the Bible was an assault on the roots of faith and theology, and thus likewise on the domain of fundamental theology. The emphasis on the historical perspective ultimately led to the emergence of a number of figures who supported an alternative understanding of revelation, tradition and truth. The impetus given by the publication of Maurice Blondel's dissertation *L'Action* in 1893 had had undermined the static vision of the Church and exposed this triptych to critique.[49] George Tyrrell and Édouard Le Roy, among others, favoured bringing history into play in relation to fundamental theology, thereby introducing the notion of development into the debate. Revelation, truth and dogma, it was argued, could also be studied from the perspective of their development and not only as fixed and unassailable formulations. It goes without saying that this perspective was pointedly rejected by the magisterium.

Both the world of biblical exegesis and that of fundamental theology witnessed a variety of controversies which, taken together, ultimately constituted the Modernist crisis. At the same time, however, Modernism also introduced a crisis in the relationship between philosophy and theology, and thereby likewise in the way in which faith was given expression. Leo XIII's response to the call for a philosophical foundation for theology, as a means to allow the Church to enter *into dialogue with* modernity on a philosophical-theological basis, evolved into a philosophical 'superstructure' with modernity *as the enemy*. Neo-scholasticism had become the norm and its theological derivatives ran counter to the Modernist emphasis on subjectivity, experience, evolution and relativity. Neo-scholasticism had become the intellectual conceptual framework of the Church's anti-modernist leadership. It had evolved into a rod for punishing those who (in the Church's mind) presented themselves as Modernist, as well as all those who did not demonstrate enough anti-Modernism. To quote Frederick Copleston, neo-scholasticism represented the 'party-line' of the Church, 'a kind of philosophical orthodoxy'.[50] According to Richard Schaeffler, the Church was more interested in Modernist deviation from neo-scholastic concepts than in Modernist ideas as such.[51]

By its being employed as a weapon in the fight against Modernism, neo-scholasticism ultimately became anti-modern.[52] The encyclical *Pascendi dominici gregis*, in which Pius X condemned Modernism, points to ignorance of and disregard for neo-scholasticism as the intellectual roots of this reprehensible intellectual movement. The study of scholastic philosophy is proposed as a remedy. Seven years later, in 1914, Pius X penned a motu proprio in which he promoted the study of Thomas in Italy, while the Congregation of Studies published a list of 24 theses establishing neo-scholasticism's basic principles and insights. The same congregation confirmed the 24 propositions as normative in 1916.[53] This was the first measure of consolidation of neo-scholastic thought and method after the death of Pius X; the pontificates of Benedict XV and Pius XI were characterized by a consolidation of neo-scholasticism. For instance, in 1917, canon 1366 of the Church's Code of Canon Law insisted that the doctrine, principles and methods of Thomas should be used in teaching philosophy and theology. In 1923, on the occasion of the 600th anniversary of Thomas's canonization, Pius XI promulgated the encyclical *Studiorum Ducem*[54] in which the Angelic Doctor's merits were lauded once again and his link with Church teaching further underlined (the promulgation date already made the point: 29 June, the Feast of Saints Peter and Paul).

The ecclesial condemnation of 'Modernism' thus caused a hardening of 'anti-modernism', the activities of which were summarized by Jan Hendrik Walgrave in 1966 as 'unbridled carnage'.[55] Paradoxically, the Church's 'creation' of an organized and systematized Modernism ultimately led to the 'creation' of a hidden, organized and systematized ecclesial anti-modernism as the only efficient antidote. The clearest expression of this reality was the secular institute Sodalitium Pianum, better known as La Sapinière, which was founded and led by Umberto Benigni in 1909. The primary task of this 'secret' international network was to detect, expose, accuse and report on Modernists. The anti-modernist movement had clearly been transformed into a form of integrism, tolerated and supported by Rome. The anti-modernist's contact vehicle at the time was the periodical *La correspondance de Rome*. While the Sodalitium Pianum was discontinued in 1921 at the end of the pontificate of Benedict XV, this did not spell the end of the integrist, anti-modernist movement, as will become clear within the context of the crisis surrounding the *nouvelle théologie*.

2.2 The Interbellum, the Second World War and the Years that Followed

In the following pages we offer a brief survey of the most important theological developments of the 1920s, 30s and 40s, developments that must be considered against the background of an internal pluralization of neo-Thomism. In order to sketch the immediate background and context of the *nouvelle théologie*, we begin with the philosophical before moving on to the theological.

The Internal Pluralization of Neo-Thomism
Following the *retour à la scolastique* – 'the return to scholastics', c. 1850–1920[56] – outlined above, neo-Thomistic philosophy enjoyed something of a golden period between 1920 and 1950 and simultaneously underwent internal pluralization.[57] It is important to note with respect to the latter that a variety of tendencies populated the Thomistic landscape, tendencies that can be organized into five clusters, which we present very briefly.

The first of these tendencies envisaged human intuition as the key to establishing a relativized Thomism capable of integrating contemporary culture within itself. Jacques Maritain is perhaps the most important representative of this line of reasoning. Referring to scholastics from the sixteenth and seventeenth century, he emphasized *l'humanisme intégral*, whereby the human person is ascribed a natural purpose (to be achieved through politics) and a supernatural purpose (to be achieved through religion and ethics).[58] Thomas's teaching serves as the basic foundation for Maritain.

The second tendency envisages the explicit return to the thought of Thomas himself. The symbolic starting point in this regard can be located in 1920, the year in which the Institut historique d'études thomistes was established by Le Saulchoir, the study house of the French Dominicans. Marie-Dominique Chenu, who had served as rector of Le Saulchoir from 1932 to 1942, can be counted among this tendency's most important representatives. His publications on theological thought in the twelfth and thirteenth centuries and his *Introduction à l'étude de saint Thomas d'Aquin* (1950) were not only intended to present a history of Thomas but also, and more importantly, to establish Thomas as a source for contemporary theology.[59] This fitted well within the spirit of *ressourcement*, emergent in the 1930s and effectively present in the 1940s (cf. Part II of this volume).

When compared with historical Thomism, the third tendency, or transcendental Thomism, was even more keen to meet the needs of modern science and counted dialogue with modernity as one of its primary goals. In line with his French confrere Pierre Rousselot, Joseph Maréchal, a Jesuit associated with Louvain's Institut supérieur de philosophie, was in fact to adopt the same point of departure as modern thought, namely the subject. Transcendental Thomism claimed direct continuity with Thomas himself, to be found, according to Maréchal, in the subject's dynamic openness with respect to absolute Being. Echoes of Maréchal can be heard in the thought of Karl Rahner and Bernard Lonergan.

A fourth tendency can be described as the interaction between transcendental Thomism, phenomenology, and the notion of 'implicit intuition'. The latter expression stems from one of the tendency's most prominent representatives, the Louvain Dominican Dominicus De Petter, who set out to rethink Thomas in light of the phenomenological analysis of consciousness.[60] To this end, he agreed with two important points of the transcendental philosophers: he shared their dissatisfaction with scholasticism's orientation towards the conceptual and wanted to validate religious epistemology in the form of a non-conceptual dynamic oriented towards the Absolute. De Petter differed nevertheless from the transcendental philosophers because he did not want to situate this dynamic in the intellect but rather in reality, i.e. the object of knowledge. In this sense, De Petter can be understood as the initiator of 'reality thinking' and the expression 'implicit intuition' as a non-conceptual insight into the infinite, based on an objective dynamic in reality and oriented towards the ground of one's own being. De Petter had an extraordinary influence on a variety of thinkers, among them Edward Schillebeeckx and Piet Schoonenberg, important figures to whom we will return in the third chapter of the second part of this volume.

Against the background of these four tendencies, Roman neo-scholasticism continued to function as a fifth Thomistic movement, which can be described succinctly as the continuation of the thought of the classic commentators on Thomas. Réginald Garrigou-Lagrange was primary in defending neo-scholasticism with his often confrontational writing skills. Based in Rome, where he taught at the Angelicum, his influence was as great as his almost caricatural single-mindedness in countering whatever appeared to deviate from the scholastic.[61]

The Second Vatican Council was to recognize and appreciate this plurality of tendencies. According to Jan van Laarhoven, it is significant in this regard that the Council fathers 'did not yield to the partially curial pressure to declare Thomas's sanctity yet again by canonising his philosophy as the pinnacle of Roman Catholic wisdom'.[62]

In addition to the aforesaid Thomistic tendencies, the period of c. 1920–50 was characterized in philosophical terms by the emergence and growth of phenomenology, which was later to be expounded – particularly under the impetus of Edmund Husserl – as existentialism (cf. Martin Heidegger and Karl Jaspers). The perception and experience of existence and reality took pride of place and were to constitute the core features of personalism.

Theological Developments

At least nine theological developments can be traced to the 1920s, 30s and 40s.[63] Let us have a look at each in the following concise survey.

The first development is at the level of ecclesiology. Where the focus prior to the 1920s was almost exclusively on the Church as institution, with a great deal of attention afforded the pope (cf. Vatican I), the authority of the magisterium (cf. the Modernist crisis), the organizational structure of the Church and the rights and obligations attached thereto (cf. the *Codex Iuris Canonici* of 1917), this widened to *include* the internal unity of the Church, the fact that the Church could be understood as 'the people of God on its way', a community of believers. Romano Guardini is particularly important in this regard, not in the least on account of his book *Vom Sinn der Kirche*.[64] The supernatural character of the Church thus acquired greater relief.

Interest in the various 'layers' of the Church went hand in hand with a more Christ-oriented spirituality. This second development was championed by, for example, the Benedictine Columba Marmion, author of *Le Christ, vie de l'âme* (1914/17), *Le Christ dans ses mystères* (1919) and *Le Christ, idéal du moine* (1922).[65]

The combination of evolutions in ecclesiology and spirituality gave rise to a vision of the Church as the mystical Body of Christ. The Belgian Jesuit Émile Mersch can be considered the main protagonist in the elaboration of this vision,[66] which was, as Roger Haight writes, 'the most authoritative twentieth-century ecclesiological teaching in the Catholic Church prior to Vatican II'.[67] In 1943, Pope Pius XII promulgated the encyclical *Mystici corporis Christi*, with Mersch's Dutch confrere Sebastiaan Tromp as its spiritual father.[68] The encyclical gives a central place to the invisible nature of the Church, although the *auctoritas* of the magisterium still was underlined. In addition to a focus on the mystical Body of Christ, interest is also shown at the Church's highest level in the historical Jesus, evidence of which can be derived from the promulgation of the encyclical *Divino afflante Spiritu* three months after the appearance of *Mystici corporis Christi*.

A fourth aspect of the historical-theological background of the interbellum was the Liturgical Movement, which focused attention on the celebration of the mysteries of the Church – liturgy – in an effort to make it more accessible to the laity and thereby encourage more conscious and active participation. Marmion likewise played a considerable role in this movement, together with its major representatives, namely the Louvain Benedictine Lambert Beauduin and his German confrere Odo Casel, who had founded the periodical *Jahrbuch für Liturgiewissenschaft* in 1921. In 1947, the most important insights of the Liturgical Movement were taken up into Pius XII's encyclical *Mediator Dei et hominum*.[69]

Casel and Guardini were also representatives of the fifth component of the theological landscape at the time, the *Verkündigungstheologie*, a leading theological movement in the German-speaking world from 1935 to 1950. In contrast to the *nouvelle théologie*, the kerygmatic theology sought a *ressourcement* that did not have exclusively scholarly or intellectual aims. The centre of gravity of this kerygmatic theology was to be found in the praxis of spirituality, preaching, liturgy and mysticism (cf. Romano Guardini, Odo Casel, Karl Adam, Hugo Rahner and Josef Andreas Jungmann).

A sixth theological development revolves around an increased interest in concrete, everyday life, evident in the emphasis on a morality that was often grafted to a Body of Christ spirituality (cf., for example, É. Mersch's *Morale et Corps mystique* of 1937).[70] Christianity's 'social action' became visible, as shown by – for example – the Jeunesse Ouvrière Chrétienne (JOC), founded by Cardinal Joseph Cardijn.[71] Even the magisterium involved itself at this juncture with the publication of Pius XI's *Casti connubii* (on marriage) in 1930 and the social encyclical *Quadragesimo anno* a year later.[72] The difficult political situation in Italy and Germany at the time inspired Pius XI to further encyclicals.[73] Several theologians endured difficulties during the Second World War, among them Yves Congar who was a prisoner of war at the time. Theological reflection on the one Mystical Body can thus be understood as a form of 'concordant thinking' against the background of a divided Europe.

The period of the years 1920–50 was also characterized by a seventh development, namely a growing interest in ecumenism.[74] The so-called Malines Conversations (the *Mechelse gesprekken*), for example, an initial dialogue between Anglicans and Catholics, took place between 1921 and 1926. The year 1926 also witnessed the first edition of the ecumenical periodical *Irénikon*. The close link between liturgical openness and ecumenical openness is demonstrated by the fact that Lambert Beauduin was the founder of the Benedictine community of Chevetogne, which was and continues to be responsible for the publication of *Irénikon*.

Two developments in France during this period are relevant on account of the geographical contextual origins of the *nouvelle théologie*. In the first – or eighth – instance, reference should be made to the large number of conversions to Catholicism in French intellectual circles. Frédéric Gugelot has analysed the different 'waves' of conversion, pointing in particular to peaks in the periods 1905–15 and 1925–35.[75] Influential thinkers such as Jacques Maritain and Gabriel Marcel can be included among their ranks. France's *renouveau catholique* or 'Catholic renewal' made a significant impression during these years, particularly in the literary world.[76]

A ninth and final development has to do with the French socio-political situation. The liberation of France took place in August 1944, thereby putting an end to the Vichy regime that had governed non-occupied France from the end of the Third Republic (1870–1940) to the transitional government of Charles de Gaulle (1944–46) and the beginning of the Fourth Republic (1946–58).[77] Against this turbulent political background, the phenomenon of the *prêtres-ouvriers* or worker-priests emerged[78] within circles of Catholic clergy who desired to evangelize among the workers. In spite of the prominence this gave to the Mission de France, the ecclesial authorities in Rome were not pleased with the activities of the worker-priests and ultimately condemned and banned them in 1954.

2.3 *Concluding Observations*

Having sketched the history of the concept and the content of the *nouvelle théologie* in the previous chapter, this second chapter was focused on the *nouvelle théologie*'s historical background and context. The first part offered a succinct survey of the prehistory of the *nouvelle théologie*: which theologians of the nineteenth century had already taken the initiative to appeal for the introduction of history in the theological endeavour? To this end, we focused our attention on the most important representatives of the *Tübinger Schule*. The Modernist crisis had been forestalled a century later, or so it seemed, and Roman anti-modernism together with a number of philosophical and theological developments during the interbellum and Second World War now served as background and context for the *nouvelle théologie*. This embeddedness is of vital importance for a complete understanding of the movement. Let us now turn to the contours of the *nouvelle théologie*.

Chapter 3

THE CONTOURS OF THE *NOUVELLE THÉOLOGIE*: FOUR PHASES

Against the background of the Modernist crisis and the various developments characteristic of the years 1920–50, a climate had been created in Catholic circles in which the *nouvelle théologie* was allowed to flourish. This does not imply, however, that anti-modernist tendencies no longer existed or that the theological developments discussed in the preceding chapter had come to an end in 1935. History is not a succession of events and movements, but rather a dynamic admixture of individuals, movements, facts, tendencies and influences to be considered within a particular context and in relation to their points of contact with other contexts.

Presenting a portrait of the *nouvelle théologie* – and of any other movement for that matter – is a difficult and delicate affair. Nevertheless, there are enough sources and already existing studies to encourage us to take up the challenge. Before embarking on such an overview of the *nouvelle théologie* in Part II, it seems advisable that we establish a sort of framework, a coat rack, as it were, on which we can hang history's many jackets. The goal of the present chapter, therefore, is to provide a broad and schematic introduction to the *nouvelle théologie* and its evolution. Four phases can be distinguished in this regard: Thomistic *ressourcement*, theological *ressourcement*, the internationalization of the movement, and its assimilation during the Second Vatican Council. The overview thus covers a period of 30 years from 1935 to 1965.

3.1 *The Four Phases or Faces of the* Nouvelle Théologie

The bipolar starting point of the so-called *nouvelle théologie* can be postulated in 1935.

On 18 January 1935, the French Dominican Yves Congar, professor at Le Saulchoir,[1] the study house of the Dominicans of the Parisian province, published an opinion piece in the Catholic newspaper *Sept* entitled 'Déficit de la théologie'.[2] Congar used the piece to formulate his critique of the practice of theology, which had become little more than a technical matter and had long lost sight of its relationship with the faith and life of ordinary men and women.

He compared neo-scholastic theology with a 'wax mask': an expressionless face, lacking any genuine connection with reality. An ambitious study of rising secularization in France was ultimately to support Congar's call for a theology rooted in faith and life, as he made clear in a second article published in June of the same year in *Vie Intellectuelle*.[3]

Congar's confrere Marie-Dominique Chenu likewise published an article in the *Revue des sciences philosophiques et théologiques* on the 'Position de la théologie'.[4] The article served as a blueprint for the third chapter of Chenu's book *Une école de théologie: le Saulchoir*, which appeared *pro manuscripto* in 1937.[5] In line with Ambroise Gardeil, the founder of Le Saulchoir, Chenu called for the reformation of theology.[6] For Chenu, theology was 'faith *in statu scientiae*' and 'faith in its intellectual mode', and the framework within which the theologian functioned was much broader than that provided by neo-scholasticism.[7] He insisted that it was not necessary to cut out the historical in order to engage in authentic theology. Indeed, the opposite was the case. For Chenu this was a logical consequence of the primary characteristic of faith as a reality made concrete in everyday life – including intellectual life: the historical perspective focuses its research on the said reality and its concretization. With this vision in mind, Chenu fashioned a project together with Congar and Henri-Marie Féret, his closest colleagues at Le Saulchoir, intended to result in a description of 'the history of theology in the West', a work – as we can read in the project proposal – that would pay specific attention to the link between theology on the one hand and cultural and spiritual life on the other.[8] While the project was never realized, its prevailing tone was representative of its three promoters and their work, emphasizing the link between reality, history, faith and theology.

A year after the appearance of *Une école de théologie*, the Belgian Dominican Louis Charlier published his *Essai sur le problème théologique*.[9] Although Charlier had not studied at Le Saulchoir – which had been housed until 1937 in a Belgian village of the same name on account of the anti-Catholic political situation in France at the time – his ideas were remarkably similar to those of Chenu. A professor at Louvain's Dominican theologate, Charlier's work caused something of a stir and was the subject of a considerable number of reviews.[10] The content of his *Essai sur le problème théologique* clearly offered food for thought. Charlier distinguished, for example, between the *côté conceptuel* – the 'conceptual dimension' – of revelation (the primary aspect of neo-scholastic theology) and the *côté réel* – the 'real dimension' – thereof (absent in theology, although Charlier himself was convinced that revelation was in the first instance a living reality and only in the second instance a collection of concepts, concepts that could never be said to enjoy any form of independence). The joint relegation of Chenu's work and Charlier's book to the Church's Index of Prohibited Books in February 1942[11] marks the end of the first phase of the *nouvelle théologie*.[12] It should be noted, nevertheless, that both works were written independently of one another. Archival research reveals that Rome's waning irritation with respect to *Une école de théologie* was rekindled by Charlier's *Essai* and the attention it had received in the review context.[13]

It was within the context of the relegation of both works to the Index that the expression *nouvelle théologie* was used for the first time, namely by Pietro Parente, who justified the condemnation in the *L'Osservatore Romano* in precisely these terms.[14] Parente argued that both works had brought neo-scholasticism into discredit with their (exaggerated) interest in the subject, experience, religious sentiment, and the notion of development. The superiors of the Dominican convent in Louvain – where Charlier had taught – likewise considered it correct to deprive Dominicus De Petter of his teaching assignment in 1942. De Petter had caused something of a stir in 1939 with the publication of his article 'Impliciete intuïtie' (Implicit intuition) in the first issue of *Tijdschrift voor Philosophie* (founded by De Petter) in which the anti-neo-scholastic tone was difficult to ignore.[15] Johan Van Wijngaarden has rightly pointed out that the sanctioning of De Petter can only be understood correctly against the background of the sanction issued against his confrere and fellow community member Charlier.[16] It is equally clear that the withdrawal of Louvain professor René Draguet's teaching assignment in July 1942 was linked to the condemnation of Charlier's *Essai*. Draguet had written in a review that Charlier had 'forgotten' to mention his primary source, namely the course he – Draguet – had taught at the Faculty of Theology in 1935.[17] Draguet was transferred to the Louvain Faculty of Arts and Philosophy at the time, although his name reappears among the staff of the Faculty of Theology in 1948. In short, in addition to Le Saulchoir, Louvain also deserves to be mentioned as an important centre of the first phase of the *nouvelle théologie*.

The fact that the Dominicans clearly played the lead role in this first phase (1935–42) is hardly surprising when one considers that they were the pre-eminent successors to the work of Thomas Aquinas, himself a Dominican. The *new theologians* of the period 1935–42 reacted against neo-scholasticism by insisting on a return to the historical Thomas, a demand that fitted well within the emerging historical interest in the Middle Ages characteristic of the time. In other words, instead of referring to authoritative commentaries on Thomas from the sixteenth and seventeenth centuries, they rather wanted to refer to Thomas himself. In this sense, the first phase can be identified with a Thomistic *ressourcement*, whereby the Thomas of the thirteenth century took pride of place over the (neo)scholastic Thomistic system. Neo-scholasticism was not abandoned completely – such would imply the dismissal of the accepted foundations of orthodoxy and, more than likely, one's own dismissal – rather it was *supplemented* in an initial step before proceeding in a second step to a theological *ressourcement*.

In the second phase of the *nouvelle théologie*, the Dominicans withdraw into the background and the Jesuits take the lead. The beginning of this phase can be related to a trilogy of publications. The first of these was Henri Bouillard's reworked doctoral dissertation, published in 1944 under the title *Conversion et grâce chez Saint Thomas d'Aquin*.[18] In the book's concluding observations, Bouillard writes that 'a theology that lacks topicality is a false theology'.[19] Such statements could only be interpreted as an attack on neo-scholasticism. The same conclusions provided the initial programmatic sketch of the goals of the second phase of the *nouvelle théologie*. The second publication was an article by Jean Daniélou published in 1946 under the title 'Orientations présentes de la pensée religieuse'.[20] Daniélou was not only explicit in arguing that Thomism had a relative value, he also insisted that a return to the Bible, liturgy and patristics was to be preferred above a theology that owed its existence to a single medieval theologian. The commotion that followed the article caused the discharge of Daniélou as editor of *Études*. The third publication, which appeared in the same year, was Henri de Lubac's *Surnaturel*.[21] Based on a historical study, de Lubac wanted to 'present a sort of essay in which contact between Catholic theology and contemporary thinking could be restored'.[22] De Lubac did not hesitate to pepper his overview with barely concealed critique of neo-scholasticism. In his opinion, the latter swallows up the mystery of faith, i.e. the supernatural as supernatural.

The desire to inject theology with a new lease of life and its associated return to the sources of the faith inspired the Jesuits to whom we have already referred and others (including Victor Fontoynont, Yves de Montcheuil and, in his own way, Pierre Teilhard de Chardin) to establish the series 'Sources chrétiennes' and 'Théologie' in 1942 and 1944 respectively.[23] Both series were based at the house of studies maintained by the order in Fourvière since 1924, even though as professor at Lyon's Institut catholique, Henri de Lubac was not a member of its staff and Jean Daniélou, as (former) editor of *Études*, was living in Paris.[24] It took little time for the house of studies and the series to be seen as vehicles of the *nouvelle théologie*, with de Lubac as the central figure.[25] We are of the opinion in this regard that de Lubac's *Surnaturel* served as a symbol in the struggle for historical theology against ongoing subjugation to the coalition between a Denzinger theology on the one hand and conclusion theology on the other. Bearing in mind the commotion caused by the work, Fergus Kerr argues that Henri de Lubac and *Surnaturel* brought about the greatest crisis twentieth-century Thomism – and perhaps even Catholic theology of the preceding century as a whole – had ever faced.[26]

This second phase is built on the first in the sense that Thomistic *ressourcement* served as its precursor and ongoing foundation. In other words, the said Thomistic *ressourcement* was not put under check in 1942. On the contrary, it acquired new impetus and dynamism in this period. The second phase can be described as theological *ressourcement*: the return to the sources of faith, whereby Rome's prescribed orientation towards neo-scholasticism and the magisterium was forced deeper into the shadows. In short, together with the first phase, the second phase constitutes a reaction to the coalition of conclusion and Denzinger theology. Via the integration of the historical perspective, theology was called upon to cross the boundaries of closed, meta-historical Thomism and meta-historical 'magisteriumism' to a historically oriented, open Thomism: a source theology.[27]

De Lubac, Daniélou and the Fourvière Jesuits were met with stiff opposition, with the reputed neo-scholastic and Roman Dominican Garrigou-Lagrange at the helm. In February 1947 he published his article 'La nouvelle théologie où va-t-elle?',[28] the text of which contained his answer: the *nouvelle théologie* is a new kind of Modernism. He considered Daniélou's article to be programmatic of the *nouvelle théologie* and – unimpeded by anachronism – the books of Bouillard and de Lubac its results. Of greater importance, however, was Garrigou's belief that the weapons used in the past to beat Modernism should be used once again to suppress the *nouvelle théologie*.[29]

Occasioned by Garrigou's article, the Jesuit authorities decided to take action. Belgian Jean-Baptiste Janssens, the order's recently elected General, set up an inquiry into the orthodoxy of Fourvière under the leadership of Édouard Dhanis, also a Belgian and a confidant of Janssens. In June 1950, this resulted, among other things, in the transfer of Henri de Lubac and Henri Bouillard from Lyon to Paris, which would have been seen as a fully fledged promotion had the circumstances been otherwise. In parallel with this discretely organized inquiry and the resulting sanctions, a war of convictions raged between the Roman Dominicans – with the *Revue thomiste* and *Angelicum* as their mouthpieces – and the Jesuits of Lyon – with the *Recherches de science religieuse* as their mouthpiece.[30]

Before the publication of Garrigou's article, Pius XII – with probable prior knowledge thereof[31] – entered the debate while addressing the participants during the Jesuit General Congregation on 17 September 1946.[32] The Pope insisted that the time had come to call a halt to discussion. Five days later, he similarly addressed the General Chapter of the Dominicans.[33] The aforementioned war of convictions, however, demonstrates that his words ultimately fell on deaf ears, and even provided the debate with new ammunition and 'publicity'. Pius XII finally promulgated *Humani generis* in 1950. This encyclical can be understood as Rome's final serious defence of neo-scholasticism as a normative framework determining the orthodoxy of theology. The spirit of *Humani generis* ran parallel with *Pascendi dominici gregis*. Strictly speaking, *Humani generis* does not mention the *nouvelle théologie*, although it condemns 13 matters it refers to as 'new'. There was clearly little to misunderstand: the *nouvelle théologie* had been rejected.[34] The Pope attacks historicism, for example, insisting that it places so much emphasis on particular facts that it thereby destroys the foundations of the universal truth of faith.

The years 1942–50 are obviously characterized by the influence of Maurice Blondel, the author of *L'Action*. His plea for the living tradition and the method of immanence became popular in theological circles – especially those of the *new theologians* – and one can speak of mutually stimulating dynamics. It is not surprising that Étienne Fouilloux, in his book *Une Église en quête de liberté*, entitled a chapter 'Blondel, Fourvière et les Pères'.[35]

After the second phase (1942–50), which was concluded like the first – with Roman censure – the *nouvelle théologie* found itself sailing into new waters, this time beyond the borders of France. The third phase concerns the period from c. 1950 up to the eve of the Second Vatican Council, a phase characterized by the internationalization of the *nouvelle théologie*. The *nouvelle théologie* pressed on in the Netherlands, for example, with scholars such as Edward Schillebeeckx and Piet Schoonenberg,[36] and in the German-speaking world with theologians like Karl Rahner[37] and Hans Urs von Balthasar.[38] In France itself, however, the *nouvelle théologie* was as good as paralyzed in the 1950s, although there are some – ourselves excluded – who defend the hypothesis that the work of the *prêtres-ouvriers* should be understood as the *nouvelle théologie*'s pastoral aspect.[39] Whatever the truth may be, the internationalization of the movement saw to the presence of a supra-francophone support basis at Vatican II, which made the acceptance of the *nouvelle théologie* in the universal Church possible. Nonetheless, it should be noted in the margin that the *nouvelle théologie* was not well received in every area. Spain, for example, had few if any representatives.[40]

The fourth and last phase of the *nouvelle théologie* is to be situated during the Second Vatican Council itself, which ultimately appropriated the central features of the ambitions of the *nouvelle théologie*. Indeed, as Thomas Guarino states, 'the names associated with this movement, such as Henri de Lubac and Hans Urs von Balthasar, were ultimately to give impetus to some of the great theological themes of Vatican II'.[41] The dogmatic constitution *Dei Verbum*, with its emphasis on the sources of the faith, can be singled out in this regard for containing definite echoes of the *nouvelle théologie*.[42] Overlooking the developments of c. 1935–65, Claude Geffré stated that 'one may say that the *Constitution on Divine Revelation* of Vatican Council II has confirmed the progress which has taken place in fundamental theology during the last thirty years'.[43] And the pastoral constitution *Gaudium et Spes* pointed out that theology 'should pursue a profound understanding of revealed truth; at the same time it should not neglect close contact with its own time that it may be able to help these men skilled in various disciplines to attain to a better understanding of the faith'.[44] During Vatican II several representatives of the *nouvelle théologie* were present as *periti* (Congar, de Lubac, Daniélou) or as a personal adviser to one of the Council fathers (Chenu, Féret).[45] Viewed from the perspective of the Council, Michael Quisinsky has described the role of Congar, Chenu and Féret as that of the pioneer, particularly with respect to the integration of history and theology.[46] It is in this sense that Bruno Forte rightly and accurately describes Vatican II as 'the Council of history'.[47] Indeed, the deposition of Roman neo-scholasticism and the assimilation of the *nouvelle théologie* allow us to speak – as Peter Eicher suggests – of the rehabilitation of Chenu, Congar and de Lubac during the Council.[48]

In the last analysis, the Council transformed the negative connotations associated with the *nouvelle théologie* into positive connotations, which reflected positively on its various representatives, several of whom were made cardinals (Daniélou in 1969, de Lubac in 1983, Congar sadly too late in 1994 and von Balthasar in 1988, although he died before the ceremony of elevation).

3.2 *Historical Note*

The phased division of the *nouvelle théologie* as we have presented it in this chapter should not be interpreted rigorously. *Humani generis*, for example, did not put an end to it, nor were the Jesuits absent from its initial phase. In the same year as the publication of Charlier's *Essai sur le problème théologique*, for example, Henri de Lubac published his *Catholicisme* with its challenging subtitle *Les aspects sociaux du dogme*, the third volume in the series 'Unam Sanctam' established by Yves Congar in 1937.[49] And just as the Jesuits were not absent from the first phase, the Dominicans continued to have a presence in the second. Archive material reveals a lively correspondence between the representatives of Le Saulchoir and La Fourvière, containing shared advice, commentary and critique.[50] Moreover, Henri-Marie Féret can be understood here as a bridge figure. The year in which his *L'Apocalypse de Saint Jean* (1943) was published – beyond the 1942 'boundary'[51] – demonstrates this. In addition to his enormous interest in the Bible, however, his involvement in the debate surrounding the so-called *théologie de l'histoire* ('the theology of history') during the second phase likewise testifies to the fact his influence was far from limited to the first phase.

In the closing considerations of the present volume, we will present some additional considerations on the division of the *nouvelle théologie* into different phases.

3.3 *Concluding Observations*

The desire of the *new theologians* to reconnect Catholic theology with the reality of the faith and with concrete everyday life forced them to rethink theology. Neo-scholasticism's manual tradition, and in particular its reduction of the faith to concepts and of theology to the art of argumentation, were bluntly denounced. The *ressourcement* of theology was obliged to take the prevailing Thomism – *in casu* Roman neo-scholasticism – as its point of departure, more specifically by returning to its historical roots and thereby to Thomas himself. Although the organization and structure of his *Summa* inclined towards the systematization of theology, the latter, as far as a growing number of philosophers and theologians was concerned, was not to be reduced to a system, as many sixteenth- and seventeenth-century thinkers had nevertheless claimed. In contrast to 'system thinking' a new 'reality thinking' emerged whereby scholars turned afresh to 'the real Thomas' of the thirteenth century. The emphasis on reality went hand in hand with an emphasis on history, which studied the reality of the past and its perception of reality in a scholarly and responsible fashion. For theology, this implied a return in the first instance to the historical Thomas and his thought. This was later transformed into a more profound and more extensive return to the sources, namely the historical sources of the faith as such and thus to the reality that constituted the research object of theology. In concrete terms, this second movement re-emphasized a connection made by the Church Fathers, one more or less taken for granted by Thomas Aquinas, the connection between Bible and theology, a connection that was reaffirmed during Vatican II by the Council Fathers.[52]

PART II

PHASES/FACES OF THE *NOUVELLE THÉOLOGIE* PRIOR TO VATICAN II

Chapter 1

LE SAULCHOIR, LOUVAIN AND ROME: DOMINICANS

The first phase of the *nouvelle théologie* spans the period from c. 1935 to 1942. In the following pages we will discuss the contributions of Yves Congar, Marie-Dominique Chenu, Henri-Marie Féret, Louis Charlier and René Draguet. With the exception of the latter, all the others were members of the Dominican order. We will conclude our discussion of each individual with the question: '*Nouvelle théologie?*' To tie up the present chapter we give an overview of some other developments during the first phase.

1.1 *Congar*

While there can be little doubt that he was unaware of the fact, Congar was the first to take clear steps in the direction of the *nouvelle théologie*. In my opinion, Congar was the creator of the preliminary programme of the *nouvelle théologie*, although such an observation can only be made with hindsight. Nevertheless, Congar did not hesitate to risk his neck on the matter from 1935 onwards. Convinced of the essence of theology's mission, he reacted against aberrations that he believed had gained the upper hand in Catholic theology.

Yves Congar
Yves Congar was born on 13 April 1904 in Sedan (France).[1] He lived through two World Wars, the second as a prisoner of war.[2] In November 1925, he entered the Dominican convent at Amiens. A little more than a year later he made his vows and was given the religious name Marie-Joseph. He was ordained to the priesthood on 25 July 1930 and defended his doctorate a year later in Le Saulchoir with a dissertation on the unity of the Church. From 1932, the year that Chenu became rector of Le Saulchoir, Congar served as professor of Fundamental Theology and actively participated in Le Saulchoir's move from Belgium to France in 1937. During this period, Congar was editorial secretary of the journal *Revue des sciences philosophiques et théologiques* and he established the series 'Unam Sanctam'. The first book in the series was by his own hand: *Chrétiens désunis*, understood to the present day as an exceptionally influential work that helped to put ecumenism on the agenda of the Roman Catholic Church.[3] Yves Congar was captivated by ecumenism

throughout his life, describing unity – in line with his doctoral dissertation – as his passion.[4] Nonetheless, his support for the ambitions of the *nouvelle théologie*, his enormous openness towards ecumenism and history, his book *Vraie et fausse réforme dans l'Église* published in 1950,[5] and his 1953 *Jalons pour une théologie du laïcat*[6] saw to it that his relationship with the magisterium was injured to such an extent that he was forced into a wilderness of personal humiliation and terrible loneliness.

Congar's interest in the eminent role of the laity and emphasis on the place of the priest in the midst of the laity exhibits parallels with Marie-Dominique Chenu. In an article written in 1954, for example, Chenu wrote about 'priesthood and the worker priests'.[7] In the same year, both Dominicans were removed from their teaching positions on account of their support for the worker-priests. Chenu left for Rouen, while Congar took up successively residence in Jerusalem, Rome and Cambridge, moving finally to Strasbourg in 1956. Both individuals had to wait until the Second Vatican Council – during which they each played an important role – before receiving renewed recognition from the magisterium.[8] In his diaries of 1946–56 Congar gives a testimony of his loneliness and difficulties. For example, he writes that the Roman system made him a broken man, 'someone killed while still alive'.[9] Within the context of his difficulties with Rome, he called the Holy Office 'a police regime of betrayal'.[10]

In spite of his troubled relationship with the magisterium, Congar's interest in Church and theology continued unabated and he was first in line among the world's theologians to fan the wind that would ultimately blow over the entire Church via Vatican II.[11] The well-wrought arguments evident in his 1946 *Dictionnaire de théologie catholique* article on the nature, methods and history of theology testify to his careful and considered approach.[12] The same year is the starting point of his theological diary of one decade:[13] the time of the *nouvelle théologie*, *Humani generis*, Rome's rejection of the worker-priests in France, the withdrawal of his own mandate to teach and his departure from Paris. This list makes Bernard Sesboüé's words comprehensible: 'it is not a surprise that Congar, with a delay of four years, experienced the same fate as the Jesuits of Fourvière did four years before.'[14] The second collection of his diaries appeared in two volumes and focuses on his activities as *peritus* during the Second Vatican Council.[15] It was only during Vatican II that his order was able to bestow on him the title of Magister in Theology, a title refused him in 1947. It is claimed, nevertheless, that the refusal had to do with the fact that both he and Henri-Marie Féret, aware of the problems encountered by Chenu (see below), had expressed the desire that Garrigou-Lagrange be excluded from the jury established to evaluate their application.[16]

In addition to his personal diaries, Yves Congar also published a large corpus of other works such as, for example, his *La Tradition et les traditions* (1960–63)[17] and his *Situation et tâches présentes de la théologie* (1967).[18] Many of Congar's works are translated into several languages.[19]

Many believed that Congar and de Lubac would be made cardinals at one and the same moment, but the February 1983 consistory only selected the Jesuit for elevation to the cardinalate. On 26 November 1994 – Congar was 90 years old at the time – he was finally made cardinal by Pope John Paul II. Prevented from attending the elevation ceremony in Rome for reasons of health, Cardinal Johannes Willebrands travelled in the Pope's name to Paris for a private ceremony of elevation.[20] Nine years earlier, Congar had terminated his activities within the International Theological Commission after a 16-year membership. A year later, in 1986, he took up residence in the Hôtel des Invalides where he died on 22 June 1995, finally granted due praise by all, but still a lonely man.

Two Articles, a Series and a Book Review

On 18 January 1935, Congar published an opinion piece entitled 'Déficit de la théologie' in the French Catholic newspaper *Sept* in which he endeavoured to weigh up the position of theology in the year 1934. Up to the present, research into the *nouvelle théologie* has not drawn attention to this article. The first part of the text establishes a pastoral point of departure while the second part points to the need for a 'theology of life'. We only focus on the second part, of which we first present the English translation:

> The position given to theology in the contemporary world, which seems to us to provide a pretty hollow result for 1934, was fixed at the very moment when the unity of mediaeval Christianity was dissolving and the new principles of the modern world were emerging. This takes us back to the constitution of the secular State (early fourteenth century), the early philosophies of immanence (Italian quattrocento followed by Campanella, Spinoza and their posterity) and the ruptures of the Renaissance and the Reformation. The result of all this was to cut the spiritual realm in two. On the one hand, there was the spiritual realm of the modern world, pursuing its development in its own way, tackling and solving the problems of life on its own, with what it was able – out of habit and thanks to traditions embedded in the institutions themselves – to retain of Christianity. On the other was the spiritual realm of the clerics, the heaven of the theologians, cut off from the world, going over and over their own problems in a different, dead language, problems that had been set once and for all, rendered eternal not so much by scholarly abstraction as by lack of scholarly faith or interest.
>
> Between these different realms only two junctions, two bridges over the gulf could be seen, equally foreign in kind to the order of vital communications: on the one hand apologetics, which struggled to restore relations between estranged brothers, and on the other the criticisms with which authority beleaguered the errant modern world.
>
> I cannot expand at length here on considerations that would require an entire volume to develop, backed up with arguments, texts and facts. But however general these considerations may be, they give us elements of the

theological balance sheet for 1934. From the point of view of the real nature of theology, the world's needs and what should be done by theologians in the world, this balance sheet is clearly in deficit.

Theology has itself become a kind of technical discipline, a thing in itself, a professional or class activity, a corporate knowledge, a special, closed domain of interest to a select few.

When on the contrary it is a form of wisdom and, where knowledge is concerned, Wisdom itself.

When it should have a living connection to the rest of knowledge and human activity, which would give all the rest its direction, measure, complement and underlying fertility.

When it should be open to all manifestations of knowledge or creation, welcoming them, adopting them all, giving an 'aim', a direction and the revelation of their true nature to many new movements that, alone, are destined to remain mere 'trends'.

When it should be 'the salt of the earth'.

We must have the courage to recognize that too many questions that are the requests of life itself have not only gone unanswered, but have not even been considered by the theologians. While *work* is one of the most important elements of human life and the modern states are seeking to give it status, where do we have a theology of work? And not just of work, but its necessary complement, a theology of leisure and rest? As long as we do not have a theology of work and rest – and not just a few grand principles from the Bible or the encyclicals, but a real *scientific* and properly theological study, with investigations, statistics, a historical dossier and elaboration of doctrine right down to the capillary details – I say that the theological balance sheet shows an absolute deficit in relation to what is by far the greatest part of human life. These are requirements so primary and so radical that, because of this initial failure, efforts made elsewhere on other matters are stricken with sterility and presumed to be worthless. And so on.

Note that I am not at all saying that the clerics have done nothing, in 1934 and before, to fulfil their divine mission in the world of men. I know very well that a great number of them have worked and continue to work with a courage and fervour that give brilliance to the supernatural beauty of the Church in the twentieth century; and I know that, as soon as they have left scholasticism of the seminary behind, many young priests put their life force into the very area I have just been discussing; and the pragmatism of their action, too mistrustful of a science of which they know little more than the wax mask, seems to me no small matter of concern for the years to come; lastly I know that, here and there, serious work has been started, promising us less hollow theological results in the future than those that have gone before. Moreover, before accusing the rest, I have too many domestic failures to deplore.

But in examining the results for 1934 I wanted to sound this note. There is an urgent need for us as clerics to turn our efforts and apply our vocation of 'salt of the earth' to theology itself, as a human *science* of the things of faith or that touch on faith. As long as we have not done the theology of all the great human realities that must be won back for Christ, we will not have done the first thing that is to be done. As long as we talk about Marxism and Bolshevism in Latin, as I've seen it done in classes and at conferences of theologians, Lenin can sleep in peace in his Moscow mausoleum. An enormous task of information, investigation, contacts and right-minded, ardent, living reflection lies before us. We must prepare, on the austere, laborious level of theological science, to reconquer the modern world. But the first condition for doing theology is believing in it.

Congar's words clearly point to the fact that theology was facing a number of challenges in the middle of the 1930s. His appeal appears to focus on the restoration of the bridge between the clergy and the laity and between two alienated spiritual universes, in short: between theology and life. The prevailing theology had turned into a 'wax mask', the exercise of a technique instead of a wisdom. Congar laments the lack of interest among theologians for the cares and activities of real life, the life of the factory worker, for example, and his wife and children. In such circumstances, theology clearly tended to circle around itself rather than around the narrative God is writing or desires to write with his people. Theology in 1934/35 was self-sufficient, detached from everyday life, and theologians were only interested in the prevailing theology and were thus inclined to be self-centred. If nothing else, however, Congar's article sounded the alarm. In his opinion, theology had to change, and in order to do so it had to leave its fortress.

Five months after the publication of the opinion piece, Congar repeated his appeal in a contribution to the French periodical *Vie Intellectuelle*. There, in June 1935, he published an article whose title translates into English as 'A theological conclusion of an inquiry on unbelief', in which his point of departure was once again pastoral: the hard reality of secularization.[21] The results of relevant research were disconcerting: secularization had taken on enormous proportions in France. In his conclusion to the article, Congar insisted that the central reason behind the growth in secularization was the rupture between faith and life. The fact that Christianity was only *part* of the world – not in the least because the Church (*in casu* the magisterium) was far too focused on itself – and the fact that people were more and more inclined to set the faith to one side in their search for happiness in life, stood in sharp contrast to the faith's inner dynamic: faith desired to permeate all of life and reveal the way to true happiness. The importance of the third part of the article is evident here, namely 'incarnation's deficit or Catholicism's deficit?'. Congar holds that Church and theology are so detached from society and reality (first of all the reality of the faith), that they cannot incarnate themselves anymore. I am inclined to support Joseph Famerée and Gilles Routhier's description of this part of the text as programmatic since Congar had already published the blueprint thereof in his January 1935 opinion piece.[22]

Congar's pastoral orientation, however, evidence of which can be found in both the opinion piece in *Sept* and the article in *Vie Intellectuelle*, did not only address itself to theologians and the Roman Catholic faithful. In 1937, he published his *Chrétiens désunis*, in which he presents the 'principles of a Catholic "ecumenism"'. Together with the following two volumes in the 'Unam Sanctam' series, *Chrétiens désunis* reveals the importance of the series for Catholic theology. While Congar's book underlined the relationship between Christians, the second book in the series focused on the unity of the Church with the publication in 1938 of *L'unité dans l'Église*, the French translation of a work by Johann Adam Möhler originally published in Tübingen in 1825(!) in which the author reveals himself to be one of the primary figures of the *Tübinger Schule*. If one bears in mind that Möhler was one of the pioneers of a theological engagement that endeavoured to fully integrate history, then there can be little doubt that the choice was far from accidental. Möhler's enormous interest in the Church Fathers was shared by Congar and Henri de Lubac, the author of the third volume in 'Unam Sanctam' series. In the same year as *L'unité dans l'Église*, de Lubac published his *Catholicisme*, subtitled *Les aspects sociaux du dogme*. The success of all three books immediately established the series' reputation.

Congar's personal involvement in the debate surrounding a number of controversial theological publications represents a further expression of his efforts to bridge the gap between faith and life. In 1939, he published a review offering comment on several publications surrounding the nature and methods of theology. We will return to this text below when we focus our attention on the commentaries that appeared in relation to Louis Charlier's essay (Section 1.4) and in our description of further developments during the first phase of the *nouvelle théologie* (Section 1.6).

Nouvelle Théologie?

The description of the opinion piece published by Congar in January 1935 as the preliminary programme of the *nouvelle théologie* does not do justice to the author's intentions at the time of writing. This is evident, for example, from his refusal to be branded one of the *new theologians*, as we can read in the letter he addressed to Emmanuel Suárez, Master General of the Dominicans, on 16 January 1950.[23] The letter compares the *nouvelle théologie* with 'La tarasque', a monster created in the human imagination, in the minds of believers, the presence of which they detected everywhere in spite of the fact that it did not exist. Congar insists in his letter that the expression *théologie nouvelle* had 'nothing to do with genuine reality'.[24] He was to repeat the *tarasque* comparison a quarter of a century later.[25]

While Congar refused to be labelled a representative of the *nouvelle théologie*, it is difficult to deny that he played an important role in support of the movement whether or not he intended to do so. As noted above, I am convinced that the 1935 opinion piece constitutes the first draft of a programme of a movement that was later to be described by its adversaries as the *nouvelle théologie*. According to Congar, the gulf between theology on the one hand, and faith, society and real life on the other could only be closed by emphasizing incarnation, history and pastoral affinity. Such an approach implied the abandonment of closed scholasticism, the system that had shackled theology and separated it from reality and everyday life.

Is this, together with his involvement in the debate (cf. *infra*: 1.6), enough to identify Congar as a *new theologian*? Perhaps not, but there are further elements that would support a positive answer to the question, including his good relations with other representatives of the *nouvelle théologie* (Chenu, Féret, Daniélou, de Lubac, etc.) with whom he exchanged ideas, critique, suggestions and comments. De Lubac's *Catholicisme* appeared, as we know, in Congar's series while Chenu and Féret were of a similar mind in the construction of a history-oriented theological project.[26] All of the aforementioned theologians encountered difficulties with Rome, yet all of them were likewise present at the Second Vatican Council.

My conviction that Congar was a representative of the *nouvelle théologie* places me in the excellent company of Étienne Fouilloux, although the latter maintains that Congar only manifested his support for the *nouvelle théologie* after the publication of *Chrétiens désunis*:[27]

> Between *Chrétiens désunis* (1937) – the first French language book on ecumenism – and *Vraie et fausse réforme dans l'Église* (1950) – proposing extensive reform without schism – the Dominican theologian, together with Chenu, Daniélou and de Lubac, became the personification of a 'new theology' in France, more concerned with a return to the Christian sources and dialogue with the major intellectual movements than the need to agree with prevailing scholasticism.

1.2 *Chenu*

The name Chenu deserves more than a brief mention in the context of any discussion of Congar's vision. He was not only rector of Le Saulchoir, the study centre at which Congar served as a professor, he was also instrumental in transforming the philosophical and theological formation offered at Le Saulchoir into fully fledged ecclesial faculties during his ten-year tenure, thereby acquiring the approval of the Church authorities.[28] Such recognition naturally implied that the official intellectual formation of the French Dominicans had a significantly neo-scholastic bias. It is something of a paradox, therefore, that the same rector Chenu was ultimately to bring himself and his house of studies into discredit in Rome. His description of Le Saulchoir's unique history, points of particular interest, work climate and methodological approach published in 1937 was met with considerable appreciation side by side with much critique.

Marie-Dominique Chenu

Marcel Chenu was born on 7 January 1895 in Soisy-sur-Seine (France) and entered the Dominican order in 1913 where he was given the religious name Marie-Dominique.[29] During the First World War he resided in Rome because his health was considered too weak for him to play an active part in the war. While in Rome he continued his studies at the Angelicum where he was granted a doctorate in theology in 1920 – a year after his ordination – on the defence of a dissertation on the topic of contemplation written under the supervision of Réginald Garrigou-Lagrange.[30] Having turned down his supervisor's request to remain at the Angelicum as a lecturer, he was then appointed Professor of the History of Dogma at Le Saulchoir. While Ambroise Gardeil had taken some initial steps as founder of Le Saulchoir towards the historical and critical understanding of Thomism, the latter is associated in particular with Chenu's tenure as the study house's rector from 1932 onwards. Chenu's enormous respect for Gardeil is evident from the foreword to the second edition of the latter's *Le donné révélé et la théologie* (1932).[31] Five years later, Chenu described this work as 'the guiding principle of the theological methodology and intellectual activity at Saulchoir' in his *Une école de théologie: le Saulchoir*, which appeared *pro manuscripto*.[32] He begins his book with an overview of intellectual formation within the Dominican order from its foundation, turns his attention to the specificity and methodology of Le Saulchoir and then focuses on the application of the said methodology in the domains of theology, philosophy and medieval studies. *Une école de théologie* enjoyed enormous success within the order. In the meantime, the study centre itself was relocated from Kain in Belgium to Étiolles near Paris in 1937.

In February 1938, Chenu was reprimanded by his order's leadership and, as a consequence, the further distribution of his book was interrupted. In spite of the many declarations of support, *Une école de théologie* was placed on the Index of Prohibited Books on 4 February 1942,[33] together with *Essai sur le problème théologique* penned by Chenu's fellow Dominican, the Belgian Louis Charlier (see Section 1.4 below). Chenu and Charlier submitted to it two months later.[34]

As a consequence of the 'indexation' of *Une école de théologie*, the Dominican authorities organized a visitation of Le Saulchoir and Chenu was removed as rector and professor. This did not prevent him, however, from continuing his teaching activities at the Sorbonne and the Institut catholique de Paris.[35] Furthermore, the second revised and enlarged edition of his successful 1927 publication *La théologie comme science au XIIIᵉ siècle* appeared in 1943, shortly after his condemnation.[36] As one would expect of a Dominican, this study of medieval theology culminates in Thomas. Indeed, the establishment of the Institut d'études médiévales in Ottawa by Chenu and his friend Étienne

Gilson in 1930 offers clear evidence of the fact that he felt very much at home in the Middle Ages.[37]

Chenu is known to have been supportive of the orthodoxy associated with Thomism, albeit with a degree of sympathy for the various Thomistic 'schools'. In his opinion, Thomism offered a useful conceptual framework for dealing with, among other things, social issues and themes. Chenu's contribution to the debate surrounding *L'Action française* in 1927, for example, was received with high esteem as 'original'.[38] Furthermore, together with Jacques Maritain and Étienne Gilson, he was to become one of the leading protagonists of the so-called 'Christian Humanism'.[39] Geared towards the formation of students, and as the belated results of his teaching at Le Saulchoir, Chenu's *Introduction à l'étude de saint Thomas d'Aquin* appeared in 1950.[40] Three years later he succeeded Gilson as editor-in-chief of the 'Bibliothèque thomiste' series, a position he was to hold until his ninetieth birthday![41] His *La théologie au XIIe siècle*, a collection of 19 articles published between 1925 and 1954, appeared in 1957.[42] Restrictions of time and space prevent us from offering a complete survey of Chenu's extensive bibliography, which consists of no fewer than 1,396 titles.[43]

The thought of Marie-Dominique Chenu can be divided along three major lines.

It is evident from the works to which we have already referred that Chenu was active in the first instance in the domain of theology, reflecting on its nature, task and methodology. Furthermore, he was particularly well qualified to speak and write about the work of Thomas Aquinas. Indeed, it would be fair to say that he grafted his vision to that of the Angelic Doctor, faithful to the inheritance of the 'historical Thomas', which he carried forward in his own writings. Chenu's rear-view mirror did not stop at scholasticism, however, although he had a more than average knowledge thereof. His continuation of the ideas of Thomas can best be described as an 'anthropologization' and 'historicization' thereof. Chenu set about his goal of forcing an opening in the Thomistic thought by introducing history into the theological endeavour as a fully fledged partner in terms of both content and methodology. For him, the crossroads of faith, theology, history and humanity is the figure of Jesus. Jesus is the core of the theandric mystery of faith, i.e. the mystery of the divine, to be found, believed in and described *in* human beings and *as* a human being.

The social life of the Church constitutes the second domain in which Chenu was active. His efforts to create an opening in theology for history are focused in the social domain on creating an opening for the full integration of the laity. His engagement in this regard, however, did not limit itself to publications, but included participation in the Jeunesse ouvrière chrétienne movement (JOC) and in the meetings of the Semaines sociales de France.[44] Indeed, Chenu was instrumental in introducing the vision of Cardinal Joseph Cardijn, the founder of the JOC, to the Dominican authorities, who offered it their support.[45]

Chenu's third domain of activity was focused on the priesthood in an effort to open it up to the reality of everyday life. He thus created a bond between pastoral care and the social reality of working people by promoting the worker-priests who took jobs as labourers and evangelized alongside their lay counterparts. In so doing, Chenu situated himself within the dynamic of the Mission de France, the French re-evangelization movement, which first saw the light of day in 1941 with Parisian Cardinal Emmanuel Célestin Suhard as one of its pioneers.[46] With a view to the 'evangelisation of the shop floor', Chenu developed a 'spirituality of labour' and published a brochure on the topic in 1947 entitled *Spiritualité du travail*.[47] According to Jean-François Six, the encyclical *Humani generis* (1950) targeted Chenu and Congar, among others, for their support for the worker-priest movement, which was considered tantamount to an expression of sympathy for Modernism and communism.[48] While Rome put an end to the worker-priest movement in 1954, Chenu published an article in the same year in which he underlined his sympathies for the movement and its goals.[49]

The commotion surrounding the worker-priests forced Chenu's superiors to expel him from Paris in February 1954 – although he remained editor-in-chief of the Le Saulchoir periodical *Bulletin thomiste*[50] – at which point he took up residence in Rouen. He was only allowed to return to the Dominican convent of Saint-Jacques in Paris in June 1962, no more than a couple of months prior to the opening of the Second Vatican Council.

Marie-Dominique Chenu played an active role during the Vatican II as personal adviser of Claude Rolland, bishop of Antsirabé (Madagascar).[51] Rolland himself had been a student at Le Saulchoir and had followed Chenu's classes.[52] He described him as someone who was always ready for action.[53]

Chenu died at the Dominican convent in Paris on 11 February 1990.

Une école de théologie: le Saulchoir

Marie-Dominique Chenu completed *Une école de théologie* in 1937. This book was not intended for publication as he himself explicitly states in the foreword. The work is written in line with Chenu's predecessors as rector, sharing their concern for Le Saulchoir's unique approach to the philosophical and theological endeavour. Chenu composed his manuscript under the 'patronage' of Thomas Aquinas and that of his predecessors as head of Saulchoir, namely Ambroise Gardeil, Antoine Lemonnyer and Pierre Mandonnet.

Une école de théologie consists of five chapters. Bearing in mind the goals of the present work, we will focus on the second, third, fourth and fifth chapters, dealing respectively with methodology, theology, philosophy and the study of the Middle Ages. The first chapter on the history of Dominican houses of formation will not be addressed.

In the second chapter of *Une école de théologie* Chenu distils Le Saulchoir's method in three points. In the first instance, the study house's goal is to examine various methodological approaches in earnest in order to determine their value in the context of the search for truth. The use of the plural within the title of the house journal *Revue des sciences philosophiques et théologiques* already indicates a level of fundamental respect for methodological pluralism. Secondly, the school is convinced that the work of Thomas Aquinas provides a charter whereby attention can be focused on the interaction between the (natural) working of human reason and the (supernatural) working of the faith, in line with the Dominican tradition and of Leo XIII's vision. Thirdly, Chenu insists that intellectual engagement of theology does not take place outside the life of faith and cannot thus be separated from it.

In the remainder of the chapter, Chenu concretizes these principles along two clear lines. The first is borrowed from Étienne Gilson. Chenu supports his vision that philosophy should not focus on itself, but rather on the concrete issues and problems of the time in which we live. This perspective is ultimately an undisguised criticism of scholasticism. Chenu dismisses the latter as a closed system, the principles of which give rise to nothing more than concepts. He considers it inappropriate to tackle questions and problems on the basis of preconceived solutions and conclusions. It is here also that we find the core of Chenu's critique of the Thomistic handbook tradition. Living reality demands open and equally living scholarship, not a system that is determined to maintain itself, that cuts itself off from reality. As far as Chenu is concerned, Thomas would have been the first to criticize contemporary scholasticism.

The second line of concretization has to do with *ressourcement*. Chenu sees such a return to the sources of the faith as a means to grant philosophy and theology a place in the actual experiential world of the faithful. Having established a number of initiatives to this end within Le Saulchoir, Chenu argues that 'the return to the sources in the historical scholarship offers us the same as the return to principles in speculative thought: the same spiritual energy, the same rejuvenation, the same productivity; and the one guarantees the other'.[54]

The third chapter of *Une école de théologie* constitutes the core of the book, an initial blueprint of which can be found in Chenu's 1935 article 'Position de la théologie'.[55] In the light of the Modernist crisis, Chenu introduces the chapters by pointing out that genuine theology is not 'anti-intellectual', rather it is painstakingly preoccupied with its own object according to its own principles. With respect to the object of theology, Chenu insists that revelation holds pride of place. Revelation is the sap of the tree of theology; theology is not a fortress surrounding revelation as the prevailing scholasticism tended to imply. Theology's task is to establish an inventory of revelation *and* to establish a speculative structure to conceptualize it. In the course of time, he adds, the tasks or functions of theology had come to develop separately, whereby the encounter between positive theology and speculative theology had frequently become a source of discord and division.

Chenu describes theology as 'faith *in statu scientiae*'[56] with revelation as its object, the faith as the unique light in which research is to be conducted, and reason as the conceptualizing, organizing and synthesizing principle.

According to Chenu, theology after the Reformation evolved into a discipline that was so detached from the faith that it was more interested in the form thereof rather than the content, i.e. the elimination of faith in favour of logical argumentation. As such, he argues that theology had lost its unique source and at the same time its connection with reality. Chenu then insists in no uncertain terms

> . . . that the unbeliever can construct a good logical argumentation on the grounds of reason as long as he respects the law of syllogism [two premises and a conclusion]. But this implies that theology is merely true and no longer godly. We are of the opinion that theology in such circumstances is dead, soulless, a rational diversion on the outskirts of revelation.[57]

Chenu goes on to argue that the stuff of revelation forms the core and context of theological reflection and not the other way round. The stuff of revelation is unassailable, not one or other theological system.

Theology is *intellectus fidei*, oriented towards the datum of revelation. Theology desires to plumb the depths of this datum *and* to live from it. This life takes shape in concrete history, for which theology must account to the full, and not in the least because Scripture and Tradition represent the datum of revelation in history. Chenu nevertheless rejects the facile schema '*probatur ex Scriptura – probatur ex Traditione – probatur ex Ratione*' as the residue of a compromise between speculative and positive theological engagement.[58] In his view, such a schema ignores the inviolable primacy of the datum of revelation, incorrectly represents the relationship between both methods, and ignores – on the basis of the evidence it claims – the experiences and thoughts of Christian men and women that underlie the texts. When Chenu relates this to Thomas's *Summa* he argues: 'The stuff of revelation is not intended to reinforce the Thomistic system, rather the Thomistic system is at the service of the faith – which transcends it – in an intelligible manner.'[59] In his book Chenu thus concludes that the faith has expressed itself in history in such a variety of forms that positive theology can play an important role in recovering, understanding and representing the datum of revelation. In his opinion, speculative theology cannot survive without positive theology.[60] It is for this reason that he emphasizes a theological endeavour rooted in faith and in contact with the life of faith.[61]

Chenu continues by posing the question that had significantly dominated the Modernist crisis: can/should theology and faith be approached from a historical-critical perspective? Without offering an explicitly positive answer to this question, Chenu insists that theologians can only achieve genuine insights by focusing on history: a history in which God has revealed Godself and in which all components of it are to be explained as links in the chain of the economy of salvation. At the centre of the history we encounter the 'theandric mystery', i.e. the mystery of the Christ of faith who is also the Christ of history. The incarnation of God in the concrete figure of Jesus Christ invites theologians to give form to the *fides quaerens intellectum* by locating themselves within the *fides ex auditu* and by allowing historical criticism to be the theological endeavour's appropriate instrument. The historical sciences and the historical-critical method are referred to in this sense as the *ancillae* of theology, and not absolutized in the sense attributed to the Modernists. Chenu is thus able to call for the integration of the historical-critical method as a fully fledged component in the palette of methods, convinced that the unity of the faith will be increased rather than diminished thereby.

In line with Gardeil, and supported by his confrere Francisco Marín-Sola,[62] Chenu argues that our knowledge of the datum of revelation is ever growing. The location of the said datum of revelation is the Church, which, as theandric reality, is the Body of Christ. The notion of tradition is thus freed of its static character by Chenu and as such 'revivified'. Tradition, after all, is the very presence of revelation, the anchor of the datum of revelation in the living Church, in the experience of Christians today, and not only the said datum as the primary element in a logical argument. Theologians are interested in 'Christianity in motion', which includes missionary work, social engagement, etc. In Chenu's mind, theologians who ignore such realities and confine their interests to publication and scholastic dispute are poor theologians. Le Saulchoir intends to contrast itself with the latter group of theologians by engaging in theology along the lines set out by the *Tübinger Schule* (cf. Johann Sebastian Drey and Johann Adam Möhler) and John Henry Newman, giving due account to the living datum of revelation and to history.[63] This explains initiatives such as the 'Unam Sanctam' series and the JOC. Two years prior to the publication of *Une école de théologie*, Chenu wrote that the JOC has taken the lead in returning to the sources – i.e. by rediscovering the theology of the Mystical Body and elaborating it according to its social dimension – in contrast to the (majority of the) theological schools.[64]

Chenu makes a distinction between 'old theology' and 'new theology'. The former remains powerless and passive in face of the mystery of God while the latter – including that of Le Saulchoir – presents itself as active.[65] Theology, for Chenu, is 'faith at work in a theological rational manner'.[66] As such, he accepts a theological rationality whereby he immediately does justice to the unity of and the distinction between revelation and theology, abolishing the gulf between mysticism and theology and between positive and speculative theology. Theology employs reason as a research tool and thus works according to the logic thereof, but faith remains central. Faith and reason are thus combined and even entangled with one another in a coherent and healthy fashion, given that theology is a human – and thus also rational – patchwork, inadequate and distinct from its inviolable object.

Chenu not only advocates theological reason's right to existence; 'even' theological systems are to be tolerated in so far as they do not try to control the datum of revelation.[67] In order to avoid the latter, Chenu follows Gardeil in making a distinction between theological science and theological systems. The science of theology guards the datum of revelation from abuse, while theological systems create a speculative structure based on reason and within a particular spirituality. As such, theology's two core tasks constitute the criterium or reason for the distinction: the protection of the datum of revelation and the creation of a speculative construction.[68]

Rooted in faith's motivating forces, which are driven in turn by the soul's restless and impatient desire to see God, Chenu believes strongly in theology's potential for progress.[69] Progress in theology no longer has to do with the pro-vision of more sophisticated or more numerous theological conclusions, or with the protection or defence of dogmas or orthodoxy, but rather, and in the first instance, with the beatific vision of God, to which the faith desires to lead us. Chenu thus insists that theology needs to stay focused on the source of faith, on revelation, and that *contemplatio* is theology's natural biotope. According to Chenu, this is the sense in which Thomas identified *sacra doctrina* and the *vita contemplativa* with one another. Theology ought thus to be a *quaedam impressio divinae scientiae*, 'an impression of divine knowledge', like the imprint left by a sandal in the sand.

Chenu places greater emphasis in his 1935 article than in his book on the idea that both the theological endeavour and contemplation are rooted in faith. Both theology and contemplation have faith as their point of departure, are faith-oriented and make progress in the light of faith. He thus states theology's position as wedded to and engaged with the life of the believer.[70] Reason in the context of theology is inseparably bound to faith and is at the service of faith. Faith predominates because it is the source, context and motivating force of theology, and it is from faith that the latter derives its scientific status – faith *in statu scientiae*.[71] For Chenu, this is the primary meaning of the concept *fides quaerens intellectum*: the search for beatific 'vision' of God, characteristic of the theological endeavour and of prayer.[72] In concrete terms, this implies that theology immerses itself in history because it is a *locus theologicus* in which God has made Godself manifest and in which faith and its aspirations are given form. In this sense, Chenu clearly adopts a position counter to the magisterial reduction of revelation to a catalogue of propositions as found in Denzinger and the like. Revelation extends beyond texts because faith first and foremost has to do with reality.

In the fourth chapter of *Une école de théologie* Chenu discusses philosophy and begins by stating that philosophy and theology are two distinct and autonomous worlds. While the former is the servant of the latter, it nevertheless employs its own methods and has its own object. Philosophy works with premises that follow the path of reason towards conclusions. As such, its primary goal is to plumb the depths of reality and steadily transform it into a culture, or at least provide the building blocks thereof. Chenu insists that philosophy and Christianity are not mutually exclusive, although the search for, examination of, and proclamation of truth makes it important to look at the said truth from every side, including the philosophical. He adds in this regard that spiritual initiatives are born at the heart of philosophy, just as the faith for its part ought to recognize its rational foundations in the *praeambula fidei* provided by philosophy. Some scholastics, he notes, appear to have forgotten this. Nevertheless, theology cherishes the faith in the first instance and not philosophy. At this level, Chenu argues, we need to 'disinfect' ourselves of 'baroque scholasticism',[73] which deduces first principles on exclusively rational grounds in line with Gottfried Wilhelm Leibniz, and as such has constructed as system bereft of fundamental contemplative attitudes and intent on presenting itself as positivistic and objective. As disinfectant, Chenu argues that we must make room for the speculative dimension, referring in this regard to Rousselot's *L'intellectualisme de saint Thomas* from 1910, the third edition of which appeared a year prior to the publication of Chenu's book.[74]

Philosophy continually recapitulates and actualizes themes and issues from history. Chenu points out, by way of example, that Thomas used history as a lever in his ideas and thought. While philosophers avail themselves of history, historians are presented with a threefold task with respect to philosophy. First, they must determine the context in which a particular philosophy came into being. Second, they must explore the context and sources of the said philosophy in order to determine its initial and irreducible spirit (the spirit that leads to new degrees of knowledge). Third, it is their task to determine the inner logic of a given philosophy whereby the progressive evolution of intuitions and systematic constructions leads towards a synthesis. Chenu likewise alludes to Thomas Aquinas at this juncture by way of example.

According to Chenu, one of the best lessons we can learn from the history of philosophy has to do with its analysis of the idea of a 'system'. A system – such as scholasticism – is guided by an organic principle and constructed on the basis of propositions and theses. The thought of Thomas Aquinas, however, is a philosophy rather than a system, because its propositions and theses are the result of a collection of organic principles. Chenu insists, nevertheless, that Thomas is first and foremost a theologian.

The fifth and final chapter of Chenu's book focuses on the study of the Middle Ages, whereby Chenu himself makes the first move in returning to the sources that are not only to be found in antiquity but also, evidently, in medieval times. According to Chenu, the Institut des études médiévales has a twofold task in line, once again, with Thomas: (1) to uncover and study the visions, texts and contexts of the period and (2) to initiate students in scholarly work.

Chenu reduces the issues surrounding higher education to the problem of methodology. It is important to bear in mind, he insists, that the call to 'reform theology' and the critique of procedures involved were initially expressed in the domain of methodology at the beginning of the twentieth century (cf. Gardeil) as well as the period that gave rise to *Une école de théologie*. Chenu sees the solution in a balanced interaction between research activity according to the various methods on the one hand, and the demands of formation – in combination with the goals maintained within the framework of orthodoxy – on the other, which he applies to the study of the Middle Ages.

Roman Condemnation and a Single Book Review

Only one single review is available of *Une école de théologie*, which is most likely due to the fact that the book appeared *pro manuscripto*. Oddly enough, the single review appeared in German, penned by Friedrich Stegmüller in 1939 in the *Theologische Revue*. Stegmüller provides an overview of the seven characteristic features of Chenu's understanding of the method of theology: (1) the datum of revelation is primary, (2) the sources are thus likewise primary, (3) the related importance of history within theology, (4) theology's involvement in the present and the future rooted in history, (5) the considerable importance of reason in theology, (6) the conviction that theological systems are relative, and (7) the independence of theological scholarship.[75]

After an investigation at the order's highest level, in which Chenu was also questioned, the latter was presented with ten theses and required to sign them in order to demonstrate that he was 'on the same wavelength as the magisterium and thus with orthodoxy'.[76] The signature, however, did not prevent other measures being taken. In a decree dated 4 February 1942, the Holy Office declared that Chenu's *Une école de théologie* had been placed on the Index of Prohibited Books.[77] The decree was published in *L'Osservatore Romano* on 6 February and a justification of the book's condemnation penned by Pietro Parente appeared three days later in the same Vatican newspaper.[78] Parente stated his conviction that *Une école de théologie* had brought the prevailing neo-scholasticism and its conceptual framework into discredit through its (exaggerated) interest in the subject, experience, religious sentiment and the notion of development. According to Parente, Chenu was to be situated in the domain of Modernism. His thought was considered harmful. Chenu even suggested that the main reason for the condemnation of his work was his preference for 'the application of the historical-critical method to the development of Christian ideas'.[79]

Nouvelle Théologie?

Having referred to Congar's 1935 opinion piece as the preliminary program-matic document of the *nouvelle théologie*, we can now describe Chenu's *Une école de théologie: le Saulchoir* as the programme itself. The third chapter of the book is of particular importance in this regard, with its draft blueprint in Chenu's article of 1935. The central elements of Chenu's programme are like-wise recognizable in the seven points of Friedrich Stegmüller's review. There can be little doubt that the goal of this sevenfold approach was to bridge the gulf between theology and faith and thereby close the gap between theology and reality. The latter takes pride of place for Chenu: the reality of revelation, i.e. the reality of the faith, and the reality of life. Theology's aim is to reflect on reality in the light of faith.

In the midst of the prevailing neo-scholastic framework, Chenu was (albeit willingly) obliged to take classical Thomism as his point of departure. Theology's implementation of history loosened the Roman neo-scholastic straightjacket, thus launching definitively the Thomistic *ressourcement* called for by Yves Congar: the return to the thirteenth-century Thomas as an alternative to the prevailing obsession with his sixteenth- and seventeenth-century commentators.

The fact that *Une école de théologie* was not distributed by a publisher necessarily limited its marketability, although it enjoyed a surprisingly large reception. Together with the book's content, this helps to explain Rome's irritation. Indeed, it was within the context of Rome's rejection of *Une école de théologie* that the expression *nouvelle théologie* emerged for the first time, although Chenu himself speaks only of the distinction between 'old' and 'new' theologians , without using the term *nouvelle théologie*.

1.3 *Féret*

Henri-Marie Féret is perhaps the least known among the theologians of Le Saulchoir.[80] While he may have been overshadowed by his confreres Congar and Chenu, his name frequently appears in company with theirs nonetheless. Féret even described them as 'the three musketeers'.[81] Féret's relative anonymity can be explained in part by the limited number of publications he produced when compared to Congar and Chenu. Féret dedicated himself in the first instance to the spoken word in preference to the written word.

Henri-Marie Féret

Henri-Marie Féret was born on 2 January 1904 in Bordeaux (France). He entered the Dominicans in 1921, studied philosophy and theology at Le Saulchoir and was granted his doctorate in theology in 1930. He was immediately appointed professor of Church History at Le Saulchoir, a task he fulfilled with considerable pleasure.

The year 1941 was an exceptional one for Féret, a year associated with three initiatives that were destined to enjoy a long and successful existence. In the first instance, he established the so-called 'Journées sacerdotales' – formation days for priests. Secondly, he established similar formation days for lay people known as the 'Cours Saint-Jacques', named after the Dominican convent in Paris. In the same year, Féret was responsible for starting the 'Groupe évangélique', a group of women who met on a monthly basis to reflect on a passage from the Bible and to pray. Of these three initiatives, the latter enjoyed the greatest longevity, continuing for no less than 50 years and only coming to an end shortly before Féret's death in 1992. It was on the instigation of the Groupe évangélique that a brochure on Féret appeared after his death: 'Henri-Marie Féret: Dominicain: 1904–1992'.[82] The women of the group clearly idolized their spiritual leader. At the height of the group's strength and to ensure it continued to be workable, Féret divided the members into several subgroups, each named after one of the apostles.[83]

Ten years after these three initiatives, Féret became a lecturer at the Institut catholique de Paris, more specifically at the then recently established Institut

Supérieur de Catéchèse. The appointment was not to last long, however. In 1954, a year before the publication of his book *Connaissance biblique de Dieu*,[84] he was deprived of his appointment for supporting the worker-priest movement.[85] As was the case with Congar, who had likewise been deprived of his authority to teach, both men were subjected to what appears to be an unequivocal sign of demotion: exile from Paris. After a short stay in Nancy, Féret made his way to Dijon, where he served as prior of the Dominican community from 1958 to 1964.

In the meantime, the Second Vatican Council was already underway. Féret was granted the opportunity to participate when Claude Flusin, the Bishop of Saint-Claude, invited him to be his personal adviser and appointed him to that post. Féret was present and at work in Rome in 1963, at the beginning of the second session of Vatican II. It was in Rome that Congar, Chenu and Féret met again for the first time in years and where they were able to continue giving shape to their emphasis on history. The postconciliar period was quick to bring a change of habitat: in 1968, six years after Chenu and a year after Féret, Congar likewise returned to Paris (promotion!) and the 'three musketeers' were united once again.

Féret was responsible for 'elaborate' articles in Festschriften for both Congar and Chenu. In a collection published on the occasion of Congar's seventieth birthday (1974) he wrote about 'concrete and historical theology and its pastoral importance today'.[86] The Festschrift for Chenu (1990) contains a contribution from Féret first published in 1964, a collection of memories of and reflection on the years in the 1940s that led up to the Second Vatican Council.[87]

Henri-Marie Féret died in Paris on 12 November 1992.

A Project

My treatment of the project shared by Congar, Chenu and Féret in the context of the contribution of the latter is far from accidental. As the trio's only Church historian, Féret's part in the shared project is quite considerable in this regard.[88]

The project shared by Congar, Chenu and Féret was never realized in the sense that it was intended. While it would be correct to say that their 'theology of history' acquired a permanent place in Catholic theology during the Second Vatican Council, their original plan was to write a 'history of theology' on an interdisciplinary basis (historical and dogmatic). In the archives of the French Dominicans, the file on Chenu contains a seven-page draft outline of the planned 'history book'.[89] The document in question offers a report of a 'reflection' on the topic by Congar and Féret (and Chenu?) that had been handed over to Chenu (hence its presence in Chenu's file, although it is also possible that Chenu acquired it because he was rector of Le Saulchoir at the time). The draft project stems from the mid-1930s although a more precise date cannot be determined.[90] The text can be situated nevertheless in Le Saulchoir, more specifically during the period of the school's 'exile' in Belgium.

The document contains three parts. The first is written in Congar's hand-writing and consists of four points. Point one stipulates that the construction of the work will require considerable effort. Chenu is thus reminded that any return to Canada would be out of the question as it would distract him with other work to such an extent that he would not be able to concentrate on the project. Point two provides further details on the project as such: the presentation of a scholarly history of theology focusing on the bond between culture and the spiritual life and thus at the service of contemporary research in the domains of Church and theology. The document proposes that the project be rooted in 'the three renaissances' without offering further explanation thereof. It goes on to reflect on the possibility of including the history of theology in the East in the project. The lack of literature on the subject was a cause for concern, however, and led to an exclusive focus on the history of theology in the West. Point three argues that one single book would not be enough to encompass the entire project as it was envisaged, although the number of potential volumes was not seen as a reason for concern. Point four divides the work between the three authors. It is worth noting at this juncture that the draft outline only speaks of the period between the twelfth century and the nineteenth century.

The second part of the draft is contained on a single page penned by Féret and dealing with the project's method. In addition to a number of practical remarks, the draft proposes that the book should give pride of place to theological thought and its development rather than official Catholic doctrine. This would make the work more interesting and less of a manual. The document insists, nevertheless, on the need for an overview of successive theological visions.

The third part consists of two pages written by Congar, with added remarks penned by both Chenu and Féret. This part of the document turns its attention to the question whether the project should limit itself to a history of theological scholarship or include a treatment of theology in the light of humanity as a whole. Congar argues that the project be expanded to include the latter and Chenu agrees. Given the remainder of the text (more detailed explanation of the implications of such an expansion), it would appear that Féret was also 'on board' in this regard.

The plan foresaw that the project would evolve in addition to the activities and publications of each of the three Dominican authors. As already noted, the draft project ultimately did not lead to a book on the history of theology in the West. Nevertheless, it would be incorrect to detach the trio's plans in this regard from their many other contributions, such as Congar's article on 'Theology' in the *Dictionnaire de théologie chrétienne* and Chenu's *Une école de théologie*. What then of Féret?

In 1943, the year in which *Divino afflante Spiritu* was promulgated, Féret published his *L'Apocalypse de Saint Jean – Vision chrétienne de l'histoire*[91], in which he explains or rather interprets history in the light of the Apocalypse (cf. his fourth chapter: 'The meaning of history after the Apocalypse'). In so doing he not only gave an initial impetus to a biblical-theological explanation of the course of history, but also evidently to a theology of history, i.e. a theological reflection on history that took history seriously and endeavoured to integrate it to the full.

Roger Aubert rightly refers to this work as the opening gambit in a polemic concerning the so-called 'théologie de l'histoire',[92] which was to continue for two decades, until Vatican II granted an unequivocal place to history and historiography in the theological endeavour.

L'Apocalypse de Saint Jean represents a uniquely personal rendition of the project Féret shared with Congar and Chenu. Written at a time in which ideologies placed history at their own service and rummaged in the course of history in search of support for their own convictions, Féret's book clearly intends to react against such abuses. In spite of this, however, his own reflections were ultimately accused of doing much the same thing.

Nouvelle Théologie?

Féret's 1943 *L'Apocalypse de Saint Jean* reveals that its author functioned more as a bridge between the first and the second phases of the *nouvelle théologie*, and did not belong exclusively to the first phase thereof. This is not only made clear by its year of publication (beyond the 1942 'boundary'), but also on account of its particular interest in the Bible. Féret's involvement in the theology of history debate during the second phase of the *nouvelle théologie*, moreover, likewise supports our conviction that his influence should not be restricted to the first phase. It thus becomes clear once again that the phased subdivision of the *nouvelle théologie* has to be approached with a degree of flexibility.

Féret's contribution to the *nouvelle théologie* can be located specifically in the fact that he constituted a bridge between the first and second phase. As one of the 'three musketeers' and 'instigator' of the most significant background debate of the second phase of the *nouvelle théologie* (i.e. the possibility and potential contours of a 'théologie de l'histoire'), he revealed himself to be a Church historian with his own unique place in the debate surrounding the nature and method of theology.

The fact that Féret supported a Thomistic *ressourcement* together with two Le Saulchoir dogmaticians gives expression to the interdisciplinary platform he shared with Congar and Chenu, a platform they used to launch their appeal for a theology rooted in reality (the reality of faith and life), taking the thirteenth-century Thomas as a trustworthy guide. As a Church historian and theologian, however, Féret's interpretation of reality from the perspective of the Bible in general and the Apocalypse in particular can only be described as ambitious. In so doing, and in his own unique manner, he introduced the biblical perspective into the hermeneutics of the reality of history.

1.4 *Charlier*

Having discussed the 'three tenors' of Le Saulchoir, our attention now turns to Louvain's most prominent representatives of the *nouvelle théologie*, namely Louis Charlier, a Belgian Dominican who in 1938 published his *Essai sur le problème théologique*.[93] The book caused significant uproar in theological circles and inspired many to offer comments and critique. Indeed, a considerable number of articles appeared on and in reaction to his essay before, during and after the Second World War. Due in part to these reactions, Charlier's work has come to be considered the most important publication of the first phase of the *nouvelle théologie*, although several suggest that the influence of his book extends beyond the first phase.

Louis Charlier

Léon Antonius Josephus Charlier was born on 29 January 1898 in Chapelle-lez-Herlaimont, in the French-speaking part of Belgium. He entered the convent of the Dominican order in La Sarte at the age of 17, i.e. during the First World War and he was given the name 'Ludovicus', a Latin name that was soon to make way for its French equivalent 'Louis'. In those days, the Dominican order still had a unitary Belgian province[94] with its provincial house of studies in Louvain where Louis Charlier studied philosophy and theology, made his vows on 10 September 1916 and was ordained priest on 17 April 1922. After his ordination, he stayed in Louvain to complete his studies at the (then also unitary) Catholic university where he graduated with a licentiate degree in history.

Charlier was appointed to teach at the order's study house in Louvain, commencing in 1927.[95] He published his first article three years later in *Ephemerides theologicae Lovanienses*, an exhaustive study of the vision of Thomas Aquinas on the will.[96] In the mid-1930s he first encountered René Draguet, professor of dogmatic theology at the Louvain Faculty of Theology, whose ideas highly influenced Charlier's only work in book form, namely his *Essai sur le problème théologique*. Four years later, this publication was placed on the Index of Prohibited Books – at the same time as Chenu's *Une école de théologie: le Saulchoir*.[97] Together with Chenu, Charlier was relieved of his teaching duties in 1942 on account of the Roman sanction.[98] He was allowed to resume teaching in 1953, this time in the study house of the French-speaking Belgian Dominicans in La Sarte. In 1954, Charlier published an article on the history of the relationship between the deposit of faith and the conclusions of theology.[99] Seven years later, he authored and published two articles, the first offering a discussion of Thomas's five-part proof for the existence of God – the written version of a lecture he had given during one of La Sarte's annual study days[100] – and the second offering a number of theological reflections on Christ as Word of God.[101] In the period between 1954 and 1961, Charlier enjoyed a period of rehabilitation, being granted the honorary academic title of 'magister' by his superiors in 1959. No further publications are recorded, however, after 1961.

Charlier died on 29 January 1981, his eighty-third birthday.

An Essay

In terms of content, Charlier's essay follows a similar line to that found in the courses taught by René Draguet at the Faculty of Theology in Louvain.[102] The latter turned his attention to the familiar triptych: theology's object of research, its concepts and its methods. In addition, the essay exhibits clear associations with Chenu's *Une école de théologie: le Saulchoir* (1937) and Ambroise Gardeil's *Le donné révélé et la théologie* (1909). In addition to the fact that both Chenu and Charlier considered Gardeil's work as foundational to their own reflections on the nature and method of theology, Charlier's essay runs quite parallel with *Le donné révélé et la théologie* in terms of structure.

Charlier's *Essai sur le problème théologique* consists of three main parts. The first deals with the relationship between theology and the revealed deposit of faith, the second discusses the link between theology and rationality, and the third examines the methods of theology and the spirit in which they are practised.

In his foreword, Charlier states clearly that the teaching of Thomas Aquinas serves as the point of departure, source and norm of his *Essai*.[103] He thus expresses his concern to remain faithful to the Angelic Doctor in both letter and spirit.[104] For Charlier, this fidelity to Thomas was the only legitimate basis upon which the emerging 'theological renewal' could be allowed to develop authentically. As such, Charlier immediately confronts an important issue, insisting that the teaching of Thomas himself was the decisive factor and not that of his commentators.

Charlier begins the first part of his essay with a clarification of its title: at the heart of the problem confronting theology one encounters a collection of questions related to its method. He then goes on to offer a preliminary description of what he understands theology to be: a human discipline relying on revelation and developing in dependence on the light of faith.[105] Three aspects are evident in this definition: theology as a human science illuminated by the light of reason and the light of faith, revelation as theology's pre-given foundation and ultimate *raison d'être*, and the idea of theology developing in complete dependence on its specific light, namely the faith.

Charlier continues his discussion with a historical overview of the concept of theology since scholasticism, supplemented with a number of observations on the relationship between theology and revelation. His central thesis argues that revelation is not only a conceptual datum – an arsenal of immutable and inviolable concepts that serve as the building blocks of the faith – but also, and in the first instance, a reality: the *donné révélé* is a *réalité donné*, pre-given revelation is a pre-given reality. This unavoidably raises the question of 'development' since every earthly reality develops. Charlier adds immediately that he does not know how revelation develops, insisting only that it evolves within the Church according to a mysterious pattern. In so doing, however, he clearly establishes the inseparable bond between revelation and the Church: revelation is located within the Church, although the Church is simultaneously part of revelation. In short, revelation develops as the Church develops and vice versa. This implies that theology cannot exist outside the magisterium if it genuinely desires to be a *théologie du donné révélé*, a theology of revelation, i.e. the only true theology.

Revelation is primary in theology and as such it is also evident that revelation is of key importance in (the history of) reality, the incarnation being its most eminent proof. Charlier thus designates the biblical history and the history of dogma as auxiliary sciences to theology.

In the second part of his *Essai* Charlier studies the role played by reason in theology. Without mentioning names, he makes a distinction between two groups of theologians, one group claiming that revelation can be understood on the basis of reason, the other claiming that reason cannot permeate the deposit of revelation but can only interpret it. For Charlier, the study of the relationship between theology and reason is akin to the question concerning the position of theology in the work of Thomas Aquinas. Rooted in Thomas's conviction that faith and reason are bound to one another inseparably, Charlier argues that they are indeed complementary. Thomas ascribes three 'functions' to reason within theology. First, the principles of reason serve as the foundation of theology's constructions as the *praeambula fidei*, which constitute an integral part of theology. Reason is thus related to faith as nature is to grace; the former precedes the latter. Secondly, Thomas argues that the principles of reason are at the service of the faith and in the domain of theology fulfil the role of 'maidservant' with respect to the supernatural truths. This role as maidservant is twofold. It is defensive in the sense that theology makes use of reason to repel the attacks directed against the principles of the faith in the name of reason. At the same time – and primarily – it is explanatory and interpretational: urged on by faith, reason does everything in its power to penetrate to the content of revelation (*fides quaerens intellectum*). A third role ascribed by Thomas to the principles of reason revolves around the deduction of different conclusions from the articles of faith.

According to Charlier, this process of deduction lies at the core of theology's problem. A strict interpretation of the conclusions thereof, Charlier argues, ultimately confronts with two inclusions and two reductions. The first inclusion implies that the entire content of the faith is embraced by the 'first truths' (God exists, God-Creator, God-Trinity). The second inclusion implies that the confession of an article of faith immediately entails (and explains) the confession of each and every article of faith (the link between the various articles is not deduction, but rather God). The Dominican sees a reduction – in fact a further inclusion – in the scholastic argument that those who believe in the Church believe in everything that the Church believes. The second reduction is the reduction of every principle of reason and scholarship to the common and universal principles of reason. Charlier does not believe that Thomas's vision of theology as science is served and recognized by such constriction. Nevertheless, he also expresses some critique of Thomas's vision. The latter's theology is constructed after all on the basis of the immutability and absoluteness of the principles of theology (the articles of faith) and not on the basis of a vision of dogmatic development. In this sense, Charlier argues, Thomas is a child of his time.

In the third part of this *Essai*, Charlier draws methodological conclusions from his self-devised idea of the continuous development of the revealed deposit of faith and from his critique of the strict interpretation of theological conclusions. He laments the fact the historical and scholastic methods have led through the centuries to two distinctive forms of theological endeavour, namely positive theology and speculative theology, a division that has endangered the unity of theology. He points out that Thomas has provided the example of a theology that can only be genuine when it first makes sure of its sources, which are present in the Church.[106] Charlier also laments the fact that many theologians lack a background in positive studies. He thus concludes that theological method comes first and only then theology's two auxiliary sciences, which ought to maintain a mutual balance. History and philosophy are secondary and at the service of theology. He insists, moreover, that theology's entire modus operandi ought to be sustained by a spirit of openness.

Charlier establishes a further inclusion in the conclusion to his *Essai*. Having started with a description of theology in the first part of his work, he concludes here that theology ultimately cannot be described in a single formula because of its complexity. On the other hand, he writes, theology as a discipline enjoys a 'simple' unity. Indeed, the *unity* of theology stems from its formal subject, God, who is both principle and goal.

Charlier concludes that theology is called – because of its nature and object – to make unremitting progress, a progress nevertheless that must follow the development of the datum of revelation within the Church. It goes without saying that the said development is a mystery since its origins are supernatural. In this sense, development is always possible in theology since we are still called to penetrate deeper into the mystery in response to a profoundly human drive. No single theological system is conclusive, therefore, not even scholasticism.

Reactions to the Essay

Charlier's *Essai* elicited a considerable number of reactions. In 1939 alone, the *Essai* was the subject of seven reviews, penned by Charlier's Dominican confreres Yves Congar,[107] Marie-Rosaire Gagnebet[108] and Mannus D. Koster,[109] the Jesuit Florian Schlagenhaufen,[110] the Benedictine Maïeul Cappuyns,[111] the Louvain university professor René Draguet[112] and the Ghent seminary professor Werner Goossens.[113] In 1940, book reviews were published by Jean Cottiaux,[114] canon of the cathedral of Liege, Coelestin Zimara S.M.B.[115] and the Jesuit Charles Boyer.[116] The *Essai* thus drew international attention.

Four reviews allude to the relationship between Charlier's *Essai* and Draguet, suggesting a degree of dependence.[117] Draguet points out in his review that Charlier's work is not a mere copy of his course 'De notione, objecto et methodo theologiae', although he insists that the Dominican made use of his course notes without his prior knowledge, did not mention the said course in his *Essai* – not even in a footnote – and abandoned a number of positions maintained therein or adapted them to fit his own vision. Others associate Charlier in more or less the same breath with Jean-François Bonnefoy, who we will discus later on in this chapter.[118]

Having situated the *Essai* in terms of its origins, we now offer a brief survey of the more positive reactions to its appearance. Koster, for example, writes that Charlier's treatment of the problem exhibits even greater depth than that of Draguet.[119] For this reason, Cottiaux refers to Charlier's work as a 'useful point of departure for a productive development'.[120] Goossens likewise alludes to the value of Charlier's work as an invitation to and meaningful point of departure for reflection on the methodology to be used in the practice of theology.[121] Cappuyns underscores the fact that Charlier's work does not lack 'envergure' and 'cohesion',[122] while Schlagenhaufen insists in addition that the *Essai* reaches to the core of the question, although Charlier's presentation of the problem is better than his solution thereto.[123] Cappuyns, however, does not hesitate to refer to the *Essai* as radically innovative and courageous.[124] Goossens similarly alludes to Charlier's candidness in approaching the given issue.[125] In his opinion, Charlier is critical of the methodological approach of several theologians. Draguet notes on the other hand that the work is primarily a critique of Dominican theologians written by a Dominican![126] Goossens concludes his review by suggesting that the theologians who consider themselves subject to the essay's criticism should take the necessary time to reflect on their method.[127]

The negative response to the *Essai*, however, was even more vigorous than the positive. Gagnebet launches a broadside against what he believes to be the essay's conceptual lack of clarity, claiming that concepts such as 'dogma' and 'positive' are insufficiently explained.[128] Zimara likewise attacks Charlier's vagueness in the articulation of his vision.[129] In my opinion, the said lack of clarity is probably best explained by the general tenor in which the work was written, a tenor described by Cappuyns as 'too mystical'.[130] Nevertheless, Charlier's critique of certain theologians is far from vague. Koster nuances this critique by exposing what he maintains to be its inadequacies: he has accounted for the thought of too few theologians and referred to too many theologians who think the same. According to Koster, Charlier's discussion of the differences between theologians in terms of vision is thus too limited. For him, therefore, the essay is to be recommended in terms of the theme it endeavours to treat but not in terms of its content.[131]

The core of Charlier's vision is a critique of a specific theological perspective and methodology. He reacts with particular vigour against many scholastic theologians who maintain their fidelity to Thomas's commentators. Three reviewers are critical of Charlier's option for Thomas himself rather than his commentators and of his endeavour to think from the perspective of the *Doctor communis*.[132] Goossens points out that Charlier's position on scholasticism is directed exclusively against those inclined to take it to its extremes.[133] Cottiaux, who shares Charlier's critical stance towards Thomas's commentators, asks himself nevertheless whether it makes sense to endeavour to interpret Thomas without accounting for his commentators.[134] Gagnebet's critique in this regard focuses on three specific points and is perhaps the most keenly formulated. He begins with a question: which scholasticism is Charlier talking about?[135] He then goes on to condemn Charlier's critique as unfounded because it is based on a historical *a priori* and on a shallow reading of the texts.[136] Gagnebet asks himself by way on conclusion whether Charlier is aware of the seriousness of his critique, bearing in mind that it is directed against scholastic theology.[137]

Gagnebet points to an apparent inconsistency in Charlier's work, arguing that someone who claims to attach considerable importance to Roman authority clearly has little respect for the (anti-modernist) statements of the said authority. Congar and Schlagenhaufen likewise draw the reader's attention to the fact that Charlier's preferential option for a positive theology goes hand in hand with his interest in the perspective of the magisterium.[138] Charlier's thought on the relationship between history and theology – especially with respect to the development of dogma – however, evidently runs counter to the magisterium's position. In the first instance, Charlier supports a vision of the development of dogma involving the evolution of both revelation and dogma, even after the apostolic period.[139] Gagnebet is critical of his positions and insists that it is only our knowledge of revelation that develops, improving as our insights improve, while revelation as such no longer develops.[140] A second observation is related to the relationship between theology and history. Cottiaux describes Charlier's vision in this regard as follows: 'Surrounded by theology's other maidservants, history is neither queen nor cindarella.'[141] Nonetheless, according to Charlier, Thomas denies the idea that theology is a science in the strict sense of the term.[142] Gagnebet, Koster and Congar offer comment on this. Gagnebet argues that Bonnefoy and Charlier cannot undermine a vision maintained by friend and foe alike for the best part of six centuries, namely that Thomas understood theology to be a science.[143] Koster writes that theology for Thomas was analogous to the other sciences, a position that runs counter to that maintained by Charlier.[144] Congar focuses on the expression *impressio divinae scientiae* employed by Thomas.[145] While Charlier likewise uses the expression and quotes Thomas correctly in this regard, Congar is convinced nevertheless that Charlier's interpretation is not entirely correct. It might be correct to refer to theology as a science in terms of its methodology but the object of theology ultimately makes it different from all the other sciences. Goossens critiques Charlier's uncommon vision of the conclusions of theology along similar lines. While the theme in question might justify Charlier's interest in Thomas research, he argues, it is a shame that he does not offer sufficient response to the question of theology's conclusions within the said Thomistic framework.[146] Similarly critical of Charlier, Cappuyns defends the classical, scholastic understanding of the conclusions of theology. In his opinion, the latter constitute the specific object of theology.[147] The Dominican Henri-Dominique Simonin likewise reacts against Charlier's position,[148] but Boyer can be singled out as perhaps the most critical. In his opinion, the exclusive focus on the knowledge of theology's conclusions that Charlier adopts is ultimately one-sided, if we bear in mind that Thomas is also interested in our knowledge of principles or antecedents. Boyer maintains that this is a contradiction of Thomas,[149] and adds that theology is the science that defends and justifies the principles of faith.[150]

Koster claims that Charlier's study raises many more questions on account of the fact that several elements – in addition to the conclusions of theology – are not studied in sufficient depth. Charlier's treatment of themes such as theology as science, the articles of faith as *praeambula*, etc., he insists, is too limited, too succinct.[151] His critique in this regard is related to the accusation of vagueness made with respect to Charlier's use of theological concepts.

Charlier harshly criticized the classical type of theology and for this reason his own vision was subjected to the same fate, a fate that led some to consider his opinions to be a misunderstanding. Zimara, for example, claims that Charlier narrows the sources of theology to the sources of revelation or the sources of faith, thereby ignoring scholasticism.[152] Charlier argues that the written representation of revelation constitutes an argument at the service of the magisterium's teaching, whereby it is the latter's task to proclaim what the sources contain as sole and unique interpreter. As such, the sources are subordinate to the magisterium; the *positive des sources* is subordinate to the *positive du magistère*.[153]

Of the critical remarks outlined above, three in particular would appear to be decisive in relation to the objectionable character of Charlier's work.

In the first instance, Charlier's vision of the development of doctrine and revelation clearly encountered substantial opposition, especially the idea that revelation itself continued to evolve and not only our knowledge thereof. Secondly, and in combination with the first, Charlier insisted on the reality character of the datum of revelation, an argument robustly substantiated in a highly detailed yet criticized study penned by Jesuit Timoteo Zapelena,[154] who limits his focus to the first part of Charlier's *Essai*. Thirdly, Charlier's critics maintained that his ideas ultimately represented an infringement of theology's speculative character, bearing in mind that he upheld a positive theology in addition to the prevailing speculative variety.

Of the quoted reviewers, it would appear that those tending more towards the speculative were the most critical of Charlier's *Essai* (Gagnebet, Koster, Boyer, Zimara, Zapelena), ranging from moderate to severe. The reviewers who did not lean explicitly in this direction appear for the most part to have favoured Charlier's vision, although their admiration for his intellectual courage was often the overriding feature of their comments (Draguet, Goossens, Cottiaux and Schlagenhaufen).

Roman Condemnation

At the beginning of February 1942, Charlier's *Essai* together with Chenu's *Une école de théologie: le Saulchoir* was added to the Index of Prohibited Books. No reason was given for sanction and no summary of arguments was provided by the magisterium itself.

Nevertheless, a brief schematic overview of the reasons – individual and combined – that motivated Rome's decision to index Charlier's work can be constructed on the basis of archive material, the aforementioned article of Parente and our own research.[155] Rome's critique can be divided into three points.

In the first instance, Charlier is guilty of bringing scholastic philosophy into discredit by (1) presenting Thomas as a child of his time, (2) placing positive theology on the same level as the hitherto universal speculative theology, and (3) devaluing the conclusions of theology by claiming that Thomas did not ascribe an independent role to human reason.

In the second instance, the *Essai* is critical of the then prevailing vision of revelation. Charlier argues (1) that revelation is [also] a reality, (2) that its place is in the Church [not in the sources], (3) that revelation did not cease with the death of the last apostle, and (4) that revelation thus continues to evolve on the basis of the fact that Christ remains a source of faith insight.

In the third instance, Charlier adheres to the idea of the development of doctrine, rooted in (1) the identification of 'reality' and 'conceptuality', and in (2) the fact that the development of revelation logically implies an accompanying development in knowledge (articulated by the magisterium).

Nouvelle Théologie?

Where Chenu's *Une école de théologie* attracted only one review, Charlier's essay elicited a veritable storm of reactions. In spite of the fact that both works were written independently of one another, however, their content and tenor is more or less the same. I thus consider it justifiable to brand Chenu's work as the programmatic text of Thomistic *ressourcement* – and thereby of the *nouvelle théologie* – while considering Charlier's *Essai* to be the first publicly available programmatic text thereof. As we know, Chenu's work appeared in the first instance *pro manuscripto* – i.e. not for general public consumption – while Charlier's work enjoyed widespread distribution as a published text. In this sense, Chenu and Charlier's involvement in the first phase of the *nouvelle théologie* clearly differ.

In spite of differences in distribution and response, however, both works reject the strict interpretation of Thomism upheld by the magisterium. In this sense, there is little reason to be surprised that the first phase of the *nouvelle théologie* emerged from within the Dominican order. Chenu and Charlier became the best-known supporters of a Thomism intent on resourcing itself in the person of Thomas, and not only or in the first instance in the scholastics of the sixteenth and seventeenth centuries. The representatives of the second phase of the *nouvelle théologie* (H. de Lubac, J. Daniélou, H. Bouillard and others) were ultimately to adopt the same aspirations.

1.5 *Draguet*

Having already noted that Louvain professor René Draguet was the most important source of inspiration for Charlier's *Essai sur le problème théologique*, we now turn our attention to Draguet himself.

René Draguet

René Draguet was born on 13 February 1896 in Gosselies near Charleroi (Belgium).[156] During the First World War, he studied philosophy and theology at the major seminary in Tournai after which he was ordained to the priesthood. Draguet was among the first to study at Louvain's Faculty of Theology when the university reopened in 1919 after the war. Albin Van Hoonacker and Alfred Cauchie were among his professors. He was granted the title of Doctor in Theology in 1924 after which he continued at the university for two years as lector in post-classical Greek. He served from 1925 to 1942 as a lecturer in Oriental Churches, although his full-time appointment as Professor of Dogmatics at the Faculty of Theology only took place in 1927. From then until his retirement – a total of 29 years – he also taught a course in Old Slavonic. Draguet was a popular teacher and served as supervisor of several doctoral dissertations, including those of, among others, Gustave Thils and Jan Hendrik Walgrave.[157]

In 1936 Draguet published a series of three articles on the method of theology in the *Revue catholique des idées et des faits*.[158] They represent the written form of two lectures given to the students of the Institut Saint-Louis in Brussels. They offer an overview of theology's methodological approach from the patristic period to his own day, coupled with an appeal in support of the historical-critical study of the Scriptures and the Fathers as a platform for genuine theology.[159] The three articles are related to Draguet's aforementioned course entitled 'De notione, objecto et methodo theologiae',[160] followed as we noted by Louis Charlier, among others. Draguet's 1939 review of Charlier's *Essai* did not go down well in Rome. As a matter of fact, Draguet himself was on the verge of facing his own problems with Rome in the period following 22 December 1941, which marked the opening of the investigation into Charlier's orthodoxy. The Holy Office called on the services of Cardinal Jozef-Ernest Van Roey, archbishop of Mechelen-Brussels, to provide information on Draguet. Van Roey only submitted the requested information after the condemnation of Charlier in February 1942, however, too late to prevent Draguet from losing his teaching mandate and perhaps even contributing to Rome's decision in this regard.[161] The said decision took place on 6 July 1942 and made clear that Draguet was no longer to be considered a member of the Faculty of Theology, although he was permitted to teach Syriac at the same faculty from 1942 onwards.[162] Incidentally, and less than a month prior to the sanction, Draguet's doctoral student Vicenze Buffon's dissertation was placed on the Index, although Rome gave him a second chance a year later, allowing him to defend a revised and corrected version of his work with success after the Second World War.[163]

We will return to the aforementioned series of articles below. For the present, however, a brief survey of related influences on Draguet's work and thought seems appropriate. Draguet developed a sympathy for the vision of doctrinal development elaborated by John Henry Newman and discussed the latter in a collection entitled *Apologétique*, published in 1937 under the editorial supervision of Maurice Brillant and Maurice Nédoncelle,[164] the Dominican who – according to Émile Poulat – had done pioneering work two years earlier on Modernism.[165] Draguet's contribution entitled 'L'évolution des dogmes', continues the line established in his 1936 series of articles. The pinnacle of his intellectual labours on the method of theology and the development of dogma is to be found in his *Histoire du dogme catholique*, published in Paris in 1941 and in a completely revised and enlarged form in 1947, after his condemnation.[166]

After a period of exile in the Faculty of Arts and Philosophy, Draguet was reinstated in 1948 and retired as a member of the Faculty of Theology in 1966. From this point onwards, however, his publication output dramatically increased.

Draguet's work focuses for the most part on patrology,[167] his translation and redaction of patristic texts being the primary source of his international reputation. He translated a work by Dadišo Qatraya (seventh century) on *Abba Isaiah*[168], for example, together with Athanasius' book on the life of Saint Anthony.[169] He also edited a number of collections on the same *Abbas Isaiah*[170], all of which were published in the series 'Corpus scriptorum christianorum Orientalium' and 'Corpus scriptorum christianorum Orientalium – Scriptores Syri'.

René Draguet died in Louvain on 23 December 1980.

A Series of Articles

Draguet's series of articles focuses on the 'theological methods of yesterday and today', addressing the method of Catholic theology by turning attention to theology in the course of its evolution and thus in its various different forms, beginning with the patristic period (up to the eighth century), through the middle ages (up to and including the fifteenth century), and modernity (from the rupture with the East, through the French Revolution, to the second half of the nineteenth century), ending with the contemporary period (from Modernism to the 1930s). According to Draguet, theology exhibits its own specific features in each of these four periods. He does not devote a separate article to the modern and contemporary periods, however, convinced as he was that the theological endeavour was confronted by more or less the same influences during these years. Before launching into the results of his research, Draguet begins with a preliminary description of what he understands theology to be: 'reason informed by faith examining the datum of revelation'. He also insists that theology is a 'human science, in spite of the supernatural light that illuminates theology's trajectory; its condition is that of every science: it perfects itself without cessation'.[171] After pointing out in addition that theology as such is continually at work between the poles of human reason and the datum of revelation, he explains what he understands research in the method of theology to be, namely an investigation of the relationship between human reason and revelation or how reason takes revelation into consideration.

During the patristic period, the theological endeavour was permanently focused on revelation. The proclamation associated with the latter served as the primary basis for the written documentation of the tradition concerning Jesus. The magisterium preserves and monitors the datum of revelation and locates its own authority to this end next to that of the Scriptures. The said authority is personalized, as it were, in the interpretation of the Apostolic Fathers and the Church Fathers. Reason is understood to be 'at the service' of such theologizing as revelation's defensive buffer, up to the third century against the 'attacks' of gnosticism, and in the fourth and fifth centuries as a weapon during councils and dogmatic disputes. As such, reason is seen as the servant of theology, which tended for the most part to hark back in those days to the Scriptures and other early authoritative voices – in short, not to the living tradition – in order to substantiate the living tradition.

In the context of medieval theology, which Draguet considers to be synonymous with scholastic theology, reason came into its own. Following the work and thought of Thomas Aquinas, reason and faith had achieved such a degree of harmony that the synthesis of both, according to Draguet, threatened to cause more confusion than clarity: 'Faith and reason infiltrate one another to such a degree that one can no longer make a systematic distinction between what is specific to the one or the other.'[172] While the theological endeavour in the patristic period had been *centripetal* (continually oriented towards Scripture, the Fathers, Tradition), the same endeavour in the scholastic period had been *centrifugal*: in search of as much knowledge as possible of the supernatural world on the basis of revelation, Scripture, the Fathers and Tradition (but no less on the basis of human reason), following the adage of Anselm of Canterbury: *fides quaerens intellectum*. The rediscovery of Aristotle transformed theology into a genuine science with its own methodology. Thomas played the primary role here as the representative of medieval scholasticism. Taking Aristotle's vision a step further, the Angelic Doctor argued that the articles of faith were the untested and untestable principles of reason and the data deduced from the said principles were reason's tested and testable conclusions. Theology became thus seen as a deductive science. According to Draguet, however, early and 'high' scholasticism were not interested in history or evolution.

'According to the scholastics, there was no essential difference between the faith of the Old Testament and that of the New', he writes.[173] By contrast, late scholasticism (fourteenth–fifteenth century) is characterized by its historical and methodological critique. The nominalists – who continued to work deductively – made a clear value distinction between various sorts of truth: the truth of the Scriptures, of the apostolic tradition and of the Church. Just as heresies and other opposition movements undermined the authority of the Church – *in casu* its magisterium – late scholasticism undermined the synthesis of faith and reason. With this at the back of his mind, Draguet characterizes Thomas Aquinas as having ploughed a furrow, as it were, and nothing more, a furrow that others were to continue and deepen in the centuries that followed.

After the middle ages, scholasticism came to the fore as a stable and stabilizing asset to Catholic theology. Speculative theology – styled thus in order to distinguish itself from the historical or positive theology that emerged during the sixteenth century – after all is *the* theology, Draguet argued, with Thomas as its most prominent point of reference, although the latter was often reduced de facto to his commentators. On the other hand, the method of scholastic theology was subjected to critique where scholars became interested in arguments that explored hitherto only implicit elements of revelation instead of revelation itself, in which theology ought to focus its interest. Draguet describes the development or growth of the said critique in a particularly systematic manner, beginning with the mysticism of the fourteenth century, through fifteenth- and sixteenth-century humanism, to the Reformation and Protestantism of the sixteenth century. In the period between the sixteenth and the eighteenth centuries, the critique became anti-ecclesial and in some instances even anti-Christian. In the nineteenth century, it gained impetus and energy because of theories relating to the emergence and development of doctrine. The Modernists were condemned at the beginning of the twentieth century because, in Draguet's opinion, they had spoken out in an unfortunate manner against the classical positions of Catholic theology, although they were completely in line with developments in historiography, which served as the seed-bed for historical or positive theology. It was here that the crux of speculative theological critique was to be located: positive theology ultimately eliminates itself as theology by adopting the method of historiography. The positive theologians reacted by arguing that they had ultimately allowed themselves to be guided by the magisterium, thereby justifying their claim to the name 'theology'.

The practice of positive theology was only 'neutralized' with true effect as it were in the second half of the nineteenth century, although the significance of this neutralization remained relative given the fact that all theological handbooks had become completely scholastic. According to Draguet, positive theology existed from the outset in two distinct forms: (1) the type that accounts for doctrinal development, to be described as *positive des sources* and (2) the type that does not account for such development, to be described as *positive du magistère*. Apart from this distinction, Draguet considered it to be one of theology's primary challenges to determine its position in the field of positive theology as knowledge of the articles of faith on the one hand, and speculative theology as knowledge of the conclusions that are drawn from the articles of faith on the other. At the time of writing, Draguet understood theology to be either positive-speculative or positive-scholastic, whereby the speculative element was becoming more and more subordinate to positive theology:[174]

> Speculative theology becomes increasingly subordinate to positive theology when [the datum of] faith can only be established in practice as pre-given and the positive method emerges as the only method of theology.

Draguet sees a second challenge to theology in the precise and unambiguous characterization of positive theology. Strangely enough, he does not formulate this challenge with respect to speculative theology, although he clearly argues that scholastic theology, in spite of its ancient pedigree, still does not know what it stands for and what its object of study is.

Draguet's series of articles concludes with a number of observations summarized here under four points. First, he insists that one can learn from both speculative and positive theology. Speculative theology teaches us that after the Middle Ages, our primeval desire for knowledge became philosophical, while positive theology makes it clear that the theological endeavour must take the sources of the faith into consideration, checking its results against them and against the magisterium. Secondly, Draguet clearly states that our attention must continue to be focused on both domains. He writes with respect to speculative theology that the small number of truths that constitute Catholic dogma ought to be explained according to relative categories. As far as positive theology is concerned, he calls for an integration of the notion of doctrinal development into Catholic thought, although he is aware that this cannot be expected in the short term. Thirdly, Draguet argues that faith has nothing to fear from historiography by virtue of its single truth. Draguet concludes with a recapitulation of his description of what theology is, serving as an *inclusio*, as it were, linking the beginning of his series of articles with the end:[175]

> Theology can be described today in two movements: in the first instance it represents scientific knowledge of God and the world based on the positive data of revelation presented to us by the magisterium of the Catholic Church; in the second instance, theology is the interpretation of revelation in terms of values that are guaranteed by reason.

Nouvelle Théologie?

Our exploration of the relevant aspects of Draguet's work has brought four main points to light. First, Draguet clearly refuses to subject himself to the norms of neo-scholastic thought. He understands Thomas and scholasticism as *one*, albeit very important, movement in the development of theological thought. In combination with this, Draguet opts in the second instance for a historical approach. He approaches the uniqueness and method of theology – and thus also the relationship between faith and theology – by casting a retrospective glance at the various methodological approaches that have manifested themselves in the course of history, and by demonstrating a clear preference at the end of his series of articles for positive theology, which prevails over speculative theology while not eliminating it completely. Thirdly, Draguet sheds light on the inter-section of history, revelation, magisterium and orthodoxy, more specifically on the development of dogma. He understands the bond between theology and the development of dogma to be indissoluble and ascribes a dynamic to both that can be explained as the ongoing exercise of making explicit that which has always been implicitly present in the deposit of revelation. In so doing, Draguet locates himself in the danger zone of Modernism as defined by the magisterium. In spite of this, a fourth feature of Draguet's vision is his con-cern to remain within the lines established by the magisterium, a concern we can deduce from his emphasis on the *positive du magistère* in addition to the *positive des sources*.

It is obvious that these four points are in line with our understanding of the *nouvelle théologie* and with our conviction that none of its representatives aimed to attack the magisterium. Whether Draguet is to be considered a *new theo-logian* or not, due to his series of articles and his influence on Louis Charlier, he could rightly be called in a way the 'ghostwriter' of Charlier's contribution to the *nouvelle théologie*.

1.6 *Further Developments During the First Phase*

In addition to the positions of Congar, Chenu, Féret, Charlier and Draguet, a further five contributions deserve our attention at this juncture if we are to touch on all the major elements of the first phase of the *nouvelle théologie*. We shall begin with a brief examination of a series of articles published by the French Friar Minor Jean-François Bonnefoy. We shall then return to the Dominicans and focus briefly on three figures working in Rome (Rosaire Gagnebet), Paris (Yves Congar revisited) and Louvain (Dominicus De Petter) respectively. We conclude with an article by the Roman Jesuit Charles Boyer. The discussion of each contribution will be succint and chronological. In a way the five points we will consider are an appendix of the present chapter: necessary in order to map the whole debate, although the developments in question tend to be considered of the second order in the debate surrounding the *nouvelle théologie*.

Jean-François Bonnefoy

Jean-François Bonnefoy was born in France in 1897 where he died in 1958. He entered the Order of Friars Minor – Franciscans – in Toulouse and defended in 1927 his doctoral dissertation on the gifts of the Holy Spirit according to

Saint Bonaventure at the Institut catholique de Toulouse, which was revised and published two years later.[176] Bonaventure continued to inspire Bonnefoy's writing, as is apparent from his 1934 *Une somme bonaventurienne de théologie mystique*.[177] His best-known work appeared three years later: *Chronique de l'Annonciade*, a chronicle of the foundress of the Order of the Blessed Virgin (Annunciade), Saint Jeanne of France, and of the confessor who was to help her in founding her monastic order.[178]

The three-part article published by Bonnefoy in *Ephemerides theologicae Lovanienses* in 1936–37 represents a significant contribution to the foundational discussion surrounding the nature, task and method of theology.[179] Bonnefoy's text is an exploration of Thomas Aquinas' concept of theology, which he begins with a distillation of two source texts, namely Thomas's *Commentary on the Sentences* and his *Summa theologiae*.

The first article begins with a piece of Thomas exegesis concerning the source texts, after which Bonnefoy focuses on the problems surrounding his chosen theme with respect to texts by Antonin-Dalmace Sertillanges and M.-D. Chenu. Bonnefoy clearly states that revelation, Scripture and theology constitute the core information required to demonstrate that the *sacra doctrina* refers to a reality. He bases his point of departure on the first article of Thomas's *Summa theologiae* and on the singular form of the expression *sacra doctrina*, describing it as a synonym for *theologia* and *sacra Scriptura*. Bonnefoy insisted that theology's task was to acquire insight into received revelation and thus contrasted his vision of the distinction between *revelata* and *revelabilia* with that of John of Saint Thomas (scholasticism's most avid representative). The latter understood the distinction to be between the formally revealed and the virtually revealed, while Bonnefoy understood the *revelata* and the *revelabilia* as two groups of formally revealed truths, 'already distinguished in the first article of the *Summa*'.[180] Bonnefoy argues that it is wrong to claim that the *revelatum* is the specific object of divine faith and the *revelabile* the specific object of theology, insisting that in so doing one upsets the evident cohesion between faith and theology, sacred doctrine and sacred Scripture.

Bonnefoy's discussion of the first nine articles of Thomas's *Summa* makes it clear that he understood theology to be a speculative science, superior to all others on account of its close bond with the Scriptures. He makes a distinction in his discussion of the tenth article between *sacra doctrina* and *sacra Scriptura* based on his conviction that the hermeneutical rules do not carry the same weight with respect to the interpretation of the Bible or the biblical commentaries and the Church Fathers. He insists nonetheless that theology and Scripture share the same origin, the same certainty (derived therefrom), the same object (God) and the same content.

Having concluded his first article by arguing that 'theology is only scientific to the extent that the Scripture is scientific',[181] his observations lead him into his discussion of the question of methodology. How does one work from principles to conclusions, from direct objects of faith (obtained without reasoning) to indirect objects of faith (obtained by reasoning)? Bonnefoy turns to the vision of Thomas and that of Bonaventure in search of an answer, reminding his reader that both maintained different opinions on the relationship between faith and reason. For Thomas, reason is faith's faithful partner, while for Bonaventure reason is 'mistress of and in theology', whereby theologians must turn to the authority of the Scriptures when reason is powerless. In any case, Bonnefoy insists that reason does not constitute a danger to faith – reason is willed by God himself – and that it can be of service to faith in three different ways: (1) it prepares the way by identifying the natural truths that faith presupposes, (2) it provides analogies for the supernatural truths, and (3) it defends the faith by exposing the imperfect arguments of its adversaries. These three tasks are extrinsic to 'theology as deductive science'.[182]

In his third article, Bonnefoy explores the specific goal of theology, namely the 'articulation of faith'. He admits, however, that such an articulation, formulated in a language invented through reasoning, is subjective and that the Church alone can establish unanimity. The article concludes by associating this with the vision of Thomas on the relationship between philosophy and theology: where philosophy is employed to explain the scriptures, one does not dilute the wine (Scripture) with water (philosophy), one changes water into wine.[183]

Marie-Rosaire Gagnebet

Rosaire Gagnebet was born in 1904 and acquired the religious name Marie-Rosaire upon entering the Dominican order in Toulouse. He obtained his doctorate in Theology in 1938 with a dissertation on the nature of speculative theology and was appointed as lecturer at the Angelicum in Rome, a post he was to hold until 1976. In spite of Gagnebet's 40-year academic career, it is surprising to find that neither the in-house periodical of the Angelicum nor any other periodical published an 'In memoriam' on his death in 1983. He was renowned, nevertheless, as a meticulous speculative theologian, a dyed-in-the-wool proponent of the classical type of theology, and equal in this sense to his colleague Réginald Garrigou-Lagrange. On the occasion of the latter's death in 1964, Gagnebet penned a fine 'In memoriam' that was published in *Angelicum*.[184] In the same year he was appointed consultor to the Holy Office. He served as *peritus* during Vatican II and proved himself an ardent defender of so-called conservative interests, especially with respect to the redaction of the dogmatic constitution *Lumen Gentium*.[185] The unity of the Church and collegiality within its ranks were his primary concerns.[186]

Gagnebet published a three-part article in the *Revue thomiste* in 1938 entitled 'La nature de la théologie spéculative', based for the most part on his dissertation.[187] The first article gives pride of place to the practice of Augustinian theology, the second article is devoted to the theology of Thomas or the practice of speculative theology, and the third article concentrates on the problems to which this latter type of theology gave rise in the sixteenth century, more specifically the thought of Luther and Erasmus.

Taking *Dei Filius* as his point of departure, Gagnebet argues in the introduction to his first article that all theology presupposes faith. In line with
Vatican I, he describes speculative theology as the human search for knowledge
of the faith via rational argument, exemplified in Thomas Aquinas. Gagnebet
is aware, nevertheless, that two types of theological practice existed side by
side in Thomas's day, namely Augustinian theology and Thomistic theology.
According to him, the main difference between the two perspectives was to be
located at two levels, both of which were methodological. In the first instance,
Thomas assimilated the Aristotelian understanding of science into theology, a
tendency Augustinian theology continually resisted. Secondly, Thomas understood action as a means to acquire knowledge, whereas Augustine held the
opposite to be true in favour of the act of love.

On the other hand, however, Gagnebet points to a parallel between Augustine
and Thomas, namely the distinction they make between faith and theology in
the search for faith insight. Gagnebet even goes so far as to describe Thomas's
vision as an 'echo of Augustine's teaching', although he immediately adds that
Thomas took the consequences of the said distinction further.

Gagnebet himself clearly has sympathy for both Doctors of the Church. This
explains his endeavour to establish a link between Augustine and Thomas – the
method of Thomas and the perspective of Augustine.[188]

Yves Congar Revisited

In *Bulletin thomiste*'s fifth year of publication, which covered 1937–39, Congar
published a review of the contributions of Bonnefoy, Gagnebet, Draguet and
Charlier.[189]

He notes in the first instance that theology is a living reality and that it is
subject to the 'laws of progress' like any other living reality.[190] For this reason,
theology is in constant need of self-reflection and renewal. In this regard, he
insists, theologians should first determine what Thomas understood the theological endeavour to be, 'a task that Bonnefoy, Charlier and Gagnebet each
included in their work'.[191] Congar applauds their determination to engage
the challenges facing theology from a historical perspective and praises their
studies for clarifying our understanding of Thomas's approach to the practice
of theology.

Congar summarizes Bonnefoy's series of articles in six points and then
goes on to point out that Charlier's book is less 'exegetical' with regard to
Thomas, describing his vision of theological methodology as 'prudently reform-
minded'.[192] Following an overview of the content of Charlier's book, Congar
offers a number of observations on the notion of theology in Thomas based on
his own detailed reflections. Congar's reflections on the notion of theology in
Thomas thus serve as a sort of touchstone for evaluating the six core points
of Bonnefoy's series of articles. We know now that Congar's personal reflections in this regard formed the basis for his contribution to the *Dictionnaire
de théologie catholique*, where he also makes reference to Bonnefoy and

Charlier.[193] Our overview of Congar's review considers both his own reflections and critical remarks.

Congar begins by focusing on two concepts. In the first instance, he argues that the expression *sacra doctrina* refers to everything within the framework of revelation that relates to revelation's transfer of knowledge, whereby (divine/supernatural) theology is of vital importance, although transcended, and the Scriptures are central. The supernatural level is thus included within the expression *sacra doctrina* (whereby the latter is employed without difficulty as a synonym for *sacra Scriptura*). The second concept to which he refers is *revelabile*. Congar points out that both John of Saint Thomas and Gardeil ascribed a strange technical significance to the concept, while Charlier's understanding thereof is more accurate, namely everything we can learn from revelation in the light of revelation.[194] He goes on to argue that the heart of the discussion has to do with the theme of theology as science. According to Congar, the key to understanding this theme is to be found in Thomas's *In Boetium de Trinitate*, which states that one can speak of science when unknown or less-known truths can be derived from better-known truths or from firm convictions.

Congar then points out that the articles of faith fulfil the role of truths that serve as principles, a conviction shared by both Bonnefoy and Charlier. Congar also follows Charlier and Gagnebet's conviction – Bonnefoy does not speak of it – that the said articles of faith can be traced back to God. For Congar, this represents the uppermost guarantee that (human) theology is the highest form of imitation of the supernatural *sacra doctrina* and that theology is as much science as it is wisdom:[195]

> Look at what theology as science ultimately is: a human imitation of divine theology, scientific reasoning acquired by speculation. *Impressio divinae scientiae*, according to Saint Thomas.

This latter statement is also borrowed from *In Boetium de Trinitate*, which Congar further explores. His understanding of Thomas's vision can be summarized in four points. First, theology for Congar is clearly a science: the human and thus secondary variant of divine science. Second, human theology is piecework, never complete, never divine. Third, human theology distinguishes itself from the divine *sacra doctrina* via the rational processes employed in the human science: unknown or insufficiently known truths are deduced from better-known truths, in particular from the (inviolable) articles of faith. Supernatural theology is characterized by perfect truths, insights and the beatific vision and does not engage in reason. Fourth, Congar insists that the deposit of faith is primary and that we can only arrive at new insights when we reason in the light of revelation, in the light of Godself. Congar thus describes Thomas's concept of theology as the rational and scientific rendition of Christian teaching, the *sacra doctrina*.

Based on his own personal reflections, Congar goes on to offer a number of critical observations with regard to Bonnefoy's articles – following the six core points distilled at the beginning of his review – and Charlier's book. He begins by criticizing Bonnefoy's static interpretation of the concept *sacra doctrina*, insisting that it needs to be broader and more flexible. He then focuses his attention on the question of theology's scientific character. Congar shares the position adopted by Gagnebet and Charlier, both of whom are critical of Bonnefoy's insensitive and shallow treatment of Thomistic texts. He insists with regard to Bonnefoy's theological principles and conclusions that both he and Charlier are guilty of over-systematizing Thomas's vision. Congar is more reserved in his understanding of the articles of faith, which serve for Thomas as the principles of theology, and is not inclined to limit them to the articles from the confession of faith. Congar then discusses the theological methodology, arguing that Bonnefoy's reference to *argumentari ex autoritate* is of little value since theology is based on *argumentari ex principiis*, albeit acquired through faith (faith being the authority). Congar ultimately accuses Bonnefoy of being disloyal to Thomas on the question of the use of reason in theology. For Bonnefoy, reason is limited to argumentation employed in explaining or demonstrating the truths of faith. For Congar however, this is not in line with Thomas's intentions and with the latter's own theological engagement, which were broader than Bonnefoy's representation thereof. Congar concludes by criticizing Bonnefoy's vision of theology as a revealed science, insisting that Thomas understood theology to be a science of revelation and about revelation.

Congar rounds off his review by pointing out that Gagnebet offers a fortunate complement to his own reflections on the concept of theology and briefly explores the latter's work. In spite of the similarities, however, he concludes that two points of conflict are evident between his own position and that established by Gagnebet.[196] He notes in the first instance that Gagnebet's rendering of the vision of Augustine and his followers focuses too readily on the speculative dimension of theology to the detriment of the positive dimension and insists, albeit without further explanation, that Gagnebet's description of the meaning of *sacra doctrina* does not square with the first article of Thomas's *Summa*.

Dominicus De Petter

Dominicus De Petter was born in Louvain in 1905 and died in the same city in 1971. He is known in the first instance for having taught Edward Schillebeeckx, Piet Schoonenberg and several of their contemporaries (see also Part II, Chapter 3 in this volume). This influential philosopher became unintentionally involved in the first phase of the *nouvelle théologie*, although his involvement only became problematic in 1942 after the condemnation of his confrere Louis Charlier. De Petter's 1939 article 'Impliciete intuitie' (Implicit intuition) offended his superiors to such a degree that they dismissed him from his position as Dean of Studies at the Dominican priory in Louvain in 1942.[197] Against the background of the condemnation of Louis Charlier, his confrere and fellow professor at the priory's house of studies, and that of René Draguet, his colleague at the university, De Petter's 'punishment' can be seen as a third component in Louvain's involvement in the *nouvelle théologie*. There can in fact be little doubt that the sanction against De Petter was a result of the measures taken against Chenu and more particularly Charlier.

The goal of De Petter's 'Impliciete intuitie' was to demonstrate a distinction between two sorts of intuition: intuition that takes certainty (inviolable and unequivocal concepts) as its point of departure with the intellect as actor (in line with Joseph Maréchal), and intuition that takes vague contact – contact with reality – within the deepest core of the intellect as its point of departure, whereby the intellect instigates a conceptualization of reality while continuing to subject every concept to critique. Indeed, De Petter argued that no single concept was adequate enough to designate the objects of reality. Reality prevails over the expressions thereof. This implied that concepts required continuous revision and adjustment. Conceptual inadequacy at the 'level of the explicit' leads one to infer the existence of an implicit level. In short, De Petter speaks not of an intuition that is cut off from reality or turned in on itself but of an intuition that belongs to the essence of human knowing as an implicit moment of intuition. Given that we cannot penetrate directly to the implicit intuition, we are left to search for points of association at the level of the explicit with the level of the implicit.

In the article's conclusion, implicit intuition – the deepest contact between man and reality – is taken to be the foundation of the act of the intellect and as such part thereof. De Petter thus insists on three levels in this regard: implicit intuition (the content of which is described as the core of the act of the intellect); an awareness of reality instigated by intuition; and an awareness that associates the level of the implicit with the level of the explicit or the third level.

Dominicus De Petter refused to lock up reality in concepts. For him, the intellect circled around reality and not vice versa. It is for this reason that he insists on giving a place to vagueness. Things are not always as clear as they seem. If such is true with respect to our thinking about reality, then it must surely apply to our thinking about the reality of the divine. De Petter's article was a slap in the face for scholasticism's adherents, who refused to accept the existence of a moment of intuition and who did not want to abandon the certainties and concepts provided by neo-scholasticism.[198]

Charles Boyer

Jesuit, professor at the Gregoriana and dyed-in-the-wool Thomist, Charles Boyer was born in France in 1884 and died in Rome in 1980. In 1940 he published an article entitled 'Qu'est-ce que la théologie' in *Gregorianum*, of which he was editor-in-chief at the time, an article with the telling subtitle: 'Réflexions sur une controverse'.[199] In similar fashion to Congar's review, Boyer's article offers a sketch of the discussion on the foundations of theology and provides some personal reflections.

In his overview, for example, Boyer points out that he has difficulty in accepting Charlier's vision on the value of theology conclusions, which sometimes offered too many concessions to a new understanding of theology, and the vision of Gagnebet, which continued to uphold a rigid Thomistic system.

Boyer then presents his own observations to the reader in two points.[200] The first of these alludes to the two orders of knowledge and their mutual relationship. Boyer is of the opinion that there is not only an order of knowledge of the principles, i.e. an order of knowledge dependent on the supernatural level, but also an order of knowledge of the conclusions. As such he completely dismisses the idea that theology is nothing more than *Konklusionstheologie*. In order to substantiate his position, Boyer briefly sketches the starting point, process and end of theological reasoning. He writes with regard to theology's starting point that theology must protect and justify its principles. In so doing it makes progress, working with other disciplines such as philosophy and history. The path followed by theology begins with the principles and makes its way to other truths. One certainty – namely the principles – demands that we go in search of other certainties. According to Boyer, however, it is wrong to narrow Thomas's vision of the task of theology to the attainment of conclusions on the basis of the principles. In his opinion, theology does not only function in the light of faith, but also in the light of reason and with other instruments.

Boyer's second point deals with the relationship between theology and the magisterium. He indicates that he has difficulty with the idea of a developing deposit of faith, which Charlier takes as his point of departure. He has problems, in addition, with the idea that theological certainty is dependent on the judgement of the magisterium alone and not on sources or rational deduction as well. 'It was possible to be certain of the Immaculate Conception of the Virgin prior to 8 December 1854', Boyer insists.[201] What the Church believes is correct, although it only believes in what is revealed.

Boyer concludes by calling upon theologians to remain alert and to be meticulous in their thoughts and reflections. He thus argues that the light of faith and the light of reason go hand in hand because they have the same source, namely God as First Cause of all things.

Boyer's ideas elicited a response from Henri de Lubac in an article published in 1948 in *Recherches de science religieuse*.[202] De Lubac discusses the theme of the development of dogma at great length and criticizes rigid ways of thinking that do not provide space for a living faith. Boyer did not hesitate to respond where the opportunity arose,[203] publishing a short but pointed reaction in the same year in *Gregorianum* in which he focuses his critique on the idea of a progressively developing vision of truth allegedly maintained by de Lubac in line with Charlier.[204]

1.7 *Concluding Observations*

In the present chapter we have discussed the visions of a number of *new theologians* and drawn attention to the critique with which they were confronted.

The central feature of the vision of the *new theologians* is to be found in their endeavour to restore the relationship between Catholic theology, the reality of faith and the reality of life as such. This implied among other things that theology had to be up to date and not only a derivative of the theology devised by scholastic thinkers of the sixteenth and seventeenth centuries. Theology had to be about faith as reality and explicitly restore contact with the latter. Faith, after all, was not to be reduced to a catalogue of concepts to be juggled by theologians according to the rules of logic. As theology's mainspring and breeding ground, faith was clearly more than this. In short, theology was confronted in the 1930s with a call to explore below the surface. In the first phase, this implied a return to the historical source of the one whose name had been associated for centuries with a system, namely Thomas Aquinas. In other words, the *new theologians* valued scholasticism, but wanted to replace 'John of Saint Thomism' – an expression of Louis Bouyer, referring to the Thomistic system represented par excellence by John of Saint Thomas[205] – with a more genuine 'Thomism'. This endeavour to open up Catholic theology from within was viewed by the magisterium with suspicion and was even subject to condemnation. The punitive measures taken against Chenu, Charlier, Draguet and De Petter demonstrate that the fear was great in leading Church circles that the ground under theology's feet was in danger of being swept away.

Chapter 2

FOURVIÈRE, TOULOUSE, PARIS AND ROME: JESUITS

In this chapter we will limit our discussion to the 'big three' among the representatives of the second phase of the *nouvelle théologie*, namely the Jesuits Henri Bouillard, Jean Daniélou and Henri de Lubac. This means that we will focus little attention on Yves de Montcheuil (†1944), Gaston Fessard and others. As with the previous chapter, we provide a biographical-bibliographical sketch of each figure, discuss their particular vision, and conclude with an evaluation of their work in relation to the *nouvelle théologie*.

After the presentation of the contributions of the three Jesuits in the period from 1942 to 1946, we also offer an overview of the polemic surrounding the *nouvelle théologie* up to 1950. We round off the chapter with a summary of some other theological contributions stemming from this period together with some concluding observations.

2.1 *Bouillard*

Henri Bouillard can be considered the instigator of the second phase of the *nouvelle théologie* and in our opinion the author of its preliminary programme.

Henri Bouillard
Henri Bouillard was born on 14 March 1908 in Charlieu (France).[1] He entered the seminary at Issy in 1926 and acquired his Master of Arts degree from the Sorbonne in Paris four years later. Bouillard entered the Society of Jesus in 1932 and continued his studies on the completion of his novitiate at Fourvière where he joined the third year of theology. He was ordained to the priesthood in 1936 after which he spent two years lecturing in Beirut. In 1938 he moved to the Gregoriana, the Jesuit university in Rome, where he specialized in dogmatic theology under the supervision of Charles Boyer. His studies were to result in a doctoral dissertation on Thomas Aquinas's understanding of the doctrine of justification entitled 'Conversion et grâce chez saint Thomas d'Aquin'. He completed and defended his dissertation in 1941 at Fourvière where he was appointed professor of dogmatic theology in the same year. Three years later, in 1944, his dissertation was published as the first book in the new 'Théologie' series of which he was one of the co-founders.[2] The foreword to his book warns

the reader against possible errors in the text due to a lack of opportunity to prepare it adequately for publication (the Second World War was raging at the time). Unfortunately, the book – and in particular its conclusions – found itself in the eye of a polemical storm surrounding what was later to go down in history as the *nouvelle théologie*. Together with his fellow Jesuits Jean Daniélou and Gaston Fessard and his confrere at the Institut Catholique de Lyon, Henri de Lubac, Bouillard was indeed considered by the Roman authorities (his Jesuit superiors and the Holy Office) to be a representative of the *nouvelle théologie*. This was one of the main reasons why he was obliged, together with de Lubac, to leave Lyon in June 1950 for Paris. In the same month and apparently for the same reason their confrere Pierre Ganne was obliged to leave Fourvière and to move to Saint-Égrève (near Grenoble).[3] One could state that disciplinary measures were taken against three outspoken 'disciples' of Maurice Blondel.[4]

Bouillard remained in Paris until his death. In 1956 he acquired a second doctorate – in Letters – at the Sorbonne under the supervision of Jean Wahl, a French philosopher who was to have a considerable influence on Bouillard. The topic of his dissertation was Karl Barth, who was present in person at the defence. As with his first dissertation, this new work was likewise published in the 'Théologie' series (three parts condensed into two volumes).[5] In 1961 he published his *Blondel et le Christianisme* in which he testified to his affinity with the thought of Blondel.[6] Three years later, he was appointed professor at the Institut Catholique de Paris. In the same year he founded the Institut de science et de théologie des religions together with Jean Daniélou. The year 1964 also saw the publication of Bouillard's *Logique de foi* – once again in the 'Théologie' series – as a sort of 'response' to his friend Eric Weil.[7] Three years later, his *Connaissance de Dieu* was published, a philosophical-theological essay on the essence of God and the possibility of knowing Him.[8] In 1971, *Comprendre ce que l'on croit* appeared on the market, the conclusion to the first chapter of which can be considered the thematic leitmotiv of his career: if one desires to understand faith one cannot ignore philosophy.[9]

Bouillard retired from teaching in 1978 and died on 22 June 1981.

The Conclusion to a Book

Bouillard's *Conversion et grace chez saint Thomas d'Aquin* appeared in 1944 as the first volume in Fourvière's 'Théologie' series. The book contained a historical study of Thomas's response to the problem of the necessary preconditions for conversion. In short, what is necessary to make conversion possible and what is the relationship in this regard between grace and conversion? Bouillard observes that the question is not new, but rather part of a 15-year-old debate in which the concrete interpretation of Thomas's vision has taken centre stage. Bouillard positions himself in the said discussion, although he notes in the opening remarks that he has no intention of being polemical and that all the important studies from past centuries will have to be accounted for in his work.

The book consists of three parts. In the first two parts, Bouillard presents the preparatory groundwork for Thomas's doctrine of grace as he describes it in his *Summa theologiae*. The said doctrine is further elaborated in the third part. Bouillard then presents a series of remarkable conclusions that were to set an extraordinary polemical debate in motion, in spite of his stated desire to avoid such complications. We will focus our attention here on the said conclusions, which present themselves as a critique of neo-scholasticism on the one hand, and as a historically grounded call for a new way of engaging in the theological endeavour on the other.

'One of the virtually unavoidable mistakes of the manuals is that they present theology as a classical science with immutable concepts, timeless problems and eternal arguments.'[10] These are the words with which Bouillard begins the conclusions to his book and he immediately launches into the attack. A historical study reveals that every form of theology has to be understood in relation to its own historical and particular context. As such, theology manifests itself as something consisting of relative concepts and its development rooted in themes and problems. Bouillard's conclusions thus make the distinction between manual theology and theology-in-context clearer.

Bouillard argues that Thomas's theology is related to the time in which he lived. The problems that came to the fore, the conceptual models he employed and the Aristotelianism he integrated all bear witness to a highly gifted thirteenth-century thinker who was embedded in the tradition of his own day. It is within this context that Thomas made clear that 'preparing for grace' and 'cooperation' are synonymous. Bouillard understands this to be the simple integration of Aristotelian concepts into theology. He argues that 'the act of love as well as that of faith – the two paths of conversion – are at the same time the ultimate disposition for grace'.[11] This implies in the first instance that leeway is created by love and faith, leeway for grace. The fact of this distinction, according to Bouillard, does not permit us to make a separation between nature and the supernatural. He refers in this regard to Thomas himself: grace is universal, embracing the natural and the supernatural. Bouillard concludes, nevertheless, that philosophers and theologians after the thirteenth century created an ever expanding gulf between the natural and the supernatural, whereby grace was reserved for the latter. Bouillard attaches his critique at this juncture of all theologians who have not made the distinction. A second critique is related to the representation of immutable truth claims. Bouillard insists: 'If the mind evolves, then the representation of the truth must evolve', an opinion he follows with a now famous comment: ' If theology is not related to contemporary life, it is a false theology.'[12] This leads Bouillard to a synthesis of both critical remarks: 'The history of theology reveals the permanence of divine truth on the one hand and the contingency of concepts and systems in which we endeavour to represent that truth on the other.'[13]

It is impossible to grasp truth and isolate it in its pure form, completely separated from life in general and from ourselves in particular. It is an inherent dimension of life that we cannot avoid representing our understanding of eternal truth in the particular concepts of our own day. Bouillard argues that 'the logic of the incarnation' is here at stake.[14] This logic implies that we have no other access to truth than human language. History as such is not an impediment, a potential source of relativism, but rather a precondition that leads to absolute truth. The succession of different concepts that have arisen in the course of history reveals that people have felt the need time and again to develop new concepts, methods and systems to represent one and the same truth and to confirm it. History thus makes it clear that our concepts, methods and systems are relative. Only the represented truth is absolute, not the representation thereof. Bouillard refers in this regard to the Council of Trent, which did not ascribe absolute value to its description of grace. 'It was certainly not the Council's intention', Bouillard continues, 'to canonise an Aristotelian concept, or a theological concept influenced by Aristotle.'[15] Bouillard takes matters even further: not only concepts, methods and systems must pass review, he insists, but there were also periods in history in which parts of the truth were forgotten or at least less emphasized. Between the twelfth and the sixteenth centuries, for example, there is virtually no mention of the Council of Orange (Aquinas and Gregory of Rimini being the exception), the Council that condemned semi-Pelagianism. Bouillard considers a knowledge of the history of Catholic dogma as interesting and essential. He concludes: 'Theology is time-bound, history-bound.'[16] This statement ultimately leads him to recognize a salutary gulf between medieval thought on the one hand and contemporary thought on the other.

Nouvelle Théologie?

In *Grace and Human Freedom in the Theology of Henri Bouillard* (2007), J. Eileen Scully correctly points out that the spirit of Bouillard's *Conversion et grâce chez saint Thomas d'Aquin* continues to be present in his later work. In line with Scully's insistence that his book is primarily a theological-historical work that only offers a few insights on hermeneutics in its final pages, I have limited myself to Bouillard's conclusions because I am inclined to argue that the observations they include represent a preliminary programme for the second phase of the *nouvelle théologie*. Having read this programme, it becomes impossible to deny its polemical character, in spite of the author's statements to the contrary. No one who writes that concepts, methods and systems are not salutary in themselves can be understood to be declaring his support for neo-scholastic theology, the derivative of the *philosophia perennis*. Furthermore, Bouillard's specific interest in the supernatural and its relationship with the natural was able to create leeway for divergent perspectives. In the last analysis, the manner with which Bouillard promoted the historical within theology was 'new'.

While Bouillard nuanced a number of matters in 1947 in an effort to distance himself from the so-called *nouvelle théologie*[17] and radically rejected the notion in 1950,[18] the conclusions to *Conversion et grâce chez saint Thomas d'Aquin* confirm that he was a genuine representative of the movement. Réginald

Garrigou-Lagrange even goes so far as to call him its leader, in conjunction with Henri de Lubac.[19] Is it mere coincidence, therefore, that both Bouillard and de Lubac were forced to leave Lyon in 1950? Nevertheless, Bouillard was always overshadowed by his confrere, and according to Karl-Heinz Neufeld he became 'virtually forgotten'.[20] Recent studies on Bouillard appear to have rescued him from the shadows, however, although they do not tend to share Garrigou-Lagrange's perhaps exaggerated opinion of him.

Henri Bouillard's contribution to the *nouvelle théologie* can be compared with that of Henri-Marie Féret in the first phase thereof. Both were bridge figures, serving to link different phases. Where Féret as a Dominican with his emphasis on the Bible appeared to be moving in the direction of the second phase, Bouillard as a Jesuit appears to take a step backwards, as it were, from the second phase. After all, we should not forget that the second phase was also characterized by Thomistic *ressourcement* as a latent undercurrent, the foundations upon which theological *ressourcement* was constructed. Bouillard's contribution demonstrates clearly that he was a herald of theological *ressourcement*: he linked the thought of the historical Thomas to the then contemporary theological reflection on grace, not only the key concept when one is speaking of the supernatural but also when one enters into the domain of dogma in general. In other words, Bouillard's vision represents the crossroads at which the first phase and the second phase visibly touch each other, where history and dogma encounter one another, where theology and Church teaching cross each other's paths. In this regard Bouillard can be understood as a pioneer in the transition between apologetics and hermeneutics. In a review, Charles Boyer, the promoter of Bouillard's doctoral thesis, defended the latter's call for an open theology, beyond the closed system of neo-scholasticism.[21] Polemic in this regard was completely unavoidable, as is shown by the debate between Bouillard on the one hand and Louis-Bertrand Guérard des Lauriers, Professor of History of Philosophy at Le Saulchoir, on the other.[22] In two articles, published in *L'Année théologique* in 1945 and 1946, Guérard des Lauriers reacts against Bouillard's relativism: in his eyes Bouillard too readily relativizes Thomas's thought in the name of history.[23] Bouillard published two reactions, one in the *Recherches de science religieuse* and the other in *L'Année théologique*, specifying his viewpoint and refuting Guérard des Lauriers' criticisms.[24]

2.2 *Daniélou*

Jean Daniélou had an eventful life and career, in both academic and ecclesial terms. Rooted in his profound knowledge of Christian antiquity, he found himself at work in the domain of the *nouvelle théologie*.

Jean Daniélou

Jean Guénolé Louis Marie Daniélou was born on 14 May 1905 in Neuilly-sur-Seine, near Paris.[25] He graduated from the Sorbonne in 1927 as a grammar teacher and entered the Society of Jesus two years later. He was ordained priest in 1938. In 1941 he returned to Paris, after a long period of formation at the study houses in Jersey and Lyon-Fourvière, interrupted in 1934–36 by a teaching assignment in Poitiers. In 1943 he acquired his doctorate in Theology at the Institut Catholique de Paris with a dissertation that was published a year later under the title *Platonisme et théologie mystique: Essai sur la doctrine spirituelle de saint Grégoire de Nysse*. His doctoral jury consisted of Yves de Montcheuil, Jules Lebreton and Guy de Broglie. In 1944 he defended the same dissertation at the Sorbonne where he was granted a doctorate in the Arts. His interest in the Church Fathers had already become apparent a year before this twofold success. The first volume of the 'Sources Chrétiennes' series – established under the impulse of Victor Fontoynont in 1942 – was *La vie de Moïse* by Gregory of Nyssa, edited by Jean Daniélou.[26] Together with his friend and fellow Jesuit Henri de Lubac, Daniélou served as the series' first editorial team, with more and more regular assistance from Claude Mondésert, who took over the series in 1960.[27] In 1943, Daniélou became the editor-in-chief of *Études* and he succeeded Jules Lebreton as Professor of the History of Christian Antiquity at the Institut Catholique de Paris. Since his first article, published in 1940 and entitled 'L'apocatastase chez Grégoire de Nysse',[28] Daniélou has written a lot of articles and books on patristics, (the contribution of the Church Fathers to the explanation and development of) the Bible, the liturgy, and the theological developments of Antiquity. In particular his interest in the historical contexts (the *Sitz im Leben*) and theological-historical developments are here to be noticed. In 1953, for example, his renowned *Essai sur le mystère de l'histoire* appeared[29] and, five years later, his *Théologie du Judéo-Christianisme*.[30] The latter was published in English translation under the title *The Development of Christian Doctrine before the Council of Nicea* in 1964. In the meantime, he had become the successor of J. Lebreton as editor of the *Bulletin des origines chrétiennes* of the periodical *Recherches de science religieuse*. His enormous productivity made him a well-known and appreciated scholar. In 1961 he was elected Dean of the Faculty of Theology of the Institut Catholique de Paris, a position he held until 1969. During the Second Vatican Council, Daniélou was both present and very active in Rome where he had been appointed as *peritus* by John XXIII. His services to the Church were rewarded with a cardinal's hat on 28 April 1969, which required his episcopal ordination a week earlier. After April 1969 his main place of work was the Curia.

Daniélou died on 20 May 1974. His death – he died during a pastoral visit in a bordello – and his life were controversial in equal measure. Reference can be made in this regard by way of example to his 1946 article in the journal *Études* (see below) in which he fires himself, as it were, as the journal's editor-in-chief. In addition to this, his insistence on the normativity of history and his sympathy for the work of Pierre Teilhard de Chardin clearly did not curry favour with Roman neo-scholastic circles on the eve of the Council. Daniélou's merits, however, remain beyond dispute, as the two special editions of the *Recherches de science religieuse* published in 1972 testify. The editions praise him for his contribution to academic reflection on Jewish Christianity.[31] Henri de Lubac described him as a 'free and evangelical man'.[32] The fact that his thought continues to be relevant in the present day was confirmed at a conference in 2005 on the occasion of the centenary of his birth. In his foreword to the conference proceedings Jacques Fontaine states that 'the works of Jean Daniélou continue to offer pertinent answers to the questions that continue to preoccupy us today'.[33]

Antoine Guggenheim saliently summarizes Daniélou's theological vision as 'fulfilment theology'.[34] For Daniélou, Christianity is indeed the fulfilment of Judaism and the endtime was inaugurated definitively by Christ. This does not imply that Christianity should ignore Judaism, however, since in so doing Christianity would ignore the very roots that make it comprehensible as the fulfilment of everything that has been predicted. It is for this reason that Daniélou speaks of Jewish Christianity. The Christ event, nevertheless, has such significance that Christianity is much more than Judaism alone. The time in which we live – between mere Judaism and the *parousia* – is the final stage in the history of the world.

Two Articles

In 1946 and 1947 respectively, Jean Daniélou published two articles in the French journal *Études*[35]: the latter intended, according to Daniélou, to further define a number of elements contained in the former.[36]

The article of April 1946 is entitled 'Les orientations présentes de la pensée religieuse' and reflects on some major methodological topics. Daniélou's point of departure here is Modernism, the representatives of which he maintains have offered the wrong answers to the correct analysis of a number of problems. He laments the fact that the adversaries of Modernism have tended to reject the analysis together with the answers. The analysis in question has two main lines of approach. In the first instance, it argues that every awareness of transcendence has disappeared: theology has become a rational enterprise that approaches God as one object among many, as an object of research. In the second instance, the analysis speaks of the 'mummification' of a closed theology: theology is understood primarily as an academic enterprise that has lost all contact with developments in philosophy and other sciences. According to Daniélou, the Modernists were wrong when they responded to the first problem by emphasizing agnosticism and the second by endorsing the aberrations of critical exegesis. Because of these errors, the Modernists did not achieve their stated goal of renewing religious thought, but were confronted rather with a hardening of positions and complete polarization, which ultimately paralyzed the efforts of researchers. Daniélou speaks here in terms of a misunderstanding between Christian intellectuals on the one hand and the magisterium on the other. But there was clearly more than a misunderstanding at work. Confronted with a revival of faith among Christian intellectuals, theology found itself isolated and plagued with shortcomings. 'The fact that theology is being called upon to participate in intellectual life today is a sign of its ultimate absence', Daniélou writes.[37] It was crystal clear to him that a gulf could be observed between theology and life. In Daniélou's opinion, this was theology's greatest problem and he set out in his article to find a solution by analysing the situation. In so doing he provided a roadmap for theology, arguing that the solution offered by the magisterium – neo-Thomism and the Pontifical Biblical Commission – could not be seen as adequate. Neo-Thomism and the Pontifical Biblical Commission may have been – and Daniélou speaks here in the past tense – the guardians of orthodox faith, but they were not the solution to the problem of the gulf between theology and life.

In his own attempt to offer a solution, Daniélou argues that theology is faced with three challenges. And it has to confront them! In the first place, theology must consider God as God and not as an object of research. Secondly, theology must accept new developments and achievements in the world of modern science. Finally, theology must also imply a dimension of activity: theology must result in a presence that serves the best interests of people and society. Daniélou concludes his overview of these three challenges by pointing out that theology cannot rise again without facing them. The remainder of his article elaborates each challenge in greater detail.

With respect to the first challenge, Daniélou points to the need for a three-fold *ressourcement*. First, he turns his attention to the increasing interest in the Bible. Following the thirteenth-century schism between theology and exegesis, theology gradually dried out. As a result, a return to the sources was badly needed in order to rediscover the living and life-giving source. The first step in this *ressourcement* was taken during the Modernist period due to the merits of thinkers such as Marie-Joseph Lagrange and Léonce de Grandmaison who – together with several others – made biblical research (more) academic. The second step, however, is more important: theology had to benefit from the rediscovery of the Bible. In short, theology had to integrate the results of biblical research. Daniélou indicates that the said integration is moving in the right direction as far as the New Testament is concerned. He makes reference in this regard to Lucien Cerfaux, for example, who published his work on the ecclesiology of Paul in 1942.[38] As far as the Old Testament was concerned, however, a great deal of work still had to be done. In the spirit of the Church Fathers, Daniélou recognizes the challenge of reassessing the texts of the Old Testament in light of their prophetic character. This challenge consists of paying renewed attention to allegorical exegesis, which is situated at the heart of the debate on the most preferable manner of engaging in exegesis. It is at this juncture that Daniélou makes use of the *nouvelle théologie* concept: 'Based on this debate we can expect the groundwork of a new theology of prophecy [*nouvelle théologie de la prophétie*], i.e. of the relationship between the Old and the New Testament, a concept that will have an important role to play in the theology of tomorrow.'[39]

Biblical *ressourcement*, for Daniélou, must go hand in hand with a patristic *ressourcement*, a fact that should come as no surprise when we realize that a considerable portion of the work of the Fathers consists of biblical commentary. In his opinion, the revival of interest in the work of the Fathers has found its reflection in the establishment of the 'Théologie' and 'Sources chrétiennnes' series. The renewal in patristic studies should be understood against the background of the parallel between the context of the patristic writings themselves and that of the 1940s. Daniélou argues more specifically that two terms should be characteristic of patristic *ressourcement*, namely 'history' and 'salvation for all'. Neither term was central to scholasticism, however, on the contrary: Daniélou refers at this juncture to Henri de Lubac's *Catholicisme*, which serves as an example of the re-introduction of the concept of 'history' in contemporary theology. The concept of 'salvation for all', moreover, is related to the emphasis on the Mystical Body of Christ. This latter idea is substantiated on the basis of the writings of the Church Fathers (Daniélou does not make specific reference to the work of Émile Mersch in this regard, but it would be difficult to imagine that he had another author than his fellow Jesuit in mind).

In addition to the need for biblical and patristic *ressourcement*, Daniélou also discusses liturgical *ressourcement*. This should also come as no surprise, he insists, since the Church Fathers devoted themselves in particular to two themes: the Bible and the liturgy. In summary, renewed interest in the Bible, patristics and liturgy stands as a synonym for a return to history. With regard to the liturgy, Daniélou underlines the mystery to which it refers. Interest in the mystery of God in the 1940s provided the precise point of connection with the return to the three aforementioned sources of faith. Liturgy's goal is thus twofold: celebrating God's mystery on the one hand, and introducing people to the various dimensions of the Catholic faith and the Christian life on the other. As such, one cannot look at the liturgy without at the same time taking the (moral) life of Christians into account.

Having offered his observations on the need for a threefold *ressourcement*, Daniélou then turns his attention to theology's second challenge, namely the need to accept the invitation of contemporary thought to engage in dialogue. Daniélou insists that the task of every theologian implies such a dialogue. Two concepts alien to scholastic theology and potential drawbacks in such a dialogue, however, are 'history' and 'subjectivity'. History underlines development, evolution, change and dynamism, while the scholastic vision is rather static and meta-historical. Despite his reservations, Daniélou also introduces his fellow Jesuit Teilhard de Chardin into the discussion at this juncture. He concludes, in fact, that Ireneus of Lyon had already liberated us from a static understanding of history in the second century. The concept 'subjectivity', he laments, is too modern in the eyes of the magisterium. Nevertheless, by using both concepts, theology will be able to enter the domain of contemporary thought and enter into dialogue with it. The negation of the notion of subjectivity implies that one does not see the human person as a free being. Daniélou concludes his explanation of this second challenge with a reference to apophatic theology. There can be little doubt, he states, that this is a reaction against neo-scholasticism in which every concept has its own exclusive meaning and every aspect of the faith a matching concept. Daniélou calls for a theology in which there is room for silence, silence in the presence of mystery.

The third segment of his 1946 article focuses on the challenge of maintaining vibrant contact between theology and life. As Daniélou himself puts it: 'Renewed by the sources of faith and reconfirmed by contact with contemporary thought, theology must account for everyday life if it wants to stay alive.'[40] This also implies that theology must pay due attention to the cares and needs of contemporary life and use them as a basis from which to approach people and society. Daniélou states the following in this regard: 'It is impossible today to maintain a separation between theology and life; a manner of thinking that is not in the first instance a testimony is an empty letter.'[41] As a consequence of this vision, Daniélou denounces the division he observed between theology and spirituality. He then formulates an appeal for a spiritual theology, which he explains by referring to the theologian's call to emphasize love of neighbour – the heart of the gospel – and to the spirituality of the laity (with specific reference to marriage). Daniélou goes on to discuss the twofold task of the theologian in response to this third challenge. He points out in the first instance that everything and everybody should be taken seriously. Neither the values of the moment nor any human reality should be open to disparagement. In the second instance, theologians should endeavour to locate such values and realities within the broader framework of the Christian vision. In doing so, however, theologians should pay attention to ideas of from the whole world and have the courage to see Christianity in opposition to all other ways of thinking (otherwise one will be unable to reflect on inculturation). This implies progress in the domain of language, more specifically in the way we give expression to the faith. Daniélou insists that this is not an attack on revelation, but rather a stimulus to encourage dogmatic progress. He concludes: 'This is the new way of theologising, which various pioneers of contemporary missionary thought have demonstrated.'

Daniélou's concluding observations run as follows:

> This is broadly speaking the threefold challenge facing Christian thought. One has to admit that the moment is a decisive one. Previous generations have collected the material and now it is time to build. For this reason it is necessary that different people present themselves who are familiar with the Christian tradition, contemplative life – which gives them access to the mystery of Christ – contemporary life, and love of neighbour: people who consider themselves free to look beyond all human forms and dare to recognise the interior bond with the Spirit.

The February 1947 article, 'Christianisme et histoire', which appeared later that year in the September issue of *Études*, discusses one of the central themes of the

1946 article, namely the relationship between Christianity and history. Daniélou wrote this article after reading Henri-Marie Féret's *Apocalypse de saint Jean* and Henri de Lubac's 1938 *Catholicisme*, among other works.[42] He points out that the title of his article alludes to the title of a chapter in Étienne Gilson's *L'esprit de la philosophie medieval*, although no such a chapter appears to exist.[43] As with the 1946 article, Daniélou makes an analysis of the current situation on the topic at hand and presents his own reflections.

The article itself was occasioned by the publication of several works in which the role of history in Christianity was the subject of discussion. Daniélou refers here to the books of Jean Guitton, Christopher Dawson, Henri de Lubac and Oscar Cullmann. After reviewing the books in question, he offers his own contribution to the debate on the meaning of history in Christianity.

In the first part of the article, Daniélou discusses Christianity as history. Two concepts require further elaboration in this regard, namely 'event' and 'progress'. Something can be seen as an event when it interrupts expected patterns and is aimed at establishing progress in the intellectual, religious and/or social order. In short, an event changes the order of things, while progress implies both continuity and discontinuity. Daniélou considers it useful to refer to both the classical Greek worldview and that of the Gnostics in order to explain the Christian worldview. The Greeks understood life to be static, immutable: the world of pure being. The Gnostics for their part maintained a dualistic worldview, which was likewise not subject to change. Both worldviews, however, did not give credit to history. Greek and Gnostic influence can be recognized in the vision of the first Christians. Ireneus of Lyon avoids the impasse by discovering the notion of history. According to Daniélou, 'this is the reality that demonstrates continuity and discontinuity in its development; there is a qualitative difference between the past and the future, but there are also sufficient similarities between the two'.[44] He refers to the Old and New Testament as history's most intriguing example of differences and similarities. Daniélou considers history to be the interpretative key par excellence to allow us to understand the Bible. In other words, history is the governess of theology. Because of the polytheistic context, for example, it was necessary to demonstrate God's unicity before emphasizing His trinity. The Old Testament thus prepares the reader step by step for the New. Daniélou quotes Paul at this juncture, who wrote that the transition from the Old Testament to the New was equal to the transition from childhood to adulthood. All the transitions in the Bible and history imply a certain component that has to be set aside – this component is designated 'old', obsolete – and one that has to be accepted (the 'new'). The latter allows us to consider the former as a prefiguration of the new and the new as the fulfilment of the prophecy of the old. The ultimate transition all human beings will have to face is our own death. Death is thus a transition from the earthly to the heavenly. It is within the context of such observations that Daniélou recognizes three characteristic features of the Christian vision of history. First, Christianity maintains a finite understanding of history: life on earth will come to an end. This conviction is closely related to the second feature: Christianity itself is the end of history. Indeed, Christianity sees itself as the final stage in history's lifespan. Thirdly, the end of history already started long ago, namely with the incarnation and the resurrection: the eschaton is already underway and is still ongoing. These three characteristics imply that Christianity is indeed the decisive phase of history: prior to Christ – in all the transitions of history – there were prefigurations and since Christ the eschaton has begun. It is our task today to remain faithful to the deposit of faith. In so doing, the core event in history as a whole is not to be located at its beginning or at its end, but in the middle.

Daniélou now turns his attention to the relationship between salvation history and profane history. In his opinion, two visions existed in this regard at the time his article was published. The first argues that Christianity is one of the many components of history that come and go, while the second insists that Christianity rises above history. Daniélou avoids both perspectives, considering Christianity to be part of history on the one hand, and history to be part of Christianity on the other. Daniélou's intentions here require further explanation.

In the first instance, he argues, Christianity is part of history. Just as Jesus manifested himself as a man of his own time and particular context, so the Church should incarnate itself in every particular context. Daniélou even insists that 'incarnation is a must'. And he goes on: 'Those who set out to place Christianity *beside* history, i.e. Christianity as a pure, non-historical entity, are making a serious mistake from the perspective of Christianity's essence'.[45]

The second part of Daniélou's vision argues that profane history is a part of salvation history. This implies on the one hand that no single historical event can have a negative influence on salvation history, and on the other that salvation history is not possible without profane history. While profane history is subordinate to salvation history, the latter – with its supernatural distinctiveness – is indebted to profane history with its natural distinctiveness. Daniélou considers himself obliged at this juncture to anticipate the criticism that this eschatological era is still characterized by a world of sin and violence. He recognizes this fact but is convinced nevertheless that the future 'perfect' world already exists as mystery in the form of the sacraments. It is here that the Church derives its *raison d'être*: the Church mediates between the 'already' and the 'not yet', in the space between inheritance and hope. In this perspective, Christians live in two worlds that exist side by side. As a result, Daniélou argues, history – temporal life – bears within it an 'important anachronistic element' and 'the life of the Church an important catachronistic element'.[46] Such a mindset includes the transfiguration of humanity through grace together with the task of not underestimating the value of profane history.

Nouvelle Théologie?

In Daniélou's first article, we were able to recognize the programme of the second phase of the *nouvelle théologie*, namely a threefold *ressourcement*; a return to the sources of faith: patristics, and via patristics the Bible and the liturgy. In the second article, Daniélou insists that Christian theology is ultimately impossible if we do not take history seriously and give due credit to historical research. This would appear to bring us to the core of the *nouvelle théologie*, but also into the nucleus of the polemic between its supporters and adversaries. The latter – in the first instance the magisterium – were radically convinced of the value of a meta-historical neo-scholasticism, centred on concepts, logical deduction and acceptable conclusions (i.e. in line with Catholic teaching).

It is part of the order of things that the confrontation between contrasting opinions always leads to polarization. People, after all, are always determined to prove themselves right. We will return to the question of polemic once we have examined the vision of Henri de Lubac. For the present we will focus briefly by way of conclusion on Daniélou's programmatic text, which represents an alternative and more explicit elaboration of the conclusions found in Bouillard's book.

Agitation towards neo-scholasticism is clearly manifest in Daniélou's 'programme' for the *nouvelle théologie*. For him, theology did not revolve around a system, but around a person, a historical figure who started a movement: the Church. Within the Church one reflects on Jesus and his message, on what people believe and on what authoritative thinkers preached and wrote in the course of history. For Daniélou, a return to that living faith – in the form of the act of faith, the liturgy, the reading and exploration of the Scriptures and meditation – meant nothing short of a motion of no confidence with respect to neo-scholasticism, which appeared to ignore the living faith and its history in favour of a closed intellectual system. His 1946 article caused such a commotion that Daniélou was obliged to resign as editor of the journal shortly after its publication. Against the background of increasing unrest concerning the position of Roman neo-scholasticism, Daniélou's article functioned as the point at which the defenders of the said neo-scholasticism took to the barricades.[47]

2.3 *De Lubac*

Of all the *new theologians*, Henri de Lubac appears to have enjoyed the greatest renown. From this perspective, it comes as no surprise that the idea of a collected edition of his entire oeuvre was born in the 1990s, in the wake of his death, a project that is still to reach completion.[48]

Henri de Lubac

Where the life of Henri Bouillard was to be divided between the years prior to 1950 and those that followed, de Lubac's also appears to be divided, on this occasion into three, with 1950 and the Second Vatican Council as the points of division.[49] In order to provide a convenient and succinct overview of de Lubac's life and work we have been obliged to restrict ourselves to a number of highlights.

In line with Bouillard, the first period in de Lubac's life stretches to 1950. Henri Sonnier de Lubac was born on 20 February 1896 in Cambrai, in the north of France. On 9 October 1913 at the age of 17 he entered the Society of Jesus in England, where the French Jesuits had taken up residence after the French anti-Church laws of the early twentieth century. With the outbreak of the First World War, the young de Lubac was conscripted into the French army. He suffered a head wound on All Saints Day 1917, an event that was to have consequences for the rest of his life. After demobilization in 1919, de Lubac continued his philosophical and theological studies in England. The French Jesuits were only to return to France in 1926, where they set up home on Fourvière Hill near Lyon. De Lubac was ordained priest on 22 August 1927. Two years later he moved from Fourvière to a Jesuit house in the city and was appointed to teach theology at the Institut Catholique de Lyon, first as Professor of Dogmatic Theology and then as Professor of the Theology of Religions. He returned to Fourvière in 1934, although he did not become a member of staff at the theologate. De Lubac's importance quickly became clear, however, and several publications appeared in rapid succession. In 1938, for example, he published his now famous book *Catholicisme*, in which the Church as continuation of the Jewish people is presented as a community – in all its facets – on its way *through history* to the *shared salvation* promised by God.[50] In 1942 he became a member of the first editoral board of the 'Sources chrétiennes' series and two years later he established together with Bouillard the 'Théologie' series. Both series were important representations of the growing desire for a fully fledged return to the sources of the faith. 'Sources chrétiennes' provided reprints of patristic texts in the original Latin and in contemporary French translation, while 'Théologie' created the opportunity for its readers to familiarize themselves with patristic and medieval topics via studies and monographs. The fact that both series were established during the Second World War does not imply that de Lubac was unrealistic and out of touch with the world. On the contrary, he was an active member of the resistance – against the official line adopted by his Jesuit superiors – and was outspoken in his reaction to anti-semitism. He was also confronted with the consequences of war on a personal level when his confrere and best friend Yves de Montcheuil was executed on 10 August 1944. In the same year as this dramatic event he published his *Le drame de l'humanisme athée*, a book in which he substantiates the thesis – in light of Karl Marx, Auguste Comte, Ludwig Feuerbach and Friedrich Nietzsche – that absolute atheism absolutizes humanity, leads to the complete negation of God, and has dramatic consequences for humanity.[51] The wave of publications that appeared after the Second World War but were written during it includes de Lubac's *Surnaturel*, which caused considerable commotion until his retirement in 1959.[52] The commotion in question was reinforced by his departure (under orders) from Lyon in June 1950 and the publication two months later of the encyclical *Humani generis*, two facts that are often linked together and not infrequently in the wrong chronological order.

The fact that de Lubac's activities were not brought to a standstill by the polemic and the disciplinary measures is made clear by his publications in the 1950s. In a single decade, he published three books on Buddhism (1951, 1952, 1955),[53] *Méditation sur l'Église* (1953)[54] and *Sur les chemins de Dieu* (1956).[55] De Lubac had returned in the meantime to Lyon – although not to Fourvière – and was back at work at the Institut Catholique de Lyon after an interruption of three years.

In the year of his retirement, de Lubac published the first part of his four-volume *Exégèse medieval*, in the 'Théologie' series (1959–64).[56] Several authors – Hans Urs von Balthasar, Yves Congar, Marie-Dominique Chenu, among others – also contributed to the Festschrift published in the same series in 1964 on the occasion of de Lubac's seventieth birthday and his fiftieth anniversary as a member of the Society of Jesus.[57] De Lubac himself likewise published his renowned *Augustinisme et théologie moderne* in the 'Theologie' series in 1965, a work which contains a reworked version of the first three chapters of *Surnaturel*.[58] The year 1965 also saw the closure of the Second Vatican Council. With regard to Vatican II, Henri de Lubac was appointed as a member of the preparatory commission in August 1960 and played a prominent role throughout the Council as a *peritus*.[59] In 2007 his conciliar notes were published.[60] De Lubac's *L'Écriture dans la Tradition* appeared in 1966 and can be understood as a continuation of the thoughts and ideas contained in *Dei Verbum*.[61] He later provided commentary to several other conciliar documents.[62]

Although de Lubac was considered a progressive theologian in the first part of his life, Vatican II served as a transition to the third part of this life in which he came to be known as a 'conservative theologian', his thoughts completely in line with the magisterium. His new attitude was rewarded with the elevation to the College of Cardinals in 1983. Joseph Ratzinger seemed to have had a similar evolution of the mind.[63] The year 1968 was a turning point for the latter, occasioning a transition from a progressive and proactive orientation to a conservative orientation in which the teaching of the magisterium was central. It should come as no surprise, therefore, that both Ratzinger and de Lubac were appointed a year later in 1969 as members of the International Theological Commission together with Hans Urs von Balthasar and Yves Congar, among others. In 1972, de Lubac founded the journal *Communio* together with Ratzinger, Urs von Balthasar, Walter Kasper and Karl Lehmann. All of these individuals were to be raised to the College of Cardinals, while the driving force behind the journal *Concilium* – Edward Schillebeeckx, Karl Rahner, Hans Küng, Johann Baptist Metz – established in 1965 were 'spared' the honour. Yves Congar is an exception in this regard, although his cardinal's hat did not arrive until six months before his death. Ratzinger's transfer from the editorial board of *Concilium* to that of *Communio* clearly serves as a symbol of the tension between both journals.

During the last 20 years of his life – with his elevation to the College of Cardinals at its midpoint – de Lubac was far from the theologian with challenging standpoints of his early life. The works he was to publish in these years reveal him, however, to be the profound believer he had always been.[64] Suffice to mention here his 1990 two-volume *Théologie dans l'histoire*, the title of which is testimony enough that theology and history cannot be taken as separate entities in de Lubac's theology.[65]

Henri de Lubac died in Paris on 4 September 1991.

Surnaturel

The work with which Henri de Lubac unleashed a polemic of considerable proportions is entitled *Surnaturel*, a historical study of places in the course of the history of the Church and theology related to the supernatural. This locates de Lubac at the crossroads of the various controversies of his day, namely the intersection between the natural and the supernatural, history and dogma, theology and reality, truth and speculation, and the positive and speculative theological method. The enormous response the book engendered has its roots in this delicate situation and in the general climate in which French theological developments were being watched in Roman circles with ever increasing concern. Before sketching the said polemic, however, we will focus some attention on *Surnaturel* itself.

Henri de Lubac insists in the foreword to the book that dogmas are more than untouchable creedal formulas. They emerged, he reminds us, within a historical context, are the work of human hands, and cannot therefore be understood beyond these associations. As far as de Lubac was concerned, the fact that dogmas had come to be seen as eternal truths essential to the faith did not change things in this regard. He points out nevertheless: 'While dogmas are established once and for all, this is much less so with regard to theology.'[66] He refers here by way of example to theories concerning the relationship between Church and state, but also to the 'technical and vague term' *Surnaturel*. The absence of any extensive historical approach to the latter serves as the immediate inspiration for his work.

Based on a historical study, de Lubac wanted to 'present a sort of essay in which contact between Catholic theology and contemporary thinking could be restored', as de Lubac formulated the aim in his *Mémoire sur l'occasion de mes écrits*.[67] De Lubac did not hesitate to pepper his overview with barely concealed critique of neo-scholasticism. In his opinion, the latter swallows up the mystery of faith, i.e. the supernatural as supernatural.

De Lubac's goal at this juncture was to try to understand the connotations hidden behind the term 'supernatural' and to examine them in their relationship to what we understand as 'natural'. While this theme can be situated perfectly within the domain of dogmatic theology, de Lubac gives priority to a historical survey of what others have already said on the matter. This explains the structure of the work, although it does not make it any easier for the reader. On the contrary, de Lubac tosses the reader into the deep end, as it were, and into the core of the polemical situation. This includes confrontation with a whole series of 'isms', among them Baianism, Jansenism, Augustinianism. These three terms are central to the first part of the book, which constitutes a recapitulation of an article de Lubac had already published in 1931, in the aftermath of the centenary of Augustine's death.[68] The entire discussion turns around Augustine's doctrine of grace and its heritage. Baianism – based on Michael Baius' thought – insists on our right to grace and denies the gratuitous character thereof. On the opposite side of the spectrum, however, Jansenism – based on Cornelius Jansenius' thought – is convinced that human beings are determined by the natural and the supernatural and denies human autonomy and freedom. For de Lubac, both perspectives represent a 'faulty' interpretation of Augustine's thought and their mutual hostility has led to the fact that Augustine and his followers have tended to be ignored since the emergence of neo-scholasticism in the middle of the nineteenth century. During the 1930s and 1940s there was a growing attention to Augustine, or, as I call it, a rediscovery of Augustine after the great silence which was a consequence of the Jansenist controversy, surrounding what Thomas Martin calls 'a tyranny of grace'.[69] In an effort to appease the situation, until the 1930s the pendulum had indeed swung to the other side and theology had become a rational discipline. God's grace had been reduced to a doctrine that excluded the *reality* of grace and the tone was thus set for the critique de Lubac was about to formulate concerning both interpretations of Augustinianism and neo-scholasticism. The latter school is discussed in the second part of *Surnaturel* against the background of a number of observations on patristic texts. In the third part of the book, de Lubac presents the various substantiations of the concept '*surnaturel*' through the ages. For de Lubac, the concept cannot be reduced to the supra-natural or the extra-natural. On the contrary, as Noel O'Sullivan writes,

> he [de Lubac] understands it as referring to the final end of the spiritual person, an end that corresponds to the biblical term 'likeness' and which is effected by the grace of Christ. For him the mystery of the supernatural is the mystery of our divine destiny and one within which all the other mysteries of revelation find their place.[70]

One can argue on the basis of this description that the longing for interiorization in Church and theology – which we have discussed in Part I, Chapter 2 of this volume – had reached its culminating point with de Lubac's emphasis of the supernatural. At the same time, however, it is not always clear to everyone what he meant by the term. The respected Jesuit and theologian Bernard Sesboüé, for example, considered himself obliged in 2002 to offer commentary on the contributions presented two years earlier at a colloquium on de Lubac's *Surnaturel* and the controversies to which it gave rise.[71] Sesboüé was particularly irritated by the incorrect presentation of the interpretation Henri de Lubac himself had given to his core concept. This explains the title of his reaction: 'Surnaturel et *Surnaturel*'.[72]

The polemic engendered by *Surnaturel* has its roots in a confluence of circumstances and reasons, the most important of which will briefly occupy our attention here. In the first instance, Henri de Lubac was evidently dissatisfied with the prevailing theological climate. Having to make do with conclusions, with concepts that had proven themselves to lack cohesion, with the strict boundaries within which 'orthodox' Catholic theology could be practised elicited enormous intellectual and spiritual frustration on de Lubac's part. Neo-scholasticism had its merits, but it had left the rails when it came to distance itself from its own object of study. This frustration gave rise to the second reason why his *Surnaturel* became the subject of such contestation, namely its method. In order to give content and substance to theological concepts, de Lubac focused himself on the history thereof: what kind of interpretations had been given to the said concepts in the course of history? In an effort to provide an answer he patiently studied a given concept and tried to understand how it functioned in the patristic period, the Middle Ages, the modern era and up to the present day. In this sense, de Lubac's book is an excellent historical study. But historical studies dealing with core theological concepts were subject to suspicion because they had the potential to raise issues that might contradict the use of the said concepts by the magisterium. A third reason behind the polemic was the introduction of Augustine into the debate. Although it had been unavoidable within the structure of de Lubac work, Augustine had been placed side by side with Thomas. It is interesting to note in this regard that de Lubac's best friend, his confrere Yves de Montcheuil, had a fondness for Augustine.[73] A fourth and final reason for the polemic reaction to *Surnaturel* is the fact that Lyon in 1946 clearly presented itself as the centre of theological *ressourcement*, with the foundation of the 'Sources Chrétiennes' series, Bouillard's book, Daniélou's article and de Lubac's *Surnaturel*.

We tie up this summary of reasons with the words of Illtyd Trethowan:

> There is no space [he is writing a review] to show how revolutionary these conclusions [of de Lubac's book] are. All that can be done is to suggest that theologians will need to make a most earnest study of this book. If P. de Lubac is right to say that modern theologians have largely departed from the teaching of the Fathers and of St Augustine on this great question [the whole development of theological thought and language], that they have misunderstood the condemnation of Baius, that they have deserted St Thomas for his commentators, that they have failed to appreciate the true significance of Ruysbroeck's teaching because they have lost the 'spiritual eye', then they must set to work and put their house in order.[74]

Nouvelle Théologie?

Henri de Lubac is considered to be the most eminent representative of the *nouvelle théologie*, invariably with reference to his *Surnaturel*. It is likewise no surprise that several recent publications on de Lubac contain a chapter or a paragraph specifically dedicated to the *nouvelle théologie*. Jean-Pierre Wagner and Antonio Russo explore the years 1946 to 1950 in this regard, while Rudolf Voderholzer continues to 1959, i.e. the eve of Vatican II.[75] In each instance, however, the use of the expression *nouvelle théologie* in relation to de Lubac's life and work is always placed in inverted commas. In so doing, the aforementioned authors endeavour to respect the fact that de Lubac never considered himself to be a *new theologian*. On the contrary: as early as 1946, he wrote a letter to the Jesuit Superior General in which he insists that he never promoted the *théologie nouvelle*.[76] In an interview concerning Vatican II and its preparations published 40 years later, moreover, de Lubac insists that the expression *nouvelle théologie* is a myth and that the label 'school' does not apply to Fourvière.[77] In the same interview he states his explicit agreement with Congar who, as we have already noted, compared the *nouvelle théologie* with an imaginary monster.[78]

The theological climate, his rejection of stringently applied neo-scholasticism, his methodological preference for a historical perspective and his interest in Augustine at the expense of Thomas seemed to serve as the four main reasons why Henri de Lubac became the subject of 'suspicion'. Nothing appeared to be the matter initially, until a mix of circumstances saw to it that de Lubac fell from grace in the eyes of his order and of the magisterium. We will examine the evolution of this process in the following pages because the history of this evolution implies most important elements of the polemic surrounding the *nouvelle théologie* in the years 1946–50.

2.4 *Henri de Lubac and Fourvière* versus *Rome and 'Roman Toulouse'*

In light of the fact that the Jesuit archives in Rome maintain a rule that archive records are only made accessible 70 years after their date, we have been forced to reconstruct de Lubac's trials and tribulations on the basis of alternative records (especially the archives of the French Jesuits in Paris), de Lubac's own *Mémoires*, material provided by his contemporaries and research that has already been conducted in this regard.[79]

September 1946–January 1947

On 15 September 1946, the Society of Jesus' 29th General Congregation elected Jean-Baptiste Janssens, a Belgian Jesuit, as its twenty-seventh General. This brought an end to a difficult period for the order. Not only had it lost many of its members to the Second World War – its former General Wladimir Ledochowski had already passed away four years earlier – but the war had also prevented the organization of a General Congregation at the time. In 1944–46, Norbert de Boynes assumed control of the order, the same confrere who was to call together the General Congregation, which took place in Rome from 6 September to 23 October 1946.[80]

In spite of his participation in the preceding General Congregation in 1938, the new General was unknown to many. As the delegate of the North Belgian province, Janssens had spent most of his life in Belgium and seems to have been quite surprised at his election.[81] He had followed a two-year course in philosophy at the Collegium Maximum in Louvain, acquired a doctorate in Law at the University there and then moved on to the Gregoriana in Rome where he added the title of Doctor in Canon Law to his academic curriculum vitae. In the years that followed, he taught Canon Law at the Jesuit College in Louvain.[82] There, he established a lasting friendship with Édouard Dhanis, who held the chair in systematic theology. Janssens was a canonist who turned to his friend and confrere in Louvain on a number of occasions in his career for theological advice. As we shall see, Janssens continued to do so after he became General.

On the day of the election of the new General, Henri de Lubac's *Surnaturel* arrived at the Curia.[83]

On the third day of Janssens' tenure, the members of the General Congregation, among them Henri de Lubac, were treated to an address by Pope Pius XII in Castel Gandolfo. According to de Lubac, the Pope's address took an unexpected swipe at the dangers of the 'nova theologia' and it insisted on the retention of Thomism.[84]

While the Pope's words were a cause of considerable unrest, they were not entirely surprising if one bears in mind that rumours concerning the theology of Fourvière had already been circulating for some time.[85] There was already considerable tension in the air in the domain of theology at the time of Janssens' election. After Bouillard's 1944 book and Daniélou's April 1946 article, the Dominicans Marie-Michel Labourdette and Garrigou-Lagrange – the former teaching in Toulouse, the latter in Rome – both published reactions a month later, Labourdette primarily in the footnotes of an article in the *Revue thomiste* – of which he was editor-in-chief – inserted just before it was despatched to the printer, while Garrigou-Lagrange's was short but to the point in *Angelicum*.[86] The May editions of both journals did not appear, however, until December 1946 (Labourdette's article) and February 1947 of the following year (Garrigou's article, see below).

During the General Congregation, de Lubac kept a diary, which offers some insight into the reaction of the Jesuits to the Pope's address.[87] On 11 September, he notes, for example, that he heard of the rumours surrounding Fourvière.[88] Further notes bear witness to the search for those who had instigated Pius' words. Labourdette's fierce attack on Daniélou in the as yet to be published article in the *Revue thomiste* – to which de Lubac had access on 19 September, prior to its appearance[89] – led him to suspect that a number of Dominicans had influenced the Pope's speech. On other occasions, however, de Lubac suspects that the papal attack concealed evidence of the influence of his own confreres, thus reducing the entire question to a Jesuit feud. At other moments, we find notes that mention different names and in his later *Mémoires*, de Lubac associates Réginald Garrigou-Lagrange with the matter.[90] Nevertheless, the precise identity of those behind the text remained a mystery.

The Jesuits of Lyon clearly considered themselves targeted and set about contacting higher powers. While the provincial of the Lyon province, Auguste Décisier, was received and reassured by General Janssens[91] on 23 September, two days after the meeting de Lubac nevertheless wrote in the ongoing context of his inquiry into the origins of the Pope's words that he had heard that the speech had been written by two German Jesuits who were said to have consulted the later cardinal, Augustin Bea.[92]

The day after his note of 25 September, de Lubac paid a personal visit to Norbert de Boynes, according to de Lubac someone who had always had a profound distrust of him.[93] In Rome he had a further meeting with Alfredo Ottaviani, Secretary of the Congregation of the Holly Office.[94] Words of reassurance appear to have been exchanged once again, as is evident from the letter de Lubac sent to Ottaviani shortly after his audience with the Secretary.[95] A meeting between Charles Chamussy, the rector of Fourvière, and N. de Boynes at the beginning of October seems to exhibit similar reassurance, although de Lubac is less positively inclined on this occasion.[96] De Lubac is still aware of the complexity of his situation, attacked and accused on the one hand, yet assured on the other that he is not at any great risk. He appears to consider the latter less and less plausible, particularly in light of the information he had received from a variety of sources in which it had become apparent that Garrigou-Lagrange and Marie-Rosaire Gagnebet were targeting the Lyon house of formation.[97] De Lubac clearly expected the support of his provincial and this was indeed forthcoming in the days that followed. In response, Décisier suggests that he and all three other French provincials co-write a letter and present it to Janssens. The letter, in which the four provincials clearly rally to the support of Fourvière and its professors, was written on 14 October and presented to the General the following day. On 15 October, de Lubac notes in his diary that Décisier had read the letter in question to him that day and that he felt reassured to have received the support of the four provincial superiors.[98] Ten days later, shortly before his departure from Rome, de Lubac was received by the General in person who reassured him that neither he nor the Pope had any opposition to Fourvière.[99] According to the notes, the General even went as far as to say that the Pope had taken advantage of the General Congregation to say something that did not in fact have anything to do with the Jesuits. De Lubac's *Mémoires* thus contain an unequivocally positive report of this meeting where the General assured him 'that he can enjoy the General's full support'.[100] De Lubac was clearly left with a sense of relief after this discussion.

At the turn of the year (1946–47), the balance was relatively positive: de Lubac had been reassured and the impression in Rome was that the matter would simply blow over. The General appears to expect no further problems nor do others, such as Stanislas Lyonnet, consider Garrigou-Lagrange to be much of a threat.[101] In short, Janssens allowed the French superiors and their theologians to continue their research.

De Lubac must indeed have considered himself at liberty to publish whatever he pleased. In November 1946, he completed his editorial work on a 16-page 'Réponse' to Labourdette's accusations.[102] On 5 December 1946, Jean Daniélou wrote in a letter to Henri de Lubac that the latter's article, to be published in the *Recherches de science religieuse*, had gone to press.[103] Moreover, if we bear in mind that he was appointed by Janssens as editor-in-chief of the *Recherches de science religieuse* on 22 January 1947, it is evident that his superiors had not lost faith in him.[104] Around the same date, the issue of the *Recherches* containing the 'Réponse' appeared, albeit by an anonymous group of Jesuits.[105]

Entrenchment: February 1947

At the beginning of February 1947, the Jesuits of Lyon still seemed to be inter-acting with one another in a relatively positive manner. When, on 2 February, the aforementioned Belgian Jesuit Édouard Dhanis contacted Henri Rondet, the Prefect of Studies at Fourvière, and presented him a number of observations and questions concerning the prolongation of the controversy after the papal address, an extremely amicable and reassuring response was despatched by Henri de Lubac four days later.[106] Dhanis' suggestions remain, nevertheless, of particular importance for the rest of our account. In his letter, Dhanis offers advice on how to react when one suspects one is being targeted by Rome. In the first instance, he insists on an examination of conscience (done by de Lubac on 6 March 1946[107]), the critical re-examination of one's own positions and the filtering out of anything that might be in error or occasion controversy. He then suggests that the individuals in question present their own positions directly to the authorities in a clear and unequivocal manner (i.e. without inviting polemic or participating therein in public fora). Dhanis concludes by pointing out the importance of acquiring the approval of the authorities for one's own ideas.

Dhanis' response to de Lubac's letter dated 18 February is likewise friendly and positive. In the interim, however, de Lubac's 'Réponse' had arrived in Rome and had caused something of a commotion. Meanwhile, the authors of the 'Réponse' nonetheless received many positive reactions. In a letter dated 4 February, for example, Daniélou wrote to de Lubac stating that Henri-Irénée Marrou, Marie-Dominique Chenu and Henri-Marié Féret, among others, fully agreed with the 'Réponse'.[108] In his reply, de Lubac mentions the fact that Yves Congar did not want to get involved in the polemic.[109] Dhanis appears at first to be relieved with respect to both de Lubac's reply to his letter and the 'Réponse'. This, however, was to be the last positive note in the entire affair.[110]

What is the 'Réponse' about? It reacts against the aforementioned article published by Labourdette in the *Revue thomiste*, which only appeared in December 1946. The Jesuits initially agree with Labourdette's resistance to exaggerated historical relativism in relation to divine truth and his opposition to the replacement of speculative truth with a more contingent truth. They go on to point out, however, that Labourdette's creation of a super heresy, finding it at work wherever he looks, is not the correct methodology and that he should have made the effort to study the various perspectives he so roundly condemns. The Jesuits draw attention to the varied nature of their group, which makes it difficult to lump them together in a single camp and condemn them without further nuance. The fact that Labourdette nevertheless does so simply testifies to his own subjectivism, the very position against which he had reacted in the first place. By pointing to a few distortions of the original Jesuit texts in Labourdette's article, the Jesuits subtly note that an adherent of the speculative truth such as Labourdette might benefit from demonstrating some degree of respect for the historical truth. They go on to resist the exclusion of relativism and subjectivism in the domain of historical studies, allowing them to insist that there is no obligation to maintain a notion of a timeless truth that overlooks the concrete and the particular. The content of the article makes it clear that its publication enjoyed the support of the French Jesuit authorities.

In February 1947, Marie-Joseph Nicolas, the Dominican provincial in Toulouse, and Bruno de Solages, Rector of the Institut Catholique de Toulouse, were likewise engaged in an exchange of letters occasioned by Labourdette's article and the Jesuit 'Réponse'.[111] De Solages, who had friends on both sides, was trying to reconcile the opposing parties and on 3 February he took the initiative of writing a letter to Nicolas. In his reply of 12 February the latter emphasized that he remains faithful to neo-scholasticism and thereby endeavours to give an albeit cautious response to the position maintained by de Solages, who quotes from one of his own articles published in the August/September 1946 edition of *Esprit* in which he argues that while revelation is immutable, human reason is not, such that a synthesis of both is always in a state of development. De Solages' attempt to establish reconciliation broke down due to the appearance of the most debated opinion in the entire crisis of the *nouvelle théologie*: the article of Réginald Garrigou-Lagrange.

Having been turned down by the *Revue thomiste*, Garrigou's article appeared in *Angelicum*, the house journal of the Roman Dominicans.[112] With continual reference to Vatican documents, Garrigou-Lagrange *retrocontextualized* the entire discussion: he located the vision of Daniélou, de Lubac and like-minded scholars within the framework sketched by ecclesial documents from the first decennium of the twentieth century of so-called 'Modernism'. Garrigou's conviction that the *nouvelle théologie* was in fact 'a new version of Modernism' serves to illustrate the anti-modernist climate that was still present in Rome, aglow under the ashes. Moreover, Maurice Blondel's thought appeared to him to be an important element of inspiration.

After the appearance of Garrigou-Lagrange's article, de Lubac received letters of support together with angry reactions to his apparent adversary. Congar and de Solages, for example, express their support of de Lubac in letters dated 25 and 26 February respectively.[113]

From the End of February 1947 to the End of 1948

What were Jean-Baptiste Janssens' preoccupations at the time? The General was intent on avoiding a condemnation. After the Pope's address and the heated discussion vented in a variety of periodicals, he considered it opportune to intervene. On 26 February, two letters made their way from the Generalate in Rome, destination France. One of the letters was addressed to the Jesuits of Fourvière and those of *Études*, two Jesuit communities that frequently tend to be reduced to the theologate and the journal respectively;[114] the other was intended for the French provincials and contained the aforementioned letter in an appendix.[115] We will examine both letters in detail.

In the first letter, Janssens refers to discussions during the last General Congregation and informs the reader that he considered himself obliged to ask the advice of a few well-disposed and competent individuals. The General begins by summarizing a number of positive evolutions.[116] After this, however, his tone is much less friendly. Janssens observes in fact that the professors in question appear to prefer to address themselves to outsiders rather than to criticize their own confreres, including those who are pleased to introduce new and potentially dangerous ideas. Janssens concludes that such lack of caution has the potential to lead to the losing sight of the teaching of the magisterium. Janssens alludes at this juncture to secret documents that were apparently in circulation. Similar allusions are made as the letter continues and the General introduces a number of directives. The professors were henceforth to avoid anything in their writings that might be understood to support Modernism and were to be on their guard against endangering the truth of dogma.

In his letter to the French provincials, Janssens refers to 'three points of varying importance', instructions to be implemented by the four superiors. In the first instance, he refers to documents in circulation that had been ascribed to Jesuit authors. While the documents in question relate to philosophical and theological issues, they had not been approved by the relevant authorities and they threatened to confuse insufficiently formed minds. The documents were to be found, nonetheless, in seminaries and houses of religious formation. Janssens requests that the provincials do everything in their power to prohibit them. In the second instance, Janssens expresses his displeasure at the gradual disappearance of Latin in study houses of the order, whereby students are no longer able to read Augustine and Thomas. Janssens insists that the provincials call a halt to this tendency and return to the use of Latin. In the third instance, the General refers to a number of published works – as opposed to the unpublished documents referred to in his first point – that had appeared without approval or the necessary censorship. According to Janssens, objective censorship was necessary, even if it concerned the writings of fellow Jesuits.

The Jesuits addressed in the first letter must have responded with the necessary haste. What then do the reports contain? We will limit ourselves to de Lubac's two-page report, which criticizes the vision represented by Garrigou-Lagrange and counters each allegation one by one.[117] De Lubac writes that he does not understand why Garrigou-Lagrange had singled him out for attack: 'I have to confess that I can find nowhere in my work that I relativize Saint Thomas, ignore truth, disrespect dogma, invent "new principles" or call into existence a heterodox *"théologie nouvelle".*'

On 4 March, a week after the letters and the reports, and prompted by the pressure of the situation, Janssens himself took the initiative and wrote to a number of Jesuit theologians asking for their judgement concerning certain publications of their colleagues of Lyon: Rondet's article 'Croyons-nous encore au péché originel', Bouillard's *Conversion et grâce chez saint Thomas d'Aquin* and two books by de Lubac: *Surnaturel* and *De la connaissance de Dieu.*[118] Janssens' round of inquiry was ultimately to last a full six months, from the end of February to the end of August. We will examine the reports supplied by the Jesuit theologians before looking at Janssens' final decision on the matter. As noted above, we will limit ourselves to the conclusions concerning de Lubac.

Four anonymous reports were found in the archives.[119] For a number of reasons, however, there is sufficient evidence to ascribe one of the reports to Dhanis: (1) the evaluation of de Lubac's work is particularly positive and is reminiscent of the correspondence between the two, (2) the report is the only one to make repeated reference to the publications of Léopold Malevez, a colleague of Dhanis, and (3) the report's concluding sentence contains a formula Dhanis employed consistently at the end of private reports he had made on Janssens' behalf as is evident from the conciliar archives.[120] Dhanis notes in his report that while he does not share de Lubac's opinion, he concedes de Lubac's freedom to maintain it. Dhanis writes with respect to *Surnaturel*. The second report likewise makes no allusion to violations of orthodoxy in *Surnaturel* and insists that de Lubac's rejection of the concept of *natura pura* does not coincide with the vision propagated thereof by authors such as Baius and Jansenius.[121] The third report makes similar allusion to Augustine's thought and likewise does not call the orthodoxy of *Surnaturel* into question, although it laments the lack of precision in the rendition of de Lubac's vision. The fourth report is more than positive and borders on unadulterated praise: '*Surnaturel* is a work of exceptional richness.'[122] The author of the last report notes, nonetheless, that de Lubac could have been more precise and indeed more prudent in his formulation of the concepts of grace and nature and the relationship between them.[123]

In the period between March and the end of August, as the reports were being submitted, several other instances and individuals took action, for the most part in reaction to Garrigou-Lagrange's article. In March, for example, the Parisian Cardinal Emmanuel Suhard's pastoral letter 'Essor ou déclin de l'Église' was published. Dated 11 February 1947, the cardinal reacts against integrism and the exlusiveness of neo-Thomism – which Garrigou-Lagrange defends – and offers his support to the search for true theology.[124] This letter was an important sign of goodwill in the eyes of the Jesuits, who did not hesitate to help the cardinal to distribute his letter. In a letter to Henri de Lubac, dated 21 May 1947, Jean Daniélou wrote that he had received a message from Stanislas Lyonnet stating that he had distributed all 20 copies of the letter Daniélou had sent to him in Rome.[125] The most vehement reaction came from Bruno de Solages. In the April issue of the *Bulletin de littérature ecclésiastique* (1947), de Solages published a damning critique,[126] dated 7 March (the feast of saint Thomas), pointing out that Garrigou-Lagrange either did not quote his sources or that he quoted them incorrectly, removed everything from its context and interpreted it in opposition to its original intention. In short, de Solages was of the opinion that Garrigou-Lagrange, 'who constantly uses Thomism as a club to crush its adversaries',[127] had abandoned the elementary rules of academic writing, and would have been better to have taken Thomas as his example in this regard. For example, Garrigou-Lagrange ascribes a scholastic description of truth to Blondel which does not square with what Blondel had actually written on the topic. He then goes on to argue that the said description, in fact the antithesis of Blondel's understanding of truth, was the foundation of Bouillard's vision of truth. De Solages concludes by noting that Garrigou-Lagrange belonged to 'the camp of those who would condemn Saint Thomas'!

Even Jean Daniélou, who was famous for his animated temperament, argued that de Solages' article was 'a bit too aggressive'.[128] The article caused several severe reactions, even a year after publication, like Mariano Cordovani's article on 'Verità e novità in Teologia' in *L'Osservatore Romano*.[129] Of course, Garrigou-Lagrange did not hesitate to write a reaction against de Solages in an article entitled 'Vérité et immutabilité du dogme', which appeared in the April issue of *Angelicum*.[130] The latter points out that the main purpose of his article of February 1947 was to react against the new definition of truth as proposed by Blondel in 1906.[131] Garrigou-Lagrange quotes Blondel in full, but insists after a number of remarks that he stands by his critique. Blondel's understanding of truth and that of the *nouvelle théologie*, he argues, would 'fatally wound the intellect'. According to Garrigou-Lagrange, the traditional definition of truth had been preserved by all the Councils and the *nouvelle théologie* had been called to task by the Pope on 19 September 1946. The same edition of *Angelicum* contains a letter penned by Maurice Blondel himself in which he reacts against the distortion of his concept of truth in Garrigou-Lagrange's February article.[132] The response of the latter, which follows immediately, insists that the many errors found in recent theological literature are due to a neglect of the traditional concept of truth and a turn to the new hypothesis that lies at its foundation and had been introduced by the philosophy of action into theological discourse. A short time later, a further article by Garrigou-Lagrange entitled 'Les notions consacrées par les conciles' appeared in *Angelicum*, written in the same spirit of absolute defence of neo-scholastic conceptual theology.[133] Henri Bouillard provided a reply in the *Recherches de science religieuse*,[134] which caused in its turn a response from Garrigou-Lagrange in *Angelicum* in which he called once again for a return to the traditional concept of truth.[135]

In the background of the ongoing debate, Bruno de Solages did not abandon his efforts to reconcile all parties involved in the debate. Although he himself had written the aforementioned polemical article against Garrigou-Lagrange in April 1947, in the same month he drew up a 'Déclaration théologique' ('Theological Declaration'), intended to be signed by all the conflicting parties. He sent a first draft to his friend Henri de Lubac, who agreed to sign while asking for a few clarifications and specifications. Finally, in May 1947, de Solages transmitted the text to all protagonists.[136] This second attempt at reconciliation broke down, however, on the appearance of a booklet dated 15 February 1947, in which Labourdette's article on theology's sources, the response of the Jesuits and the Dominican response – which was scheduled for publication in the *Revue thomiste*, but never appeared – were bundled together.[137] The Toulousian Dominicans Raymond-Léopold Bruckberger (who introduced the debate), Labourdette (who provided the text of the reply to the Jesuit 'Réponse') and Nicolas (who provided a *post scriptum* on both the progress of theology and fidelity to Saint Thomas) were the official authors. Labourdette writes concerning the Jesuit response that the debate was threatening to remain within the boundaries of mere rivalry between religious orders.[138]

In its 26 March, 4 July and 17 July editions of 1947, the bimonthly newsletter published on behalf of the bishops by the Secretariat of the French Episcopate summarized the polemic, detailing the publications and positions that had fired the discussion in chronological order.[139] It is also evident from the 4 July edition that the secret responses from the Jesuits of Lyon – secret according to the orders of General Janssens – had been passed on to the French bishops. The edition informed the bishops of the reactions of the Jesuits to the allegations of Garrigou-Lagrange,[140] publishing excerpts from the reports of Bouillard, de Lubac, Fessard, Daniélou and Teilhard de Chardin. The said reports represent a basic reworking of their first reaction to Garrigou-Lagrange's allegations, as requested by Janssens at the end of February. De Lubac upholds his vision.

Janssens waited until the end of August 1947 to write to the provincials of Lyon and Paris with his findings and directives on the matter.[141] In his report, Janssens makes a distinction between the training given at Fourvière and the orthodoxy of the standpoints maintained by the Jesuits of Lyon. With respect to the former, the General is short and to the point: questions at the core of theological debate ought to be studied. His response to the orthodoxy question is more detailed. In the first instance, he relativizes attacks against the Jesuits of Lyon and expresses his appreciation for all the reports upon which his letter is based. The General is clearly concerned with content and has an eye for orthodoxy, not in the least in order to avoid magisterial involvement. Janssens then moves on to 'the weak point of the so-called Fourvière school, both its professors and its publicists'. In order to designate the core of the problem, he begins by quoting from the most general passages of the censors' reports. In the first instance, he quotes a passage from the fourth report word for word in which it is observed that the staff of Fourvière all too frequently give the impression that Thomism is no longer adequate as a response to modern themes and problems.[142] Janssens continues with the text of Dhanis' report, pointing out that several publications of the French Jesuits have 'an aspect of *nouvelle théologie*' because of the disdain with which they approach scholasticism and hark back to Augustine, other Fathers or the Scriptures 'without beating about the bush'.[143] He continues: 'The thought constructed around Thomas is considered to be "old".' Janssens then introduces some remarks of his own: 'Although this representation of the vision of the Jesuits of Fourvière may not coincide with what they themselves think, it is nevertheless the way in which the "school of Fourvière" is perceived.' He then warns against potential misadventures if this perception were to continue.

Against the background of the General's inquiry and final report, it comes as no suprise that the Jesuits of Lyon were willing to reconcile themselves with the Dominicans of Toulouse. Once again, Bruno de Solages took the initiative in this regard. In May 1947, after the appearance of the booklet entitled *Dialogue théologique* – considered a revised version of his 'Theological Declaration' – he made his third attempt to reconcile the protagonists and invited them to meet at Carmaux, in the house of his nephew. A first appointment, scheduled for 13 June, was cancelled by the Jesuits as a result of the publication of the aforementioned booklet and Labourdette himself cancelled a second meeting scheduled for 4 October. The meeting was never to take place. A month earlier, Labourdette published an article in the *Revue thomiste*, dated Easter 1947.[144] While Labourdette clearly wanted to go beyond the level of polemic, the title, content and publication of his article demonstrated that the debate was far from over. This was reinforced by the publication of other articles in the *Revue thomiste*, such as those by Labourdette and Nicolas on the status of the truth and the unity of theology that were scheduled for the third edition of 1947, but only appeared in 1948.[145] The article in question was a response to an earlier contribution by Jesuit Jean-Marie Le Blond in the *Recherches de science religieuse* in which he reflected on the theological debate from a philosophical perspective.[146] Reference has already been made to the debate that raged between Garrigou-Lagrange, Blondel and Bouillard in 1947/48.

The Jesuit 'camp' had been rendered more or less powerless in the debate (and the various subdebates) by their General. De Lubac in particular was evidently encouraged to desist from engaging in the debate in the public forum. In a letter dated 10 November 1947, Janssens expresses approval of de Lubac's low profile 'for publications that are intended for a particular readership [and] are read in reality by people one ought to be wary of.'[147] Roughly two weeks later, an article appeared in *Gregorianum* penned by the Roman Jesuit Charles Boyer in which de Lubac is heavily criticized for his *Surnaturel*.[148] Boyer himself sent his article to de Lubac who, the day after he received it, replied with a letter in which he lamented the limitedness of his own freedom of opinion.[149] On this account, de Lubac writes in his *Mémoires*: 'He [Boyer] seems to be incapable of passing from the juridical level to the level of the religious intuition.'[150] De Lubac was determined to react: he wrote a letter to his provincial in order to obtain the General's permission to react.[151] Because there were so many attacks against him – he mentions Garrigou-Lagrange, Boyer, Jacques de Blic,[152] Guy de Broglie and Gagnebet – de Lubac states in his letter that it was very hard to remain calm and silent. On 21 March 1948, Janssens granted him permission to react, although he insisted that de Lubac's article first be submitted to the censorship of the Jesuit Province and the Roman ecclesial authorities before publication, noting that 'the experience of the past proves that this is necessary'.[153] The same approach was also employed by Bouillard, who wished to respond to Garrigou-Lagrange. On 17 May 1948, Bouillard was ordered by Janssens to moderate the tone of his article – which was otherwise acceptable in terms of content – out of respect for 'le vieux professeur'.[154]

When de Lubac received the General's response from his provincial, he addressed a letter to the latter in which he expresses his disappointment.[155] De Lubac laments the fact that reference is constantly made to the authority to which he owes his obedience, while he has never called the said authority into question. He also finds it difficult to accept that he has been branded as a 'suspect' theologian within the Church.[156]

Spring 1949–Summer 1951

In Spring 1949, a year after the imposition of the twofold censure, a visitation took place at Fourvière – a task ascribed by the General to his confidant Dhanis – a logical follow-up to the first measure stated in Janssens' conclusions that emerged at the end of August 1947.

In addition to investigations and critique from within his order, de Lubac continued to be the subject of external critique. In a letter to his friend Daniélou, he laments the never ending attacks of the *Revue thomiste*, as demonstrated by Dominicans Marie-Rosaire Gagnebet[157] and Maurice Corvez.[158] Written in 1948 and published in 1950, articles by both Dominicans are representative of the ongoing debate.

In 1950, a combination of the visitation, the ongoing polemic and Rome's continuing irritation resulted in at least three sanctions.

First, General Janssens ordered that de Lubac was to be removed as head of the *Recherches de science religieuse*, the house journal of the French Jesuits and their primary mouthpiece in the debate. In a letter to Daniélou dated 30 May 1950, de Lubac writes that he had already known about this measure for three months. In his *Mémoires*, he states that he had received a confidential letter from Janssens in which the latter informed him that he was to be relieved of his duties as editor-in-chief in the spring.[159] The discharge finally took place in June, shortly after the letter to Daniélou. De Lubac was ultimately replaced by a group of four Jesuits: Charles Baumgartner, Joseph Lecler, André Lefèvre and Henri Rondet.[160]

The second level of sanctions against the *nouvelle théologie* is related to Fourvière. Two months prior to the promulgation of the encyclical *Humani generis*, the General ordered a number of Jesuits to resign as professors at the study house and required them to move out of Lyon. Such measures were taken against Émile Delaye on 28 May 1950, occasioned by the publication of his book *Qu'est-ce qu'un catholique?*[161] According to de Lubac, however, the real storm to hit Fourvière came a month later.[162] Measures were taken against the latter on 12 June, followed a couple of days later by Henri Bouillard, Alexandre Durand and Pierre Ganne. In July 1951, a little more than a year after these events, Henri Rondet was obliged to step down as Prefect of Studies at Fourvière. By coincidence or design, Jean Louisgrand ended his term as Rector of Fourvière on 31 July 1951, precisely two years after succeeding Chamussy on 1 August 1949. His resignation serves as the final chapter in the study house's 'decontamination'.

The third and final level of sanctions took place on the level of publications. On 25 October 1950, in the aftermath of *Humani generis*, Jean-Baptiste Janssens despatched a circular 'Ad omnes provinciarum praepositos'.[163] The latter document instructs the provincials of the order to remove a number of Jesuit publications from the libraries of the order's houses of formation. The publications in question were authored by Henri de Lubac (three books and an article), Henri Bouillard (one book and three articles), Yves de Montcheuil (two books), Jean Daniélou (one book and one article) and Jean-Marie Le Blond (one article).[164] Their affinity with Blondel's thought is striking. Reference can be made by way of conclusion to René d'Ouince, editor-in-chief of *Études*, who felt himself obliged under pressure from Rome to alter and supplement his journal's reporting of *Humani generis* after the publication of an article on the encyclical by his adjunct Robert Rouquette.[165] In the conclusion to his contribution, d'Ouince wisely points out that in spite of the continued commentary on the encyclical, 'nothing can replace a reading of the document itself'.[166]

On 11 February 1951, General Janssens offered some explanation – in French! – by considering the measures in light of *Humani generis*:

> If I had not taken these measures, I would have failed in my task of maintaining fidelity to the church's doctrine within the Society. I realise that the said measures were exceptionally severe, but the pressure brought to bear by the encyclical's warning 'concerning a number of opinions that threaten to ruin the foundations of Catholic doctrine' testifies to the equally severe situation in which I found myself. Such a warning from the Vicar of Our Lord Jesus Christ has to be accepted in a spirit of faith.[167]

Later in his text he underlines the need to defend the application of the *philosophia perennis*, the exclusive basis of every good philosophy and theology.[168]

According to Jean-Pierre Wagner, 'the *new theologians* were accused of misunderstanding the relationship between the supernatural and human nature, of falsifying Thomism by subjecting it to a historical perspective, and of relativising dogmas'.[169] It should be noted at this juncture that Rome's fear of a resurgence of Modernism was likewise fanned into flame. It would appear that

Janssens had no choice in the matter and was obliged to intervene in order to protect his theologians and spare the order from a new period of difficulty.

2.5 *Further Developments During the Second Phase*

During the second phase of the *nouvelle théologie*, a number of other works were published in addition to those of the Jesuits in which the relationship between theology, faith and reality was the primary subject or which touched on related themes. While it would take us far beyond our present goals to examine this material in detail, three works of specific importance and an ongoing debate deserve to be mentioned nonetheless. We do not presuppose that the following contributions are expressions of the *nouvelle théologie*, although it would be difficult to deny any relationship with this movement of *ressourcement*.

The 1945 book *Le problème de l'acte de foi* by Louvain historian Roger Aubert continues to the present day to be a standard work on theological methodology in the period between the First Vatican Council and the year of its publication,[170] and its four editions are far from accidental. In a well organized and detailed manner, Aubert provides the reader access to the developments in theological methodology whereby the tension between positive and speculative theology serves as a sort of leitmotiv. It is striking that the first part of the book deals with the period prior to Vatican I, paying significant attention to the Scriptures, the Church Fathers – in particular Augustine – the theology of Thomas Aquinas, the role of the magisterium and finally the conclusions of Vatican I itself (the constitution *Dei Filius*).

Five years after the creation of 'Sources chrétiennes', Eligius Dekkers, a Benedictine of the Abbey of Saint Peter in Steenbrugge (near Bruges), introduced the idea of a 'Corpus Christianorum' series of critical editions of Christian literature from late antiquity to the late Middle Ages. The series took concrete form in the course of the following years and at a later stage the Latin series acquired its Greek counterpart.

In 1947–49, Gustave Thils, a Louvain professor of theology, published his two-volume *Théologie des réalités terrestres*.[171] Where Aubert had examined the relationship between theology and faith from the perspective of methodology and Dekkers had taken the initiative to establish a series that was to contribute to the formation of a theology of sources, Thils underlines the bond between theology and the reality of everyday life. From the perspective of both theology and concrete life, this bond is associated inseparably with a focus on the history of faith, Church and theology.

Against the background of the *nouvelle théologie*, a debate can be observed in various periodicals (including *Angelicum* and the *Revue thomiste*) on the question of 'truth'. The debate reached its height in the first five years after the Second World War and had its roots in a similar debate at the time of the Modernist crisis. The same two main parties can be recognized, namely – and without using either term in its proper sense – the dogmaticians on one side and the historians on the other. The former group continued to uphold the concept of an immutable eternal truth that was not open to discussion. The latter group did not deny the value of a concept of the truth, but found it difficult to accept that truth – a human understanding of something divine – was not open to development in line with the evolution of human knowledge.

2.6 *Concluding Observations*

As with the first phase of the *nouvelle théologie*, the second phase was also characterized by polemic, whereby Rome – the magisterium and the superiors of religious orders – served as both player and umpire on the theological playing field. During this period, Jean Daniélou and the Jesuits of Lyon – the theologians of Fourvière and Henri de Lubac – manifested themselves as pioneers of a 'sources theology' at the expense of a 'conclusion theology'. The sources of the faith were given pride of place over the neo-scholastic conceptual system. The conclusions of the work of Henri Bouillard, the programme of Daniélou and the controversy surrounding Henri de Lubac's *Surnaturel* ultimately forced the superiors of the Society of Jesus to investigate claims that *nouvelle théologie* was being practised in Lyon. The said investigation constitutes the nucleus of the so-called *affaire Fourvière* and was to result in disciplinary measures being taken against, among others, Bouillard and de Lubac. Both men continued to insist, however, that they had never presented themselves as representatives of this movement.

Chapter 3

THE PHASE OF THE INTERNATIONALIZATION OF THE *NOUVELLE THÉOLOGIE*. CASE STUDY: THE LOW COUNTRIES

After the promulgation of *Humani generis* and the implementation of disciplinary measures against so-called *new theologians*, the *nouvelle théologie* entered a period of paralysis in France. The present chapter demonstrates, however, that the two phases of the *nouvelle théologie* as an intellectual movement was not exclusively French. As a matter of fact, the *nouvelle théologie*, the encyclical, the polemic and the sanctions attracted a considerable international response, which did lead to the spread of the movement throughout the world, although not everywhere. In Spain and Great Britain, for example, the *nouvelle théologie* enjoyed little if any success. In the Netherlands and German-speaking countries, on the other hand, the theological renewal movement found some acceptance. We shall begin our survey of the third phase of the *nouvelle théologie* with some general observations and then focus on one of its most important components, namely the increasing success of the *nouvelle théologie* in the Low Countries (Flanders and the Netherlands).

3.1 *General Observations: The Third Phase*

It is striking that the internationalization of the French language *nouvelle théologie* took place first and foremost in two non-Latin languages, Dutch and German. The initial impetus in this regard had its roots in a healthy curiosity concerning the building blocks of the French polemic and the various positions represented in the debate. It was far from simple for 'outsiders' to distinguish the different nuances involved and reconstruct the chronology of the debate, let alone determine their own position on the matter. It has to be said nevertheless that many of the representatives of the first and second phases of the *nouvelle théologie* were considered to be prominent intellectuals outside France and, in some instances, important teachers.

It goes without saying that our discussion of the third phase will focus on the question of reception: the integration of the *nouvelle théologie* in a specific language and in a specific theological context. While such reception was obviously an important component of the third phase, an additional component also deserves our attention: the ongoing development of the *nouvelle théologie* itself. This development can be observed from a variety of different perspectives, including the geographical and linguistic. By expanding towards Germany in the East, for example, and the Netherlands in the North, the *nouvelle théologie* extended its support base within theological circles.

The pillars of the *nouvelle théologie* remain the same as in the preceding two phases. The same reaction is evident, for example, to 'dead' theology, or as the German Jesuit Karl Rahner expressed it in 1943: 'handbook theology lacks nothing whatsoever, except life.'[1] This explains the latter's critique of neo-scholasticism's meta-historical doctrine of grace as excessively abstract.[2] In the second instance, the underestimation and virtual negation of history and historiography is also the subject of criticism. It is not accidental that Karl Lehmann lists Rahner's greatest merit as his 'return to the sources of theology, a theology that was imprisoned in its own tradition and dogma'.[3] Reaction against neo-scholasticism and meta-historical research constitutes a third point of similarity with the early phases of the movement: the return to the 'basics'. The neo-scholastic theological edifice had evolved into an ivory tower with access for only the happy few, leading more and more people to focus their attention on the bricks instead of the building, on reality instead of speculation. This position shared common ground with the French *nouvelle théologie*, which was warmly appreciated by those who shared the desire for a 'theology of reality'. The fact that this attitude was not appreciated in Roman circles is confirmed by its rejection of demonstrations of interest and sympathy towards the *new theologians* and their ideas. The Jesuit Sebastiaan Tromp, for example, a senior figure in the Roman Curia, was sent to the Netherlands – the country of his birth – in 1954 in an effort to guard its theology and theologians against the *nouvelle théologie*. In spite of the resignation of Klaas Steur, a professor at the seminary of Warmond and a *nouvelle théologie* sympathizer, van Tromp's mission enjoyed little success.[4] On the contrary, it appeared to be part of the last death spasms of *Humani generis*. The spasms managed to inflict a considerable amount of pain nevertheless, by ensuring, for example, that certain books were not published. It is apparent here that greater freedom existed among the Dominicans in this regard than among the Jesuits, who had a reputation for their unmediated fidelity to the Pope (cf. the fourth of the Jesuit vows). After the intrigues of the 1940s and the fact that the *nouvelle théologie* had become associated with them after the second phase, moreover, the Jesuits clearly wanted to keep a low profile. It is against this background that Karl Rahner around 1950 was refused permission from his superiors to publish his hefty book on the Assumption of the Blessed Virgin Mary.[5] Around the same period, the Dutch Jesuits also refused to grant permission to Piet Schoonenberg to publish his doctoral dissertation. Signs of the times . . .

The reception of the *nouvelle théologie* is one thing, its continuation another. While the period of reception was beset with difficulties, the central ambitions of the *nouvelle théologie* seemed unstoppable. It had to be continued, whatever the cost. In the present chapter we will discuss the thought of two of the most important and influential Dutch-speaking theologians of the second half of the twentieth century from this perspective: Edward Schillebeeckx, the Belgian Dominican who became a professor of Theology in the Netherlands in 1958, and the Dutch Jesuit Piet Schoonenberg, who became Schillebeeckx's colleague in Nijmegen in 1964 and who consistently enjoyed more appreciation in Belgium than in his native Netherlands. In so doing, however, we are making a choice that will leave the contribution of the likes of Rahner, Hans Urs von Balthasar and others undiscussed.[6] Our focus on the Low Countries, and on Schillebeeckx and Schoonenberg in particular, is appropriate for a number of reasons. Side by side with the predominantly French academic world, a fully fledged Dutch-speaking academy evolved, thereby opening the door for the Dutch-speaking world as a serious dialogue partner. Moreover, the Low Countries served in those days as a crossroads between the *nouvelle théologie* and the German *Verkündigungstheologie*. Thirdly, our choice allows us to give voice to a Dominican and a Jesuit. Last, but not least, we are of the opinion that parallels can be observed with regard to prominent theologians of the Low Countries, between Dutch Jesuits and Belgian Dominicans on the one hand (pro *nouvelle théologie*) and Dutch Dominicans and Belgian Jesuits on the other (contra *nouvelle théologie*). This hypothesis represents the central feature of our present research activities and is due for further elaboration at a later date.

In our discussion of the relationship between Schillebeeckx, Schoonenberg and the *nouvelle théologie* we follow our biographical-bibliographical sketch with two further sections, one on the reception of the *nouvelle théologie*, the other on its ongoing elaboration. Given the extent to which Schillebeeckx and Schoonenberg travelled significantly parallel paths leading up to the Vatican II period, we have opted for a different approach to both scholars. Bearing in mind that much more has been written about Schillebeeckx' thought than that of Schoonenberg, we will limit ourselves to a number of 'moments' in the former's career while focusing with greater intensity on the latter's personal vision.

3.2 *Schillebeeckx*

As noted above, Belgium had already played an important role in the *nouvelle théologie* prior to 1950. Two centres of the first phase of the *nouvelle théologie* were housed within the Belgian borders: Louvain and the study house of the Belgian Dominicans, with Charlier and De Petter in residence, and Le Saulchoir, the Walloon village in which the French Dominicans had set up their study house after their expulsion from France at the beginning of the century. Chenu served as Rector of Le Saulchoir from 1932 to 1942, the last five years being spent in the study centre's new location in Étiolles near Paris from 1937.

Schillebeeckx had contact with both centres. He commenced his studies in Louvain in 1935 and was to depart ten years later for a year in Paris. A further ten years later he moved from Belgium to the Netherlands. In short, Schillebeeckx' career is a perfect illustration of the spread of the *nouvelle théologie* from France, via Belgium to the Netherlands.

Edward Schillebeeckx

Edward Cornelis Florent Alfons Schillebeeckx was born in Antwerp on 12 November 1914.[7] After his secondary school studies at the Jesuit college in Turnhout he entered the Order of Preachers at the age of 19 years, starting his noviciate in the Dominican convent in Ghent in 1934. After his noviciate, he spent three years studying philosophy at the order's study house in Louvain, completed his military service in 1938, was reconscripted after a brief return to Louvain because of the imminent war and only recommenced his theological studies in Louvain in the middle of 1940. Schillebeeckx was ordained to the priesthood in 1941, was appointed lector in Theology a year later[8] and lecturer at the order's study house immediately thereafter.

The end of the war created the possibility for Schillebeeckx to continue his studies in Paris at Le Saulchoir where he was in residence from 1945 to 1947. At the same time – in fact primarily – he took classes at other institutes, including the École des Hautes Études at the Sorbonne, where he got to know Chenu. He was recalled to Louvain in 1947 where he resumed his position as Lecturer in Systematic Theology, teaching a long list of systematic-theological topics over a four-year cycle until his departure for Nijmegen ten years later. Schillebeeckx' 1952 book *De sacramentele heilseconomie* on the sacramental economy of salvation served as his doctoral dissertation at Le Saulchoir.[9] In the latter part of 1957, Schillebeeckx was appointed professor at the Catholic University of Nijmegen (presently Radboud University) where he started to teach classes in January 1958. He served for 25 years as Professor of Dogmatics and the History of Theology at Nijmegen's Faculty of Theology where he retired from in 1983. While he devoted a great deal of energy teaching the large numbers of students at the faculty – many of whom were drawn there by Schillebeeckx himself – publication commanded the lion's share of his time. In addition to establishing the Dutch journal *Tijdschrift voor Theologie* in 1961 and being a member of the editorial board of *Concilium*, Schillebeeckx published a string of monographs and articles. Perhaps the most important and certainly the best-known of his works are the three books he published on the figure of Christ and Christology,[10] together with his *De sacramentele heilseconomie, Openbaring en Theologie*[11] and his *Pleidooi voor mensen in de kerk*.[12]

In the period leading up to Vatican II and the four sessions of the Council itself, Schillebeeckx served as executive adviser to the bishops of the Netherlands and as an influential observer. Nevertheless, his ideas and writings – before, during and after the Council – were the subject of scrutiny from the Roman authorities. For a variety of reasons – particularly Christological – Schillebeeckx was called to account on a number of occasions by the same authorities,[13] although he was never condemned. Schillebeeckx died in Nijmegen on 23 December 2009.

Reception of the Nouvelle Théologie

With respect to Edward Schillebeeckx' reception of the *nouvelle théologie*, we will refer to six moments in his career up to and including Vatican II.

The first moment represents a turning point in his theological studies. When Schillebeeckx encountered philosophy in action in the work of De Petter, theology must have appeared immobile in comparison, static and indeed old fashioned. The kind of theology he was exposed to was based exclusively on the Church's Thomistic manual tradition, which had enjoyed a revival after Leo XIII's *Aeterni Patris* promoted Thomism anew and which, as we have noted, had reduced Catholic theology in the wake of Modernism to a series of manuals or handbooks. Schillebeeckx distanced himself from this fossilized, lifeless speculative thinking and chose exegesis as his specialization instead of systematic theology. John Bowden states the following in this regard: 'Because of his discontent with speculative theology he devoted his last two years' study to exegesis.'[14] This is completely in line with what he himself writes in his 'theological testament', where we read that his memories of the 'traditional and old fashioned' Dominican theologate in Louvain were 'not exactly the best'.[15] The results of his new specialization, however, did not enjoy the kind of historical-critical underpinning one might have come to expect from the later Schillebeeckx. He completed his lector's thesis – what we would now call his Master's thesis – on Paul's view on the sinful history prior to Christianity in November 1942.[16]

The second moment took place during the months prior to November 1942 as he prepared his thesis for submission. At this juncture, two of Schillebeeckx' teachers were sanctioned by the Roman authorities for their work and for the vision it represented. The first of these took place at the beginning of February 1942 when the *Essai sur le problème théologique* by Louvain Professor of Theology Louis Charlier was placed on the Index of Prohibited Books. As already noted, Chenu's *Une école de théologie: le Saulchoir* was also added to the Index at the same time. Schillebeeckx was upset by these sanctions and the fact that both of his confreres had lost their licence to teach in Dominican study houses. The second sanction was the dismissal of De Petter by the Dominican authorities. De Petter had been responsible for coordinating the order's studies and in this capacity – but also as a philosopher and dialogue partner who occasionally passed on forbidden (indexed) literature to Schillebeeckx – the man was important to him and the dismissal was a shock to him.[17] Rome's rejection of the *nouvelle théologie* thus resounded within the walls of Schillebeeckx' own Dominican house.

The third moment can be dated 16 September 1943, the day on which Schillebeeckx delivered his inaugural address at the Dominican study house in Louvain. The address was entitled: 'Naar een nieuwe levenstheologie?' (Towards a new theology of life?').[18] Schillebeeckx distanced himself from the non-scientific manner in which kerygmatic theology endeavoured to establish a relationship between theology and life and likewise rejected the separation or radical division of theology and life as promoted by Georg Koepgen, for example, in his 1939 book *Die Gnosis des Christentums*.[19] Schillebeeckx positioned his own vision in contrast to these two schools of thought. As Erik Borgman writes: 'It was very important for him that faith was not just an existential experience, as the kerygmatic theologians emphasized, or an unconditional submission to the absolute mystery, as it was for Koepgen. Faith was also a form of real, albeit diffuse, knowledge of God.'[20] One page earlier, Borgman had already noted that Schillebeeckx' lecture promoted a scholarly theology in touch with a living faith. Borgman points out in addition: 'Although he did not spell this out, here at the same time he indicated that the dominant scholastic theology which exclusively occupied itself with the statements defined by the magisterium as "truths of faith", did not meet the demand for a scholarly theology as seen by Thomas Aquinas, the one who by its own account was *the* philosophical and theological authority.'[21]

The fourth moment took place shortly afterwards and is related to an issue in the background of Schillebeeckx' intellectual development. Four days after Schillebeeckx' inaugural address Pope Pius XII promulgated the encyclical *Divino afflante Spiritu* in which the door was thrown open to the implementation of the historical-critical method in biblical research. This event was of considerable significance if we bear in mind the magisterium's consistent aversion of the method up to that point. It is also important within the context of Schillebeeckx' interest in the Bible and exegesis (cf. his thesis a year earlier and his use of the Bible in his later writings).

The fifth moment can be dated to the post-war years. During the second phase of the *nouvelle théologie*, Schillebeeckx was influenced by a protagonist of the first phase, namely Marie-Dominique Chenu. As we have noted, Schillebeeckx attended Chenu's classes at the École des Hautes Études in Paris from 1945 to 1947 against a background of existentialism that was blossoming in France at the time. As a historian, Chenu was responsible for courses on the history of the Middle Ages. The classes definitively confirmed the value of a historical perspective for Schillebeeckx, a perspective that harked back further in time than Thomas's commentators and that considered all theology and every theologian to be a child of its/his/her time.[22] Schillebeeckx states in his theological testament:[23]

> Under Chenu I studied the twelfth century and Thomas from a historical perspective, in the context of his time. Every course of study at Le Saulchoir adopted this perspective. Later, in my own teaching, I endeavoured to explain every tractate from the Old Testament to the twentieth century. An impossible task. But I was convinced nevertheless that faith, history and our reflection on faith must be studied in close relationship with one another.

At Le Saulchoir, Schillebeeckx also got to know Yves Congar who had just returned from captivity. Schillebeeckx certainly shared the opinion of Chenu found in Congar's diary: Chenu is a 'homme magnifique'.[24] Schillebeeckx himself had greater respect for Chenu than for Congar because the former's personality reflected what he considered to be important, while the latter came across as withdrawn and detached in his dealings with others.

Our final 'moment' is also situated in the post-war years. There can be little doubt that Schillebeeckx must have followed the French polemic surrounding the *nouvelle théologie* with considerable interest. As noted above, Schillebeeckx was studying in Paris between 1945 and 1947, years in which theology's self-understanding was evolving as never before. This continued to fascinate the young Schillebeeckx in the years that followed. The polemic attracted the attention of the Pope and the Dominican authorities ,who reacted vehemently to the advancing *nouvelle théologie,* as we have seen. Congar's authoritative contribution to the *Dictionnaire de théologie catholique* in 1946 likewise exhibited a degree of sympathy towards the likes of Charlier and Draguet.[25] In his 'In memoriam' for Congar, Schillebeeckx felt obliged to write that the condemnation of the *nouvelle théologie* in *Humani generis* also targeted the deceased.[26] One of the high points in the polemic surrounding the *nouvelle théologie* was the article published by Réginald Garrigou-Lagrange, Schillebeeckx' influential confrere. Against the background of an increasing pluralization and historicization of Thomism, both men were clearly poles apart. As Fergus Kerr writes: 'He [Schillebeeckx] was particularly interested in phenomenology, Husserl and problems of the intentionality of consciousness; from the outset, this directed Schillebeeckx away from anything that Garrigou-Lagrange could have recognized as Thomism.'[27] Having witnessed Garrigou-Lagrange's radical rejection of the *nouvelle théologie* in 1946, Schillebeeckx was aware that the gloves would soon be off. Indeed, in 1950 *Humani generis* appeared. As Robert Schreiter points out, however, the years 1945–47 meant a great deal to Schillebeeckx, even after 1950:[28]

> The two years in Paris provided the second major intellectual influence on his theology [after De Petter]. Le Saulchoir was very much at the center of the *Nouvelle Théologie* movement. This movement promoted a *ressource-ment,* or return to the patristic and medieval sources, as the way to engage in theological reflection, rather than continuing to rely on later commentators and manuals of theology. The movement embraced methods of historical-critical research as the way to rediscover the Great Christian thinkers. This emphasis on doing historical research has clearly marked Schillebeeckx' own theology, most notably his work on the sacraments, marriage, eucharist, and ministry. In the 1970s he was to extend this 'back-to-the-sources' approach to include a study of the exegetical research on the scriptures in preparation of his books on Jesus.

Continued Evolution of the Nouvelle Théologie

With regard to the continued evolution of the *nouvelle théologie* in Schillebeeckx' own theology, we will focus once again on a number of moments in Schillebeeckx' life.

As Francis Schüssler Fiorenza has argued, Schillebeeckx' early work is strongly influenced by the *nouvelle théologie*.[29] His *De sacramentele heilseconomie*, with its subtitle that translates as 'a theological reflection on Saint Thomas's teaching on the sacraments in light of the tradition and of contemporary issues relating to the sacraments', deserves to be mentioned first in this regard. In addition to a detailed historical survey of the definition of sacrament, the book's foreword is of particular interest because of its rejection of the division between faith and theology. For Schillebeeckx, genuine scholarly theology is bound together with the faith and thereby involved with everyday life. Schillebeeckx writes: 'Therefore, we resolutely reject any division between theology conceived as scholarly and so-called kerygmatic theology, and we are completely convinced that only an appropriately theological, scholarly reflection on faith that allows itself to be inspired by the structure of the deposit of faith can give rise to a kerygmatic theology.'[30] With these words, Schillebeeckx not only combines theology, faith and everyday life, but also theology as a scholarly science and theology as a pastoral framework. This explains his reaction against rigid, meta-historical neo-scholasticism, a characteristic feature of the book.

Our second moment took place in 1953, during a lecture given in Brussels at a meeting of the Vlaams Werkgenootschap voor Theologie ('Flemish Theological Fellowship').[31] The lecture brands the opposition between neo-scholastic theology and genuine theology as a false one. Indeed, without concepts, theology would be impossible. Furthermore, speculative theology should not be reduced to neo-scholasticism, and a theology that turns around experience and nothing more has few prospects. Schillebeeckx argues therefore that the said opposition must be transcended and he takes the initiative in this regard by offering a twofold warning against extreme positions. The first points out that the absolutization of conceptual theology – in which there is scarcely room for experience – brings forth a theology that bears no relation to reality and is thus false and disingenuous. The second warning addresses the opposite situation: a theology that distances itself completely from speculative thinking alienates itself from the salvific character of history and from the interpretation of history as salvific history. In short, Schillebeeckx calls for a balanced theological endeavour, and although he is aware that the commotion caused by the *nouvelle théologie* and *Humani generis* did not make such a balance any easier, he still considers it necessary.

A lecture given in 1954 in Ghent, once again to the Vlaams Werkgenootschap voor Theologie, constitutes the next 'moment' in the continued evolution of the *nouvelle théologie*.[32] Schillebeeckx situates the *nouvelle théologie* and the crisis surrounding it in the aftermath of Modernism, pointing out that the Modernist crisis served as the interpretative key employed by Rome to judge and condemn the *nouvelle théologie*. According to Schillebeeckx this in itself comes as no surprise. After all, the *nouvelle théologie* had re-opened a question left unanswered by Modernism, namely that of the restoration of the relationship between experience and concept. Schillebeeckx points out nevertheless that 'two distinct spiritual worlds' continue to oppose one another in spite of the many shared and generally accepted insights:[33] the substantial group of people who emphasize the bond between theology and reality on the one hand, and a smaller group who uphold a conceptual theology and accuse the larger group of relativism on the other. Schillebeeckx makes it clear in his use of Maréchal and De Petter that he himself belongs to the larger of the two groups.

The fourth moment is related to the remarkable fact that every contribution on themes considered a 'hot item' within the framework of the *nouvelle théologie* published in the three-volume Dutch theological dictionary *Theologisch Woordenboek* of 1952–58 were penned by Schillebeeckx, namely the lemmas 'Development of dogma', 'Theology', 'History' and '*Humani generis*'.[34] Schillebeeckx was also responsible for the lemma '*Nouvelle théologie*', although it is uncharacteristically short: 'For the most part [however] the *nouvelle théologie* is associated with the exhortations of *Humani generis* against modernising theological tendencies, at least in as far as the latter deny or minimise the significance of speculative thought in theology.'[35] Under the lemma 'Development of dogma', Schillebeeckx goes into considerable detail on Charlier's essay and Draguet's series of articles. He also makes mention of both representatives of the *nouvelle théologie* in his discussion of the term 'Theology'. In so doing, however, Schillebeeckx takes sides. He lashes out at Jean-François Bonnefoy and Charlier, for example, accusing them both of bias and inaccuracy in their interpretation of the concept *revelabilia*.[36] Congar is praised for drawing attention to positive theology's service to the Church in his book *Vraie et fausse réforme dans l'Église*, although Schillebeeckx adds that the same can be said for speculative theology.[37] His sympathy towards the *nouvelle théologie* is implied nevertheless throughout the contribution, although it is perhaps at its most explicit when he writes that

> . . . theology is both positive *and* speculative in all its functions. It is imposs-
> ible to be a good dogmatician if one does not apply oneself in the Sacred
> Scriptures, patristics, high scholasticism, including St Thomas in particular
> etc., as well as contemporary philosophy. Thomas himself serves as our
> example in this regard.[38]

Schillebeeckx thus takes Thomas as the model theologian who combined Scripture, tradition and the concrete context, a theologian who embraced all these elements and took them fully into account in his theologizing. Schillebeeckx was clearly not afraid of ruffling the sensitivities of the magisterium. Barely disguised critique of *Humani generis* resounds a couple of columns further in the theological dictionary when Schillebeeckx writes:[39]

Theology's very function as servant to the Church implies a certain freedom
for the theologian and for theological reflection (in line with the demands of
the content of revelation) within the boundaries established by the Church's
magisterium). Indeed, theology would not be able to exercise its function as
service to the Church if serious new [theological] endeavours are not even
given the chance to affirm themselves.

The fifth moment in the continued evolution of the *nouvelle théologie* in
Schillebeeckx' theology has to do with his move to the Netherlands and
represents a geographical element in the spread of the movement. In the year
in which the last volume of the *Theologisch Woordenboek* appeared, the
Radboud Universiteit – then Catholic University of Nijmegen – was set to
appoint a successor to Gerard Kreling, Professor of Dogmatic Theology. In
those days, Nijmegen's Faculty of Theology only offered a graduate – Master's
– programme and Dogmatic Theology had been entrusted to a Dominican since
the foundation of the university in 1923. The clear candidate to succeed Kreling
was Andreas H. Maltha, but the faculty authorities had their doubts about him
because of his extreme neo-scholastic profile. Given Schillebeeckx' credentials
and reputation, the provincial of the Flemish Dominicans was asked if he would
send him to Nijmegen. The provincial refused, however, and the authorities in
Nijmegen considered themselves obliged to bring the matter to the Dominican
Master General in Rome. Their appeal was met with a positive response and
Schillebeeckx started work as Professor of Dogmatic Theology in January 1958.[40]

The sixth moment is closely related to Schillebeeckx's appointment in
Nijmegen. From the beginning of his first full year in Nijmegen, more precisely
from October 1958, Schillebeeckx was responsible for courses in fundamental
dogmatic theology together with a separate course on the history of theology.
His activities on behalf of the Second Vatican Council, however, saw to it that
he had to abandon plans for the latter. For Schillebeeckx, on the other hand,
the history of theology had its place in systematic theology. The characteristic
manner with which he approached themes such as Christ and grace testified
to this: first collecting every last detail of primary information from Scripture
and Tradition and only then endeavouring to delve deeper into the subject in
search of new insights and a synthesis. This preparatory collection of material
is clearly biblical-theological and historical-theological, and Schillebeeckx'
approach in this regard can be seen as being in line with the developments in
French theology in the 1930s and 1940s. His inaugural lecture in Nijmegen on
9 May 1959 was entitled 'Op zoek naar de levende God' (The search for the
living God).[41] The popular internet encyclopaedia Wikipedia notes in relation to
the lecture that Schillebeeckx thereby introduced the *nouvelle théologie* into the
Netherlands. This is incorrect in one sense, since he himself was not responsible
for introducing the movement into the Netherlands, although it is correct in the
sense that Schillebeeckx was clearly aligned with those in the Netherlands who
promoted the *nouvelle théologie*.[42]

The seventh moment likewise establishes a connection between 1958 and 1959 and is related to Schillebeeckx' reaction to the work of one of his confreres. In 1958, Andreas Maltha published a book entitled *De nieuwe theologie: Informatie en oriëntatie* ('The New Theology: Information and Orientation'), translated into several languages but not English.[43] The following year, Schillebeeckx discusses the work of this hardline anti-*new theologian* in a Dominican periodical.[44] Schillebeeckx argues that his confrere has given his book the wrong title, that he is more interested in the *nouvelle théologie*'s lack of orthodoxy than its content and value, and that he most probably used Thomism as his basis for slating the movement. The word 'probably' is clearly a euphemism, as is evident in the remainder of Schillebeeckx' discussion. Schillebeeckx asks himself *which* Thomism Maltha is maintaining: that of the fifteenth, sixteenth, eighteenth or twentieth century? 'And in the latter instance', he continues, 'the Thomism of Garrigou-Lagrange, Manser, Sertillanges, Gilson, Kreling, de Raeymaeker, Fabro, Hayen or Maltha?'[45] The pluralization of Thomism had clearly reached fever pitch, but this inevitably led to a devaluation of Roman neo-scholasticism.

The eighth moment is the Second Vatican Council announced by John XXIII on 25 January 1959. For Schillebeeckx, the Council was to represent years of hard work as adviser to the Dutch episcopate, with Cardinal Bernard Jan Alfrink at its head.[46] His wide-ranging activities as a writer, speaker and avid debater inspired some to see him as a manipulator and someone to be feared, and others as a welcome source of inspiration. In reality, however, no one doubted his influence, and this is important when we look at themes close to the heart of the *nouvelle théologie* such as Scripture and revelation (cf. *Dei Verbum*).

Nouvelle Théologie?

Our overview of 'significant' moments in Edward Schillebeeckx' career in the period from c. 1940 to 1965 makes it clear that he was among the heirs of the French *nouvelle théologie* and was evidently someone who could continue to give form to the movement in the Dutch-speaking world.[47] Schillebeeckx continues to insist on his affinity with Marie-Dominique Chenu, his French confrere and a pioneer of theological reform. Both men – and others besides – shared the opinion that neo-scholasticism had evolved into a dead theology, alienated from the object of its study, namely living faith. Schillebeeckx, by contrast, is an important representative and promoter of a 'theology of reality', in which he defended historical-critical exegesis, a spirited understanding of the tradition, and a theology oriented towards the sources of the faith.

Schillebeeckx' contribution *to* theology and his significance *for* theology cannot he fully understood, interpreted and assessed without taking the legacy of French theology into account. His activities in Flanders, his appointment in the Netherlands and his influence during Vatican II are all components in the internationalization of the *nouvelle théologie* and stepping-stones in the direction of its ultimate assimilation during the Council itself.

3.3 *Schoonenberg*

When the Catholic University of Nijmegen decided to supplement its master's programme with a bachelor's programme in 1964, new lecturers were clearly needed to share the burden of teaching. In spite of the 'rule' whereby a member of the Dominican order was generally assigned to the Chair of Dogmatic Theology, a Jesuit was chosen for the bachelor's programme. On the day of his priestly silver jubilee, Piet Schoonenberg was appointed Professor of Dogmatic Theology. He was thus to become a colleague of the younger Edward Schillebeeckx, although the two were not destined to be the best of friends. In spite of his late vocation as a university professor, Schoonenberg already had a considerable amount of experience as a lecturer and had acquired something of a reputation on the basis of his various publications.

Piet Schoonenberg

Petrus Johannes Albertus Maria Schoonenberg was born in Amsterdam on 1 October 1911.[48] After completing his secondary education at the Jesuit college in Amsterdam (1924–30), he joined the society on 7 September 1930. After two years as a novice, a year as a junior in Maastricht and three years as a student of philosophy in Nijmegen, Schoonenberg completed his theological studies in 1940 at the Canisianum, the study house of the Dutch Jesuits in Maastricht. His ordination to the priesthood took place in the meantime on 15 August 1939. The war prevented him from continuing his theological studies in Rome. Instead, he spent the war years teaching at the Faculty of Theology in Maastricht. In 1946–47, he was finally given the opportunity to specialize in exegesis at the Biblicum in Rome, where he took classes with the French exegete Stanislas Lyonnet, among others, who had outspoken sympathies for the *nouvelle théologie* and who had been professor at Fourvière in 1938–43.

On 20 April 1948, Piet Schoonenberg was granted the degree of Doctor in Theology on the defence of a dissertation entitled 'Theologie als geloofsvertolking – Een kritische samenvatting van de leerstellige inhoud der hedendaagse katholieke Franse literatuur over de verhouding der speculatieve theologie tot het geloof' ('Theology as an Articulation of Faith. A Critical Summary of the Doctrinal Content of Contemporary Catholic French Literature on the Relationship between Speculative Theology and Faith'). After graduation, Schoonenberg took an active part for several years in Dutch Jesuit formation and initiated what was to be a lengthy engagement with the Hoger Katechetisch Instituut (Higher Institute for Catechetics) in Nijmegen. In the latter capacity, he worked on *De Nieuwe Katechismus* (The new catechism), the so-called 'Dutch Catechism', which caused considerable commotion among the Roman Curia and far beyond when it appeared in 1966.[49] Schoonenberg's first project – a theology with pastoral intentions – had already been published under the title *Het geloof van ons doopsel* (The faith of our baptism), a dogmatic handbook on the articles of faith of which four parts appeared between 1955 and 1962.[50]

In 1964, Schoonenberg was appointed as Professor of Dogmatic Theology at the Catholic University of Nijmegen. From that point until his retirement in 1976, Schoonenberg contributed to the renewal of Dutch Catholic theology that was attracting international attention, in particular with publications on the Christian doctrine, the theology of sin and Christology. After the publication of a first collection of articles under the title *Gods wordende wereld* (God's world in the making) in 1962,[51] he published a detailed study on the doctrine of original sin in the dogmatic handbook *Mysterium Salutis* in 1968.[52] Early drafts of his Christology appeared in the renowned volume *Hij is een God van mensen: Twee theologische studies* (The Christ – a study of the God-man relationship in the whole of creation and in Jesus Christ), which appeared in 1969.[53] In several later articles, Schoonenberg joined colleagues such as Schillebeeckx and Ansfried Hulsbosch in drafting a new approach to Christology 'from below', taking humanity, the world and history as its points of departure. This new Christology also attracted considerable criticism in the Netherlands and abroad. It is probable, in fact, that this led to the Roman Jesuit authorities refusing him permission to publish his 1984 study *De Geest, het Woord en de Zoon* (The Spirit, the Word and the Son). His proposed Spirit Christology was finally published, nevertheless, in 1991 by a number of Louvain theologians and later translated into German and Spanish.[54] The number of Schoonenberg's works that have been translated is quite remarkable. His international renown was also given expression in the time he spent abroad and the many guest lectures he gave during the latter part of his academic career in Germany, Austria, Belgium and the United States. Contact with the charismatic renewal in the USA inspired him to develop a particular interest in the theology of the Spirit, in addition to his focus on the Trinity and Christology. From the beginning of the 1990s onwards, Schoonenberg gradually withdrew from public life. He died in Nijmegen on 21 September 1999, shortly after his eighty-eighth birthday.

De Geest, het Woord en de Zoon was the last book Schoonenberg was to publish. One might be at liberty to argue, therefore, that his entire academic career started and ended with two works that drew reaction as well as rejection. Both his final book and his first comprehensive work – his doctoral dissertation – encountered publication problems.

Reception of the Nouvelle Théologie

Piet Schoonenberg's doctoral dissertation examines the debate that took place in the French-speaking world between 1935 and 1942 on the specificity and method of Catholic theology. His choice thus focused on what was later to be a turning point in the development of twentieth-century Catholic theology, in which the transition was made from a classical, scholastic type of theology to a contemporary, biblically inspired and existentially motivated expression of the Christian faith. Left unpublished until 2008, the 1948 dissertation[55] thus represented 'an unknown key' to a better understanding of Piet Schoonenberg's own theology.[56] In these early reflections on theology's specificity and method,

Schoonenberg formulated a number of points of departure that were to continue to characterize his later thought and cannot be separated from his sympathy for the *nouvelle théologie*.

Schoonenberg's choice of topic for his dissertation is in line with the thesis on philosophy and theology as existential sciences entitled 'Wijsbegeerte en theologie als zijns-wetenschappen' that he presented for the degree of Master in Theology in 1940 in Maastricht.[57] Both studies demonstrate his interest in the renewal of theology in France, an interest inspired by his promoter and fellow Jesuit Felix Malmberg, a specialist in apologetics who had been able to enthuse his students since the 1930s with the new theological ideas of authors such as Marie-Dominique Chenu.[58]

Schoonenberg's choice of research focus, however, was to put him in a precarious position. Indeed, in the years that he was working on his dissertation, several authors alluded to and quoted in it were to become victims of smear campaigns and sanctions. In September 1946, the year in which Schoonenberg commenced his studies at the Biblicum, Pius XII addressed the Jesuit authorities in person and explicitly criticized the 'nova theologia', as we have seen before. Although the works of the targeted theologians were rarely if ever mentioned in the dissertation, it was clear that the publication of his work would have been far from opportune at the time. His superiors requested him to rework several parts of his text, in particular his own synthesis.

Around 1951 Schoonenberg presented a revised version of his dissertation to his superiors. In spite of the corrections, however, the provincial of the Jesuits in the Netherlands, Constant Kolfschoten, refused permission for its publication. A variety of reasons combined to substantiate this ruling: tensions with colleagues at the Canisianum, internal critique of his 1948 tractate on grace, his sympathy towards theologians associated with the *nouvelle théologie* alluded to in his dissertation . . .[59] There can be little doubt, nevertheless, that the primary reason behind the prohibition was the climate that prevailed after the promulgation of *Humani generis* and which Jean-Baptiste Janssens – a Belgian and the General of the Jesuits – discussed in his circular letter of October 1950.[60]

What is the relationship between faith and theological reason? For Schoonenberg, this was the central question that dominated Catholic theology in the 1930s and 1940s. The question was most pertinent in relation to speculative theology, in which the characteristic modus operandi was reason, deduction and conclusion. In the years in question, this neo-scholastic perspective on theology increasingly came to be considered inadequate as an expression of the fullness of theological reflection on the Christian faith.

The seven chapters of Schoonenberg's dissertation survey the debate surrounding the transition from neo-scholastic theology to a 'source theology'. He begins with a presentation of 'Classical theology' (chapter II), in which the division between faith and theology is real and tangible; discusses a number of endeavours to bridge the division in chapter III; and then goes on to explain how the endeavour to substantiate a historical interpretation (chapter IV), in which the concept of theology of Thomas Aquinas is central, implies a struggle to create a synthesis between faith and reason (chapter V). Schoonenberg then offers his own proposed synthesis based on a renewed and integrative understanding of 'The relationship between faith and theology' (chapter VI), which serves as the foundation of his vision of 'Theology as an articulation of faith' (chapter VII). Let us have a closer look at each of these stepping-stones of Schoonenberg's reconstruction and his own vision.

The relationship between faith and theology in classical reflection had been reduced to a question of succession: faith provides the concepts with which theology then operates according to a purely rational logic. In his initial exploratory reflections of the first chapter of his dissertation, Schoonenberg endeavours to nuance this conceptualistic understanding of theology from a number of different perspectives. From the theological standpoint, the question presented itself of whether faith should be more than a set of conceptual premises and also supply a reality that can enlighten theology. Schoonenberg is primarily interested in the intuitive dimension of knowledge, which had also evolved as part of scholastic philosophy. He believed he had found an epistemological model in the De Petter's 'masterly essay' on implied intuition (1939) that made it possible to conceptualize the relationship between faith and reason in a more refined manner.[61] De Petter holds that faith provides more that conceptual premises; rather it becomes the intuition of the reality of revelation that enlightens theology on an ongoing basis. Schoonenberg illustrates this alternative model for theology as follows: in theological reflection, one does not only attach the red thread of reason to the blue thread of faith, both threads are continually intertwined.

According to Schoonenberg, the classical type of theological reflection is best described by John of Saint Thomas, the most important representative of late scholasticism (seventeenth century). In this second chapter we see 'theology in succession to faith' at work, whereby faith, which provides knowledge of principles, is distinguished from theology, which derives knowledge of the conclusions from the said principles. Only the conceptual content of faith is passed on, which theology used to formulate conclusions by way of deduction. The only further connection that theology has with faith is the certainty it enjoys concerning the supernatural that it receives from faith. Of the twentieth-century representatives of this classical form of speculative theology – criticized as *Konklusionstheologie* ('conclusion theology') – Schoonenberg makes reference to the French Dominican Ambroise Gardeil. Gardeil, the first rector of Le Saulchoir, was a pioneer of theological renewal because of the emphasis he placed on the ongoing priority of the datum revelation in theological reflection.[62] At the same time, however, he continued to be a representative of classical theology because he continued to understand the theological endeavour as a matter of deducing conclusions through the introduction of rational principles. According to Schoonenberg, this position, in which the distinction between faith and theology prevails, still had its adherents, although it was gradually being revised in the direction of a unity of faith and theology.

In the third chapter of his dissertation, Schoonenberg makes reference to his former teacher Malmberg as an example of a theologian who endeavoured to demonstrate the unity of faith and theology. Malmberg insisted that a permanent bond exists between faith and theology that implies reciprocal influence: faith already contains the rudiments of theology and continues to be present in theology. Marie-Dominique Chenu likewise underlines the reciprocal immanence of faith and theology by emphasizing the presence of faith in the activity of the theologian. According to Chenu, theology is faith '*in statu scientiae*' (cf. Part II, Chapter 1 in this volume). Theology is thus located within faith and theological reflection is thereby guided by the light of faith. Schoonenberg goes into greater detail on the vision of the Belgian Jesuit Émile Mersch, 'a great leader and driving force of contemporary theological renewal',[63] which he has demonstrated especially in his posthumously published book *La théologie du Corps mystique* (The theology of the mystical body) (1944).[64] Mersch's introduction of the idea of the *Christus totus* broadens the subject (*subiectum*) of theology. Theology not only deals with God (as He is) but with God as one with us in the total Christ (human and divine). Through Christ's incarnation we have been taken up into the consciousness of God.

This new insight – that faith and reason influence and pervade one another in a balanced understanding of theology – has been explored in greater depth in numerous theological discussions and serves as the main theme of the fourth chapter. Logically speaking, these discussions took place within the framework of a historical re-interpretation of the theology of Thomas Aquinas in an effort to determine whether the alternative vision – different from the neo-scholastic one – agreed with the perspective of Thomas. As always in his dissertation, Schoonenberg's primary intention here is to distinguish the methodological-theological position of these studies rather than their historical correctness. The methodological considerations of René Draguet, for example, focused in the first instance on positive theology, and more specifically on the connection between theology and the development of dogma. In his historical survey of Catholic theology, Draguet envisaged a new theology emerging as the successor to scholastic theology, a theology that was positive in the first instance, a theology in which the reality of revelation would finally be grasped under the guidance of the magisterium (Draguet maintained the concept of *théologie positive du magistère* in this regard as opposed to *positive des sources*). As such, theology becomes an ongoing 'interpretation of revelation'. According to Schoonenberg, this is no longer a speculative theology that operates as a sort of continuation of revealed truth, but a theology that understands itself as an *articulation* of truth: interpretation of revelation. Schoonenberg also encounters this designation of theology as interpretation, as articulation of revelation and faith, in the vision of the French Franciscan Jean-François Bonnefoy. Bonnefoy deals with the method and task of theology in his historical study of Thomas Aquinas in which he characterizes the latter's theological perspective as 'explication de la foi', an expression closely akin to Schoonenberg's own interpretation of theology as articulation of faith. Bonnefoy demonstrates in a number of what Schoonenberg describes as 'revolutionary' arguments that Thomas's concept of theology may in fact be closer to the new theological understanding than the interpretations of late scholasticism. Bonnefoy draws particular attention to the fact that Thomas's *sacra doctrina* is an *intellectus*, grasping truth by way of the *intuitus* and *intelligentia*, which is more than mere deduction of the truth via *ratio*. Schoonenberg points out that this interpretation attracted a great deal of reaction, especially from Marie-Rosaire Gagnebet, Bonnefoy's harshest critic. At the same time, however, Gagnebet, whose theology is rooted in a more Augustinian vision, appears to accept with Bonnefoy that something of the light of faith permeates theological argument.

In the fifth chapter, Schoonenberg concludes his *status quaestionis* on the relationship between faith and theology with a detailed presentation of a single work by a single author, Louis Charlier's *Essai sur le problème théologique*. Up to this point, he argues, the authors discussed have tended to attach more importance to one of the two poles – reason (John of Saint Thomas, Gardeil, Gagnebet) and faith (Chenu, Bonnefoy) – or they point in only general terms in the direction of a possible synthesis (Malmberg, Mersch). Schoonenberg is of the opinion, however, that Charlier's *Essai* represents a detailed endeavour to establish a genuine synthesis between both elements. In his sometimes complicated work, which continually adopts a critical attitude to neo-scholastic ideas, Charlier stresses a number of important aspects in theology's approach. In the relationship between theology and the deposit of faith, for example, he insists that faith leads to the reality of revelation. Faith is not only familiar with the conceptual content of revelation (the 'côté conceptuel'), it is also in permanent contact with the reality of revelation (the 'côté réel'). This real subject is Christ who lives on as the source of faith's insights. This reality, which is more important than practical conclusions, is theology's final goal, in Schoonenberg's presentation of Charlier's vision. Theology thus emerges from faith as faith's reflection on itself, an essentially collective faith given expression in the doctrine of the Church. As far as the reason element in theology is concerned, Charlier insists in what Schoonenberg describes as 'revolutionary Thomas exegesis' that theology for Thomas is the explanation of the articles of faith. This position implies a critical assessment of the use of reason as a premise in determining theological conclusions, which only derive their certainty and applicability from the magisterium. Charlier's reflections on the validity of classical theological argument drew enormous criticism, which Schoonenberg discusses in considerable detail. In presenting the discussion, however, Schoonenberg exhibits a degree of sympathy for Charlier's standpoint and he closes this part of his work with a comparison of the latter's vision with a number of magisterial documents in an effort to distinguish the points in Charlier's essay that ultimately attracted sanction.

When Schoonenberg endeavours to formulate his own synthesis of the relationship between faith and reason in theology from chapter six onwards, he immediately abandons the impersonal, bookish presentational style. From this point on we are given occasional glimpses of Schoonenberg the 'stylist', as we know him from his later writings, with his balanced, stirring yet harmonious prose. In an initial explanation of the epistemological relationship between faith and theology, he harks back to De Petter and the intuitive moment present in our knowledge, the implicit intuition that immediately grasps reality and continues to be present in the concepts that explain this knowledge. In a study of Scripture (the New Testament) and Tradition, Schoonenberg observes that such an intuitive moment is also present in faith as an immediate 'knowing' contact with God in his salvific reality. When further specifying the reality encountered by the intuition of faith he harks back to the idea of the *Christus totus*, although he notes in this regard that this can be replaced by other concepts such as the Kingdom of God. In a second comparison of theology with faith – in this instance with respect to their degree of supernaturality – he draws on Malmberg for inspiration. In theological reflection, there is always unity and difference between natural reason and the implicitly present supernatural faith to which it refers. In the process of theological reflection, there is a moment of transition from the said intuition to the conceptual, a process of individuation in which reason becomes aware of itself as an entity formally bound to faith. Theological reason enriched by faith is continually aware that it must return to the facts of revelation, that it is 'a continuously listening rendition and articulation of revelation'.[65] Schoonenberg ties in at this juncture with the scholastic formulation of the relationship between faith and theology, which he was later to present as his own vision:[66] theology is a natural science that uses reason in the same way as other sciences, but – in contrast to the other sciences – it has a supernatural character. Here, in this unity of natural reason and supernatural faith, theology is aware of its natural rational procedures and its supernatural origins. The latter is more than a mere point of departure, however, since 'the supernaturality of its origins in faith is to be felt in every aspect of its existence; theology is rooted in it as in a rich and fertile breeding ground, and the sap from its roots reaches to the finest leaves and branches'.[67]

Schoonenberg's seventh chapter draws a number of conclusions from his understanding of theology as articulation of faith. He begins with what he considers to be an adequate definition of theology: 'Reason, inspired by faith as intuition and rooted at the same time in its concepts, which engages in the theological endeavour, gives expression to the content of faith, articulates what is believed with all the means it has as its disposal, with the technique of a science.'[68] He then provides a number of short observations on topics such as the scientific character of theology and the contribution of philosophy. His explanation of the relationship between positive and speculative theology, however, deserves particular attention. Schoonenberg argues that the bonds between positive and speculative theology should be reinforced. His own image of two interwoven rather than knotted threads also functions here: speculative theology does not begin where positive theology leaves off, both rather are present as two elements of a single process of reflection. The difference between them is not to be found in their relative distance to the deposit of faith, but in their degree of knowledge. For Schoonenberg, speculative theology must allow positive theology – which, after all, provides its sources – to determine the formation of its concepts, but must also allow itself to be continually reshaped in accordance with advancing positive knowledge. Its unique contribution to the single reflection process consists in the greater degree of reflexivity with which it can clarify the deposit of faith.

In a final series of conclusions, Schoonenberg holds that only our knowledge of the entire deposit of faith that is given in Scripture and Tradition, which we can trace with the help of positive theology, can guarantee the continuity of theological argumentation. Indeed, in theology, it is a historical continuity that binds theological concepts with the sources of Christianity. The concepts that provide a more precise analysis of a topic (e.g. in later magisterial documents) are less capable of grasping the wealth and significance of the mystery present in the original documents. Harking back to original concepts is thus important. The theological clarification of concepts must function as historical development. This implies taking the Scripture as point of departure, in which the mysteries of faith of the New Covenant – e.g. in the witness of the apostles – are contained in all their original unity and richness. The same reality, however, is expressed in its turn using images and concepts found in the Old Testament and this presents us with an additional priority: 'In this sense, the Old Testament is the first source of theological concept formation.'[69]

Schoonenberg thus concludes his presentation of his new theological perspective with this relatively surprising vision, a theological perspective orientated towards balance, in which 'fact and construct, positive research and metaphysical speculation' go hand in hand: 'We want a scholasticism that is able to go deeply into the richness of the Fathers and the Scriptures with all its keenness.'[70] Openness to the mystery, to the supernatural, must characterize every speculative theology. Schoonenberg concludes with an appeal for the continuation of theological renewal. Up to this point, the renewal had led to a revised understanding of philosophy as a primary instrument. Now, according to Schoonenberg, we must 'renew the renewal' by attuning philosophy to the deposit of faith by supporting positive research.[71] Schoonenberg gave an initial impetus to such a renewed theology, in which positive and speculative research are integrated, when he elaborated a biblically founded reflection on the deposit of faith a few years later in the first part of his *Het geloof van ons doopsel*, written in the awareness that Christian theology must address the core of the faith driven by reality: 'For the world of today asks its questions of faith, questions which compel the theologian to unearth the whole treasure of the faith and, particularly, to make visible the deepest roots of the latest growths.'[72]

Continued Evolution of the Nouvelle Théologie

After his 1940 thesis and during his formation year in Rome (1946–47), Schoonenberg was able to familiarize himself further with the *nouvelle théologie* to which he was particularly well disposed. He felt at home in the inductive approach, and abandoned the exclusivity of the deductive method of scholasticism. He had already indicated in his doctoral dissertation that the theological renewal had in fact taken place at the philosophical level – Thomistic *ressourcement* – and that it was important that the said renewal continue with greater emphasis on the Bible and patristics. Schoonenberg thus positioned himself clearly as a 'critical renewer'.

On the eve of the Second Vatican Council, Piet Schoonenberg introduced the first article in his collection *God's World in the Making* with the following words: 'The vision of Teilhard de Chardin has stimulated Catholic thought in a new way. We can foresee that it, together with the biblical renewal, will provide materials for a new theological synthesis.'[73] Familiarization with the thought of Teilhard signified a turning point in Schoonenberg's theology. Up to that point, and in spite of his neo-scholastic formation, he had exhibited clear sympathies for the *nouvelle théologie* without explicitly engaging himself therein.

After reading Teilhard's *Le phénomène humain* (1955) and *Le milieu divin* (1957),[74] Schoonenberg was so taken with Teilhard's evolutionary thought that the *nouvelle théologie* acquired a new face for him which reflected, tested and inspired his own thought. Teilhard was an exceptional representative of the *nouvelle théologie*. More than Henri Bouillard, Henri de Lubac and Jean Daniélou, Teilhard de Chardin placed the human person in the central position in the world, history and faith. In his vision, the human person is in constant development on their way to the omega point, to Christ. In line with Teilhard, Schoonenberg was in search of a synthesis. With this in mind, he found in Teilhard's writings the necessary 'building blocks', although he must certainly have realized that this carried the risk of encroaching on the territory of so-called Modernism, which he had described in his dissertation as a 'crisis of growth' on the one hand and 'a unhealthy exponent of what had been slowly developing in the theology of the day: the use of new historical methods of research and a more critical stance towards concept and deduction'.[75]

Schoonenberg's idea of putting together a series of publications that would discuss the Catholic articles of faith – *Het geloof van ons doopsel* – served as the framework for an initial draft of his thought on Jesus and his relationship to God. He reveals himself to be particularly influenced by the *nouvelle théologie* in this regard, especially by Teilhard. In line with the final two chapters of his dissertation, Schoonenberg concretized his ideas with strong emphasis on the Bible and patristics. Jesus is present in the first instance as a human being, whereby Schoonenberg explicitly and resolutely relegates the dogma of Chalcedon (451) to the background. In the third book of the series (1958), and inspired by Karl Rahner, he makes reference to the historical 'defensive context' of that dogma. He also alludes to the meaning of a dogma as such in the eyes of the magisterium[76] and is even inclined to openly question the dogma of Chalcedon:[77]

> It is questionable, however, when one denies the human act of existence or act of being in the humanity of Christ because he is not a human person. Setting aside the philosophical questions that thus present themselves, we are inclined to wonder nevertheless whether the dogma of Chalcedon on Christ's true humanity continues to be upheld by this theory in all its consequences. Neither Chalcedon nor any other statement of the Church's magisterium has spoken out directly concerning this theological opinion. It seems appropriate, therefore, that we should at least call into question the orthodoxy of theologians who would deny Christ's created act of existence. The question remains, however, whether this theological opinion represents a genuine and unabridged articulation of the faith of Chalcedon. While it is possible to equate nature without act of existence with the nature of humankind that Chalcedon ascribed to Christ, the question remains whether the latter was not intended to be a great deal more concrete, and thus to include the act of human existence. Moreover, can the absence of the act of existence be squared with the fact that God's Son is our likeness in all things but sin? Does this not lead inevitably to the denial of the reality of Christ's humanity, to a certain docetism? Furthermore, is it not a contradiction in itself, and a parody of the doctrine of the real distinction between nature and act of existence, because it loses sight of the real unity of both?

In the same year, 1958, Teilhard's *Le milieu divin* appeared in a Dutch translation. In line with Teilhard, and expanding on his own 1957 contribution on theology as articulation of faith,[78] Schoonenberg now turned – Bible in hand – not only to the extremely broad interpretation of 'evolution', but in particular to the human element thereof, which he refers to as 'history'. Jesus is located in history as 'our fellow human being', whereby God becomes our Father and the Spirit is granted us.[79] The same Jesus represents God's encounter with humanity at its most eminent, precisely because Jesus is present *in* history *as* human. That is why the fullness of God has been made manifest to us in Christ, at the same time bringing to an end the period of revelation. But not the end of history, a history that is *also present in that fullness*! The latter demonstrates both the humanity of God's son and the path we must follow – Schoonenberg offers us a glimpse here of his pastoral disposition – to continue to write history – salvation history – *with* and *like* him. In Schoonenberg's own words:[80]

> This eternal Son of God is also truly and fully man. Consequently, He will make history with us and we with Him. That is why, as man, He not only grew in age but also 'in wisdom and grace before God and men' (Lk 2,52). It was principally for that reason that He desired to enter into our history and existence, and in order that we could be taken up into His own life, He in us

and we in Him. Since the coming of Christ, there is still a further development of what is human, a development of which we are today discovering
unsuspected dimensions. This constructive development is significant for salvation, and this applies even to today's industrial revolution. Besides, there is
a progress in the history of salvation that is woven into human history.

In this vision, suffering is granted a significant role. As a matter of fact,
Schoonenberg associates the suffering and death of Jesus with titles such as 'the
eternal Son of God' and 'Christ' together with concepts such as 'human' and
'history', and does so without batting an eyelid. It seems clear to Schoonenberg
that the suffering and death of Jesus – indeed, his entire humanity! – were
oriented towards being the image of God's being on the one hand, and being
an example for human beings of the highest form of human being known to
history on the other.

The reflection on history to which Schoonenberg adheres is thus explicitly
introduced into his Christological reflection. Jesus is a human being in human
history, although he is *the* human being, as it were, the only divine human
being. In this period, Schoonenberg is still able to square his vision with that
of Chalcedon:[81]

> God the Son thus works in the highest manner when He admits humanity
> into his Person. The transformation this brings about in Christ's humanity
> is now a higher identification of humanity with itself, the elevation is a
> deepening in its own essence, the divinisation is a humanisation. Christ's
> humanity remains human, not in spite of its admission to the Divine Person,
> but by virtue of this admission. Indeed, it becomes more human through
> the said admission. We do not need to uphold the dogma of Chalcedon in
> spite of Ephesus, but in the mysterious relationship between God and his
> creatures we find a link between both dogmas, and it is for this reason that
> our theology also endeavours to express 'the mutual relationship between
> mysteries' (Dz 1796).

In his *De Geest, het Woord en de Zoon*, which places his Logos Christology
side by side with a Spirit Christology, Schoonenberg was to distance himself
definitively from the exclusivity of Chalcedon. In all of the phases that lead
up to this moment – which are not discussed here – the *nouvelle théologie* is
consistently present in the background.

Nouvelle Théologie?

In the introduction to his doctoral dissertation, Piet Schoonenberg wrote that he
planned to ignore the historical perspective. It is all the more striking, therefore,
that the remainder of his work is constantly confronted with the temptation to
integrate the historical perspective in spite of his initial intentions. The two final
chapters of his dissertation ultimately demonstrate that Schoonenberg implicitly

accepted that the historical perspective could not be excluded. In the last analysis, the evolution from neo-scholastic theology to source theology turns around the revaluation of the historical sources of the faith: the Old Testament, the New Testament, the Apostolic Fathers, and the Church Fathers. In short, the return to Scripture and Tradition was the key required to reconnect theology and faith and to understand the latter as a reality instead of an array of concepts.

While Schoonenberg's dissertation tends to build more on the first phase of the *nouvelle théologie* (Charlier is given a central place), its author is also clearly in line with his French confreres of the second phases: Daniélou, Bouillard and de Lubac. Indeed, it seems that the history of the second phase had impeded the publication of his dissertation in the first place. *Humani generis* and J.-B. Janssens' circular letter inclined the Dutch Jesuits to forbid the publication of works that would be likely to offend Rome, including Schoonenberg's planned book.

Schoonenberg did not give up, however. Under the auspices of the Higher Institute for Catechetics, he set about establishing a book series *Het geloof van ons doopsel*. When asked about the need for such a new dogmatic handbook in a period of secularization he consistently responded that it was important 'to know the faith one intended to abandon'.[82] The series was never completed, although the four books that were ultimately published can be typified on the basis of their return to the Bible and patristics. The same can also be said for his *God's World in the Making* (1962), a collection of five essays in which the connection between faith and history takes centre stage. Inspired by his fellow Jesuit Pierre Teilhard de Chardin, a singular representative of the *nouvelle théologie*, the collection focuses on the notion of evolution.

It is particularly in the domain of Christology that Schoonenberg has made a name for himself. His thought is described as a *nouvelle christologie* ('a new Christology'), and he is respected together with Schillebeeckx as the pacesetter of this uniquely 'Dutch theological tradition'[83] in which the dogma of Chalcedon was subject to criticism. The fact that both he and Schillebeeckx were questioned by Vatican representatives in the 1970s cannot be understood without reference to the inheritance of the *nouvelle théologie* and its further evolution.

3.4 *Concluding Observations*

As was the case with Edward Schillebeeckx, Piet Schoonenberg became fully acquainted with the *nouvelle théologie* outside the Netherlands: Schillebeeckx in Paris under his favourite teacher Chenu, and Schoonenberg in Rome under the French professor Stanislas Lyonnet. As a result, both the Dominicans and the Jesuits found themselves with a leading figure of the *nouvelle théologie* in the Low Countries. Both men were not only successful in promoting this theological renewal movement in the Low Countries, they also took it a step further in their own writings. As such they became ambassadors of the *nouvelle théologie*.

The critique with which both Schillebeeckx and Schoonenberg were confronted made it clear that they not only represented the reception and continuation of the *nouvelle théologie* in the Low Countries, they also inspired a continuation of the critical stance maintained by some towards the movement itself. The Dominican Andreas H. Maltha deserves particular mention in this regard, although there were others Dominicans and Jesuits too who were inclined to reject the theological direction being taken by the thought of both Schillebeeckx and Schoonenberg.

PART III

Closing Considerations

Closing Considerations

What is the *nouvelle théologie*? This was the question with which the present volume opened and we conclude it with the same question. The *nouvelle théologie* emerged for the first time in France and Belgium, moved into its second phase in Lyon, into its third outside the French-speaking world, and into its fourth when its central features were assimilated into Catholic theology. A precise description of the theological renewal movement continues, nevertheless, to elude us. The absence of a conclusive definition might be seen to place any theology historian writing on the *nouvelle théologie* in a position of weakness because it exposes him or her to critique with regard to everything that he or she writes (or does not write) and everyone he or she includes (or does not include) under the said heading (conclusive criteria for inclusion or exclusion are also lacking). Nevertheless, the absence of a conclusive definition can be understood as one of the core characteristics of the *nouvelle théologie* if one (1) does not reduce the latter to its description by the magisterium, and if one (2) takes the denial of the existence of the *nouvelle théologie* by numerous representatives thereof seriously while envisaging the movement's approach in broader terms than those claimed by the said representatives, and if one (3) remains faithful to the historical reality that a movement once existed that, in spite of the fact that it came to be designated collectively as the *nouvelle théologie*, was made up of a variety of components and exhibited divergent points of emphasis, depending on the representatives one studies.

The expression *nouvelle théologie* is a cluster concept: a banner representing a variety of visions, as became evident in our study of the various theologians associated with it. At the same time, however, the core ambition of each of the thinkers discussed in these pages is ultimately the same: to restore contact between theology and the living faith and thus also with the sources of the faith. To this end, the *new theologians* rejected every theological system that revolved around the system itself rather than around the faith: a system that caused the sources to clot and congeal, that reduced theologians from days long past to an authority while ignoring the actual content of their works in the name of the system. From the 1930s onwards, neo-scholasticism came to be criticized more and more openly as a closed system. The *new theologians* revealed themselves to be representatives of a movement determined to depose such neo-scholasticism in the name of a return to the sources of faith and tradition. Their ambition was to return to the Thomas Aquinas of the thirteenth century, to the patristic period, and via the Church Fathers to the Bible and the liturgy.

The *nouvelle théologie* did not end with its representatives of the 1930s and 1940s. Based for the most part on the latter's writings, more and more theologians began to echo their aspirations. In this sense, the *nouvelle théologie* can be understood as a movement within a broader *ressourcement* movement. This has at least three implications. In the first instance, the *nouvelle théologie* cannot be strictly confined as a 'theological school': a vague zone remains. Secondly, the representatives of the *nouvelle théologie* are more than *new theologians* alone: our biographical-bibliographical portraits of Chenu, Congar, Bouillard, de Lubac and others make this abundantly clear. As a matter of fact, the theologians in question tended to be unhappy with the idea of being reduced to the label *new theologian*. In our opinion, the expression can only be applied to the period in their lives and the specific contributions that connect them with the *nouvelle théologie*, whereby each of them introduced his own accents. Thirdly, the previous two remarks stress the question posed at the end of each vision discussed: '*Nouvelle théologie?*' Indeed, historians are ultimately obliged to respect the question mark and leave it in place. This need not suggest that the present volume is redundant. On the contrary, there is more than enough historical evidence available to defend the idea that the *nouvelle théologie* existed, but the same abundance of evidence also makes a conclusive definition of the movement impossible.

The expression *nouvelle théologie* is a paradox as such, given the fact that there is little apparent 'newness' in a return to the 'old' sources of the faith. The roots of the expression have a role to play in this regard, however, since the term 'new' within the Roman Catholic Church has often been taken as a reproach (with the exception of the 'New Testament', the 'new Adam', etc.). A lengthy series of *novi heretici* – 'new heretics' – can be pointed to in the course of the Church's history, and it should be clear from the present volume that the Church authorities considered the *new theologians* to be among their ranks. They represented a tendency that the Church authorities understood to be a renewed version of Modernism, which was described in 1907 as the 'synthesis of all heresies'. Associations sought – as with Modernism – between the so-called *nouvelle théologie* and Protestant academic theological research only served to reinforce suspicions. According to the prominent neo-scholastic Réginald Garrigou-Lagrange, it was imperative that the Church fight the *nouvelle théologie* with anti-modernist weapons. Condemnations and the *Humani generis* encyclical were thus the weapons of choice. Pope Pius XII, however, did not opt to present a new *Syllabus errorum*, something some people had wished and others expected with fear.

In researching the history of theology of the period from c. 1935 to 1965, it is important that the researcher does not succumb to the temptation to construct his or her own system and endeavour to provide a definitive answer to the question surrounding the content of the *nouvelle théologie*. None of the theologians discussed in the present volume has been absorbed by the *nouvelle théologie*, as it were. Each of the said theologians is clearly more than a *new theologian*, and the *nouvelle théologie* we have endeavoured to picture is clearly more than the picture we have been able to sketch. No matter how much we once hoped to provide an exhaustive account of the *nouvelle théologie*, the present limited accessibility of some archives and the state of international research on the topic ultimately stands in the way, and the question remains whether such exhaustiveness will ever be possible.

The expression *nouvelle théologie* is open to discussion. It is a 'loaded' expression. In like fashion to the term Modernism, *nouvelle théologie* became a label applied to an image that the movement's adversaries had established of it. Due to the succession of expressions of rejection by the Church authorities – including the Pope – the *nouvelle théologie* acquired such a negative connotation that it comes as no surprise when we read that many of the thinkers discussed in these pages did not want to be associated with it. Since the Second Vatican Council – especially *Dei Verbum* – the *nouvelle théologie* was set free of this negative connotation and likewise from the 'system' its adversaries had made of it (the parallel with Modernism is also striking in this regard; cf. the abolition of the 'anti-modernist oath' in 1966). As a result, an equally paradoxical situation has arisen whereby the expression *nouvelle théologie* continued to be used after the Council, while the content of the concept remained variable on account of the number of different visions and perspectives it represented.

Our decision to use the Roman rejection of the *nouvelle théologie* and the beginning of the Second Vatican Council as the keys to subdividing the movement into phases was a completely conscious one. In the last analysis, the consignment of the works of Chenu and Charlier to the Index, the sanctions against some French Jesuits and the promulgation of the *Humani generis* encyclical, and the beginning of the Council had an enormous influence on the evolution of the *nouvelle théologie*, as the phases described in the present volume confirm. Are we guilty of latent schematism in this regard? The answer to this question must be no, although the subdivision into phases is indeed relative. While our subdivision is historically accurate, it should not be understood in this strict sense for equally historical reasons. The goal of the subdivision is to help create a degree of clarity with respect to the development of the *nouvelle théologie*. Indeed, it is impossible to ignore the fact that the Thomistic *ressourcement* was followed by a theological *ressourcement*, and that the French-speaking implantation of the *nouvelle théologie* was followed by a period of internationalization that contributed to a broader support base for the assimilation of the central points of the *nouvelle théologie* during Vatican II.

In this sense, the *nouvelle théologie* can be described as a catalyst of an intellectual movement; it contributed to the return to a source theology that was clearly propagated in the conciliar document *Dei Verbum*. In order to arrive at such a source theology, the *new theologians* turned their attention to the Church Fathers, eminent protagonists of the tradition who were soundly attached to the Scripture as the source of faith, pastoral practice and theology. By highlighting patristic research, the Church Fathers were placed side by side with scholasticism and ultimately above it. The deficit facing Catholic theology at the time had its roots in the derailment of neo-scholasticism: a discourse technique within the framework of a theological system.

'System theology' became subject to critique by a renewed emphasis on the sources of faith and theology. The said emphasis on the part of the *new theologians* was in line with a more general tendency within Christian spirituality, within which an ever increasing interest in the mystery, Christ, the gospel and the interior life of the Church can be discerned from the 1920s onwards. This tendency was thus carried through at the academic theological level with the focus on the Scriptures and the Church Fathers, a focus that was ultimately to lead to the dismantlement of neo-scholastic theology and the replacement of 'system theology' with a 'source theology'. According to Jean Daniélou and Bernard Sesboüé, it is the return to the sources that marks the 'originality' of Catholic theology in the twentieth century;[1] Hans Boersma calls this rightly the 'return to mystery', to the deepest essence of faith and theology.[2]

Without pretending to be exhaustive, our book has endeavoured to expose this originality from the perspective of the specificity, representatives, contribution and significance of the so-called *nouvelle théologie*.

It is clear that a generation of theologians can be designated as the inheritors of Modernism and the forerunners of the Second Vatican Council. The ambition of the *new theologians* to restore contact between Catholic theology and the reality of the faith and concrete everyday life confronted them with the need to rethink theology and ultimately to re-source it. This return to the origins of Catholic theology focused its critique in the first instance on the neo-scholastic handbook tradition, its reduction of the faith to concepts, and theology to rhetoric. The *ressourcement*'s only possible point of departure was the prevailing Thomism, *in casu* Roman neo-scholasticism, more specifically by returning to its historical roots and to Thomas's own thought. While his *Summa* occasioned a systematization of theology, a growing number of philosophers and theologians had come to realize that theology could not be reduced to a system, in spite of the best efforts of numerous sixteenth- and seventeenth-century thinkers. 'Reality thinking' took the place of 'system thinking' and scholars addressed themselves anew to 'the real Thomas' who had wanted to provide an answer to 'real' problems and issues with his theological reflections.[3] This emphasis on reality went hand in hand with an emphasis on history, which studied the reality of the past and the perception of reality in the past. In theological terms, this implied a return in the first instance to the historical Thomas and his thought. In a second wave, scholars dug deeper and deeper into the past in a return to the historical sources of the faith and thus to the reality that was seen to be theology's research object. In concrete terms, the second wave re-emphasized the bond the Church Fathers had made between Bible, faith and theology, a bond that been self-evident for Thomas Aquinas. In addition to this, however, attention was drawn to the non-notional aspect of the faith: revelation as reality, the faith's conceptual articulation side by side with its devotion and emotional dimension (experience, sentiment . . .), and so on. This latter, non-exclusively intellectual dimension of the faith found an ally in the re-assessment of Augustine, notably in the aftermath of the celebration of the 1,500th anniversary of his death in 1930). Known for his *theologia affectiva*, Augustine was employed as a sort of crowbar, as it were, to help break through the monopoly of neo-scholasticism. It is not by accident thinkers inspired by Augustine came to enjoy success, and it is likewise not by accident that all the *new theologians* mentioned in the present volume were interested in Augustine, the *doctor gratiae*.

NOTES

Notes to Part I, Chapter 1: Nouvelle Théologie: *Concept and Content*

1 Jan Sperna Weiland, *Oriëntatie: Nieuwe wegen in de theologie* (Theologische Monografieën), Baarn: Het Wereldvenster, 1966. Published in French as *La nouvelle théologie: Tillich, Bultmann, Bonhoeffer, Fuchs, Ebeling, Robinson, Van Buren, Michalson, Winter, Cox, Hamilton, Altizer, Sölle*, Bruges: Desclée De Brouwer, 1969.

2 Étienne Gilson, *Le thomisme: Introduction à la philosophie de Saint Thomas d'Aquin* (Études de philosophie médiévale, 1), Strasbourg: Vix, 1919; ⁶Paris: Vrin, 1964; 7th repr. of the 6th edn, 1997, pp. 153–89.

3 George Tyrrell, *Through Scylla and Charybdis or the Old Theology and the New*, London: Longmans, 1907.

4 John R. Campbell, *The New Theology*, London: Chapman & Hall, 1907, pp. v–vi.

5 Cf., for example, Hans Küng, *Theologie im Aufbruch: Eine Ökumenische Grundlegung*, Munich/Zurich: Piper, 1987. See also the schema in Hans Küng, *Das Christentum: Wesen und Geschichte*, Munich/Zurich: Piper, 1994, inside front cover; Lieven Boeve, *God onderbreekt de geschiedenis: Theologie in tijden van ommekeer* (Mens en Tijd), Kapellen: Pelckmans, 2006.

6 Pietro Parente, 'Nuove tendenze teologiche', in *L'Osservatore Romano*, 9–10 February 1942, p. 1.

7 Parente, 'Nuove tendenze teologiche', p. 1.

8 Mariano Cordovani, 'Per la vitalità della teologia cattolica', in *L'Osservatore Romano*, 22 March 1940, p. 3 (= *Angelicum* 17 [1940] 133–46).

9 'Il venerato Discorso del Sommo Pontifice alla XXIX Congregazione Generale della Compagnia di Gesù', in *L'Osservatore Romano*, 19 September 1946, p. 1 (= *Acta Apostolicae Sedis* 38 [1946] 381–85, esp. p. 385).

10 'Fervido Discorso del Sommo Pontifice ai Capitolari dell'Ordine dei Frati Predicatori', in *L'Osservatore Romano*, 23–24 September 1946, p. 1 (= *Acta Apostolicae Sedis* 38 [1946] 385–89).

11 Réginald Garrigou-Lagrange, 'La nouvelle théologie où va-t-elle?', in *Angelicum* 23 (1946) 126–45.

12 Garrigou-Lagrange, 'La nouvelle théologie où va-t-elle?', p. 143.

13 *Pascendi dominici gregis*, encyclical of Pope Pius X, 7 September 1907, in *Acta Sanctae Sedis* 40 (1907) 593–650, p. 632.

14 *Humani generis*, encyclical of Pope Pius XII, 12 August 1950, in *Acta Apostolicae Sedis* 42 (1950) 561–78.

15 *Humani generis*, p. 578.

16 'Une récente et importante controverse théologique: À propos des Collections

"Sources chrétiennes" et "Théologie'", in Secrétariat de l'Épiscopat, Note 17/47, 26 March 1947, pp. 1–6; 'La controverse théologique relative aux Collections "Sources chrétiennes" et "Théologie'", in Secrétariat de l'Épiscopat, Note 32/47, 4 July 1947, pp. 1–8; ibid., in Secrétariat de l'Épiscopat, Note 33/47, 17 July 1947, pp. 1–6.

17 Hugo Rahner, 'Wege zu einer "neuen" Theologie?', in *Orientierung* 11 (1947) 213–17.

18 'La nouvelle théologie', in *Katholiek Archief* 2 (1947–48) 941–44.

19 Philip J. Donnelly, 'Theological Opinion on the Development of Dogma', in *Theological Studies* 8 (1947) 668–99, p. 681. This is the second part of the overview. The first part: 'On the Development of Dogma and the Supernatural', in *Theological Studies* 8 (1947) 471–91.

20 James M. Connolly, *The Voices of France: A Survey of Contemporary Theology in France*, New York: MacMillan, 1961, esp. pp. 176–90; John Auricchio, *The Future of Theology*, Staten Island, NY: St. Paul, 1970, esp. pp. 257–316.

21 Aloïs van Rijen, 'Een nieuwe stroming in de Theologie', in *Nederlandse Katholieke Stemmen* 44 (1948) 177–88. See also his article '"Nieuwe" en "katholiek-oecumenische" theologie', in *Studia Catholica* 24 (1949) 209–37.

22 Avelino Esteban Romero, 'Nota bibliográfica sobre la llamada "Teología Nueva'", in *Revista Española de teologia* 9 (1949) 303–18 [187 titles], 527–46 [166 titles].

23 Adolf Darlapp, 'Nouvelle théologie', in *Lexikon für Theologie und Kirche* 7 (1962) 1060–61.

24 Albert Raffelt, 'Nouvelle théologie', in *Lexikon für und Kirche* 7 (1998, ³2006) 935–37.

25 For example, Raffelt, 'Nouvelle théologie'; Henri Rondet, 'Nouvelle théologie', in *Sacramentum Mundi* 3 (1969) 816–20; Raymond Winling, 'Nouvelle Théologie', in *Theologische Realenzyklopädie* 24 (1994) 668–75; Hendricus Schillebeeckx, 'Nouvelle théologie', *in Theologisch Woordenboek* 3 (1958) 3519–20; Donald K. McKim, *Westminster Dictionary of Theological Terms*, Louisville, KY: Westminster John Knox, 1996, p. 190.

26 Étienne Fouilloux, '"Nouvelle théologie" et théologie nouvelle (1930–1960)', in B. Pellistrandi (ed.), *L'histoire religieuse en France et Espagne* (Collection de la Casa Velázquez, 87), Madrid: Casa de Velázquez, 2004, pp. 411–25 (417).

27 Cf. Étienne Fouilloux, '"Nouvelle théologie" et théologie nouvelle (1930–1960)'.

28 Some researchers, for example Hans Boersma (*'Nouvelle Théologie' and Sacramental Ontology: A Return to Mystery*, Oxford: Oxford University Press, 2009), use the term '*nouvelle* theologian'. While the latter expression clearly refers to the proper name *nouvelle théologie*, the expressions '*nouvelle* theologian' and '*nouvelle* theologians' do not coincide with the French original terms '*nouveau théologien*' and '*nouveaux théologiens*'. With respect to the French original, we prefer to use the terms '*new theologian*' and '*new theologians*', always making use of italics.

29 Yves Congar, *Situation et tâches présentes de la théologie* (Cogitatio fidei, 27), Paris: Cerf, 1967, p. 14.

30 Cf. the letter of Congar to Emmanuel Suárez, 16 January 1950, in the Archives de la province dominicaine de France, 'Corr Congar, Janvier 1950'; *Jean Puyo interroge*

le Père Congar: 'Une vie pour la vérité' (Les interviews), Paris: Centurion, 1975, p. 99.

31 Henri de Lubac, *Entretiens autour de Vatican II: Souvenirs et Réflexions* (Théologies), Paris: France Catholique/Cerf, 1985, ²2007, p. 12.

32 Cf. Henri de Lubac, *Mémoire sur l'occasion de mes écrits* (Oeuvres complètes, 33), Paris: Cerf, 2006, p. 270.

33 Henri Bouillard, *Vérité du christianisme* (Théologie), Paris: Desclée De Brouwer, 1989, pp. 401, 406.

34 Cf. John Allen, *Cardinal Ratzinger: The Vatican's Enforcer of the Faith*, London/ New York: Continuum, 2000, re-edited as *Pope Benedict XVI: A Biography of Joseph Ratzinger*, London/New York: Continuum, 2005, pp. 89–118.

35 Cf. Christoph Frey, *Mysterium der Kirche, Öffnung zur Welt: Zwei Aspekte der Erneuerung französischer katholischer Theologie* (Kirche und Konfession, 14), Göttingen: Vandenhoeck & Ruprecht, 1969; Tarcisus Tshibangu, *La théologie comme science au XXème siècle*, Kinshasa: Presses universitaires, 1980, pp. 79–110; Raymond Winling, *La théologie contemporaine (1945–1980)*, Paris: Centurion, 1985; Jean-Claude Petit, 'La compréhension de la théologie dans la théologie française au XXe siècle: La hantise du savoir et de l'objectivité: l'exemple d'Ambroise Gardeil', in *Laval théologique et philosophique* 45 (1989) 379–91; 'La compréhension de la théologie dans la théologie française au XXe siècle: Vers une nouvelle conscience historique: G. Rabeau, M.-D. Chenu, L. Charlier', in *Laval théologique et philosophique* 47 (1991) 215–29; 'La compréhension de la théologie dans la théologie française au XXe siècle: Pour une théologie qui réponde à nos nécessités: la nouvelle théologie', in *Laval théologique et philosophique* 48 (1992) 415–31; Rosino Gibellini, *Panorama de la théologie au XXe siècle* (Théologies), Paris: Cerf, 1994, pp. 186–96; Evangelista Vilanova, *Histoire des théologies chrétiennes* (Initiations), Vol. 3: *XVIIIe-XXe siècle*, Paris: Cerf, 1997, pp. 901–27; Étienne Fouilloux, *Une Église en quête de liberté. La pensée catholique française entre modernisme et Vatican II (1914–1962)* (Anthropologiques), Paris: Declée de Brouwer, 1998; Mark Schoof, *A Survey of Catholic Theology, 1800–1970*, Eugene: Wipf and Stock, 2008, pp. 188–210 (repr. of *Beginnings of the New Catholic Theology* [Logos Books], Dublin: Gill and MacMillan, 1970).

36 Cf. A.N. Williams, 'The Future of the Past: The Contemporary Significance of the Nouvelle Théologie', in *International Journal of Systematic Theology* 7 (2005) 347–61 (348).

37 The concept 'Denzinger theology' is also used by Franco Giulio Brambilla in his interesting article entitled '"Theologia del Magistero" e fermenti di rinnovamento nella teologia cattolica', in G. Angelini and S. Macchi (eds), *La teologia del Novecento: Momenti maggiori e questioni aperte* (Lectio, 7), Milan: Glossa, 2008, pp. 189–236 (190).

38 Cf., for example, Piet Schoonenberg, 'Roeping, vrijheid en onvrijheid van de theoloog', in *Bijdragen* 43 (1982) 2–29.

39 Johannes Beumer, 'Konklusionstheologie?', in *Zeitschrift für katholische Theologie* 63 (1939) 260–365.

150   *Notes to Pages 15–19*

Notes to Part I, Chapter 2: Theological Background and Context

1   On Johann Sebastian Drey, see Michael Kessler and Ottmar Fuchs (eds), *Theologie als Instanz der Moderne: Beiträge und Studien zu Johann Sebastian Drey und zur Katholischen Tübinger Schule* (Tübinger Studien zur Theologie und Philosophie, 22), Tübingen: Francke, 2005.

2   On Johann Adam Möhler, see Michel Deneken, *Johann Adam Möhler* (Initiations aux théologiens), Paris: Cerf, 2007.

3   Cf. Johann Sebastian Drey, *Die Apologetik als wissenschaftliche Nachweisung der Göttlichkeit des Christentums in seiner Erscheinung*, 3 vols, Mainz: Kupferberg, 1838–47, repr.: Frankfurt am Main: Minerva, 1967.

4   Johann Adam Möhler, *Die Einheit in der Kirche, oder das Prinzip des Katholizismus: Dargestellt im Geiste der Kirchenväter der drei ersten Jahrhunderte*, Tübingen: Laupp, 1825.

5   See, for example, John Henry Newman, *The Church of the Fathers* (The Works of Cardinal John Henry Newman, Birmingham Oratory Millennium Edition, 5), Notre Dame: Gracewing/University of Notre Dame, 2002. On Newman, see Ian Ker and Terrence Merrigan, *The Cambridge Companion to John Henry Newman*, Cambridge: Cambridge University Press, 2009.

6   John Henry Newman, *An Essay on the Development of Christian Doctrine*, London: Toovey, 1845; ⁶(Notre Dame Series in the Great Books), Notre Dame, IN: University of Notre Dame, 1989.

7   John Henry Newman, *An Essay in Aid of a Grammar of Assent*, London: Burns and Oates, 1870; Notre Dame, IN: University of Notre Dame, 2001.

8   Cf. Roger Aubert, *Le pontificat de Pie IX (1846–1878)* (Histoire de l'Église depuis les origines à nos jours, 21), Paris: Bloud & Gay, 1952. The encyclical: *Mirari Vos*, encyclical of Pope Gregory XVI, 15 August 1832, in *Acta Sanctae Sedis* 4 (1868) 336–45.

9   *Quanta Cura*, encyclical of Pope Pius IX, 8 December 1864, in *Acta Sanctae Sedis* 3 (1867) 160–67. The appendix: *Syllabus complectens praecipuos nostrae aetatis errores qui notantur in encyclicis aliisque apostolicis litteris Sanctissimi Domini nostri Pii Papae IX*, in *Acta Sanctae Sedis* 3 (1867) 168–76.

10   Cf. Roger Aubert, 'L'intervention de Montalembert au Congrès de Malines en 1863', in *Collectanea Mechliniensia* 35 (1950) 525–51.

11   Cf. Wolfgang Klausnitzer, 'Döllingers Theologierede vom 28. September 1863 in ihrem theologiegeschichtlichen Kontext', in G. Denzler and E.L. Grasmück (eds), *Geschichtlichkeit und Glaube: Zum 100. Todestag Johann Joseph Ignaz von Döllingers (1799–1890)*, Munchen: Wewel, 1990, pp. 417–45.

12   Cf. Ulrich G. Leinsle, *Einführung in die scholastische Theologie* (UTB für Wissenschaft – Uni-Taschenbücher, 1865), Paderborn/Munich/Vienna/Zürich: Schöning, 1995, p. 341; Roger Aubert, 'Die Enzyklika 'Aeterni Patris' und die weiteren päpstlichen Stellungnahmen zur christlichen Philosophie', in E. Coreth, W. Neidl and R. Pfligersdorffer (eds), *Christliche Philosophie im katholischen Denken des 19. und 20. Jahrhunderts*, Vol. 2, Graz/Vienna/Cologne: Styria, 1988, pp. 310–32.

13   Cf. Thomas F. O'Meara, *Thomas Aquinas Theologian*, Notre Dame, IN/London: University of Notre Dame, 1997, esp. p. 167.

14   Matteo Liberatore, *Institutiones logicae et metaphysicae*, Mediolani: Rossi, 1846; Joseph Kleutgen, *Die Theologie der Vorzeit*, 3 vols, Münster: Theissing,

1853–60; idem, *Die Philosophie der Vorzeit*, 2 vols, Münster: Theissing, 1860–63, ²1878.

15 Cf. Abelardo Lobato, 'León XIII y el Neotomismo', in Á.G. García and J.B. Barquilla (eds), *León XIII y su tiempo* (Bibliotheca Salmanticensis: Estudios, 264), Salamanca: Universidad Pontificia, 2004, pp. 397–417; Serge-Thomas Bonino, 'Le fondement doctrinal du projet léonin: "Aeterni Patris" et la restauration du thomisme', in P. Levillain and J.-M. Ticchi (eds), *Le pontificat de Léon XIII: Renaissances du Saint-Siège?* (Collection de l'École française de Rome, 368), Rome: École Française de Rome, 2006, pp. 267–74.

16 *Aeterni Patris*, encyclical of Pope Leo XIII, 4 August 1879, in *Acta Sanctae Sedis* 12 (1879) 97–115.

17 *Pastor Aeternus*, dogmatic constitution of Vatican I, 18 July 1870, in *Acta Sanctae Sedis* 6 (1870–71) 40–47.

18 *Dei Filius*, dogmatic constitution of Vatican I, 24 April 1870, in *Acta Sanctae Sedis* 5 (1869) 460–68. On Vatican I, see Klaus Schatz, *Vaticanum I* (Konziliengeschichte. A: Darstellungen), 3 vols, Paderborn: Schöningh, 1992–94; Aubert, *Le pontificat de Pie IX (1846–1878)*, pp. 311–67.

19 *Dei Filius*, p. 467.

20 Lucien Laberthonnière, 'Dogme et théologie', in *Annales de philosophie chrétienne* 69 (1908) 479–521 (511): 'Avec les protestants libéraux c'était la foi sans croyance: maintenant c'est la croyance sans foi.'

21 *Pascendi dominici gregis*, encyclical of Pope Pius X, 7 September 1907, in *Acta Sanctae Sedis* 40 (1907) 593–650, p. 632.

22 *Lamentabili sane exitu*, decree of Pope Pius X, 7 July 1907, in *Acta Sanctae Sedis* 40 (1907) 470–78; *Praestantia Scripturae*, motu proprio of Pope Pius X, 18 November 1907, in *Acta Sanctae Sedis* 40 (1907) 723–26. Reference is made to *Providentissimus Deus*, encyclical of Pope Leo XIII, 18 November 1893, in *Acta Sanctae Sedis* 26 (1893–94) 269–92.

23 *Sacrorum antistitum*, motu proprio of Pope Pius X, 1 September 1910, in *Acta Apostolicae Sedis* 2 (1910) 669–72.

24 Pierre Colin, *L'audace et le soupçon: La crise du modernisme dans le catholicisme français 1893–1914* (Anthropologiques), Paris: Desclée De Brouwer, 1997, p. 241.

25 Thomas Michael Loome, *Liberal Catholicism – Reform Catholicism – Modernism: A Contribution to a New Orientation in Modernist Research* (Tübinger Theologische Studien, 14), Mainz: Matthias-Grünewald, 1979, p. 196.

26 Cf. Charles J.T. Talar, 'The French Connection: The Church's "Eldest Daughter" and the Condemnation of Modernism', in *US Catholic Historian* 25 (2007) 55–69.

27 Édouard Le Roy, *Dogme et critique* (Études de philosophie et de critique religieuse), Paris: Bloud, 1907. On Le Roy's thought, see Rudolf M. Schmitz, *Dogma und Praxis: Der Dogmenbegriff des Modernisten Édouard Le Roy kritisch dargestellt* (Studi tomistici, 51), Vatican: Libr. ed. Vaticana, 1993.

28 Albert Houtin, *La question biblique chez les catholiques de France en XIXe siècle*, Paris: Picard, 1902. On his life and work, see the two volumes of his autobiography: Albert Houtin, *Une vie de prêtre: Mon experience, 1867–1912*, Paris: Rieder, 1926 and *Mon experience II: Ma vie laïque, 1912–1926: Documents et souvenirs*, Paris: Rieder, 1928.

29   Cf. Henri Bremond, *Histoire littéraire du sentiment religieux en France depuis
      la fin des guerres de religion jusqu'à nos jours*, 12 vols, Paris: Bloud & Gay,
      1916–33. On the latter, see Émile Goichot, *Henri Bremond, historien du sentiment
      religieux: Genèse et stratégie d'une entreprise littéraire*, Paris: Ophrys, 1982.

30   Cf. Friedrich Heiler, *Der Vater des katholischen Modernismus: Alfred Loisy
      (1857–1940)* (Ernst Reinhardt Bücherreihe), Munich: Erasmus, 1947. On 8
      March 1908, after several works of Loisy were put on the Index, Loisy was
      excommunicated, which he learned about from the newspapers. Cf. Alfred Loisy,
      Mémoires pour servir à l'histoire religieuse de notre temps, 3 vols, Paris: Nourry,
      1930–31. On his contribution to Modernism, see Émile Goichot, *Alfred Loisy et
      ses amis* (Histoire), Paris: Cerf, 2002; Harvey Hill, *The Politics of Modernism:
      Alfred Loisy and the Scientific Study of Religion*, Washington, DC: Catholic
      University of America, 2002; Claus Arnold, 'Alfred Loisy (1857–1940)', in
      F.W. Graf (ed.), *Klassiker der Theologie*, Vol. 2: *Von Richard Simon bis Karl
      Rahner*, Munchen: Beck, 2005, pp. 155–70; Otto Weiss, 'Alfred Firmin Loisy
      (1857–1940)', in *Theologische Revue* 103 (2007) 17–28.

31   On J. Turmel, see Kurt-Peter Gertz, *Joseph Turmel (1859–1943): Ein
      theologiegeschichtlicher Beitrag zum Problem der Geschichtlichkeit der Dogmen*
      (Disputationes theologicae, 2), Bern/Frankfurt am Main: Lang, 1975.

32   On F. Von Hügel, see James J. Kelly, 'Modernism: A Unique Perspective:
      Friedrich von Hügel', in *The Downside Review* 122 (2004) 94–112; idem,
      Baron Friedrich von Hügel's Philosophy of Religion (Bibliotheca ephemeridum
      theologicarum Lovaniensium, 62), Louvain: University Press, 1983.

33   On M. Petre, see Clyde F. Crews, *English Catholic Modernism: Maude Petre's
      Way of Faith*, Notre Dame, in: University of Notre Dame Press, 1984; James J.
      Kelly, *The Letters of Baron Friedrich von Hügel and Maude Petre: The Modernist
      Movement in England* (Annua nuntia Lovaniensia, 44), Louvain: Peeters, 2003.

34   On G. Tyrrell, see David G. Schultenover, *George Tyrrell: In Search of
      Catholicism*, Shepherdstown: Patmos, 1981.

35   On Modernism in Italy, see Maurilio Guasco, *Modernismo: I fatti; le idée,
      i personaggi*, Cinisello Balsamo: San Paolo, 1995, pp. 59–70.

36   On Modernism in Germany, see Otto Weiss, *Der Modernismus in Deutschland:
      Ein Beitrag zur Theologiegeschichte*, Regensburg: Pustet, 1995. On Modernism
      in Belgium, see Lieve Gevers, 'Belgium and the Modernist Crisis: Main Trends in
      the Historiography', in A. Botti and R. Cerrato (eds), *Il modernismo tra cristianità
      e secolarizzazione: Atti del Convegno Internazionale di Urbino, 1–4 ottobre 1997*
      (Studi e testi, 2), Urbino: Quattro Venti, 2000, pp. 285–94. On Modernism in the
      Netherlands, see Ludovicus J. Rogier and Nicolaas De Rooij, *In vrijheid herboren:
      Katholiek Nederland 1853–1953*, The Hague: Pax, 1953, pp. 511–68.

37   Hendrik Andreas Poels, 'Examen critique de l'histoire du sanctuaire de l'Arche',
      doctoral dissertation in Theology, Louvain, 1897. Only the first part was
      published: *Examen critique de l'histoire du sanctuaire de l'Arche* (Universitas
      Catholica Lovaniensis. Dissertationes ad gradum doctoris in Facultate theologica
      consequendum conscriptae. Series 1, 47), Louvain: Vanlinthout, 1897.

38   Cf. Johannes P. de Valk, *Roomser dan de paus? Studies over de betrekkingen
      tussen de Heilige Stoel en het Nederlands katholicisme, 1815–1940* (KDC bronnen
      en studies, 36), Nijmegen: Valkhof, 1998, pp. 173–91.

39   *Testem benevolentiae*, letter of Pope Leo XIII to Cardinal James Gibbons,

Archbishop of Baltimore, 22 January 1899, in *Acta Sanctae Sedis* 31 (1898–99) 470–79. Cf. Margaret M. Reher, 'Americanism and Modernism: Continuity or Discontinuity?', in *US Catholic Historian* 1 (1981) 87–103.

40 Cf. Émile Poulat, *Histoire, dogme et critique dans la crise moderniste* (Religion et sociétés), Tournai: Casterman, 1962, ³(Bibliothèque de l'Évolution de l'Humanité), Paris: Albin Michel, 1996, p. xxiv: 'L'âge d'or du biblicisme'. On the development of twentieth-century exegesis, see François Laplanche, *La crise de l'origine: L'histoire et la science catholique des Évangiles au XXe siècle* (L'Évolution de l'humanité), Paris: Albin Michel, 2006 and my review of which in *Revue d'histoire ecclésiastique* 101 (2006) 1294–302.

41 For more information and literature, see Claus Arnold, 'Neuere Forschungen zur Modernismuskrise in der katholischen Kirche', in *Theologische Revue* 99 (2003) 91–104; Colin, *L'audace et le soupçon*; Jürgen Mettepenningen, 'Malheur devenu bénédiction: Un siècle de modernisme', in *Revue d'histoire ecclésiastique* 101 (2006) 1039–70; Poulat, *Histoire, dogme et critique dans la crise moderniste*.

42 Maurice d'Hulst, 'La question biblique', in *Le Correspondant* 50 (1893) 201–51. Cf. Francesco Beretta, *Monseigneur d'Hulst et la science chrétienne: Portrait d'un intellectuel* (Textes, dossiers, documents, 16), Paris: Beauchesne, 1996, pp. 99–123.

43 Alfred Loisy, *L'Évangile et l'Église*, Paris: Picard, 1902; idem, *Autour d'un petit livre*, Paris: Picard, 1903.

44 Alfred Loisy, *Le quatrième évangile*, Paris: Picard, 1903.

45 On M.-J. Lagrange, see Bernard Montagnes, *Marie-Joseph Lagrange: Une biographie critique* (Histoire – Biographie), Paris: Cerf, 2004.

46 Cf. *Vigilantiae studiique*, apostolic letter of Pope Leo XIII, 30 October 1902, in *Acta Sanctae Sedis* 35 (1902–3) 234–38. On the Pontifical Biblical Commission and the development of biblical research, see Joseph G. Prior, *The Historical Critical Method in Catholic Exegesis* (Tesi Gregoriana. Serie Teologia, 50), Rome: Pontificia Università Gregoriana, 1999 and Laplanche, *La crise de l'origine*.

47 *Spiritus Paraclitus*, encyclical of Pope Benedict XV, 15 September 1920, in *Acta Apostolicae Sedis* 12 (1920) 385–422.

48 *Divino afflante Spiritu*, encyclical of Pope Pius XII, 30 September 1943, in *Acta Apostolicae Sedis* 35 (1943) 297–325.

49 Maurice Blondel, *L'Action: Essai d'une critique de vie et d'une science de pratique* (Bibliothèque de philosophie contemporaine), Paris: Alcan, 1893. Reprinted on the occasion of its centenary: (Quadrige, 170), Paris: Presses Universitaires de France, 1993.

50 Frederick C. Copleston, *A History of Philosophy*, Vol. 9: *Modern Philosophy: From the French Revolution to Sartre, Camus, and Lévi-Strauss*, New York/London/Toronto/Sydney/Auckland: Doubleday, 1974, ⁴(A History of Philosophy, 9), London: Continuum, 2003, p. 250.

51 Richard Schaeffler, 'Modernismus', in *Historisches Wörterbuch der Philosophie* 6 (1984) 64.

52 Cf. Étienne Fouilloux, 'Courants de pensée, piété, apostolat, II: Le catholicisme', in J.-M. Mayeur (ed.), *Guerres mondiales et totalitarismes (1914–1958)* (Histoire du christianisme des origines à nos jours, 12), Paris: Desclée, 1990, pp. 116–86, esp. p. 167.

53 *Doctoris Angelici*, motu proprio of Pope Pius X, 29 June 1914, in *Acta Apostolicae*

Sedis 6 (1914) 336–41. The 24 theses are written in a decree of 27 July 1914, in *Acta Apostolicae Sedis* 6 (1914) 383–86. For its confirmation by the Congregation, see *Acta Apostolicae Sedis* 8 (1916) 156–57.

54 *Studiorum Ducem*, encyclical of Pope Pius XI, 29 June 1923, in *Acta Apostolicae Sedis* 15 (1923) 309–26.

55 Jan Hendrik Walgrave, *Geloof en theologie in de crisis* (Bezinning en bezieling, 1), Kasterlee: De Vroente, 1966, p. 14.

56 Cf. Gonzague Truc, *Le retour à la scolastique* (Bibliothèque internationale de critique: Religion et philosophie, 20), Paris: La Renaissance du Livre, 1919.

57 On nineteenth-century and twentieth-century Thomism, see Emerich Coreth, Walter M. Neidl and Georg Pfligersdorffer (eds), *Christliche Philosophie im katholischen Denken des 19. und 20. Jahrhunderts*, 3 vols, Graz/Vienna/Cologne: Styria, 1987–90; Gerald A. McCool, *From Unity to Pluralism: The Internal Evolution of Thomism*, New York: Fordham University Press, 1989, ⁴2002; idem, *Nineteenth-Century Scholasticism: The Search for a Unitary Method*, New York: Fordham University Press, 1989, ³1999; idem, *The Neo-Thomists* (Marquette Studies in Philosophy, 3), Milwaukee, WI: Marquette University Press, 1994; Géry Prouvost, *Thomas d'Aquin et les thomismes: Essai sur l'histoire des thomismes* (Cogitatio fidei, 195), Paris: Cerf, 1996; Philippe Chenaux, 'La seconde vague thomiste', in Pierre Colin (ed.), *Intellectuels chrétiens et esprit des années 1920: Actes du colloque Institut catholique de Paris, 23–24 septembre 1993* (Sciences humaines et religions: nouvelle série), Paris: Cerf, 1997, pp. 139–67; Thomas F. O'Meara, *Thomas Aquinas Theologian*; James C. Livingston, *Modern Christian Thought*, Vol. 1: *The Enlightenment and the Nineteenth Century*, Minneapolis, MN: Fortress Press, 1997, ²2006, pp. 342–55; David Berger, *Thomismus: Grosse Leitmotive der thomistischen Synthese und ihre Aktualität für die Gegenwart*, Cologne: Editiones thomisticae, 2001, pp. 59–126; Fergus Kerr, *After Aquinas: Versions of Thomism*, Malden, MA: Blackwell, 2002; Brian J. Shanley, *The Thomist Tradition* (Handbook of Contemporary Philosophy of Religion, 2), Dordrecht/Boston/London: Kluwer, 2002; John F.X. Knasas, *Being and Some Twentieth-Century Thomists*, New York: Fordham University Press, 2003; Linda Bendel-Maidl, *Tradition und Innovation: Zur Dialektik von historischer und systematischer Perspektive in der Theologie: Am Beispiel von Transformationen in der Rezeption des Thomas von Aquin im 20. Jahrhundert* (Religion – Geschichte – Gesellschaft. Fundamentaltheologische Studien, 27), Münster: LIT, 2004; Peter Gangl, *Franz Ehrle (1845–1934) und die Erneuerung der Scholastik nach die Enzyklika 'Aeterni Patris'* (Quellen und Studien zur neueren Theologiegeschichte, 7), Regensburg: Pustet, 2006, pp. 18–52.

58 Cf. Jacques Maritain, *Humanisme intégral: Problèmes temporels et spirituels d'une nouvelle chrétienté* (Bibliothèque philosophique), Paris: Aubier, 1936.

59 Marie-Dominique Chenu, *Introduction à l'étude de Saint Thomas d'Aquin* (Publications de l'Institut d'études médiévales, 11), Montréal/Paris: Université de Montréal/Institut d'études médiévales, 1950, ²1954, ³1974. On Chenu, see Part II, Chapter 1 in this volume.

60 Cf. Dominicus-Maria De Petter, 'Impliciete intuïtie', in *Tijdschrift voor Philosophie* 1 (1939) 84–105.

61 Cf. Shanley, *The Thomist Tradition*, p. 5: '. . . and he came to be seen by some as

a kind of Thomistic dinosaur.' See also Richard Peddicord, *The Sacred Monster of Thomism: An Introduction to the Life and Legacy of Reginald Garrigou-Lagrange, O.P.*, South Bend, IN: St. Augustine's Press, 2004.

62   Jan van Laarhoven, 'Thomas op Vaticanum II', in *De praktische Thomas: Thomas van Aquino: De consequenties van zijn theologie voor hedendaags gedrag* (Theologie en samenleving, 10), Hilversum: Gooi en Sticht, 1987, pp. 113–24 (123). See also Ralph McInerny, *Praeambula Fidei: Thomism and the God of the Philosophers*, Washington, DC: University of America, 2006.

63   For some overviews, see Roger Aubert, *La théologie catholique au milieu du XXe siècle* (Cahiers de l'actualité religieuse, 3), Tournai: Casterman, 1954; Gustave Thils, *Orientations de la théologie* (Bibliotheca ephemeridum theologicarum Lovaniensium, 11), Louvain: Ceuterick, 1958; Joseph Comblin, *Vers une théologie de l'action* (Études religieuses, 767), Brussels: La pensée catholique, 1964; Jacques Guillet, *La théologie catholique en France de 1914 à 1960*, Paris: Médiasèvres, 1988; Leo Scheffczyk, 'Grundzüge der Entwicklung der Theologie zwischen dem Ersten Weltkrieg und dem Zweiten Vatikanischen Konzil', in *Die Weltkirche im 20. Jahrhundert* (Handbuch der Kirchengeschichte, 7), Fribourg/ Basel/Vienna: Herder, pp. 263–301; Evangelista Vilanova, *Histoire des théologies chrétiennes* (Initiations), Vol. 3: *XVIIIe-XXe siècle*, pp. 849–911; Roger Aubert, *Le problème de l'acte de foi: Données traditionnelles et résultats des controverses récentes* (Universitas Catholica Lovaniensis – Dissertationes ad gradum magistri in Facultate Theologica vel in Facultate Iuris Canonici consequendum conscriptae, II/36), Louvain/Paris: Warny, 1945, ⁴1969.

64   Romano Guardini, *Vom Sinn der Kirche: Fünf Vorträge*, Mainz: Matthias-Grünewald, 1922, ⁴1955.

65   Columba Marmion, *Le Christ, vie de l'âme*, Maredsous: Abbaye de Maredsous, 1914; idem, *Le Christ dans ses mystères*, Maredsous: Abbaye de Maredsous, 1919; idem, *Le Christ, idéal du moine: Conférences spirituelles sur la vie monastique et religieuse*, Maredsous: Abbaye de Maredsous, 1922.

66   Cf. Émile Mersch, *Le Corps mystique du Christ: Étude de théologie historique* (Museum Lessianum: Section théologique, 28–29), 2 vols, Louvain: Museum Lessianum, 1933; idem, *La théologie du Corps mystique* (Museum Lessianum: Section théologique, 38–39), 2 vols, Paris: Desclée De Brouwer, 1944. On É. Mersch, see Gregory E. Malanowski, *Émile Mersch, S.J. (1890–1940): Un christocentrisme unifié*, in *Nouvelle revue théologique* 112 (1990) 44–66.

67   Roger Haight, *Christian Community in History*, Vol. 2: *Comparative Ecclesiology*, New York: Continuum, 2005, p. 384.

68   *Mystici corporis Christi*, encyclical of Pope Pius XII, 29 June 1943, in *Acta Apostolicae Sedis* 35 (1943) 200–43.

69   *Mediator Dei et hominum*, encyclical of Pope Pius XII, 20 November 1947, in *Acta Apostolicae Sedis* 39 (1947) 521–95. Like *Mystici corporis Christi*, this encyclical was written by S. Tromp.

70   Émile Mersch, *Morale et Corps mystique* (Museum Lessianum: Section théologique, 34), Brussels: Desclée De Brouwer, 1937, ²1941.

71   On the JOC, see Paul Wynants and Fernand Vanneste, 'Jeunesse ouvrière chrétienne', in *Dictionnaire de l'histoire et de géographie ecclésiastique* 27 (2000) 1254–80, with references to additional literature. See also, Thierry Keck, *Jeunesse de l'Église (1936–1955): Aux sources de la crise progressiste en France*

(Signes des temps), Paris: Karthala, 2004. On Catholic Action, see Gerd-Rainer Horn, *Western European Liberation Theology: The First Wave (1924–1959)*, Oxford: Oxford University Press, 2008, esp. pp. 5–53.

72 *Casti connubii*, encyclical of Pope Pius XI, 31 December 1930, in *Acta Apostolicae Sedis* 22 (1930) 539–92; *Quadragesimo anno*, encyclical of Pope Pius XI, 15 May 1931, in *Acta Apostolicae Sedis* 23 (1931) 177–228.

73 Cf. the Italian encyclical *Non abbiamo bisogno* of Pius XI, 29 June 1931, in *Acta Apostolicae Sedis* 23 (1931) 285–312 and the German encyclical *Mit brennender Sorge* of Pius XI, 14 March 1937, in *Acta Apostolicae Sedis* 29 (1937) 145–67.

74 Cf. Étienne Fouilloux, *Les catholiques et l'unité chrétienne du XIXe au XXe siècle: Itinéraires européens d'expression française*, Paris: Centurion, 1982, pp. 125–924.

75 Cf. Frédéric Gugelot, *La conversion des intellectuels au catholicisme en France, 1885–1935*, Paris: CNRS, 1998, esp. pp. 25–53.

76 Cf. Hervé Serry, *Naissance de l'intellectuel catholique* (L'espace de l'histoire), Paris: La Découverte, 2004.

77 On this period, see for example Étienne Fouilloux, *Les chrétiens français entre crise et liberation, 1937–1947* (XXe siècle), Paris: Seuil, 1997.

78 Cf. Émile Poulat, *Les prêtres-ouvriers: Naissance et fin* (Religion et sociétés), Tournai: Casterman, 1965, ²(Histoire), Paris: Cerf, 1999; François Leprieur, *Quand Rome condamne: Dominicains et prêtres-ouvriers* (Terre humaine), Paris: Plon, 1989.

Notes to Part I, Chapter 3: The Contours of the Nouvelle Théologie*: Four Phases*

1 On Le Saulchoir, see Jean-Pierre Jossua, 'Le Saulchoir: une formation théologique replacée dans son histoire', in *Cristianesimo nella storia* 14 (1993) 99–124.

2 Yves Congar, 'Déficit de la théologie', in *Sept*, 18 January 1935.

3 Asked for his observations on the survey, Congar declared that the gulf between faith and everyday life was the rise in secularization's primary cause. Cf. Yves Congar, 'Une conclusion théologique à l'enquête sur les raisons actuelles de l'incroyance', in *Vie Intellectuelle* 37 (1935) 214–49.

4 Marie-Dominique Chenu, 'Position de la théologie', in *Revue de science philosophique et théologique* 24 (1935) 232–57.

5 Marie-Dominique Chenu, *Une école de théologie: Le Saulchoir*, Kain: pro manuscripto, 1937; re-issued by Giuseppe Alberigo, *et al.*, *Une école de théologie: le Saulchoir* (Théologies), Paris: Cerf, 1985, pp. 91–173 (chapter on theology: pp. 129–50). Given the fact that the book was not commercially available, only one review exists, penned by Franz Stegmüller in *Theologische Revue* 38 (1939) 48–51.

6 Chenu alludes here to Ambroise Gardeil, *Le donné révélé et la théologie* (Bibliothèque théologique, 4), Paris: Cerf, 1909, ²1932. Chenu provided a foreword to the second edition: Marie-Dominique Chenu, 'Préface pour la deuxième édition', in Gardeil, *Le donné révélé et la théologie*, ²1932, pp. vii–xiv.

7 Chenu, 'Position de la théologie', p. 233; idem, *Une école de théologie*, p. 145.

8 The text of the project as found in the folder 'Chenu, Congar, Féret: Projet d'histoire de la théologie. Kain années 30' in the Archives de la province dominicaine de France was published in the footnotes of Michael Quisinsky, *Geschichtlicher Glaube in einer geschichtlichen Welt: Der Beitrag von M.-D. Chenu, Y. Congar und H.-M. Féret zum II. Vaticanum* (Dogma und Geschichte, 6), Berlin: LIT, 2007, pp. 47–51 (with pictures of the relevant archive pages on pp. 568–74).

9 Louis Charlier, *Essai sur le problème théologique* (Bibliothèque Orientations. Section scientifique, 1), Thuillies: Ramgal, 1938.

10 Cf. Jürgen Mettepenningen, 'L'Essai de Louis Charlier (1938): Une contribution à la nouvelle théologie', in *Revue théologique de Louvain* 39 (2008) 211–32.

11 Cf. *Acta Apostolicae Sedis* 34 (1942) 37. See also Étienne Fouilloux, 'Autour d'une mise à l'Index', in *Marie-Dominique Chenu, Moyen-Âge et modernité* (Les Cahiers du Centre d'études du Saulchoir, 5), Paris: Cerf, 1997, pp. 25–56.

12 The idea that *nouvelle théologie* evolved in a number of phases is also supported by Rosino Gibellini, Tarcisus Tshibangu and Étienne Fouilloux. In 1980, Tarcisus Tshibangu described the *nouvelle théologie* as a crisis in two phases (Tshibangu, *La théologie comme science au XXème siècle*, pp. 79–110). Six years later, Robert Guelluy suggested that the Dominican contributions of 1935–42 served as the antecedent to *Humani generis* (Robert Guelluy, 'Les antécédents de l'encyclique "Humani generis" dans les sanctions romaines de 1942: Chenu, Charlier, Draguet', in *Revue d'histoire ecclésiastique* 81 [1986] 421–97). In a series of three articles published between 1989 and 1992, Jean-Claude Petit agreed with Guelluy (Petit, 'La compréhension de la théologie dans la théologie française au XXe siècle'). In 1994 and 1998 Gibellini and Fouilloux confirmed respectively that the *nouvelle théologie* was to be divided into two phases, although the precise dating of each phase differs from scholar to scholar (Gibellini, *Panorama de la théologie au XXe siècle*, pp. 186–96; Fouilloux, *Une Église en quête de liberté*, pp. 193–300). While Fouilloux appears to suggest that the movement consisted of three phases (cf. Fouilloux, '"Nouvelle théologie" et théologie nouvelle [1930–1960]'), he does not discuss the third phase explicitly.

13 Cf., for example, the letter of Chenu to Henri-Dominique Gardeil, 28 February 1939, 5 pp., in the Archives de la Province dominicaine de France, 'Corr Chenu Février 1939', p. 2: Chenu writes that the Dominicans experience internal conflict because the younger generation wanted to free itself from the prevalence of Thomism. He notes in the margins: 'Je présume que l'incident Charlier (Louvain) est à l'origine de cette recrudescence.'

14 Pietro Parente, 'Nuove tendenze teologiche'.

15 Dominicus-Maria De Petter, 'Impliciete intuïtie'. In the same year, in *The Thomist*, another new journal, an article appeared on seven kinds of intuition: Mary de Munnynck, 'Notes on Intuition', in *The Thomist* 1 (1939) 143–68.

16 Johan Van Wijngaerden, 'Voorstudie tot het denken van E. Schillebeeckx: D.M. De Petter o.p. (1905–1971): Een inleiding tot zijn leven en denken. Deel 1: Een conjunctureel-historische situering', unpublished masters thesis, K.U.Leuven, Louvain, 1988–89, pp. 114–17.

17 René Draguet, review [Charlier, *Essai sur le problème théologique*], in *Ephemerides theologicae Lovanienses* 16 (1939) 143–45. Cf. Guelluy, 'Les antécédents de l'encyclique "Humani generis" dans les sanctions romaines de 1942'.

18   Henri Bouillard, *Conversion et grâce chez saint Thomas d'Aquin: Étude historique* (Théologie, 1), Paris: Aubier, 1944. Bouillard defended his doctoral dissertation at La Fourvière in 1941.

19   Bouillard, *Conversion et grâce chez saint Thomas d'Aquin*, p. 219.

20   Jean Daniélou, 'Les orientations présentes de la pensée religieuse', in *Études*, Vol. 79, nr. 249, April 1946, pp. 5–21.

21   Henri de Lubac, *Surnaturel: Études historiques* (Théologie, 8), Paris: Cerf, 1946. On the context of the publication of *Surnaturel*, see Étienne Fouilloux, 'H. de Lubac au moment de la publication de "Surnaturel"', in *Revue thomiste* 101 (2001) 13–30.

22   Henri de Lubac, *Mémoire sur l'occasion de mes écrits*, Namur: Culture et Vérité, 1989, ²1992, (Œuvres complètes, 33), Paris: Cerf, 2006, p. 34.

23   Excellent books have recently been published on Y. de Montcheuil and P. Teilhard de Chardin: Bernard Sesboüé, *Yves de Montcheuil (1900–1944): Précurseur en théologie* (Cogitatio fidei, 255), Paris: Cerf, 2006 and Patrice Boudignon, *Pierre Teilhard de Chardin: Sa vie, son œuvre, sa réflexion* (Cerf Histoire), Paris: Cerf, 2008.

24   On Fourvière, see Étienne Fouilloux, 'Une "école de Fourvière"?', in *Gregorianum* 83 (2002) 451–59; idem, *Une Église en quête de liberté*, pp. 172–91; Dominique Avon, 'Une école théologique à Fourvière?', in É. Fouilloux and B. Hours (eds), *Les jésuites à Lyon: XVIe-XXe siècle* (Sociétes, espaces, temps), Lyon: ENS, 2005, pp. 231–46. The connection between Fourvière and the *nouvelle théologie* is also made by Wilhelm Geerlings, 'Sources chrétiennes', in *Lexikon für Theologie und Kirche*, Vol. 9, ³2000, c. 747. On the link between 'Sources chrétiennes' and the *nouvelle théologie*, see Étienne Fouilloux, *La collection 'Sources chrétiennes': Éditer les Pères de l'Église au XXe siècle*, Paris: Cerf, 1995, pp. 113–52. On 'Sources chrétiennes', see also *Les Pères de l'Église au XXe siècle: Histoire, littérature, théologie: L'aventure des Sources chrétiennes* (Patrimoines: Christianisme), Paris: Cerf, 1997.

25   On de Lubac and the difficulties he was facing at the time, see Bernard Comte, 'Le Père de Lubac, un théologien dans l'Église de Lyon', in J.-D. Durand (ed.), *Henri de Lubac: La rencontre au cœur de l'Église*, Paris: Cerf, 2006, pp. 35–89, esp. pp. 73–81; Étienne Fouilloux, 'Autour d'un livre (1946–1953)', in Durand (ed.), *Henri de Lubac*, pp. 91–107, esp. pp. 93–95. For a more general study, see Joseph A. Komonchak, 'Theology at Mid-Century: The Example of Henri de Lubac', in *Theological Studies* 51 (1990) 579–602.

26   Fergus Kerr, *After Aquinas*, p. 134. The colloquium 'Surnaturel: une controverse au cœur du thomisme au XXe siècle' took place in 2000 and its proceedings appeared in *Revue thomiste* 109 (2001) 5–351. Reference can also be made at this juncture to John Milbank, *The Suspended Middle: Henri de Lubac and the Debate concerning the Supernatural*, Grand Rapids, MI/Cambridge: Eerdmans, 2005.

27   Within the methodological framework, special attention needs to be given here to the different understanding and appreciation of history during the modernist crisis and the period of the *nouvelle théologie*. While Modernists and *new theologians* were attempting to implement the historical-critical method in order to reconnect Catholic theology with modern sciences, this did not square with the magisterium's historical consciousness. The latter understood history in (what we would presently call) a meta-historical way: something is in line with history if it is in line with Catholic (dogmatic) tradition, rather than with historical events.

28 Réginald Garrigou-Lagrange, 'La nouvelle théologie où va-t-elle?'.

29 The concept 'retrocontextualization', whereby one relocates something to a context in the past, is first used in Jürgen Mettepenningen, 'Truth as Issue in a Second Modernist Crisis? The Clash between Recontextualization and Retrocontextualization in the French-Speaking Polemic of 1946–47', in M. Lamberigts, L. Boeve and T. Merrigan (eds), *Theology and the Quest for Truth: Historical- and Systematic-Theological Studies* (Bibliotheca ephemeridum theologicarum Lovaniensium, 202), Louvain: Peeters, 2006, pp. 119–41, esp. p. 141.

30 For an insight into the polemics surrounding the *nouvelle théologie*, see Étienne Fouilloux, 'Dialogue théologique? (1946–1948)', in S.-T. Bonino (ed.), *Saint Thomas au XXe siècle: Colloque du centenaire de la 'Revue thomiste' (1893–1992), Toulouse, 25–28 mars 1993*, Paris: Saint-Paul, 1995, pp. 153–95; idem, 'Autour d'un livre (1946–1953)'; Aidan Nichols, 'Thomism and the Nouvelle Théologie', in *The Thomist* 64 (2000) 1–19; Mettepenningen, 'Truth as Issue in a Second Modernist Crisis?'.

31 For chronology, redaction and actual publication of articles, see Mettepenningen, 'Truth as Issue in a Second Modernist Crisis?'. The fact that a number of journals had faced a chronological backlog makes it difficult to reconstruct the sequence of 'reactions to reactions'.

32 Cf. *Il venerato Discorso del Sommo Pontifice alla XXIX Congregazione Generale della Compagnia di Gesù*.

33 Cf. *Fervido Discorso del Sommo Pontifice ai Capitolari dell'Ordine dei Frati Predicatori*.

34 Cf. Étienne Fouilloux, '"Nouvelle théologie" et théologie nouvelle (1930–1960)', in B. Pellistrandi (ed.), *L'histoire religieuse en France et Espagne* (Collection de la Casa Velázquez, 87), Madrid: Casa de Velázquez, 2004, pp. 411–25.

35 Fouilloux, *Une Église en quête de liberté*, pp. 149–91.

36 On both theologians, see Part II, Chapter 3 in this volume.

37 Cf. Bernard Sesboüé, *Karl Rahner* (Initiations aux théologiens), Paris: Cerf, 2001, pp. 193–95.

38 Cf. Rudolf Voderholzer, 'Die Bedeutung der sogenannten "Nouvelle Théologie" (insbesondere Henri de Lubacs) für die Theologie Hans Urs von Balthasars', in W. Kasper (ed.), *Logik der Liebe und Herrlichkeit Gottes: Hans Urs von Balthasar im Gespräch*, Ostfildern: Matthias Grünewald, 2006, pp. 204–28.

39 Wolfgang W. Müller suggests that the phenomenon of the *prêtres-ouvriers* represents the pastoral expression of the *nouvelle théologie* (Wolfgang W. Müller, 'Was kann an der Theologie neu sein? Der Beitrag der Dominikaner zur "nouvelle théologie"', in *Zeitschrift für Kirchengeschichte* 110 [1999], pp. 86–104 [103]). Wolfgang Pauly would also appear to support this argument, cf. Wolfgang Pauly, 'Theologien im 20. Jahrhundert', in idem (ed.), *Geschichte der christlichen Theologie*, Darmstadt: Primus, 2008, pp. 197–229 (209). In line with Étienne Fouilloux (confirmed during a personal discussion in Lyon on 18 December 2008), I am inclined to argue that this is not correct. The *nouvelle théologie* was an academic-theological enterprise while the phenomenon of the *prêtres-ouvriers* – supported by Congar, Chenu and Féret – is better understood as a re-integration of faith and Church in everyday life, *in casu* the life of the factory worker and better described as a sort of re-evangelization. Nevertheless, the fact that Congar

and Chenu sympathized with the *prêtres-ouvriers* makes it comprehensible that people emphasize a connection between the *nouvelle théologie* on the one hand and the phenomenon of the *prêtres-ouvriers* on the other.

40 Cf. Étienne Fouilloux, 'La "nouvelle théologie" française vue d'Espagne (1948–1951)', in *Revue d'histoire de l'Église de France* 90 (2004) 279–93.

41 Thomas G. Guarino, *Foundations of Systematic Theology* (Theology for the Twenty-First Century), New York/London: T&T Clark, 2005, p. 288.

42 *Dei Verbum*, dogmatic constitution of Vatican II, 18 November 1965, in *Acta Apostolicae Sedis* 58 (1966) 817–35.

43 Claude Geffré, 'Recent Developments in Fundamental Theology: An Interpretation', in J.B. Metz (ed.), *The Development of Fundamental Theology* (Concilium, 46), New York/ Paramus, NJ: Paulist Press, 1969, pp. 5–27 (10).

44 *Gaudium et Spes*, pastoral constitution of Vatican II, 7 December 1965, in *Acta Apostolicae Sedis* 58 (1966) 1025–120 (1084).

45 For those among them who were faced with Roman sanctions, the Council signified a rehabilitation, albeit without apology or explicit re-instatement (something alien to the Holy Office). In order to explore the 'rehabilitation' it would be necessary to account for the period preceding it, but this would take us beyond the boundaries of the present study. Reference can be made, for example, to Yves Congar, *Journal d'un théologien 1946–1956*, Paris: Cerf, 2001.

46 For Quisinsky's work, see n. 8 above.

47 Bruno Forte, 'Le prospettive della ricera teologica', in R. Fisichella (ed.), *Il Concilio Vaticano II. Recezione e attualità alla luce del Giubileo*, Milan: San Paolo, 2000, pp. 419–29 (423).

48 Cf. Peter Eicher, 'Von den Schwierigkeiten bürgerlicher Theologie mit den katholischen Kirchenstrukturen', in K. Rahner and H. Fries (eds), *Theologie in Freiheit und Verantwortung*, Munich: Kösel, 1981, pp. 96–137 (101), reissued in W. Kern (ed.), *Die Theologie und das Lehramt* (Quaestiones Disputatae, 91), Freiburg/Basel/Vienna: Herder, 1982, pp. 116–51.

49 Henri de Lubac, *Catholicisme: Les aspects sociaux du dogme* (Unam Sanctam, 3), Paris: Cerf, 1938, ⁷1983; (Œuvres complètes, 7), Paris: Cerf, 2003.

50 Cf. the letters of Congar and Chenu (in the Archives de la province dominicaine de France, Paris) and of H. de Lubac (in the Archives françaises de la Compagnie de Jésus, Vanves).

51 Henri-Marie Féret, *L'Apocalypse de Saint Jean: Vision chrétienne de l'histoire* (Témoignages chrétiens), Paris: Corrêa, 1943. Here Féret provides, among other things, an explanation and interpretation of history based on the Apocalypse.

52 Cf. Silouane Ponga, *L'Écriture, âme de la théologie: Le problème de la suffisance matérielle des Écritures* (Théologies), Paris: Cerf, 2008, esp. the chapter on 'La nouvelle théologie': pp. 69–105.

Notes to Part II, Chapter 1: Le Saulchoir, Louvain and Rome: Dominicans

1 On Congar, see Jean-Pierre Jossua, *Le Père Congar: La théologie au service du peuple de Dieu* (Chrétiens de tous les temps, 20), Paris: Cerf, 1967; Marie-Joseph Le Guillou, 'P. Yves M.-J. Congar O.P.', in H. Vorgrimler and R. Vander Gucht (eds), *Bilanz der Theologie im 20. Jahrhundert: Bahnbrechende Theologen,*

Freiburg/Basel/Vienna: Herder, 1970, pp. 99–199; *Jean Puyo interroge le Père Congar: 'Une vie pour la vérité'* (Les interviews), Paris: Centurion, 1975; Yves-Marie Congar, *Entretiens d'automne* (Théologies), Paris: Cerf, 1987; Étienne Fouilloux, 'Frère Yves, Cardinal Congar, dominicain: Itinéraire d'un théologien', in *Revue des sciences philosophiques et théologiques* 79 (1995) 379–404; André Vauchez (ed.), *Cardinal Yves Congar 1904–1995* (Histoire), Paris: Cerf, 1999; Gabriel Flynn (ed.), *Yves Congar: Theologian of the Church* (Louvain Theological Pastoral Monographs, 32), Louvain/Paris/Dudley, MA: Peeters, 2005; Fergus Kerr, *Twentieth Century Catholic Theologians: From Neoscholasticism to Nuptial Mysticism*, Malden, MA/Oxford/Victoria: Blackwell, 2007, pp. 34–51; Johannes Bunnenberg, 'Yves Congar OP (1904–1995): Mit dem Konzil über das Konzil hinaus', in T. Eggensperger and U. Engel (eds), *'Mutig in die Zukunft': Dominikanische Beiträge zum Vaticanum II* (Dominikanische Quellen und Zeugnisse, 10), Leipzig: Benno, 2007, pp. 39–63; Joseph Famerée and Gilles Routhier, *Yves Congar* (Initiations aux théologiens), Paris: Cerf, 2008.

2   On his trials and tribulations during the First World War, see Yves Congar, *Journal de la guerre 1914–1918*, ed. S. Audoin-Rouzeau and D. Congar, Paris: Cerf, 1997.

3   Yves-Marie-Joseph Congar, *Chrétiens désunis: Principes d'un œcuménisme catholique* (Unam Sanctam, 1), Paris: Cerf, 1937.

4   Yves Congar, *Une passion: L'unité: Réflexions et souvenirs: 1929–1973* (Foi vivante, 156), Paris: Cerf, 1974. On his desire for unity, see Jean-Pierre Jossua, 'In Hope of Unity', in Flynn (ed.), *Yves Congar*, pp. 167–81.

5   Yves-Marie-Joseph Congar, *Vraie et fausse réforme dans l'Église* (Unam Sanctam, 20; Essais sur la communion catholique, 4), Paris: Cerf, 1950, ²(Unam Sanctam, 72), Paris: Cerf 1968. Avery Dulles considered this book to be 'the most searching theological treatise on our subject [Church, Church Reform, and Society]', cf. Avery Cardinal Dulles S.J., *Church and Society: The Laurence J. McGinley Lectures 1988–2007*, New York: Fordham University Press, 2008, p. 405. On the problems surrounding the book, see Étienne Fouilloux, 'Recherche théologique et magistère romain en 1952: Une "affaire" parmi d'autres', in *Recherches de science religieuse* 71 (1983) 269–86.

6   Cf. Yves-Marie-Joseph Congar, *Jalons pour une théologie du laïcat* (Unam Sanctam, 23), Paris: Cerf, 1953. ³1964.

7   Marie-Dominique Chenu, 'Le sacerdoce des prêtres-ouvriers', in *Vie Intellectuelle* 1 (1954) nr. 2, 175–81.

8   On Congar in this regard, see Étienne Fouilloux, 'Comment devient-on expert au Vatican II? Le cas du Père Yves Congar', in *Le deuxième concile du Vatican (1959–1965)* (Collection de l'École Française de Rome), Rome: École française de Rome, 1989, pp. 307–31.

9   Yves Congar, *Journal d'un théologien 1946–1956*, ed. É. Fouilloux, Paris: Cerf, 2001, p. 427.

10   Congar, *Journal d'un théologien 1946–1956*, p. 195.

11   Cf. Paul D. Murray, 'Roman Catholic Theology after Vatican II', in D.F. Ford and R. Muers (eds), *The Modern Theologians: An Introduction to Christian Theology Since 1918*, Malden, MA/Oxford/Victoria: Blackwell, 2005, pp. 265–86, esp. p. 268.

12   Marie-Joseph Congar, 'Théologie', in *Dictionnaire de théologie chrétienne* 15 (1946) 341–502. A slightly revised English translation of this article was published almost 20 years later: Yves-Marie-Joseph Congar, *A History of Theology*, Garden City, NY: Doubleday, 1968. In 2005, Fergus Kerr sketched the content of the article in his 'Yves Congar and Thomism', in Flynn (ed.), *Yves Congar*, pp. 67–97.

13   See n. 10.

14   Bernard Sesboüé, 'Le drame de la théologie au XXe siècle: A propos du "Journal d'un théologien (1946–1956)" du P. Yves Congar', in *Recherches de science religieuse* 89 (2001) 271–87.

15   Yves Congar, *Mon Journal du Concile*, ed. É. Mahieu, 2 vols, Paris: Cerf, 2002. On Congar's journal and his contribution to Vatican II, see Alberto Melloni, 'The System and the Truth in the Diaries of Yves Congar', in Flynn (ed.), *Yves Congar*, pp. 278–302; Mary Cecily Boulding, 'Yves Congar: Faithful Critic of the Church in "Mon Journal du Concile"', in *Louvain Studies* 29 (2004) 350–70. See also the numerous references to Congar in Alberigo and Komonchak (eds), *History of Vatican II*.

16   Cf. the draft text of 22 February 1947 from the prior of Saint-Jacques, the final version of which was sent to the Dominican authorities in Rome on 26 February of the same year without reference to Garrigou-Lagrange, in the Archives de la province dominicaine de France, 'Courrier Yves Congar 1948', 1 p. For further reference to this turbulent month, see Jürgen Mettepenningen, 'Truth as Issue in a Second Modernist Crisis?', pp. 129–31. On the allocation of the title of magister, see the letter of provincial superior Kopf in *Ut sint unum: Bulletin de liaison de la province de France*, 13, 180, 1 October 1963 (also in the Archives de la province dominicaine de France, 'Congar, Frère Yves – V-832/83').

17   Yves-Marie-Joseph Congar, *La Tradition et les traditions* (Le signe), 2 vols, Paris: Fayard, 1960–63.

18   Yves Congar, *Situation et tâches présentes de la théologie* (Cogitatio fidei, 27), Paris: Cerf, 1967.

19   For an overview of English translations of his work and English contributions on his life and thought, see J.R. Emond and J.A. Driscoll (eds), *A Dominican Bibliography and Book Reference, 1216–1992: A List of Works in English by and about Members of the Friars Preachers, Founded by St. Dominic de Guzman (c. 1171–1221) and Confirmed by Pope Honorius III, 22 December 1216*, New York, *et al.*: Lang, 2000, pp. 168–74.

20   Congar's health prevented him from attending the ceremony of elevation in Rome. A separate ceremony was organized on his behalf in the Cathedral of the Military Diocese, Saint Louis des Invalides, on 8 December 1994, presided over by Cardinal Johannes Willebrands.

21   Marie-Joseph Congar, 'Une conclusion théologique à l'enquête sur les raisons actuelles de l'incroyance', in *Vie Intellectuelle* 37 (31 July 1935) 214–49.

22   Cf. Famerée and Routhier, *Yves Congar*, p. 23, n. 3.

23   Letter of Congar to Emmanuel Suárez, dated 16 January 1950, in the Archives de la province dominicaine de France, 'Corr Congar, January 1950'.

24   Letter of Congar to Emmanuel Suárez, dated 16 January 1950.

25   *Jean Puyo interroge le Père Congar*, p. 99.

26   See Part I, Chapter 3, n. 7 in this volume.

27 Étienne Fouilloux, 'Présentation générale', in Congar, *Journal d'un théologien 1946–1956*, p. 12.
28 Under Chenu's leadership, both programmes were to be adapted to the new 1931 guidelines as found in *Deus scientiarum Dominus*, apostolic constitution of Pius XI, 24 May 1931, in *Acta Apostolicae Sedis* 23 (1931) 241–62.
29 On Chenu, see *Jacques Duquesne interroge le Père Chenu: 'Un théologien en liberté'* (Les interviews), Paris: Centurion, 1975; *L'hommage différé au Père Chenu* (Théologies), Paris: Cerf, 1990; Joseph Doré, 'Un itinéraire-témoin: Marie-Dominique Chenu', in P. Colin (ed.), *Les catholiques français et l'héritage de 1789: D'un centenaire à l'autre* (Bibliothèque Beauchesne: Religions, société, politique, 17), Paris: Beauchesne, 1989, pp. 313–39; Claude Geffré, 'Théologie de l'incarnation et théologie des signes des temps chez le Père Chenu', in *Marie-Dominique Chenu, Moyen-Âge et modernité* (Les Cahiers du Centre d'études du Saulchoir, 5), Paris: Cerf, 1997, pp. 131–53; Christophe F. Potworowski, *Contemplation and Incarnation: The Theology of Marie-Dominique Chenu* (McGill-Queen's Studies in the History of Ideas, 33), Montreal: McGill-Queen's University Press, 2001; Emmanuel Vangu Vangu, *La théologie de Marie-Dominique Chenu: Réflexion sur une méthodologie théologique de l'intégration communautaire*, Paris: L'Harmattan, 2007; Christian Bauer, 'Marie-Dominique Chenu OP (1895–1990): Gottes messianisches Volk unter den Zeichen der Zeit', in Eggensperger and Engel (eds), *'Mutig in die Zukunft'*, pp. 105–46.
30 Chenu's unpublished doctorate 'De contemplatione' is to be found in Paris: Archives de la province dominicaine de France, Archive Chenu, file 1920/2 (file 1920/1 contains his diploma). A partial publication appeared in 1991: Carmelo G. Conticello, '"De contemplatione" (Angelicum, 1920): La thèse inédite de doctorat du P. M.-D. Chenu', in *Revue des sciences philosophiques et théologiques* 75 (1991) 363–422. Potworowski points out that the text anticipates several aspects of Chenu's later work, especially his rejection of dualism and its destruction of the integral unity of the human person (Potworowski, *Contemplation and Incarnation*, p. 6). On the context, see Étienne Fouilloux, *Au cœur du XXe siècle religieux* (Églises/Sociétés), Paris: Ouvrières, 1993, pp. 203–58.
31 Ambroise Gardeil, *Le donné révélé et la théologie* (Bibliothèque théologique, 4), Paris: Lecoffre, 1910, ²1932.
32 Marie-Dominique Chenu, *Une école de théologie: Le Saulchoir*, Kain: *pro manuscripto*, 1937; re-issued by Giuseppe Alberigo, *et al.*, *Une école de théologie: le Saulchoir* (Théologies), Paris: Cerf, 1985, p. 119.
33 Cf. the chronicles of Le Saulchoir, drafted by Henri-Marie Féret, in the Archives de la province dominicaine de France, 'Corr Chenu 1938', '13 Janvier – 23 Février', 3 pp. See also Étienne Fouilloux, 'Autour d'une mise à l'Index', in *Marie-Dominique Chenu, Moyen-Âge et modernité*, pp. 25–56. Declarations of support for Chenu were written, among others, by Henri de Lubac (letter of de Lubac to M.-D. Chenu, dated 18 March 1938, in the Archives de la province dominicaine de France, 'Corr Chenu Mars 1948', 2 pp.), Yves Congar (letter of Congar to M.-D. Chenu, dated 1 February 1938, in the Archives de la province dominicaine de France, 'Corr Chenu, février 1938', 4 pp.) and Lucien Cerfaux (letter of Cerfaux to M.-D. Chenu, dated 14 January 1938, in the Archives de la province dominicaine de France, 'Corr Chenu, Janvier 1938', 1 p.).

34   *Acta Apostolicae Sedis* 34 (1942) 148.

35   Cf. the text justifying the condemnation presented by visitator Thomas Philippe
      to the Dominicans of Le Saulchoir on 8 and 9 June 1942, i.e. during the visitation
      itself (May–June 1942): *Cours du T.R.P. Thomas Philippe: Le 8 & 9 Juin 1942*, in
      the Archives de la province dominicaine de France, 'Visite canonique au Saulchoir
      par le P. Th. Philippe. L'affaire de la Revue des Sciences Phil. et Théol. 1942–43
      (dont il avait décidé de changer le comité de direction)', 5 pp. As a result of the
      visitation and condemnation, Chenu was replaced as senior editor of the *Revue
      des sciences philosophiques et théologiques* by Guérard des Lauriers, cf. the letter
      from T. Philippe to M.-D. Chenu, dated 24 January 1943, in the Archives de la
      province dominicaine de France, 'Chenu, Visite canonique au Saulchoir par le
      P. Th. Philippe', 1 p. In a personal note, Chenu offers critique of the visitation,
      not in the least on account of the visitator's lack of competence: 'Note sur les
      conditions de la visite canonique au Saulchoir en 1942', in the Archives de la
      province dominicaine de France, 'Chenu, Visite canonique au Saulchoir par
      le P. Th. Philippe', 3 pp. On the condemnation, see also: 'Pièces relatives à la
      condamnation du Père Chenu', in the Archives de la province dominicaine de
      France, 'Chenu, 1942–1946/1942. Autour de la mise à l'Index', 13 pp. For Chenu's
      response to the various accusations, see 'À propos de l'opuscule du P. Chenu:
      Accusations, et réponse par les textes mêmes', in the Archives de la province
      dominicaine de France, 'Chenu, 1942–1946/1942. Autour de la mise à l'Index',
      5 pp.

36   Marie-Dominique Chenu, *La théologie comme science au XIIIe siècle*, 1927,
      ²1943, ³(Bibliothèque thomiste, 33), Paris: Vrin, 1957; ⁴1969. On this work, see
      Henri Donneaud, 'Histoire d'une histoire: M.-D. Chenu et "La Théologie comme
      science au XIIIe siècle"', in *Les Dominicains en Europe* (Mémoire Dominicaine,
      9), Paris: Cerf, 1996, pp. 41–50, esp. pp. 46–50.

37   On the positive relationship between Chenu and Gilson, see, for example,
      Francesca A. Murphy, 'Correspondance entre É. Gilson et M.-D. Chenu: Un choix
      de lettres (1923–1969)', in *Revue thomiste* 112 (2005) 25–87.

38   Cf. Jacques Prévotat, *Les catholiques et l'Action française: Histoire d'une
      condamnation 1899–1939* (Pour une histoire du XXe siècle), Paris: Fayard,
      2001, p. 458. Cf. Marie-Dominique Chenu, book review [Maritain, *Primauté du
      Spirituel*], in *Revue des sciences philosophiques et théologiques* 16 (1927) 21*.

39   Cf. Philippe Chenaux, 'La seconde vague thomiste', in Pierre Colin (ed.),
      *Intellectuels chrétiens et esprit des années 1920: Actes du colloque Institut
      catholique de Paris, 23–24 septembre 1993* (Sciences humaines et religions:
      nouvelle série), Paris: Cerf, 1997, pp. 139–67, esp. p. 167.

40   Marie-Dominique Chenu, *Introduction à l'étude de saint Thomas d'Aquin*
      (Publications de l'Institut d'études médiévales, 11), Montréal: Université de
      Montréal; Paris: Institut d'études médiévales, 1950, ²1954, ³1974.

41   The series was started in 1921 by Pierre Mandonnet, then co-rector of Le Saulchoir,
      who continued his association until 1938. Étienne Gilson assumed responsibility
      with a first publication in 1942. Chenu followed in his footsteps 11 years later, in 1953.

42   Marie-Dominique Chenu, *La théologie au XIIe siècle* (Études de philosophie
      médiévale, 45), Paris: Vrin, 1957, ²1966, ³1976.

43   For a complete bibliography, see: Potworowski, *Contemplation and Incarnation*,
      pp. 237–321. For a list of English translations of his work and English language

studies of his life and legacy, see Emond and Driscoll (eds), *A Dominican Bibliography and Book Reference, 1216–1992*, pp. 144–46.

44 The Semaines sociales de France is a series of symposia organized on an annual basis since 1904. Its central themes focus on social existence considered in the first instance from the Christian perspective.

45 Cf. Joseph Cardijn, 'Théologie du travail, théologie pour l'homme', in *L'hommage différé au Père Chenu*, pp. 19–21, esp. p. 21.

46 For additional background information on the Mission de France, see the dated but nonetheless well-ordered work of Jacques Faupin, *La mission de France: Histoire et Institution*, Tournai: Casterman, 1960.

47 Marie-Dominique Chenu, *Spiritualité du travail* (Études religieuses, 604–5), Liège: La pensée catholique, 1947.

48 Jean-François Six, *Cheminements de la Mission de France*, Paris: Seuil, 1967, p. 60.

49 Marie-Dominique Chenu, 'Le sacerdoce des prêtres-ouvriers', in *Vie Intellectuelle* 1 (1954), nr. 2, pp. 175–81.

50 The first volume of the *Bulletin thomiste* is dated 1924–25 and appeared under Pierre Mandonnet as editor-in-chief. Chenu took over the position from the ninth volume, beginning in January 1932, and held the post until 1965. The *Bulletin* did not only change editor at that point, it also continued under a new name: *Rassegna di letteratura tomistica*.

51 Cf. Quisinsky, *Geschichtlicher Glaube in einer geschichtlichen Welt*; Giuseppe Alberigo, '"Un concile à la dimension du monde": Marie-Dominique Chenu à Vatican II d'après son journal', in *Marie-Dominique Chenu, Moyen-Âge et modernité*, pp. 155–72; Giovanni Turbanti, 'Il ruolo del P. D. Chenu nell'elaborazione della constituzione "Gaudium et spes"', in *Marie-Dominique Chenu, Moyen-Âge et modernité*, pp. 173–212. See also the following note.

52 Claude Rolland, 'Le Père Chenu, théologien au Concile', in *L'hommage différé au Père Chenu*, pp. 249–56, esp. 250; Marie-Dominique Chenu, *Notes quotidiennes au Concile: Journal de Vatican II: 1962–1963* (Histoire à vif), Paris: Cerf, 1995.

53 Rolland, 'Le Père Chenu, théologien au Concile', p. 255.

54 Chenu, *Une école de théologie: le Saulchoir*, p. 127.

55 Marie-Dominique Chenu, 'Position de la théologie', in *Revue des sciences philosophiques et théologiques* 24 (1935) 232–57.

56 Chenu, *Une école de théologie: le Saulchoir*, p. 130.

57 Chenu, *Une école de théologie: le Saulchoir*, p. 131.

58 Chenu, *Une école de théologie: le Saulchoir*, p. 133.

59 Chenu, *Une école de théologie: le Saulchoir*, p. 133.

60 Cf. Chenu, *Une école de théologie: le Saulchoir*, p. 132.

61 Chenu, *Une école de théologie: le Saulchoir*, p. 134.

62 Francisco Marín-Sola, *La evolución homogénea del dogma católico* (Biblioteca de tomistas españoles, 1), Madrid: La Ciencia tomista, 1923, ²1923, ³(Biblioteca de autores cristianos, 84; biblioteca de tomistas españoles, 14), Madrid: Biblioteca de autores cristianos, 1952.

63 Cf. Chenu, *Une école de théologie: le Saulchoir*, pp. 140–41.

64 Cf. Chenu, 'Position de la théologie', p. 243.

65 Chenu refers here to 'la chrétienté en travail' ('Christianity at work') (Chenu, *Une école de théologie: le Saulchoir*, p. 142).

66 Chenu, *Une école de théologie: le Saulchoir*, p. 145. The article refers to both 'la foi en œuvre d'intelligence théologale' and 'la foi en œuvre d'intelligence théologique', cf. Chenu, 'Position de la théologie', esp. pp. 233, 252.

67 Chenu, *Une école de théologie: le Saulchoir*, p. 147; Chenu, 'Position de la théologie', p. 247.

68 Cf. Chenu, 'Position de la théologie', pp. 241–46

69 Cf. Chenu, 'Position de la théologie', p. 234.

70 Chenu, 'Position de la théologie', p. 252.

71 Chenu, 'Position de la théologie', p. 249 (= *Une école de théologie: le Saulchoir*, p. 149).

72 Chenu, 'Position de la théologie', p. 253.

73 Chenu, *Une école de théologie: le Saulchoir*, p. 155.

74 On Rousselot's vision, see, for example, Thomas Sheehan, 'Pierre Rousselot and the Dynamism of Human Spirit', in *Gregorianum* 66 (1985) 241–67; Hans Boersma, 'A Sacramental Journey to the Beatific Vision: The Intellectualism of Pierre Rousselot', in *The Heythrop Journal* 49 (2008) 1015–34. Francis Schüssler Fiorenza explicitly locates Rousselot in 'the background and context of the *nouvelle théologie*', cf. Francis Schüssler Fiorenza, 'The New Theology and Transcendental Thomism', in J.C. Livingston and F. Schüssler Fiorenza (eds), *Modern Christian Thought: The Twentieth Century*, Minneapolis, MN: Fortress, 2006, pp. 197–232, esp. p. 200. In 1910 Rousselot has published his famous article on the (two) eyes of faith, emphasizing the complementarity of positive and speculative methodology: Pierre Rousselot, 'Les yeux de la foi', in *Recherches de science religieuse* 1 (1910) 241–59, 444–75.

75 Friedrich Stegmüller, review, in *Theologische Revue* 38 (1939) 48–51.

76 On this investigation and the theses, see Fouilloux, 'Autour d'une mise à l'Index'; idem, 'Le Saulchoir en process (1937–1942)', in G. Alberigo, *et al.*, *Une école de théologie: le Saulchoir*, pp. 37–59. The theses: Giuseppe Alberigo, 'Christianisme en tant qu'histoire et "théologie confessante"', in G. Alberigo, *et al.*, *Une école de théologie: le Saulchoir*, pp. 9–35 (35).

77 Cf. *Acta Apostolicae Sedis* 34 (1942) 37.

78 Pietro Parente, 'Nuove tendenze teologiche'.

79 *Jacques Duquesne interroge le Père Chenu*, p. 122.

80 On Féret, see 'Henri-Marie Féret: Dominicain: 1904–1992', unpublished brochure of the Groupe évangélique, Paris, 1992; Michael Quisinsky, 'Henri-Marie Féret OP (1904–1992): Auf dem Weg zu einer "konkreten und geschichtlichen Theologie"', in Eggensperger and Engel (eds), *'Mutig in die Zukunft'*, pp. 65–103.

81 'Henri-Marie Féret: Dominicain', p. 3.

82 See n. 80 above.

83 On the Groupe évangélique, see 'Henri-Marie Féret: Dominicain', pp. 24–33.

84 Henri-Marie Féret, *Connaissance biblique de Dieu* (Epiphanie), Paris: Cerf, 1955.

85 Cf. François Leprieur, *Quand Rome condamne*.

86 Henri-Marie Féret, 'La théologie concrète et historique et son importance pastorale présente', in *Théologie: Le service théologique dans l'Église: Mélanges offerts à Yves Congar pour ses soixante-dix ans*, Paris: Cerf, 1974, pp. 193–247.

87 Henri-Marie Féret, 'Dans les cheminements de la sagesse de Dieu', in *L'hommage différé au Père Chenu*, pp. 208–38.

88 Fouilloux describes the trio as 'une équipe ardente et soudée', cf. Étienne Fouilloux, 'Présentation générale', in Yves Congar, *Journal d'un théologien 1946–1956*, p. 10.

89 In the Archives de la province dominicaine de France, file 'Chenu, Congar, Féret: Projet d'histoire de la théologie. Kain années 30'. See also Part I, Chapter 3 in this volume.

90 Quisinsky suggests between the end of 1933 and the beginning of 1936, cf. Quisinsky, *Geschichtlicher Glaube in einer geschichtlichen Welt*, pp. 53–54.

91 Henri-Marie Féret, *L'Apocalypse de saint Jean: Vision chrétienne de l'histoire* (Témoignages chrétiens), Paris: Corrêa, 1943.

92 Roger Aubert, 'Discussions récentes autour de la Théologie de l'Histoire', in *Collectanea Mechliniensia* 33 (1948) 129–49.

93 Louis Charlier, *Essai sur le problème théologique* (Bibliothèque Orientations. Section scientifique, 1), Thuillies: Ramgal, 1938.

94 On the division of the Belgian Dominican province in 1958 into a Flemish province (the 'Provincia S. Rosae in Flandria') and a Walloon province ('Vicariatus generalis S. Thomae Aquinitatis in Belgio'), see the *Catalogus generalis Ordinis Praedicatorum: Conspectus generalis Ordinis Fratrum Praedicatorum necnon index monasteriorum, congregationum et fraternitatum*, Rome: Curia generalitia, 1992, pp. 182–83 and p. 231.

95 Charlier gave courses on 'De Deo Uno', 'De Justitia originali' and 'De Sacramentis' (present in the Archive of the Flemish Dominican Province, Louvain, untitled file).

96 Louis Charlier, 'Puissance passive et désir naturel selon saint Thomas', in *Ephemerides theologicae Lovanienses* 7 (1930) 5–28, 639–62.

97 Cf. Guelluy, 'Les antécédents de l'encyclique "Humani generis" dans les sanctions romaines de 1942'; Jean-Claude Petit, 'La compréhension de la théologie dans la théologie française au XXe siècle: Vers une nouvelle conscience historique: G. Rabeau, M.-D. Chenu, L. Charlier'.

98 A letter was sent from the Holy Office to Cardinal Jozef-Ernest Van Roey, archbishop of Mechelen-Brussels on 22 December, in which reference is made to the condemnation of the *Essai sur le problème théologique*. Cf. letter of Cardinal Francesco Marchetti Selvaggiani to Cardinal Jozef-Ernest Van Roey, dated 22 December 1941, in the Archive of the Archdiocese of Mechelen-Brussels, 'Fonds Van Roey', IV5a.

99 Louis Charlier, 'Histoire des principales mises en ordre des données de la foi et des grandes synthèses théologiques: L'organisation des études sacrées au cours de l'histoire', in *Formation doctrinale des religieuses* (Problèmes de la religieuse aujourd'hui, 9), Paris: Cerf, 1954, pp. 231–70.

100 Louis Charlier, 'Les cinq voies de saint Thomas: Leur structure métaphysique', in *L'existence de Dieu* (Cahiers de l'actualité religieuse, 16), Tournai: Casterman, 1961, pp. 181–228.

101 Louis Charlier, 'Le Christ, Parole de Dieu: Réflexions théologiques', in *La Parole de Dieu en Jésus-Christ* (Cahiers de l'actualité religieuse, 15), Tournai: Casterman, 1961, pp. 121–39.

102 The following presentation of the essay and the different critiques is a reworked (English) version of Jürgen Mettepenningen, 'L'Essai de Louis Charlier (1938): Une contribution à la nouvelle théologie', in *Revue théologique de Louvain* 39 (2008) 211–32.

103   Charlier, *Essai sur le problème théologique*, pp. 7–8.
104   Charlier, *Essai sur le problème théologique*, p. 7.
105   Cf. Charlier, *Essai sur le problème théologique*, p. 12.
106   In this sense, Charlier speaks not only of a 'positive des sources', but also of a 'positive du magistère'. Cf. Charlier, *Essai sur le problème théologique*, pp. 61–62.
107   Marie-Joseph Congar, review, in *Bulletin thomiste* 5 (1937–39) 490–505.
108   Marie-Rosaire Gagnebet, 'Un essai sur le problème théologique', in *Revue thomiste* 45 (1939) 108–45.
109   Mannus D. Koster, review, in *Theologische Revue* 38 (1939) 41–48.
110   Florian Schlagenhaufen, review, in *Zeitschrift für katholische Theologie* 63 (1939) 366–71.
111   Maïeul Cappuyns, review, in *Recherches de théologie ancienne et médiévale* 11 (1939) [13]–[15].
112   René Draguet, review, in *Ephemerides theologicae Lovanienses* 16 (1939) 143–45.
113   Werner Goossens, 'Notion et méthodes de la théologie: "L'Essai" du P. L. Charlier"', in *Collationes Gandavenses* 26 (1939) 115–34.
114   Jean Cottiaux, review, in *Revue d'histoire ecclésiastique* 36 (1940) 459–62.
115   Coelestin Zimara, 'Theologie: Eine Denkaufgabe', in *Divus Thomas* 18 (1940) 89–112.
116   Charles Boyer, 'Qu'est-ce que la théologie: Réflexions sur une controverse', in *Gregorianum* 21 (1940) 255–66.
117   Congar, review, p. 490; Koster, review, c. 41; Boyer, 'Qu'est-ce que la théologie', pp. 255–56; Draguet, review, p. 143. The fact that Charlier had never studied at the Faculty of Theology, however, is evident from the registers contained in the *Acta Sacrae Facultatis Theologiae Universitatis Lovaniensis*, 1910/11–1946/47 (Archive of the Faculty of Theology, Maurits Sabbe Library).
118   Cf. Congar, review, p. 490; Gagnebet, 'Un essai sur le problème théologique', p. 123; Cottiaux, review, p. 459.
119   Koster, review, c. 41.
120   Cottiaux, review, p. 462.
121   Goossens, 'Notion et méthodes de la théologie', pp. 131, 134.
122   Cappuyns, review, p. [14].
123   Schlagenhaufen, review, p. 366.
124   Cappuyns, review, p. [13].
125   Goossens, 'Notion et méthodes de la théologie', p. 131.
126   Draguet, review, p. 145.
127   Goossens, 'Notion et méthodes de la théologie', p. 134.
128   Gagnebet, 'Un essai sur le problème théologique', pp. 114, 119, 129 and 142.
129   Zimara, 'Theologie', p. 107.
130   Cappuyns, review, p. [14].
131   Koster, review, c. 48.
132   Draguet, review, p. 145; Congar, review, p. 490.
133   Goossens, 'Notion et méthodes de la théologie', p. 131.
134   Cottiaux, review, p. 459.
135   Gagnebet, 'Un essai sur le problème théologique', p. 111.
136   Gagnebet, 'Un essai sur le problème théologique', pp. 113–14.

137   Gagnebet, 'Un essai sur le problème théologique', p. 118.
138   Congar, review, p. 494; Schlagenhaufen, review, p. 371.
139   Charlier aligns himself here with the Modernist proposition condemned by Rome, which upheld that revelation did not stop at the end of the apostolic period. Cf. *Lamentabili sane exitu*, esp. p. 473 (proposition 21).
140   Cf. Gagnebet, 'Un essai sur le problème théologique', pp. 117–18.
141   Cottiaux, review, p. 460.
142   Charlier, *Essai sur le problème théologique*, p. 148.
143   Gagnebet, 'Un essai sur le problème théologique', pp. 122–23.
144   Koster, review, c. 45.
145   Congar, review, p. 498.
146   Goossens, 'Notion et méthodes de la théologie', pp. 132–33.
147   Cappuyns, review, p. [15].
148   Henri-Dominique Simonin, 'De la nécessité de certaines conclusions théologiques', in *Angelicum* 16 (1939) 72–83.
149   Boyer, 'Qu'est-ce que la théologie', p. 259.
150   Boyer, 'Qu'est-ce que la théologie', p. 260.
151   Koster, review, c. 45.
152   Cf. Zimara, 'Theologie', pp. 105–6.
153   Cf. Zimara, 'Theologie', pp. 106–7.
154   Timoteo Zapelena, 'Problema theologicum', in *Gregorianum* 24 (1943) 23–47, 287–326; 25 (1944) 38–73, 247–82.
155   We base ourselves here in terms of archive material on the file '1942. Autour de la mise à l'Index', in the Archives de la Province dominicaine de France, Archive Chenu, 15 pp., where Charlier is mentioned on the reverse of p. 2 – handwritten – in addition to the references (with Draguet) on pp. 10–14.
156   On Draguet, see Joseph Coppens, 'In memoriam R. Draguet (1896–1980)', in *Ephemerides theologicae Lovanienses* 57 (1981) 194–200.
157   Gustave Thils, 'La note de catholicité de l'Église dans la théologie catholique d'Occident, du XVIe au XIXe siècle', unpublished doctoral dissertation, Faculty of Theology, K.U.Leuven, Louvain 1935; Jan Hendrik Walgrave, 'Newman's theorie over de ontwikkeling van het dogma: Een poging tot synthese', unpublished doctoral dissertation, Faculty of Theology, K.U.Leuven, Louvain, 1942.
158   René Draguet, 'Méthodes théologiques d'hier et d'aujourd'hui', in *Revue catholique des idées et des faits* 15/42 (10 January 1936) 1–7; 15/46 (7 February 1936) 4–7; 15/47 (14 February 1936) 13–17.
159   Cf. Coppens, 'In memoriam R. Draguet (1896–1980)', p. 198.
160   Cf. the Archives de l'Université catholique de Louvain-la-Neuve, C II 4335: handwritten notes by Gustave Thils, academic year 1934–35, 105 pp.
161   Cf. Dirk Claes, 'Theologie in tijden van verandering: De theologische faculteit te Leuven in de twintigste eeuw, 1900–1968', unpublished doctoral dissertation, K.U.Leuven, Louvain, 2004, p. 79.
162   Cf. Guelluy, 'Les antécédents de l'encyclique "Humani generis" dans les sanctions romaines de 1942'.
163   Cf. Vicenze Buffon, 'Chiesa di Cristo e Chiesa romana nelle opere e nelle lettere di fra Paolo Sarpi', unpublished and unsuccessful doctoral dissertation, Faculty of Theology, K.U.Leuven, Louvain, 1939; idem, 'Il pensiero del Sarpi alla luce della doctrina cattolica', unpublished doctoral dissertation, Faculty of Theology,

K.U.Leuven, Louvain, 1946. On this question see: *Acta Sacrae Facultatis Theologiae Lovaniensis*, I (1910–47) 484.

164 René Draguet, 'L'évolution des dogmes', in M. Brillant and M. Nédoncelle (eds), *Apologétique: Nos raisons de croire, réponses aux objections*, Paris: Bloud & Gay, 1937, ²1939, ³1948, pp. 1166–92. This publication also appeared seperately as *L'évolution des dogmes*, Saint-Dizier: Brulliard, 1937.

165 Maurice Nédoncelle, *La pensée religieuse de Friedrich von Hügel (1852–1925)* (Bibliothèque d'histoire de la philosophie), Paris: Vrin, 1935. For Poulat's appreciation, see Émile Poulat, 'Préface', in L. Courtois, *et al.* (eds), *Écrire l'histoire du catholicisme des 19ᵉ et 20ᵉ siècles: Bilan, tendances récentes et perspectives (1975–2005): Hommage au professeur Roger Aubert à l'occasion de ses 90 ans*, Louvain-la-Neuve: ARCA, 2005, pp. 11–16 (14).

166 René Draguet, *Histoire du dogme catholique*, Paris: Albin Michel, 1941, ²1947.

167 See, for example, René Draguet, 'Pièces de polémique antijulianiste: Le Pacte d'Union de 797 entre les jacobites et les julianistes du patriarcat d'Antioche', in *Le Muséon* 54 (1941) 59–106.

168 Dadišo Qatraya, *Commentaire du livre d'Abba Isaïe (logoi I–XV)* (Corpus scriptorium christianorum Orientalium, 326–7; Corpus scriptorium christianorum Orientalium. Scriptores Syri, 144–5), 2 vols, Louvain: Corpus scriptorium christianorum Orientalium, 1972. Draguet is mentioned for his redactional activities by Karl Pinggéra: 'Dadischo Qatraya', in *Biographisches-Bibliographisches Kirchenlexikon* 23 (2004) 249–52, pp. 249, 251.

169 Athanasius of Alexandria, *La vie primitive de S. Antoine conservée en syriaque* (Corpus scriptorium christianorum Orientalium, 417–18; Corpus scriptorium christianorum Orientalium. Scriptores Syri, 183–84), 2 vols, Louvain: Corpus scriptorium christianorum Orientalium, 1980.

170 Abbas Isaias, *Les cinq recensions de l'Ascéticon syriaque d'Abba-Isaïe* (Corpus scriptorium christianorum Orientalium, 289, 290, 293 and 294; Corpus scriptorium christianorum Orientalium. Scriptores Syri, 120, 121, 122 and 123), 4 vols, Louvain: Corpus scriptorium christianorum Orientalium, 1968; *Commentaire anonyme du livre d'Abba Isaïe (fragments)* (Corpus scriptorium christianorum Orientalium, 336–7; Corpus scriptorium christianorum Orientalium. Scriptores Syri, 150–51), 2 vols, Louvain: Corpus scriptorium christianorum Orientalium, 1973.

171 Draguet, 'Méthodes théologiques' (10 January 1936) 1.

172 Draguet, 'Méthodes théologiques' (7 February 1936) 6.

173 Draguet, 'Méthodes théologiques' (7 February 1936) 5.

174 Draguet, 'Méthodes théologiques' (14 February 1936) 17.

175 Draguet, 'Méthodes théologiques' (14 February 1936) 17.

176 Jean-François Bonnefoy, *Le Saint-Esprit et ses dons selon Saint Bonaventure* (Étude de philosophie médiévale, 10), Paris: Vrin, 1929.

177 Jean-François Bonnefoy, *Une somme bonaventurienne: Le De triplice via*, Paris: Vrin, 1934.

178 Jean-François Bonnefoy, *Chronique de l'Annonciade: Vies de la Bienheureuse Jeanne de France et du Bienheureux Gabriel-Maria*, Villeneuve-sur-Lot: Monastère de l'Annonciade, 1937, ²1950.

179 Jean-François Bonnefoy, 'La théologie comme science et l'explication de la foi selon saint Thomas d'Aquin', in *Ephemerides theologicae Lovanienses* 14 (1937) 421–46, 600–31; 15 (1938) 491–516. This series also appeared in the form of a

book entitled *La nature de la théologie selon saint Thomas d'Aquin*, Paris: Vrin, 1939.

180 Bonnefoy, 'La théologie comme science', p. 436.

181 Bonnefoy, 'La théologie comme science', p. 446.

182 Bonnefoy, 'La théologie comme science', p. 627.

183 Bonnefoy, 'La théologie comme science', p. 514.

184 Marie-Rosaire Gagnebet, 'L'œuvre du P. Garrigou-Lagrange: itineraire intellectuel et spirituel vers Dieu', in *Angelicum* 17 (1965) 7–31.

185 *Lumen Gentium*, dogmatic constitution of Vatican II, in *Acta Apostolicae Sedis* 57 (1965) 5–71. The role played by Gagnebet during the Council and in the preparatory period is explained in detail in the work of G. Alberigo and J.A. Komonchak (eds), *History of Vatican II*.

186 Cf., for example, the article he published prior to the Council entitled 'L'origine de la Jurisdiction collegiale du corps épiscopal au Concile selon Bolegni', in *Divinitas* 5 (1961) 431–93. See also F. Alvarez Alonso, 'La posizione del Laterano sui problemi ecclesiologici nella fase preparatoria del Concilio', in P. Chenaux (ed.), *L'Università del Laterano e la preparazione del Concilio Vaticano II: Atti del convegno internazionale di studi, Città del Vaticano, 27 gennaio 2000* (Studi e documenti sul Concilio Vaticano II, 1), Rome: Pontificia Università Lateranense, 2001, pp. 67–80, esp. pp. 76–78.

187 Marie-Rosaire Gagnebet, 'La nature de la théologie spéculative', in *Revue thomiste* 44 (1938) 1–39, 213–55, 645–74.

188 Gagnebet published another article along similar lines entitled 'Le problème actuel de la théologie et la science aristotélicienne d'après un ouvrage récent', in *Divus Thomas* 43 (1943) 237–70.

189 Congar, review (see n. 107).

190 Congar, review, p. 490.

191 Congar, review, p. 490.

192 Congar, review, p. 492.

193 Marie-Joseph Congar, *Théologie*, pp. 417, 430 and 446.

194 Congar quotes Charlier, *Essai sur le problème théologique*, pp. 145–46. Cf. Congar, review, p. 496.

195 Congar, review, p. 498.

196 Congar, review, p. 503, n. 3.

197 Dominicus-Maria De Petter, 'Impliciete intuitie', in *Tijdschrift voor Philosophie* 1 (1939) 84–105.

198 Cf. De Petter, 'Impliciete intuitie', p. 87.

199 Boyer, 'Qu'est-ce que la théologie' (see n. 116).

200 Although Boyer does not divide his article into paragraphs, the twofold subdivision is clear nonetheless.

201 Boyer, 'Qu'est-ce que la théologie', p. 264.

202 Henri de Lubac, 'Le problème du développement du dogme', in *Recherches de science religieuse* 35 (1938) 130–60.

203 Avon, 'Une école théologique à Fourvière?', pp. 236–37.

204 Charles Boyer, 'Sur un article des Recherches de science religieuse', in *Gregorianum* 29 (1948) 152–54.

205 Louis Bouyer, *La décomposition du catholicisme* (Présence et pensée, 13), Paris: Aubier Montaigne, 1968, p. 119.

Notes to Part II, Chapter 2: Fourvière, Toulouse, Paris and Rome: Jesuits

1   For helpful literature on Bouillard's life and work, see Karl H. Neufeld, 'Fundamentaltheologie in gewandelter Welt: H. Bouillards theologischer Beitrag: Zur Vollendung seines 70. Lebensjahres', in *Zeitschrift für katholische Theologie* 100 (1978) 417–40; Thomas Guarino, 'Henri Bouillard and the Truth-Status of Dogmatic Statements', in *Science et esprit* 39 (1987) 331–43; Xavier de Montclos, 'Bouillard Henri', in Xavier de Montclos (ed.), *Lyon: Le Lyonnais – Le Beaujolais* (Dictionnaire du monde religieux dans la France contemporaine, 6), Paris: Beauchesne, 1994, pp. 74–75; Joseph Doré, 'Théologie et philosophie chez Henri Bouillard', in *Nouvelle revue théologique* 117 (1995) 801–20; Auguste Demoment, 'Bouillard, Henri', in C.E. O'Neill and J.M. Domínguez (eds), *Diccionario histórico de la Compañia de Jesus: Biográfico-temático*, Madrid: Universidad Ponticia Comillas; Rome: Institutum historicum, 2001, pp. 506–7; Michel Castro, 'Henri Bouillard (1908–1981): Éléments de biographie intellectuelle', in *Mélanges de science religieuse* 60 (2003) nr. 4, 43–58 and 63 (2006) nr. 2, pp. 47–59; J. Euleen Scully, *Grace and Human Freedom in the Theology of Henri Bouillard*, Bethesda, MD: Academica, 2007 ; Joseph Doré, 'Henri Bouillard: Un grand théologien jésuite à l'Institut Catholique de Paris', in *Transversalités*, nr. 109, January–March 2009, pp. 141–48.

2   Henri Bouillard, *Conversion et grâce chez saint Thomas d'Aquin* (Théologie), Paris: Aubier, 1944. Cf. Étienne Fouilloux, 'Henri Bouillard et Saint Thomas d'Aquin (1941–1951)', in *Recherches de science religieuse* 97 (2009) 173–83.

3   Cf. Étienne Fouilloux, 'Itinéraire d'un théologien contrarié (1904–1979)', in M. Fédou (ed.), *Pierre Ganne (1904–1979): La théologie chrétienne pédagogie de la liberté: Colloque janvier 2009, Centre Sèvres – Facultés des Jésuites de Paris* (Théologie, 149), Paris: Médiasèvres, 2009, pp. 13–22 (17–20). See also Étienne Fouilloux, 'Pierre Ganne et l'affaire de Fourvière', in *Pierre Ganne: La liberté d'un prophète* (Cahiers de Meylan), Meylan: Centre Théologique de Meylan-Grenoble, 2005, pp. 29–54.

4   De Lubac, Bouillard and Ganne are inheritors of the so-called 'second school of Lyon', which was in favour of Blondel. On this second school and on the influence of Blondel on French Jesuits, see Étienne Fouilloux, 'La seconde 'École de Lyon' (1919–1939)', in E. Gabellieri and P. de Cointet (eds), *Blondel et la philosophie française*, Paris: Parole et Silence, 2007, pp. 263–73 ; Peter Henrici, 'La descendance blondélienne parmi les jésuites français', in Gabellieri and de Cointet (eds), *Blondel et la philosophie française*, pp. 305–22.

5   Henri Bouillard, *Karl Barth* (Théologie, 38–39), Paris: Aubier, 1957.

6   Henri Bouillard, *Blondel et le christianisme*, Paris: Seuil, 1961.

7   Henri Bouillard, *Logique de la foi* (Théologie, 60), Paris: Aubier, 1964.

8   Henri Bouillard, *Connaissance de Dieu: Foi chrétienne et théologie naturelle* (Foi vivante, 45), Paris: Aubier Montaigne, 1967.

9   Henri Bouillard, *Comprendre ce que l'on croit* (Intelligence de la foi), Paris: Aubier, 1971, esp. p. 42.

10 Bouillard, *Conversion et grâce chez saint Thomas d'Aquin*, p. 211.

11 Bouillard, *Conversion et grâce chez saint Thomas d'Aquin*, p. 215.

12 Bouillard, *Conversion et grâce chez saint Thomas d'Aquin*, p. 219.

13 Bouillard, *Conversion et grâce chez saint Thomas d'Aquin*, p. 219.

14 Bouillard, *Conversion et grâce chez saint Thomas d'Aquin*, p. 220.

15 Bouillard, *Conversion et grâce chez saint Thomas d'Aquin*, pp. 221–22.

16 Bouillard, *Conversion et grâce chez saint Thomas d'Aquin*, p. 223.

17 Bouillard, *Vérité du christianisme*, p. 401: '. . . Encore ne prétendrons-nous jamais faire une théologie nouvelle. Et si nous renouvelons un peu la théologie, ce sera sans l'avoir cherché. En outre, nous ne formons pas une école. Nous avons en commun les mêmes soucis apostoliques, la conscience des mêmes besoins, certaines méthodes de travail scientifique qui sont celles de tous les travailleurs d'aujourd'hui, avec cela, une compréhension mutuelle et une bonne entente fraternelle. Mais bien des divergences d'idées et de mentalité séparent ceux que nos critiques rassemblent arbitrairement. Chacun, dans ses écrits, n'engage que lui-même.'

18 Bouillard, *Vérité du christianisme*, p. 406: 'Je [Bouillard, 19 June 1950] n'ai jamais eu l'intention de créer une "théologie nouvelle" qui irait on se sait où.'

19 Réginald Garrigou-Lagrange, 'La nouvelle théologie où va-t-elle?'.

20 Karl-Heinz Neufeld, *Fundamentaltheologie in gewandelter Welt*, p. 421.

21 Charles Boyer, review, in *Gregorianum* 27 (1946) 157–60.

22 This fact makes clear that Le Saulchoir was not a monolitic bloc and is not to reduce to the viewpoint of Congar, Chenu and Féret.

23 Louis-Bertrand Guérard des Lauriers, 'La théologie de Saint Thomas et la grâce actuelle', in *L'Année théologique* 6 (1945) 276–325; idem, 'La théologie historique et le développement de la théologie', in *L'Année théologique* 7 (1946) 15–55.

24 Henri Bouillard, 'À propos de la grâce actuelle chez saint Thomas d'Aquin', in *Recherches de science religieuse* 33 (1946) 92–114; idem, 'Notes sur le développement de la théologie: À propos d'une controverse', in *L'Année théologique* 7 (1946) 254–64.

25 The biographical sketch offered here is based on Karl H. Neufeld, 'Daniélou', in *Lexikon für Theologie und Kirche*, Vol. 3, [3]2006, pp. 16–17; Marguerite Harl, 'In memoriam: Jean Daniélou', in *Bulletin des amis du Cardinal Daniélou*, nr. 10, April 1984, pp. 54–62; Johannes Hofmann, 'Daniélou', in *Biographisch-Bibliographisches Kirchenlexikon*, Vol. 15, 1999, pp. 453–61; Paul Lebeau, *Jean Daniélou* (Théologiens et spirituels contemporains, 4), Paris: Fleurus, 1967; Paul Duclos, 'Daniélou', in O'Neill and Domínguez (eds), *Diccionario histórico de la Compañía de Jesús*, pp. 1044–46. His mémoires appeared in 1974: Jean Daniélou, *Et qui est mon prochain? Mémoires*, Paris: Stock, 1974. His spiritual journal appeared 1993: Jean Daniélou, *Carnets spirituels* (Intimité du christianisme), ed. M.-J. Rondeau, Paris: Cerf, 1993, [2]2007. A posthumous commemorative Festschrift appeared a year after his death: *Jean Daniélou 1905–1974*, Paris: Cerf/Axes, 1975. On the occasion of the centenary of Daniélou's birthday, the following work appeared: Jacques Fontaine (ed.), *Actualité de Jean Daniélou* (Paris: Cerf), 2006.

26 Gregory of Nyssa, *La vie de Moïse ou traité de la perfection en matière de vertu* (Sources Chrétiennes, 1), ed. J. Daniélou, Paris: Cerf, 1942, [3]1968, repr. 2000.

27 On the relationship between Daniélou and de Lubac, see Marie-Josèphe Rondeau, 'Le Père de Lubac et le Père Daniélou', in *Bulletin des amis du Cardinal Daniélou*, nr. 19, October 1993, pp. 49–65.

28 Jean Daniélou, 'L'apocatastase chez Saint Grégoire de Nysse', in *Recherches de science religieuse* 30 (1940) 328–47.

29   Jean Daniélou, *Essai sur le mystère de l'histoire* (La Sphère et la Croix), Paris: Seuil, 1953.

30   Jean Daniélou, *Théologie du Judéo-Christianisme* (Bibliothèque de théologie. Histoire des doctrines chrétiennes avant Nicée, 1), Paris: Cerf, 1958, ²1991.

31   'Judéo-christianisme: Recherches historiques et théologiques offertes en hommage au Cardinal Jean Daniélou', in *Recherches de science religieuse* 60 (1972) 5–323. For a list of Daniélou's contributions on the theme, see 'Bibliographie des travaux du Cardinal J. Daniélou sur le Judéo-Christianisme', in *Recherches de science religieuse* 60 (1972) 11–18.

32   Henri de Lubac, 'Un homme libre et évangélique', in *Cahiers de l'actualité religieuse et sociale* 81 (1974) 413–16, reprinted in Henri de Lubac, *Mémoire sur l'occasion de mes écrits* (Œuvres complètes, 33), Paris: Cerf, ⁹2001, pp. 166–68.

33   Jacques Fontaine, 'Préface', in Fontaine (ed.), *Actualité de Jean Daniélou*, p. 8.

34   Antoine Guggenheim, 'La théologie de l'accomplissement de Jean Daniélou', in *Nouvelle revue théologique* 128 (2006) 240–57, repr.: 'La théologie de l'accomplissement', in Jacques Fontaine (ed.), *Actualité de Jean Daniélou*, pp. 165–87.

35   Jean Daniélou, 'Les orientations présentes de la pensée religieuse', in *Études*, Vol. 79, nr. 249 (1946), pp. 5–21; idem, 'Christianisme et histoire', in *Études*, Vol. 80, nr. 254, September 1947, pp. 166–84.

36   Cf. letter from Daniélou to de Lubac, dated 28 February 1947, in *Bulletin des amis du Cardinal Daniélou*, nr. 21, November 1995, p. 43.

37   Daniélou, 'Les orientations présentes de la pensée religieuse', p. 5.

38   Lucien Cerfaux, *La théologie de l'Église suivant saint Paul* (Unam Sanctam, 10), Paris: Cerf, 1942.

39   Daniélou, 'Les orientations présentes de la pensée religieuse', p. 9.

40   Daniélou, 'Les orientations présentes de la pensée religieuse', p. 17.

41   Daniélou, 'Les orientations présentes de la pensée religieuse', p. 17.

42   Henri de Lubac, *Catholicisme: Les aspects sociaux du dogme* (Unam Sanctam, 3), Paris: Cerf, 1938, ⁷1983, (Œuvres complètes, 7), Paris: Cerf, 2003.

43   Daniélou refers to Étienne Gilson, *L'esprit de la philosophie médiévale* (Études de philosophie médiévale, 33), Paris: Vrin, 1932, pp. 369–71. The pages in question are to be found in the chapter entitled 'Le moyen age et l'histoire'.

44   Daniélou, 'Christianisme et histoire', p. 170.

45   Daniélou, 'Christianisme et histoire', p. 177.

46   Daniélou, 'Christianisme et histoire', p. 183.

47   Cf. Fouilloux, 'Dialogue théologique? (1946–1948)', pp. 159–60.

48   Œuvres completes series, Paris: Cerf.

49   On Henri de Lubac, see Henri de Lubac, *Mémoire sur l'occasion de mes écrits*; idem, *Entretien autour de Vatican II: Souvenirs et Réflexions* (Théologies), Paris: France Catholique/Cerf, 1985, ²2007; Herbert Vorgrimler, 'Henri de Lubac', in H. Vorgrimler and R. Vander Gucht (eds), *Bilanz der Theologie im 20. Jahrhundert: Bahnbrechende Theologen*, Freiburg/Basel/Vienna: Herder, 1970, pp. 199–214; Joseph A. Komonchak, 'Theology and Culture at Mid-Century: The Example of Henri de Lubac', in *Theological Studies* 51 (1990) 579–602; Ekkart Sauser, 'Lubac, Henri Marie Joseph Sonnier de', in *Biographisch-Bibliographisches Kirchenlexikon* 5 (1993) 282–86; Joseph Doré, 'Henri de Lubac (1896–1991): La vie et l'œuvre d'un théologien exemplaire', in *Bulletin de*

littérature ecclésiastique 94 (1993) 39–46; X. de Montclos, 'Lubac Henri Sonier de', in Xavier de Montclos (ed.), *Lyon: Le Lyonnais – Le Beaujolais*, pp. 279–81; Antonio Russo, *Henri de Lubac* (Biographie), Paris: Brepols, 1997; Antonio Russo, *Henri de Lubac: Biographie*, Paris: Brepols, 1997; Rudolf Voderholzer, *Henri de Lubac begegnen* (Zeugen des Glaubens), Augsburg: Sankt Ulrich, 1999; Jean-Pierre Wagner, *Henri de Lubac* (Initiations aux théologiens), Paris: Cerf, 2001; Jacques Guillet, 'Lubac, Henri de', in O'Neill and Domínguez (eds), *Diccionario histórico de la Compañía de Jesús*, pp. 2430–32; John Milbank, 'Henri de Lubac', in David F. Ford and R. Muers (eds), *The Modern Theologians: An Introduction to Christian Theology Since 1918*, Malden, MA/Oxford/ Victoria: Blackwell, ³2005, pp. 76–91; David Grumett, *De Lubac: A Guide for the Perplexed* (Guides for the Perplexed), London/New York, 2007; Fergus Kerr, *Twentieth Century Catholic Theologians*, pp. 67–86; Georges Chantraine, 'Henri de Lubac (1896–1991) : Une vue panoramique', in *Nouvelle revue théologique* 129 (2007) 212–34; Georges Chantraine, *Henri de Lubac*, Vol. 1: *De la naissance à la démobilisation (1896–1919)* (Études Lubaciennes, 6), Paris: Cerf, 2007, Vol. 2: *Les années de formation (1919–1929)* (Études Lubaciennes, 7), Paris: Cerf, 2009.

50 De Lubac, *Catholicisme*.

51 Henri de Lubac, *Le drame de l'humanisme athée*, Paris: Spes, 1944, (Œuvres complètes, 2), Paris: Cerf, 1998.

52 Henri de Lubac, *Surnaturel: Études historiques* (Théologie, 8), Paris: Aubier, 1946.

53 Henri de Lubac, *Aspects du bouddhisme* (La sphère et la croix), 2 vols, Paris: Seuil, 1951 and 1955; idem, *La rencontre du bouddhisme et de l'Occident* (Théologie, 24), Paris: Aubier, 1952.

54 Henri de Lubac, *Méditation sur l'Église* (Théologie, 27), Paris: Aubier, 1953, (Œuvres complètes, 8), Paris: Cerf, 2003.

55 Henri de Lubac, *Sur les chemins de Dieu*, Paris: Aubier, 1956, (Œuvres complètes, 1), Paris: Cerf, 2006.

56 Henri de Lubac, *Exégèse médiévale: Les quatre sens de l'Écriture* (Théologie, 41–42), 4 vols, Paris: Aubier, 1959–64.

57 *L'homme devant Dieu: Mélanges offerts au Père Henri de Lubac* (Théologie, 56–58), 3 vols, Paris: Aubier, 1963–64.

58 Henri de Lubac, *Augustinisme et théologie moderne* (Théologie, 63), Paris: Aubier, 1965; (Œuvres complètes, 13), Paris: Cerf, 2009.

59 Cf. Henri de Lubac, *Entretien autour de Vatican II*; idem, *Mémoire sur l'occasion de mes écrits*, pp. 117–22.

60 Henri de Lubac, *Carnets du Concile*, ed. L. Figoureux, 2 vols, Paris: Cerf, 2007.

61 Henri de Lubac, *L'Écriture dans la Tradition*, Paris: Aubier, 1966.

62 For example, Henri de Lubac, *Athéisme et sens de l'homme: Une double requête de Gaudium et Spes* (Foi vivante, 67), Paris: Cerf, 1968.

63 Cf. John Allen, *Pope Benedict XVI*, pp. 113–18.

64 For example, Henri de Lubac, *Pic de La Mirandole: Études et discussions*, Paris: Aubier, 1974; idem, *La postériorité spirituelle de Joachim de Flore*, 2 vols, Paris/ Namur: Lethielleux, 1979–81; idem, *Théologies d'occasion*, Paris: Desclée De Brouwer, 1984.

65 Henri de Lubac, *Théologie dans l'histoire* (Théologie), 2 vols, Paris: Desclée De Brouwer, 1990.

66   De Lubac, *Surnaturel*, p. 6.

67   Henri de Lubac, *Mémoire sur l'occasion de mes écrits*, p. 34.

68   Henri de Lubac, 'Deux augustiniens fourvoyés', in *Recherches de science religieuse* 21 (1931) 422–43, 513–40.

69   Thomas F. Martin, *Our Restless Heart: The Augustinian Tradition* (Traditions of Christian Spirituality Series), Maryknoll, NY: Orbis, 2003, p. 139.

70   Noel O'Sullivan, 'Henri de Lubac's "Surnaturel": An Emerging Christology', in *Irish Theological Quarterly* 72 (2007) 3–31, esp. p. 30.

71   The colloquium took place at the Institut Saint-Thomas-d'Aquin in Toulouse. For the proceedings, see the special double edition of *Revue thomiste*, January–June 2001.

72   Bernard Sesboüé, 'Surnaturel et "Surnaturel"', in *Recherches de science religieuse* 90 (2002) 179–86. See also his article 'Le surnaturel chez Henri de Lubac: Un conflit autour d'une théologie', in *Recherches de science religieuse* 80 (1992) 373–408.

73   Bernard Sesboüé describes Yves de Montcheuil as 'un augustinien de coeur', cf. Sesboüé, *Yves de Montcheuil (1900–1944)*, p. 100.

74   Illtyd Trethowan, review [De Lubac, *Surnaturel*], in *The Downside Review* 65 (1947) 70–72, p. 72.

75   Russo, *Henri de Lubac*, pp. 145–68 (entitled: 'Le débat sur la nouvelle théologie'); Wagner, *Henri de Lubac*, 21–24 (entitled: 'Les années silencieuses: L'affaire de la nouvelle théologie'); Voderholzer, *Henri de Lubac begegnen*, pp. 46–61 (entitled: 'Eine "Neue Theologie"?').

76   De Lubac, *Mémoire sur l'occasion de mes écrits*, p. 270 (in a letter to Superior General Jean Baptiste Janssens, 6 March 1946).

77   De Lubac, *Entretien autour de Vatican II*, pp. 12, 93.

78   De Lubac, *Entretien autour de Vatican II*, p. 12.

79   Most important historical research in this regard is done by Étienne Fouilloux: see his article 'Dialogue théologique? (1946–1948)'. An article by myself and K. Schelkens only adds that the information provided by both Fouilloux's overview and de Lubac's *Mémoire* are in line with the documents found in the Archives de la province de Belgique méridionale, as Fouilloux rightly seems to suggest in his 'Itinéraire d'un théologien contrarié (1904–1979)', p. 19, n. 16. Cf. Jürgen Mettepenningen and Karim Schelkens, '"Quod immutabile est, nemo turbet et moveat": Les rapports entre H. de Lubac et le P. Général J.-B. Janssens dans les années 1946–1948: À propos de documents inédits', in *Cristianesimo nella storia* 29 (2008) 139–72. What follows here is a much corrected, reworked and supplemented version of the third and fourth paragraph of the latter article.

80   More information on the Congregation can be found in the *Acta Romana Societatis Iesu* 11 (1946–50) 7–68; for an English translation see J.L. McCarthy, M.D. O'Keefe and J.W. Padberg (eds), *For Matters of Greater Moment: The First Thirty Jesuit General Congregations: A Brief History and A Translation of the Decrees* (Jesuit Primary Sources in English Translations, 12), Saint Louis, MO: Institute of Jesuit Sources, 1994, pp. 620–46.

81   Cf. Janssens' letter to Dhanis, dated 20 September 1946, in the Archives des Jésuites de la Province Belge Méridionale: Corr. 4.

82   On the Louvain Jesuit College at this time, cf. Camille Dumont, 'L'enseignement

théologique au Collège jésuite de Louvain: Louvain 1838 – Bruxelles 1988', in *Nouvelle revue théologique* 111 (1989) 556–76.

83 Cf. de Lubac, *Mémoire sur l'occasion de mes écrits*, p. 253.

84 Cf. de Lubac, *Mémoire sur l'occasion de mes écrits*, pp. 61–62.

85 See, for example, Fouilloux, 'Dialogue théologique? (1946–1948)', pp. 157–60.

86 Marie-Michel Labourdette, 'La théologie et ses sources', in *Revue thomiste* 46 (May–August 1946) 353–71; Garrigou-Lagrange, *La nouvelle théologie où va-t-elle?*. In the first issue of the 1949 edition of *Revue thomiste*, Labourdette had already published an article on theology that appeared to have caused little if any commotion: Marie-Michel Labourdette, 'La théologie, intelligence de la foi', in *Revue thomiste* 46 (1946) 5–44. On Labourdette's Thomism, see Serge-Thomas Bonino, 'Le thomisme du père Labourdette', in *Revue thomiste* 92 (1992) 88–122.

87 See de Lubac, *Mémoire sur l'occasion de mes écrits*, pp. 253–59.

88 De Lubac, *Mémoire sur l'occasion de mes écrits*, p. 253.

89 On 19 September, de Lubac writes in his diary that he received the text of Labourdette's article: see de Lubac, *Mémoire sur l'occasion de mes écrits*, p. 254. As a member of the editorial board of the *Recherches de science religieuse*, however, de Lubac probably had knowledge of the article before 19 September because it had been refused by the *Recherches* and by the *Bulletin de Littérature ecclésiastique* – with de Lubac's friend Bruno de Solages as a member of the editorial board – before it appeared in Labourdette's 'own' *Revue thomiste* (cf. letter from de Lubac to Philip John Donnelly, dated 9 April 1947, in *Bulletin des amis du Cardinal Daniélou*, nr. 22, October 1996, pp. 45–46, p. 46).

90 De Lubac, *Mémoire sur l'occasion de mes écrits*, pp. 61–62.

91 De Lubac, *Mémoire sur l'occasion de mes écrits*, p. 254.

92 De Lubac, *Mémoire sur l'occasion de mes écrits*, p. 254.

93 De Lubac, *Mémoire sur l'occasion de mes écrits*, p. 254.

94 Under Pius XII, the Secretary was second only to the Pope who was himself Prefect of the Congregation. This situation was to change under the papacy of Pope Paul VI.

95 Archives françaises de la Compagnie de Jésus: Letter from de Lubac to Msgr. A. Ottaviani, dated 3 October 1946.

96 H. de Lubac, Extract from daily notes, 4 October 1946, see de Lubac, *Mémoire sur l'occasion de mes écrits*, p. 253.

97 Extract from daily notes, 9 October 1946; 12 October 1946: see de Lubac, *Mémoire sur l'occasion de mes écrits*, pp. 255–56. On 17 October 1946, de Lubac wrote to Blondel to inform him of 'les représentants de ce qu'on appelle "la théologie nouvelle" qui compromettent gravement l'immutabilité du dogme', and to accuse his addressee in one fell swoop. He refers in this regard to the publication of the papal address in *L'Osservatore Romano*. Blondel replied in his own defence on 25 October. Both letters are to be found in the Archives françaises de la Compagnie de Jésus.

98 De Lubac, *Mémoire sur l'occasion de mes écrits*, p. 256.

99 De Lubac, *Mémoire sur l'occasion de mes écrits*, p. 258.

100 Cf. de Lubac, *Mémoire sur l'occasion de mes écrits*, pp. 62–63 (63).

101 Cf. Stanislas Lyonnet's letter addressed to de Lubac, dated 13 December 1946 (to be found in the Archives françaises de la Compagnie de Jésus): 'Le P. Fessard

vous a apporté de nos nouvelles et vous voyez qu'elles ne sont pas mauvaises. Ici on ne parle pas beaucoup de "théologie nouvelle", mais je ne pense pas que ce silence prépare une tempête. Le P. Garrigou devient vraiment complètement "pezzo". Votre réponse certes ne les convaincra pas; mais elle en "convertera" d'autres et vous faites bien de ne pas "laisser tomber" . . .'

102 'La théologie et ses sources: Réponse', in *Recherches de science religieuse* 33 (1946) 385–401. On the completion of the work, see, for example, a letter from Daniélou to de Lubac, dated 27 November 1946, in *Bulletin des amis du Cardinal Daniélou*, nr. 21, November 1995, p. 24: 'Je vous renvoie le texte de notre commune réponse au P. Labourdette. Il me paraît excellent et aborde toutes les questions essentieles. Le seul point que j'aimerais voir développer un peu plus serait la question de notre soi-dissant "subjectivisme".' The text was dated 20 November 1946, i.e. prior to the appearance of Labourdette's article in the *Revue thomiste* and, according to the authors – de Lubac in this instance – two months after they had read the text (two days after Pius XII's public comments on the *nouvelle théologie*). This date, however, is not in line with Daniélou's letter dated 27 November 1946.

103 Cf. letter from Daniélou to de Lubac, dated 5 December 1946, in *Bulletin des amis du Cardinal Daniélou*, nr. 21, November 1995, p. 25.

104 Cf. de Lubac, *Mémoire sur l'occasion de mes écrits*, p. 63.

105 While no specific authors are named in the article, M.-M. Labourdette, M.-J. Nicolas and R.-L. Bruckberger allege that the following Jesuits were responsible for its contents: H. de Lubac, J. Daniélou, H. Bouillard, G. Fessard and H. Urs von Balthasar. Cf. Marie-Michel Labourdette, Marie-Joseph Nicolas and Raymond-Léopold Bruckberger, *Dialogue théologique: Pièces du débat entre "La Revue Thomiste" d'une part et les R.R. P.P. de Lubac, Daniélou, Bouillard, Fessard, von Balthasar, S.J., d'autre part*, Toulouse: Saint-Maximin, 1947. In reality, de Lubac wrote the text and the others offered their personal remarks and approved the final version.

106 Archives françaises de la Compagnie de Jésus: Letter from de Lubac to Dhanis, dated 6 February 1947.

107 De Lubac, *Mémoire sur l'occasion de mes écrits*, p. 270.

108 Cf. letter from Daniélou to de Lubac, dated 4 February 1947, in *Bulletin des amis du Cardinal Daniélou*, nr. 21, November 1995, p. 31.

109 Cf. letter from de Lubac to Daniélou, dated 7 February 1947, in *Bulletin des amis du Cardinal Daniélou*, nr. 21, November 1995, p. 35.

110 Archives françaises de la Compagnie de Jésus: Letter from Dhanis to de Lubac, dated 18 February 1947.

111 Bruno de Solages and Marie-Joseph Nicolas, 'Autour d'une controverse', in *Bulletin de littérature ecclésiastique* 48 (1947) 3–17.

112 Garrigou-Lagrange, 'La nouvelle théologie où va-t-elle?'. Garrigou-Lagrange was furious about this refutation and refused to write any contributions for the *Revue thomiste* until 1949. In a letter to Henri de Lubac, Labourdette (the editor-in-chief at the time) writes that Garrigou's article was refused by the editorial board of the *Revue* (letter from Labourdette to de Lubac, dated 1 March 1947, in the Archives françaises de la Compagnie de Jésus).

113 Archives françaises de la Compagnie de Jésus: Letter from Congar to de Lubac, dated 25 February 1947; Letter from de Solages, dated 26 February 1947.

114 Archives des Jésuites de la Province Belge Méridionale: Letter from Janssens to the Fathers at Fourvière and *Études* [two Jesuit communities, 26 February 1947], published by Marie-Josèphe Rondeau, *Quatre lettres du Père de Lubac au Père d'Ouince 1948–1950*, in *Bulletin des amis du Cardinal Daniélou*, nr. 26–27, 2000–1, pp. 53–96 (62–64).

115 Archives des Jésuites de la Province Belge Méridionale: Letter from Janssens to the Provincials, dated 26 February 1947.

116 Archives des Jésuites de la Province Belge Méridionale: Letter from Janssens to the Fathers at Fourvière and the *Études*, dated 26 February 1947.

117 Published by Marie-Josèphe Rondeau in the *Bulletin des amis du Cardinal Daniélou*, nr. 21, November 1995, pp. 37–38.

118 Henri Rondet, *Problèmes pour la réflexion chrétienne: Le Péché originel; L'Enfer et autres études*, Paris: Spes, 1945, pp. 9–39; Bouillard, *Conversion et grâce chez saint Thomas d'Aquin*; De Lubac, *Surnaturel*; and de Lubac, *De la connaissance de Dieu*, Paris: Cerf, 1941.

119 Cf. de Lubac, *Mémoire sur l'occasion de mes écrits*, pp. 262–67 (we present the reports, however, in a different order for we have taken the versions present in the archives as our source, to be found in the Archives des Jésuites de la Province Belge Méridionale in Brussels).

120 'Haec omnia, sincere, coram Domino et salvo meliori judicio'. See the archives of the Gregorian University, Rome, Fonds Dhanis, Vatican II, 4, in which several *sub secreto* reports are to be found which Dhanis wrote for the Superior General during the Council.

121 Archives des Jésuites de la Province Belge Méridionale: Second report, p. 5.

122 Archives des Jésuites de la Province Belge Méridionale: Third report, p. 1.

123 Archives des Jésuites de la Province Belge Méridionale: Fourth report, p. 3.

124 Cardinal Emmanuel Suhard, 'Essor ou déclin de l'Église', in *La semaine religieuse de Paris*, 15 and 22 March 1947, repr.: *Essor ou déclin de l'Église: Lettre pastorale, Carême de l'an de grâce 1947* (Livre de vie, 32), Paris: Lahure, 1962.

125 Letter from Daniélou to de Lubac, dated 21 May 1947, in *Bulletin des amis du Cardinal Daniélou*, nr. 22, October 1996, pp. 5–6 (6).

126 Bruno de Solages, 'Pour l'honneur de la théologie: Les contre-sens du R. P. Garrigou-Lagrange', in *Bulletin de litérature ecclésiastique* 48 (1947) 65–84, repr. in *Bulletin de Litérature ecclésiastique* 99 (1998) 257–72. The page numbers of the quotations in the following notes refer to the original article. Fifty years later, in 1998, J.-M. Glé and A. Dupleix both published an article on the contribution of de Solages: Jean-Marie Glé, '"Pour l'honneur de la théologie": Bruno de Solages le défenseur de Henri Bouillard', in *Bulletin de litérature ecclésiastique* 99 (1998) 157–65; André Dupleix, '"Pour l'honneur de la théologie": Bruno de Solages le défenseur de Teilhard', in *Bulletin de litérature ecclésiastique* 99 (1998) 167–79. On the contribution of Nicolas, see Étienne Fouilloux, 'Le "dialogue théologique" selon Marie-Joseph Nicolas', in *Bulletin de littérature ecclésiastique* 103 (2002) 19–32.

127 De Solages, 'Pour l'honneur de la théologie', p. 66.

128 Letter from Daniélou to de Lubac, dated 4 April 1947, in *Bulletin des amis du Cardinal Daniélou*, nr. 21, November 1995, pp. 43–44 (44).

129 Mariano Cordovani, 'Verità e novità in Teologia', in *L'Osservatore Romano*, 15–16 March, 1948(!), pp. 1–2.

130 Réginald Garrigou-Lagrange, 'Vérité et immutabilité du dogme', in *Angelicum* 24 (1947) 124–39.

131 On the truth-debate, see Agnès Desmazières, 'La "nouvelle théologie", prémisse d'une théologie herméneutique? La controverse sur l'analogie de la vérité (1946–1949)', in *Revue thomiste* 104 (2004) 241–72.

132 'Correspondance', in *Angelicum* 24 (1947) 210–14 (210–11).

133 Réginald Garrigou-Lagrange, 'Les notions consacrées par les conciles', in *Angelicum* 25 (1948) 217–30.

134 Henri Bouillard, 'Notions conciliaires et analogie de la vérité', in *Recherches de science religieuse* 35 (1948) 251–71.

135 Réginald Garrigou-Lagrange, 'Nécessité de revenir à la definition traditionnelle de la vérité', in *Angelicum* 25 (1948) 145–98.

136 For the text of this 'Déclaration théologique', see *Bulletin des amis du Cardinal Daniélou*, nr. 22, October 1996, pp. 36–41. The text contains seven paragraphs: 'Évolution et histoire', 'Relativisme partiel de la pensée et absolu de la vérité', 'Équivalence possible de notions ou de systèmes', 'Tâche des théologiens', 'Liberté des Écoles et controverse', 'Place et rôle du thomisme', 'Place et rôle d'autres penseurs chrétiens'. Daniélou had received this text on 30 May 1947, cf. his letter to de Lubac, dated 30 May 1947, in *Bulletin des amis du Cardinal Daniélou*, nr. 22, October 1996, pp. 8–9 (8).

137 Labourdette, Nicolas and Bruckberger, *Dialogue théologique*.

138 Labourdette, Nicolas and Bruckberger, *Dialogue théologique*, p. 104.

139 See Part I, Chapter 1, n. 16 in this volume.

140 Secrétariat de l'Épiscopat, *La controverse théologique*, 4 July 1947, p. 1: 'Le débat ne s'étant pas arrêté là [the February publications], le Secrétariat d'Épiscopat pense être utile à NN.SS. les Évêques en leur adressant une nouvelle note composé avec les remarques ou observations faites par les théologiens de la Compagnie de Jésus sur l'article paru dans Angelicum. [. . .] Ces observations rédigées à l'intention du T.R.Père Janssens, préposé général de la Compagnie de Jésus, ne sont point destinées au public.'

141 Archives des Jésuites de la Province Belge Méridionale: Letter from Janssens to the provincials of Lyon and Paris, dated 27 August 1947.

142 Cf. Archives des Jésuites de la Province Belge Méridionale: Fourth report, pp. 3–4.

143 Cf. Archives des Jésuites de la Province Belge Méridionale: First report, p. 3.

144 Marie-Michel Labourdette, 'Fermes propos', in *Revue thomiste* 47 (1947) 5–19.

145 Marie-Michel Labourdette and Marie-Joseph Nicolas, 'L'analogie de la vérité et l'unité de la science théologique', in *Revue thomiste* 47 (1947) 417–66. In the same issue: Marie-Michel Labourdette and Marie-Joseph Nicolas, 'Autour du "Dialogue théologique"', in *Revue thomiste* 47 (1947) 577–85.

146 Jean-Marie Le Blond, 'L'analogie de la vérité: Réflexion d'un philosophe sur une controverse théologique', in *Recherches de science religieuse* 34 (1947) 129–41.

147 Archives françaises de la Compagnie de Jésus: Letter from Janssens to de Lubac, dated 10 November 1947.

148 Charles Boyer, 'Nature pure et surnaturel dans le "Surnaturel" du Père de Lubac', in *Gregorianum* 28 (1947) 379–95.

149 Archives françaises de la Compagnie de Jésus: Letter from de Lubac to Boyer, dated 29 November 1947.

150 De Lubac, *Mémoire sur l'occasion de mes écrits*, p. 64.

151 Letter from de Lubac to Décisier, dated 16 March 1948, in de Lubac, *Mémoire sur l'occasion de mes écrits*, pp. 274–75.

152 Cf. Jacques de Blic, 'Quelques vieux textes sur la notion de l'ordre surnaturel', in *Mélanges de science religieuse* 3 (1946, part 1) 359–62. For de Lubac's respons and de Blic's reply, see 'À propos de la conception médiévale de l'ordre surnaturel', in *Mélanges de science religieuse* 4 (1947) 365–79 [365–73: de Lubac; 373–79: de Blic]. In 1949, de Lubac published an article in which he summarized his vision: Henri de Lubac, 'Le mystère du surnaturel', in *Recherches de science religieuse* 36 (1949) 80–121.

153 Letter from Janssens to Décisier, dated 21 March 1948, in de Lubac, *Mémoire sur l'occasion de mes écrits*, p. 275 (Décisier transmitted de Lubac the 'good' news in a letter, dated 24 March 1948).

154 Archives françaises de la Compagnie de Jésus: Letter from Janssens to Bouillard, dated 17 May 1948. Also published: Bouillard, *Vérité du christianisme*, p. 404; de Lubac, *Mémoire sur l'occasion de mes écrits*, p. 268.

155 Letter from de Lubac to Décisier, dated 25 March 1948, in de Lubac, *Mémoire sur l'occasion de mes écrits*, pp. 275–76.

156 Archives françaises de la Compagnie de Jésus: Letter from de Lubac to Décisier, dated 25 March 1948.

157 Rosaire Gagnebet, 'L'amour naturel de Dieu chez saint Thomas et ses contemporains', in *Revue thomiste* 48 (1948) 394–446; 49 (1949) 31–102.

158 Maurice Corvez, 'De la connaissance de Dieu', in *Revue thomiste* 48 (1948) 511–24; idem, 'Gratia Christi', in *Revue thomiste* 48 (1948) 525–37. The mentioned letter: Letter from de Lubac to Daniélou, dated 2 February 1950, in *Bulletin des amis du Cardinal Daniélou*, nr. 26–27, 2000–1, pp. 35–36 (36).

159 De Lubac, *Mémoire sur l'occasion de mes écrits*, p. 66.

160 See de Lubac, *Mémoire sur l'occasion de mes écrits*, p. 71.

161 Émile Delaye, *Qu'est qu'un catholique? Exposé d'ensemble de la doctrine catholique*, Paris: Spes, 1948.

162 De Lubac, *Mémoire sur l'occasion de mes écrits*, p. 68.

163 See *Acta Romana Societatis Iesu*, Vol. 11, 1946–50, pp. 882–83.

164 Respectively, Henri de Lubac, *Surnaturel*; idem, *De la connaissance de Dieu*, Paris: Témoignage chrétien, 1941, ²1948; idem, *Corpus Mysticum: L'Eucharistie et l'Église au Moyen Âge: Étude historique* (Théologie, 3), Paris: Aubier, 1944, ²1949; Henri Bouillard, *Conversion et grâce chez saint Thomas d'Aquin*; idem, 'Notions conciliaires et analogie de la vérité'; idem, 'L'intention fondamentale de Maurice Blondel et la théologie', in *Recherches de science religieuse* 36 (1949) 321–402; idem, 'L'idée chrétienne du miracle', in *Cahiers Laënnec* 8 (1948), nr. 4, pp. 25–37; Maurice Blondel, *Pages religieuses* (Bibliothèque philosophique), ed. Y. de Montcheuil, Paris: Aubier, 1942; idem, *Leçons sur le Christ*, Paris: Epi, 1949; Jean Daniélou, *Dialogues avec les marxistes, les existentialistes, les protestants, les juifs, l'hindouisme* (Catholique), Paris: Le Portulan, 1948; idem, 'Les orientations présentes dans la pensée religieuse'; Le Blond, 'L'analogie de la vérité: Réflexions d'un philosophe sur une controverse théologique'.

165 Robert Rouquette, 'L'encyclique "Humani generis"', in *Études*, Vol. 83, nr. 267, October 1950, pp. 108–16; René d'Ouince, 'Quelques commentaires de l'encyclique "Humani generis"', in *Études*, Vol. 83, nr. 267, December 1950, pp. 353–73.

166   D'Ouince, 'Quelques commentaires de l'encyclique "Humani generis"', p. 368.
167   Jean-Baptiste Janssens, 'De exsecutione Encyclicae "Humanae generis"', in *Acta Romana Societatis Iesu*, Vol. 12, nr. 1, 1951, pp. 47–72, p. 47.
168   Jean-Baptiste Janssens, 'De exsecutione Encyclicae "Humanae generis"', pp. 62–64.
169   Wagner, *Henri de Lubac*, p. 22.
170   Roger Aubert, *Le problème de l'acte de foi*.
171   Gustave Thils, *Théologie des réalités terrestres*, 2 vols, Bruges: Desclée De Brouwer, 1947–49.

Notes to Part II, Chapter 3: The Phase of the Internationalization of the Nouvelle Théologie.

1   From a memorandum signed by a group of theologians but penned in fact by Rahner himself. See in this regard Bernard Sesboüé, *Karl Rahner* (Initiations aux théologiens), Paris: Cerf, 2001, p. 23.
2   Cf. Heribert Mühlen, 'Gnadenlehre', in H. Vorgrimler and R. Vander Gucht (eds), *Bilanz der Theologie im 20. Jahrhundert: Perspektiven, Strömungen, Motive in der christlichen und nichtchristlichen Welt*, Vol. 3, Freiburg/Basel/Vienna: Herder, 1970, pp. 148–92, esp. p. 169.
3   Karl Lehmann, 'Karl Rahner', in H. Vorgrimler and R. Vander Gucht (eds), *Bilanz der Theologie im 20. Jahrhundert: Bahnbrechende Theologen*, Freiburg/Basel/ Vienna: Herder, 1970, pp. 143–81 (150).
4   On K. Steur, see Jan Y.H.A. Jacobs, 'Dr. Klaas Steur (1905–1985): Geloofsdenker in dienst van verkondiging en toerusting', in *Trajecta* 6 (1997) 53–73. On the education at the seminary of Warmond, see Lodewijk Winkeler, 'Het onderwijs op Warmond, 1799–1967', in *Trajecta* 9 (2000) 134–63.
5   Karl Rahner, *Maria, Mutter des Herrn: Mariologische Studien* (Sämtliche Werke, 9), Freiburg/Basel/Vienna, 2004.
6   On both theologians, see in this regard Karl-Heinz Neufeld, 'Le paysage théologique des années 1930–1960 et deux itinéraires', in H.-J. Gagey and V. Holzer (eds), *Balthasar, Rahner: Deux pensées en contraste* (Theologia, 218), Paris: Bayard, 2005, pp. 31–46; Bernard Sesboüé, 'La genèse d'une œuvre ou comment sortir de la "néoscolastique"?', in H.-J. Gagey and V. Holzer (eds), *Balthasar, Rahner*, pp. 47–67. On Balthasar, see Rudolf Voderholzer, 'Die Bedeutung der sogenannten 'Nouvelle Théologie' (insbesondere Henri de Lubacs) für die Theologie Hans Urs von Balthasars', in W. Kasper (ed.), *Logik der Liebe und Herrlichkeit Gottes:Hans Urs von Balthasar im Gespräch*, Ostfildern: Matthias-Grünewald, 2006, pp. 204–28.
7   On Schillebeeckx, see Edward Schillebeeckx, *Theologisch testament: Notarieel nog niet verleden*, Baarn: Nelissen, 1994; idem, *I Am a Happy Theologian*, London: SCM, 1994; Huub Oosterhuis and Piet Hoogeveen, *God is ieder ogenblik nieuw: Gesprekken met Edward Schillebeeckx*, Baarn: Ambo, 1982; Erik Borgman, *Edward Schillebeeckx: Een theoloog in zijn geschiedenis*, Vol. 1: *Een katholieke cultuurtheologie (1914–1965)*, Baarn: Nelissen, 1999 (published in English as: *Edward Schillebeeckx: A Theologian in His History*, Vol. 1: *A Catholic Theology of Culture (1914–1965)*, London/New York: Continuum, 2003); Ambroos Remi

Van de Walle, 'Theologie over de werkelijkheid: Een betekenis van het werk van Edward Schillebeeckx', in *Tijdschrift voor Theologie* 14 (1974) 463–90; John Bowden, *Edward Schillebeeckx: Portrait of a Theologian*, London: SCM, 1983; Edward Schillebeeckx, *The Schillebeeckx Reader*, ed. by Robert Schreiter, New York: Crossroad, 1984; Fergus Kerr, *Twentieth-Century Catholic Theologians*, pp. 52–66; Francis Schüssler Fiorenza, *The New Theology and Transcendental Thomism*, pp. 197–232, esp. pp. 221–27.

8   Schillebeeckx acquired the degree of Lector in Theology with a thesis entitled 'De zondige voor-geschiedenis van het christendom volgens Sint-Paulus' (unpublished lector's thesis, Louvain, 1941–1942).

9   Edward Schillebeeckx, *De sacramentele heilseconomie*, Antwerp: 't Groeit, 1952.

10   Edward Schillebeeckx, *Jezus, het verhaal van een levende*, Bloemendaal: Nelissen, 1974; *Gerechtigheid en Liefde: Genade en Bevrijding*, Bloemendaal: Nelissen, 1977; *Mensen als verhaal van God*, Baarn: Nelissen, 1989.

11   Edward Schillebeeckx, *Openbaring en theologie* (Theologische Peilingen, 1), Bilthoven: Nelissen, 1964.

12   Edward Schillebeeckx, *Pleidooi voor mensen in de kerk: Christelijke identiteit en ambten in de kerk*, Baarn: Nelissen, 1985.

13   Ted Schoof, *De zaak Schillebeeckx: Officiële stukken*, Bloemendaal: Nelissen, 1980.

14   John Bowden, *Edward Schillebeeckx*, p. 28.

15   Schillebeeckx, *Theologisch testament*, p. 25.

16   See n. 7 above.

17   Cf. Borgman, *Edward Schillebeeckx: A Theologian in His History*, pp. 41–51; Van de Walle, *Theologie over de werkelijkheid*, pp. 470–71.

18   Unpublished address, to be found in the Archief Edward Schillebeeckx, nr. 358 (see Borgman, *Edward Schillebeeckx: A Theologian in His History*, pp. 61–67).

19   Georg Koepgen, *Die Gnosis des Christentums*, Salzburg: Müller, 1939, ²1940, ³(Occidens, 4), Trier: Spee, 1978.

20   Borgman, *Edward Schillebeeckx: A Theologian in His History*, p. 65.

21   Borgman, *Edward Schillebeeckx: A Theologian in His History*, p. 64.

22   See also Edward Schillebeeckx, 'In memoriam M.-D. Chenu (1895–1990)', in *Tijdschrift voor Theologie* 30 (1990) 184–85.

23   Edward Schillebeeckx, *Theologisch testament*, p. 28.

24   Yves Congar, *Journal d'un théologien 1946–1956*, p. 58. We base this presupposition on what Schillebeeckx says about Chenu in the two preceding notes.

25   Marie-Joseph Congar, 'Théologie' (see Part I, Chapter 1, n. 11).

26   Edward Schillebeeckx, 'In memoriam Yves Congar, 1904–1995', in *Tijdschrift voor Theologie* 35 (1995) 271–73.

27   Kerr, *Twentieth-Century Catholic Theologians*, p. 52.

28   Robert Schreiter, 'Edward Schillebeeckx: An Orientation to His Thought', in Schillebeeckx, *The Schillebeeckx Reader*, pp. 1–24 (2).

29   Cf. Schüssler Fiorenza, 'The New Theology and Transcendental Thomism', p. 222.

30   Schillebeeckx, *De sacramentele heilseconomie*, p. v.

31   Schillebeeckx, *Concept of Truth and Theological Renewal*, New York: Sheed and Ward, 1968, pp. 79–105).

32   Edward Schillebeeckx, *Het waarheidsbegrip en aanverwante problemen*, in

Katholiek Archief 17 (1962) 1169–1180. Published in English as: *Concept of Truth and Theological Renewal*, New York: Sheed and Ward, 1968, pp. 5–29.

33 Schillebeeckx, *Concept of Truth and Theological Renewal*, p. 29.

34 Henricus Schillebeeckx, 'Dogma-ontwikkeling: A. Historisch overzicht van het vraagstuk, B. Perspectieven op een synthese', in *Theologisch Woordenboek*, 3 vols, Roermond/Maaseik: Romen and Zonen, 1952–58, c. 1087–106; idem, 'Theologie', c. 4485–542; 'Geschiedenis', c. 1838–40; '"Humani generis"', c. 2300–2.

35 Henricus Schillebeeckx, 'Nouvelle théologie', in *Theologisch Woordenboek*, c. 3519–520.

36 Cf. Schillebeeckx, 'Theologie', esp. c. 4498–500.

37 Cf. Schillebeeckx, 'Theologie', c. 4539.

38 Schillebeeckx, 'Theologie', c. 4537.

39 Schillebeeckx, 'Theologie', c. 4539–40.

40 On the said appointment, see Willem K. Grossouw, *Alles is van u: Gewijde en profane herinneringen*, Baarn: Ambo, 1981, pp. 285–86; Schillebeeckx, *Theologisch testament*, pp. 33–34; Borgman, *Edward Schillebeeckx: A Theologian in His History*, pp. 285–89.

41 Edward Schillebeeckx, 'Op zoek naar de levende God', in Edward Schillebeeckx, *God en mens* (Theologische Peilingen, 2), Bilthoven: Nelissen, 1965.

42 See the Wikipedia article on Edward Schillebeeckx at http://nl.wikipedia.org/wiki/Edward_Schillebeeckx (accessed on 23 January 2007) (in Dutch).

43 Andreas H. Maltha, *De Nieuwe Theologie: Informatie en Oriëntatie*, Bruges: Desclée de Brouwer, 1958.

44 Edward Schillebeeckx, '"Nieuwe theologie"?', in *Kultuurleven* 26 (1959) 122–25.

45 Schillebeeckx, '"Nieuwe theologie"?', p. 124.

46 Cf. Ton H.M. van Schaik, *Alfrink: Een biografie*, Amsterdam: Anthos, 1997.

47 See also Jürgen Mettepenningen, 'Edward Schillebeeckx: Herodero y promotor de la "nouvelle théologie"', in *Mayeuticá* 78 (2008) 285–302.

48 On Schoonenberg, see Jürgen Mettepenningen, 'Schoonenberg', in *Biographisch-Bibliographisches Kirchenlexikon* 30 (2009) 1297–300; Herwi W.M. Rikhof, 'Schoonenberg, Piet', in *Christelijke Encyclopedie*, ed. G. Harinck, 3 vols, Kampen: Kok, 2005, pp. 1612–13; Herwi Rikhof, 'Uit oud en nieuw de schatten: P. Schoonenberg', in J. Beumer (ed.), *Zo de ouden zongen . . . Leraar en leerling zijn in de theologie-beoefening (tussen 1945 en 2000)*, Baarn: Ten Have, 1996, pp. 199–220; Anton Houtepen, *Theologen op zoek naar God: Twintig portretten van katholieke theologen uit de tweede helft van de 20ste eeuw*, Zoetermeer: Meinema, 2001, pp. 74–82; Wilhelm Zauner, 'Schoonenberg, Piet', in *Lexikon für Theologie und Kirche* 9 (2000, 2006) 214.

49 *De Nieuwe Katechismus: Geloofsverkondiging voor volwassenen*, Hilversum/Antwerp: Paul Brand, 1966.

50 Piet Schoonenberg, *Het geloof van ons doopsel: Gesprekken over de Apostolische Geloofsbelijdenis*, Vol. 1: *God, Vader en Schepper: Het eerste geloofsartikel*, 's-Hertogenbosch: L.C.G. Malmberg, 1955; Vol. 2: *Jezus, de Christus, de Zoon Gods: Het tweede geloofsartikel*, 's-Hertogenbosch: L.C.G. Malmberg, 1956; Vol. 3: *De Mensgeworden Zoon van God: Het derde geloofsartikel*, 's-Hertogenbosch: L.C.G. Malmberg, 1958; Vol. 4: *De macht der zonde: Inleiding*

op de verlossingsleer, 's-Hertogenbosch: L.C.G. Malmberg, 1962.

51   Piet Schoonenberg, *Gods wordende wereld: Vijf theologische essays* (Woord en Beleving, 13), Tielt/The Hague: Lannoo, 1962.

52   Piet Schoonenberg, 'Der Mensch in der Sünde', in J. Feiner and M. Löhrer (eds), *Mysterium Salutis: Grundriß heilsgeschichtlicher Dogmatik*, Vol. 2: *Die Heilsgeschichte vor Christus*, Einsiedeln/Zurich/Cologne: Benziger, 1967, pp. 845–941.

53   Piet Schoonenberg, *Hij is een God van mensen: Twee theologische studies*, 's-Hertogenbosch: L.C.G. Malmberg, 1969.

54   Piet Schoonenberg, *De Geest, het Woord en de Zoon: Theologische overdenkingen over Geest-christologie, Logos-christologie en drieëenheidsleer*, Averbode: Altiora; Kampen: Kok, 1991.

55   Piet Schoonenberg, *Theologie als geloofsvertolking: Het proefschrift van 1948* (Documenta Libraria, 36), ed. by L. Kenis and J. Mettepenningen, Louvain: Maurits Sabbebibliotheek/Faculteit Godgeleerdheid/Peeters, 2008. The following presentation of the dissertation is a revised and English version of Leo Kenis and Jürgen Mettepenningen, 'Inleiding', in Schoonenberg, *Theologie als geloofsvertolking*, pp. 7*–22*.

56   Cf. Leo Bakker, 'Schoonenberg's theologie: Spiegel van onze eigen ontwikkeling?', in *Tijdschrift voor Theologie* 11 (1971) 353–82 (355).

57   Piet Schoonenberg, 'Wijsbegeerte en theologie als zijns-wetenschappen', unpublished lector's thesis, Canisianum Maastricht, 1940, 43 p., in Archief Piet Schoonenberg, III, 1.

58   See Schoonenberg's testimony in 'Roeping, vrijheid en onvrijheid van de theoloog', in *Bijdragen* 43 (1982) 2–29 (3).

59   See Jürgen Mettepenningen, 'Naar theologie als geloofsvertolking: Piet Schoonenbergs proefschrift (1948/1951) als theologische zelfreflectie op het kantelmoment tussen modernisme en Vaticanum II', unpublished doctoral dissertation, K.U.Leuven, Louvain, 2008, pp. 282–84.

60   *Altera patris nostri adhortatio ad PP. Provinciarum Procuratores*, 30 September 1950, in *Acta Romana Societatis Iesu* 11 (1946–50) 865–77.

61   Schoonenberg, *Theologie als geloofsvertolking*, p. 34.

62   Cf. Gardeil's book *Le donné révélé et la théologie*.

63   Piet Schoonenberg, 'Een Theoloog van Christus' Mystiek Lichaam: Emile Mersch S.J. en zijn laatste boek', in *Katholiek Cultureel Tijdschrift* 2 (1946, 1) 93–96 (93).

64   Émile Mersch, *La théologie du Corps mystique* (Musseum Lessianum: Section théologique, 38–39), 2 vols, Paris: Desclée de Brouwer, 1944, ⁴1954.

65   Schoonenberg, *Theologie als geloofsvertolking*, p. 246.

66   Cf. Piet Schoonenberg, 'Theologie in zelfbezinning', in *Annalen van het Thijmgenootschap* 44 (1956) 225–36.

67   Schoonenberg, *Theologie als geloofsvertolking*, p. 243.

68   Schoonenberg, *Theologie als geloofsvertolking*, p. 251.

69   Schoonenberg, *Theologie als geloofsvertolking*, p. 276.

70   Schoonenberg, *Theologie als geloofsvertolking*, p. 286.

71   Schoonenberg, *Theologie als geloofsvertolking*, p. 287.

72   Schoonenberg, *Covenant and Creation*, p. xiv.

73   Schoonenberg, *God's World in the Making*, p. 1.

74 Pierre Teilhard de Chardin, *Le phénomène humain* (Œuvres de Pierre Teilhard de Chardin, 1), Paris: Seuil, 1955; idem, *Le milieu divin: Essai de vie intérieure*, Paris: Seuil, 1957.
75 Schoonenberg, *Theologie als geloofsvertolking*, p. viii.
76 Cf. Schoonenberg, *Het geloof van ons doopsel: Gesprekken over de Apostolische Geloofsbelijdenis*, Vol. 3: *De Mensgeworden Zoon van God*, p. 108. Schoonenberg refers in a footnote to Karl Rahner, 'Chalkedon: Ende oder Anfang?', in A. Grillmeyer and H. Bacht (eds), *Das Konzil von Chalkedon: Geschichte und Gegenwart*, Vol. 3: *Chalkedon heute*, Wurzburg: Echter Verlag, 1954, pp. 3–49.
77 Schoonenberg, *Het geloof van ons doopsel: Gesprekken over de Apostolische Geloofsbelijdenis*, Vol. 3: *De Mensgeworden Zoon van God*, p. 131.
78 See n. 62 above.
79 Schoonenberg, *Gods wordende wereld*, pp. 61–99. This is a detailed redraft of 'De menswording', in *Verbum* 27 (1960) 453–66.
80 Schoonenberg, *God's World in the Making*, p. 99.
81 Cf. Schoonenberg, *Het geloof van ons doopsel: Gesprekken over de Apostolische Geloofsbelijdenis*, Vol. 3: *De Mensgeworden Zoon van God*, p. 139.
82 Quoted by George Harinck and Lodewijk Winkeler, 'De Twintigste Eeuw', in Herman J. Selderhuis (ed.), *Handboek Nederlandse Kerkgeschiedenis*, Kampen: Kok, 2006, pp. 723–912 (838).
83 Cf. Robrecht Michiels, 'Het nieuwe christologische dossier', in *Collationes* 6 (1976) 480–512, esp. p. 485, n. 6.

Notes to Part III: Closing Considerations

1 Jean Daniélou, 'Catholicisme au XXe siècle', unpublished text in Archives français de la Compagnie de Jésus, H Dan 51/27, 73 pp., p. 2: 'Ce qui marque le christianisme du XXe siècle, ce qui est à la source de ce qu'il a suscité et de ce qu'il suscite valable, ce n'est pas d'abord les changements de structure ou les courants théologiques. Ceux-ci ne sont que des conséquences. C'est d'abord une certaine expérience spirituelle. Et cette expérience spirituelle est celle d'un retour à l'Évangile. Et c'est dans le cœur des saints qu'elle est apparue. Ce qui marque le christianisme du XXe siècle, c'est la soif d'un retour aux sources, d'un retour à l'Évangile, d'un renouveau évangélique'; Bernard Sesboüé, *La théologie au XXe siècle et l'avenir de la foi: Entretiens avec Marc Leboucher*, Paris: Desclée de Brouwer, 2007, p. 11: 'L'originalité du XXe siècle, en cela héritier des questions redoutable posées lors de la "crise moderniste" du tout début de ce siècle, a été d'opérer un retour magistral aux "Sources chrétiennes", comme le dit symboliquement le titre d'une fameuse collection.'
2 Hans Boersma, *'Nouvelle Théologie' and Sacramental Ontology: A Return to Mystery*, Oxford/New York: Oxford University Press, 2009.
3 In this regard, Pope John Paul II was right to state the following in 1998: 'The most influential Catholic theologians of the present century, to whose thinking and research the Second Vatican Council is much indebted, were products of this revival of Thomistic philosophy.' Cf. the English translation of *Fides et ratio*, encyclical of Pope John Paul II, 14 September 1998, in *Acta Apostolicae Sedis* 91 (1999) 5–88, p. 51 (nr. 58). Online: http://www.vatican.va

BIBLIOGRAPHY

Ecclesiastical Documents *[in chronological order]*

Mirari Vos, encyclical of Pope Gregory XVI, 15 August 1832, in *Acta Sanctae Sedis* 4 (1868) 336–45.

Quanta Cura, encyclical of Pope Pius IX, 8 December 1864, in *Acta Sanctae Sedis* 3 (1867) 160–67.

Syllabus complectens praecipuos nostrae aetatis errores qui notantur in encyclicis aliisque apostolicis litteris Sanctissimi Domini nostri Pii Papae IX, in *Acta Sanctae Sedis* 3 (1867) 168–76.

Dei Filius, dogmatic constitution of Vatican I, 24 April 1870, in *Acta Sanctae Sedis* 5 (1869) 460–68.

Pastor Aeternus, dogmatic constitution of Vatican I, 18 July 1870, in *Acta Sanctae Sedis* 6 (1870–71) 40–47.

Aeterni Patris, encyclical of Pope Leo XIII, 4 August 1879, in *Acta Sanctae Sedis* 12 (1879) 97–115.

Providentissimus Deus, encyclical of Pope Leo XIII, 18 November 1893, in *Acta Sanctae Sedis* 26 (1893–94) 269–92.

Testem benevolentiae, letter of Pope Leo XIII to Cardinal James Gibbons, archbishop of Baltimore, 22 January 1899, in *Acta Sanctae Sedis* 31 (1898–99) 470–79.

Vigilantiae studiique, apostolic letter of Pope Leo XIII, 30 October 1902, in *Acta Sanctae Sedis* 35 (1902–3) 234–38.

Lamentabili sane exitu, decree of Pope Pius X, 7 July 1907, in *Acta Sanctae Sedis* 40 (1907) 470–78.

Pascendi dominici gregis, encyclical of Pope Pius X, 7 September 1907, in *Acta Sanctae Sedis* 40 (1907) 593–650.

Praestantia Scripturae, motu proprio of Pope Pius X, 18 November 1907, in *Acta Sanctae Sedis* 40 (1907) 723–26.

Sacrorum antistitum, motu proprio of Pope Pius X, 1 September 1910, in *Acta Apostolicae Sedis* 2 (1910) 669–72.

Doctoris Angelici, motu proprio of Pope Pius X, 29 June 1914, in *Acta Apostolicae Sedis* 6 (1914) 336–41.

Spiritus Paraclitus, encyclical of Pope Benedict XV, 15 September 1920, in *Acta Apostolicae Sedis* 12 (1920) 385–422.

Studiorum Ducem, encyclical of Pope Pius XI, 29 June 1923, in *Acta Apostolicae Sedis* 15 (1923) 309–26.

Casti connubii, encyclical of Pope Pius XI, 31 December 1930, in *Acta Apostolicae Sedis* 22 (1930) 539–92.

Quadragesimo anno, encyclical of Pope Pius XI, 15 May 1931, in *Acta Apostolicae Sedis* 23 (1931) 177–228.

Deus scientiarum Dominus, apostolic constitution of Pius XI, 24 May 1931, in
      Acta Apostolicae Sedis 23 (1931) 241–62.
Non abbiamo bisogno, encyclical of Pius XI, 29 June 1931, in *Acta Apostolicae
      Sedis* 23 (1931) 285–312.
Mit brennender Sorge, encyclical of Pius XI, 14 March 1937, in *Acta Apostolicae
      Sedis* 29 (1937) 145–67.
Mystici corporis Christi, encyclical of Pope Pius XII, 29 June 1943, in *Acta
      Apostolicae Sedis* 35 (1943) 200–43.
Divino afflante Spiritu, encyclical of Pope Pius XII, 30 September 1943, in *Acta
      Apostolicae Sedis* 35 (1943) 297–325.
*Il venerato Discorso del Sommo Pontifice alla XXIX Congregazione Generale
      della Compagnia di Gesù*, in *L'Osservatore Romano*, 19 September 1946, p. 1
      (= *Acta Apostolicae Sedis* 38 [1946] 381–85, esp. p. 385).
*Fervido Discorso del Sommo Pontifice ai Capitolari dell'Ordine dei Frati
      Predicatori*, in *L'Osservatore Romano*, 23–24 September 1946, p. 1 (= *Acta
      Apostolicae Sedis* 38 [1946] 385–89).
Mediator Dei et hominum, encyclical of Pope Pius XII, 20 November 1947, in
      Acta Apostolicae Sedis 39 (1947) 521–95.
*Une récente et importante controverse théologique: À propos des Collections
      'Sources chrétiennes' et 'Théologie'*, in Secrétariat de l'Épiscopat, Note
      17/47, 26 March 1947, pp. 1–6.
*La controverse théologique relative aux Collections 'Sources chrétiennes' et
      'Théologie'*, in Secrétariat de l'Épiscopat, Note 32/47, 4 July 1947, pp. 1–8;
      Note 33/47, 17 July 1947, pp. 1–6.
Humani generis, encyclical of Pope Pius XII, 12 August 1950, in *Acta
      Apostolicae Sedis* 42 (1950) 561–78.
Lumen Gentium, dogmatic constitution of Vatican II, in *Acta Apostolicae Sedis*
      57 (1965) 5–71.
Dei Verbum, dogmatic constitution of Vatican II, 18 November 1965, in *Acta
      Apostolicae Sedis* 58 (1966) 817–35.
Gaudium et Spes, pastoral constitution of Vatican II, 7 December 1965, in *Acta
      Apostolicae Sedis* 58 (1966) 1025–120.
Fides et ratio, encyclical of Pope John Paul II, 14 September 1998, in *Acta
      Apostolicae Sedis* 91 (1999) 5–88.

Archives

Archives de la province dominicaine de France, Paris.
Archive of the Flemish Dominican Province, Louvain.
Archive of the Archdiocese of Mechelen-Brussels, Mechelen.
Archives de l'Université catholique de Louvain-la-Neuve, Louvain-la-
      Neuve.
Archives des Jésuites de la Province Belge Méridionale, Brussels.
Archives françaises de la Compagnie de Jésus, Vanves.
Archive of Piet Schoonenberg, Louvain.
Archive of t the Katholieke Documentatiecentrum (KDC), Nijmegen.
Archive of the Dutch Jesuits, Nijmegen.

Books [monographs and volumes]

Abbas Isaias, *Les cinq recensions de l'Ascéticon syriaque d'Abba-Isaïe*
(Corpus scriptorium christianorum Orientalium, 289, 290, 293 and 294;
Corpus scriptorium christianorum Orientalium. Scriptores Syri, 120, 121,
122 and 123), 4 vols, Louvain: Corpus scriptorium christianorum
Orientalium, 1968.

Alberigo, Giuseppe, *et al.*, *Une école de théologie: le Saulchoir* (Théologies),
Paris: Cerf, 1985.

Alberigo, Giuseppe and Joseph A. Komonchak (eds), *History of Vatican II*,
5 vols, Louvain: Peeters; Maryknoll: Orbis, 1995–2006.

Allen, John, *Cardinal Ratzinger: The Vatican's Enforcer of the Faith*, London/
New York: Continuum, 2000 (= *Pope Benedict XVI: A Biography of Joseph
Ratzinger*, London/New York: Continuum, 2005).

Athanasius of Alexandria, *La vie primitive de S. Antoine conservée en syriaque*
(Corpus scriptorium christianorum Orientalium, 417–18; Corpus scriptorium
christianorum Orientalium. Scriptores Syri, 183–84), 2 vols, Louvain: Corpus
scriptorium christianorum Orientalium, 1980.

Aubert, Roger, *Le pontificat de Pie IX (1846–1878)* (Histoire de l'Église depuis
les origines à nos jours, 21), Paris: Bloud & Gay, 1952.

—— *Le problème de l'acte de foi: Données traditionnelles et résultats des
controverses récentes* (Universitas Catholica Lovaniensis – Dissertationes
ad gradum magistri in Facultate Theologica vel in Facultate Iuris Canonici
consequendum conscriptae, II/36), Louvain/Paris: Warny, 1945, ⁴1969.

—— *La théologie catholique au milieu du XXe siècle* (Cahiers de l'actualité
religieuse, 3), Tournai: Casterman, 1954.

Auricchio, John, *The Future of Theology*, Staten Island, NY: St. Paul, 1970.

Bendel-Maidl, Linda, *Tradition und Innovation: Zur Dialektik von historischer
und systematischer Perspektive in der Theologie: Am Beispiel von
Transformationen in der Rezeption des Thomas von Aquin im 20. Jahrhundert*
(Religion – Geschichte – Gesellschaft. Fundamentaltheologische Studien, 27),
Münster: LIT, 2004.

Beretta, Francesco, *Monseigneur d'Hulst et la science chrétienne: Portrait
d'un intellectuel* (Textes, dossiers, documents, 16), Paris: Beauchesne,
1996.

Berger, David, *Thomismus: Grosse Leitmotive der thomistischen Synthese und
ihre Aktualität für die Gegenwart*, Cologne: Editiones thomisticae, 2001.

Blondel, Maurice, *L'Action: Essai d'une critique de vie et d'une science de
pratique* (Bibliothèque de philosophie contemporaine), Paris: Alcan, 1893;
repr.: ibid. (Quadrige, 170), Paris: Presses Universitaires de France, 1993.

—— *Pages religieuses* (Bibliothèque philosophique), ed. Y. de Montcheuil,
Paris: Aubier, 1942.

Boersma, Hans, *'Nouvelle Théologie' and Sacramental Ontology: A Return to
Mystery*, Oxford/New York: Oxford University Press, 2009.

Boeve, Lieven, *God onderbreekt de geschiedenis: Theologie in tijden van
ommekeer* (Mens en Tijd), Kapellen: Pelckmans, 2006. Published in English
as *God Interrupts History: Theology in a Time of Upheaval*, New York/
London: Continuum, 2007.

Bonnefoy, Jean-François, *Chronique de l'Annonciade: Vies de la Bienheureuse Jeanne de France et du Bienheureux Gabriel-Maria*, Villeneuve-sur-Lot: Monastère de l'Annonciade, 1937, [2]1950.

—— *La nature de la théologie selon saint Thomas d'Aquin*, Paris: Vrin, 1939.

—— *Le Saint-Esprit et ses dons selon Saint Bonaventure* (Étude de philosophie médiévale, 10), Paris: Vrin, 1929.

—— *Une somme bonaventurienne: Le De triplice via*, Paris: Vrin, 1934.

Borgman, Erik, *Edward Schillebeeckx: Een theoloog in zijn geschiedenis*, Vol. 1: *Een katholieke cultuurtheologie (1914–1965)*, Baarn: Nelissen, 1999. Published in English as *Edward Schillebeeckx: A Theologian in His History, Vol. 1: A Catholic Theology of Culture (1914–1965)*, London/New York: Continuum, 2003.

Boudignon, Patrice, *Pierre Teilhard de Chardin: Sa vie, son œuvre, sa réflexion* (Cerf Histoire), Paris: Cerf, 2008.

Bouillard, Henri, *Blondel et le christianisme*, Paris: Seuil, 1961. Published in English as *Blondel and Christianity*, Washington, DC: Corpus, 1969.

—— *Comprendre ce que l'on croit* (Intelligence de la foi), Paris: Aubier, 1971.

—— *Connaissance de Dieu: Foi chrétienne et théologie naturelle* (Foi vivante, 45), Paris: Aubier Montaigne, 1967. Published in English as *The Knowledge of God*, New York: Herder & Herder, 1968.

—— *Conversion et grâce chez saint Thomas d'Aquin: Étude historique* (Théologie, 1), Paris: Aubier, 1944.

—— *Karl Barth* (Théologie, 38–39), Paris: Aubier, 1957.

—— *Logique de la foi* (Théologie, 60), Paris: Aubier, 1964. Published in English as *The Logic of the Faith*, New York: Sheed and Ward, 1967.

—— *Vérité du christianisme* (Théologie), Paris: Desclée De Brouwer, 1989.

Bouyer, Louis, *La décomposition du catholicisme* (Présence et pensée, 13), Paris: Aubier Montaigne, 1968.

Bowden, John, *Edward Schillebeeckx: Portrait of a Theologian*, London: SCM, 1983.

Bremond, Henri, *Histoire littéraire du sentiment religieux en France depuis la fin des guerres de religion jusqu'à nos jours*, 12 vols, Paris: Bloud & Gay, 1916–33.

Campbell, John R., *The New Theology*, London: Chapman & Hall, 1907.

Catalogus generalis Ordinis Praedicatorum: Conspectus generalis Ordinis Fratrum Praedicatorum necnon index monasteriorum, congregationum et fraternitatum, Rome: Curia generalitia, 1992.

Cerfaux, Lucien, *La théologie de l'Église suivant saint Paul* (Unam Sanctam, 10), Paris: Cerf, 1942.

Chantraine, Georges, *Henri de Lubac*, Vol. 1: *De la naissance à la demobilisation (1896–1919)* (Études Lubaciennes, 6), Paris: Cerf, 2007.

—— *Henri de Lubac*, Vol. 2: *Les années de formation (1919–1929)* (Études Lubaciennes, 7), Paris: Cerf, 2009.

Charlier, Louis, *Essai sur le problème théologique* (Bibliothèque Orientations. Section scientifique, 1), Thuillies: Ramgal, 1938.

Chenu, Marie-Dominique, *Introduction à l'étude de saint Thomas d'Aquin* (Publications de l'Institut d'études médiévales, 11), Montréal: Université de Montréal ; Paris: Institut d'études médiévales, 1950, [2]1954, [3]1974.

—— *La théologie au XIIe siècle* (Études de philosophie médiévale, 45), Paris: Vrin, 1957, ²1966, ³1976.

—— *La théologie comme science au XIIIe siècle*, 1927, ²1943, ³(Bibliothèque thomiste, 33), Paris: Vrin, 1957; ⁴1969.

—— *Spiritualité du travail* (Études religieuses, 604–5), Liège: La pensée catholique, 1947.

—— *Une école de théologie: Le Saulchoir*, Kain: *pro manuscripto*, 1937.

Colin, Pierre, *L'audace et le soupçon: La crise du modernisme dans le catholicisme français 1893–1914* (Anthropologiques), Paris: Desclée de Brouwer, 1997.

Comblin, Joseph, *Vers une théologie de l'action* (Études religieuses, 767), Brussels: La pensée catholique, 1964.

Commentaire anonyme du livre d'Abba Isaïe (fragments) (Corpus scriptorium christianorum Orientalium, 336–37; Corpus scriptorium christianorum Orientalium. Scriptores Syri, 150–51), 2 vols, Louvain: Corpus scriptorium christianorum Orientalium, 1973.

Congar, Yves-Marie-Joseph, *Chrétiens désunis: Principes d'un œcuménisme catholique* (Unam Sanctam, 1), Paris: Cerf, 1937. Published in English as *Divided Christendom: A Catholic Study of the Problem of Reunion*, London: Bles, 1939.

—— *La Tradition et les traditions* (Le signe), 2 vols, Paris: Fayard, 1960–63. Published in English as *Tradition and Traditions : An Historical and a Theological Essay*, London: Burns & Oates, 1966.

—— *Jalons pour une théologie du laïcat* (Unam Sanctam, 23), Paris: Cerf, 1953. ³1964. Published in English as *Lay People in the Church: A Study for a Theology of Laity*, Westminster: Newman, 1967.

—— *Situation et tâches présentes de la théologie* (Cogitatio fidei, 27), Paris: Cerf, 1967.

—— *A History of Theology*, Garden City, NY: Doubleday, 1968.

—— *Vraie et fausse réforme dans l'Église* (Unam Sanctam, 20; Essais sur la communion catholique, 4), Paris: Cerf, 1950, ²(Unam Sanctam, 72), Paris: Cerf 1968.

—— *Une passion: L'unité: Réflexions et souvenirs: 1929–1973* (Foi vivante, 156), Paris: Cerf, 1974.

—— *Entretiens d'automne* (Théologies), Paris: Cerf, 1987.

—— *Journal de la guerre 1914–1918*, ed. S. Audoin-Rouzeau and D. Congar, Paris: Cerf, 1997.

—— *Journal d'un théologien 1946–1956*, ed. É. Fouilloux, Paris: Cerf, 2001.

—— *Mon Journal du Concile*, ed. É. Mahieu, 2 vols, Paris: Cerf, 2002.

Connolly, James M., *The Voices of France: A Survey of Contemporary Theology in France*, New York: MacMillan, 1961.

Copleston, Frederick C., *A History of Philosophy*, Vol. 9: *Modern Philosophy: From the French Revolution to Sartre, Camus, and Lévi-Strauss*, New York/London/Toronto/Sydney/Auckland: Doubleday, 1974, ⁴(A History of Philosophy, 9), London: Continuum, 2003.

Coreth, Emerich, Walter M. Neidl and Georg Pfligersdorffer (eds), *Christliche Philosophie im katholischen Denken des 19. und 20. Jahrhunderts*, 3 vols, Graz/Vienna/Cologne: Styria, 1987–90.

Crews, Clyde F., *English Catholic Modernism: Maude Petre's Way of Faith*, Notre Dame, IN: University of Notre Dame Press, 1984.

Daniélou, Jean, *Carnets spirituels* (Intimité du christianisme), ed. M.-J. Rondeau, Paris: Cerf, 1993, ²2007.

—— *Dialogues avec les marxistes, les existentialistes, les protestants, les juifs, l'hindouisme* (Catholique), Paris: Le Portulan, 1948.

—— *Essai sur le mystère de l'histoire* (La Sphère et la Croix), Paris: Seuil, 1953.

—— *Et qui est mon prochain? Mémoires*, Paris: Stock, 1974.

—— *Théologie du Judéo-Christianisme* (Bibliothèque de théologie. Histoire des doctrines chrétiennes avant Nicée, 1), Paris: Cerf, 1958, ²1991. Published in English as *The Development of Christian Doctrine before the Council of Nicea*, London: Darton, 1964.

Delaye, Émile, *Qu'est qu'un catholique? Exposé d'ensemble de la doctrine catholique*, Paris: Spes, 1948.

De Lubac, Henri, *Catholicisme. Les aspects sociaux du dogme* (Unam sanctam, 3), Paris: Cerf, 1938, ⁷1983; (Œuvres complètes, 7), Paris: Cerf, 2003. Published in English as *Catholicism: Christ and the Common Destiny of Man*, San Francisco, CA: Ignatius, 1988.

—— *De la connaissance de Dieu*, Paris: Témoignage chrétien, 1941, ²1948.

—— *Le drame de l'humanisme athée*, Paris: Spes, 1944, (Œuvres complètes, 2), Paris: Cerf, 1998.

—— *Corpus Mysticum: L'Eucharistie et l'Église au Moyen Âge: Étude historique* (Théologie, 3), Paris: Aubier, 1944, ²1949. Published in English as *Corpus mysticum: The Eucharist and the Church in the Middle Ages: Historical Survey*, London: SCM, 2006.

—— *Surnaturel: Études historiques* (Théologie, 8), Paris: Cerf, 1946.

—— *Aspects du bouddhisme* (La sphère et la croix), 2 vols, Paris: Seuil, 1951 and 1955.

—— *La rencontre du bouddhisme et de l'Occident* (Théologie, 24), Paris: Aubier, 1952.

—— *Méditation sur l'Église* (Théologie, 27), Paris: Aubier, 1953, (Œuvres complètes, 8), Paris: Cerf, 2003.

—— *Sur les chemins de Dieu*, Paris: Aubier, 1956, (Œuvres complètes, 1), Paris: Cerf, 2006.

—— *Exégèse médiévale: Les quatre sens de l'Écriture* (Théologie, 41–42), 4 vols, Paris: Aubier, 1959–64. Published in English as *Medieval Exegesis: The Four Senses of Scripture* (Ressourcement), 2 vols, Grand Rapids, MI: Eerdmans, 1998–2000.

—— *Augustinisme et théologie moderne* (Théologie, 63), Paris: Aubier, 1965; (Œuvres complètes, 13), Paris: Cerf, 2009. Published in English as *Augustinianism and Modern Theology*, New York: Crossroad/Herder, 2000.

—— *L'Écriture dans la Tradition*, Paris: Aubier, 1966. Published in English as *Scripture in the Tradition* (Milestones in Catholic Theology), New York: Crossroad, 2000.

—— *Athéisme et sens de l'homme: Une double requête de Gaudium et Spes* (Foi vivante, 67), Paris: Cerf, 1968.

—— *Pic de La Mirandole: Études et discussions*, Paris: Aubier, 1974.

—— *La postériorité spirituelle de Joachim de Flore*, 2 vols, Paris/Namur: Lethielleux, 1979–81.

—— *Théologies d'occasion*, Paris: Desclée De Brouwer, 1984.

—— *Entretiens autour de Vatican II: Souvenirs et Réflexions* (Théologies), Paris: France Catholique/Cerf, 1985, ²2007.

—— *Mémoire sur l'occasion de mes écrits* (Chrétiens aujourd'hui, 1), Namur : Culture et Vérité, 1989, repr.: (Œuvres complètes, 33), Paris: Cerf, 2006. Published in English as *At the Service of the Church: Henri de Lubac Reflects on the Circumstances that Occasioned his Writings*, San Francisco, CA: Ignatius, 1993.

—— *Théologie dans l'histoire* (Théologie), 2 vols, Paris: Desclée De Brouwer, 1990. Published in English as *Theology in History*, San Francisco, CA: Ignatius, 1997.

—— *Carnets du Concile*, ed. L. Figoureux, 2 vols, Paris: Cerf, 2007.

De Montcheuil, Yves, *Leçons sur le Christ*, Paris: Epi, 1949.

Deneken, Michel, *Johann Adam Möhler* (Initiations aux théologiens), Paris: Cerf, 2007.

De Valk, Johannes P., *Roomser dan de paus? Studies over de betrekkingen tussen de Heilige Stoel en het Nederlands katholicisme, 1815–1940* (KDC bronnen en studies, 36), Nijmegen: Valkhof, 1998.

Draguet, René, *L'évolution des dogmes*, Saint-Dizier: Brulliard, 1937.

—— *Histoire du dogme catholique*, Paris: Albin Michel, 1941, ²1947.

Drey, Johann Sebastian, *Die Apologetik als wissenschaftliche Nachweisung der Göttlichkeit des Christentums in seiner Erscheinung*, 3 vols, Mainz: Kupferberg, 1838–47, repr,: Frankfurt am Main: Minerva, 1967.

Dulles, Avery, *Church and Society: The Laurence J. McGinley Lectures 1988–2007*, New York: Fordham University Press, 2008.

Emond, James R. and James A. Driscoll (eds), *A Dominican Bibliography and Book Reference, 1216–1992: A List of Works in English by and about Members of the Friars Preachers, Founded by St. Dominic de Guzman (c. 1171–1221) and Confirmed by Pope Honorius III, 22 December 1216*, New York, et al.: Lang, 2000.

Famerée, Joseph and Gilles Routhier, *Yves Congar* (Initiations aux théologiens), Paris: Cerf, 2008.

Faupin, Jacques, *La mission de France: Histoire et Institution*, Tournai: Casterman, 1960.

Féret, Henri-Marie, *L'Apocalypse de saint Jean: vision chrétienne de l'histoire* (Témoignages chrétiens), Paris: Corrêa, 1943.

—— *Connaissance biblique de Dieu* (Epiphanie), Paris: Cerf, 1955.

Flynn, Gabriel (ed.), *Yves Congar: Theologian of the Church* (Louvain Theological Pastoral Monographs, 32), Louvain/Paris/Dudley, MA: Peeters, 2005.

Fontaine, Jacques (ed.), *Actualité de Jean Daniélou*, Paris: Cerf, 2006.

Fouilloux, Étienne, *Les catholiques et l'unité chrétienne du XIXe au XXe siècle: Itinéraires européens d'expression française*, Paris: Centurion, 1982.

—— *Au cœur du XXe siècle religieux* (Églises/Sociétés), Paris: Ouvrières, 1993.

—— *La collection 'Sources chrétiennes': Éditer les Pères de l'Église au XXe siècle*, Paris: Cerf, 1995.

—— *Les chrétiens français entre crise et liberation, 1937–1947* (XXe siècle), Paris: Seuil, 1997.

—— *Une Église en quête de liberté. La pensée catholique française entre modernisme et Vatican II (1914–1962)* (Anthropologiques), Paris: Declée de Brouwer, 1998.

Frey, Christoph, *Mysterium der Kirche, Öffnung zur Welt: Zwei Aspekte der Erneuerung französischer katholischer Theologie* (Kirche und Konfession, 14), Göttingen: Vandenhoeck & Ruprecht, 1969.

Gangl, Peter, *Franz Ehrle (1845–1934) und die Erneuerung der Scholastik nach die Enzyklika 'Aeterni Patris'* (Quellen und Studien zur neueren Theologiegeschichte, 7), Regensburg: Pustet, 2006.

Gardeil, Ambroise, *Le donné révélé et la théologie* (Bibliothèque théologique, 4), Paris: Cerf, 1909, ²1932.

Gertz, Kurt-Peter, *Joseph Turmel (1859–1943): Ein theologiegeschichtlicher Beitrag zum Problem der Geschichtlichkeit der Dogmen* (Disputationes theologicae, 2), Bern/Frankfurt am Main: Lang, 1975.

Gibellini, Rosino, *Panorama de la théologie au XXe siècle* (Théologies), Paris: Cerf, 1994.

Gilson, Étienne, *Le thomisme: Introduction à la philosophie de Saint Thomas d'Aquin* (Études de philosophie médiévale, 1), Strasbourg: Vix, 1919; ⁶Paris: Vrin, 1964; 7th repr. of the 6th edn, 1997.

—— *L'esprit de la philosophie médiévale* (Études de philosophie médiévale, 33), Paris: Vrin, 1932.

Goichot, Émile, *Henri Bremond, historien du sentiment religieux: Genèse et stratégie d'une entreprise littéraire*, Paris: Ophrys, 1982.

—— *Alfred Loisy et ses amis* (Histoire), Paris: Cerf, 2002.

Gregory of Nyssa, *La vie de Moïse ou traité de la perfection en matière de vertu* (Sources Chrétiennes, 1), ed. J. Daniélou, Paris: Cerf, 1942, ³1968, repr. 2000.

Grossouw, Willem K., *Alles is van u: Gewijde en profane herinneringen*, Baarn: Ambo, 1981.

Grumett, David, *De Lubac: A Guide for the Perplexed* (Guides for the Perplexed), London/New York: T&T Clark, 2007.

Guardini, Romano, *Vom Sinn der Kirche: Fünf Vorträge*, Mainz: Matthias-Grünewald, 1922, ⁴1955.

Guarino, Thomas G., *Foundations of Systematic Theology* (Theology for the Twenty-First Century), New York/London: T&T Clark, 2005.

Guasco, Maurilio, *Modernismo: I fatti; le idée, i personaggi*, Cinisello Balsamo: San Paolo, 1995.

Gugelot, Frédéric, *La conversion des intellectuels au catholicisme en France, 1885–1935*, Paris: CNRS, 1998.

Guillet, Jacques, *La théologie catholique en France de 1914 à 1960*, Paris: Médiasèvres, 1988.

Haight, Roger, *Christian Community in History*, Vol. 2: *Comparative Ecclesiology*, New York: Continuum, 2005.

Heiler, Friedrich, *Der Vater des katholischen Modernismus: Alfred Loisy (1857–1940)* (Ernst Reinhardt Bücherreihe), Munich: Erasmus, 1947.

Henri-Marie Féret: Dominicain: 1904–1992, unpublished brochure of the Groupe évangélique, Paris, 1992.

Hill, Harvey, *The Politics of Modernism: Alfred Loisy and the Scientific Study of Religion*, Washington, DC: Catholic University of America, 2002.

L'hommage différé au Père Chenu (Théologies), Paris: Cerf, 1990.

L'homme devant Dieu: Mélanges offerts au Père Henri de Lubac (Théologie, 56–58), 3 vols, Paris: Aubier, 1963–64.

Horn, Gerd-Rainer, *Western European Liberation Theology: The First Wave (1924–1959)*, Oxford: Oxford University Press, 2008.

Houtepen, Anton, *Theologen op zoek naar God: Twintig portretten van katholieke theologen uit de tweede helft van de 20ste eeuw*, Zoetermeer: Meinema, 2001.

Houtin, Albert, *La question biblique chez les catholiques de France en XIXe siècle*, Paris: Picard, 1902.

—— *Une vie de prêtre: Mon experience, 1867–1912*, Paris: Rieder, 1926.

—— *Mon experience II: Ma vie laïque, 1912–1926: Documents et souvenirs*, Paris: Rieder, 1928.

Jacques Duquesne interroge le Père Chenu: 'Un théologien en liberté' (Les interviews), Paris: Centurion, 1975.

Jean Daniélou 1905–1974, Paris: Cerf/Axes, 1975.

Jean Puyo interroge le Père Congar: 'Une vie pour la vérité' (Les interviews), Paris: Centurion, 1975.

Jossua, Jean-Pierre, *Le Père Congar: La théologie au service du peuple de Dieu* (Chrétiens de tous les temps, 20), Paris: Cerf, 1967.

Keck, Thierry, *Jeunesse de l'Église (1936–1955): Aux sources de la crise progressiste en France* (Signes des temps), Paris: Karthala, 2004.

Kelly, James J., *Baron Friedrich von Hügel's Philosophy of Religion* (Bibliotheca ephemeridum theologicarum Lovaniensium, 62), Louvain: University Press, 1983.

—— *The Letters of Baron Friedrich von Hügel and Maude Petre: The Modernist Movement in England* (Annua nuntia Lovaniensia, 44), Louvain: Peeters, 2003.

Ker, Ian and Terrence Merrigan (eds), *The Cambridge Companion to John Henry Newman*, Cambridge: Cambridge University Press, 2009.

Kerr, Fergus, *After Aquinas: Versions of Thomism*, Malden, MA: Blackwell, 2002.

—— *Twentieth-Century Catholic Theologians: From Neoscholasticism to Nuptial Mysticism*, Malden, MA/Oxford/Victoria: Blackwell, 2007.

Kessler, Michael and Ottmar Fuchs (eds), *Theologie als Instanz der Moderne: Beiträge und Studien zu Johann Sebastian Drey und zur Katholischen Tübinger Schule* (Tübinger Studien zur Theologie und Philosophie, 22), Tübingen: Francke, 2005.

Kleutgen, Joseph, *Die Theologie der Vorzeit*, 3 vols, Münster: Theissing, 1853–60.

—— *Die Philosophie der Vorzeit*, 2 vols, Münster: Theissing, 1860–63, ²1878.

Knasas, John F.X., *Being and Some Twentieth-Century Thomists*, New York: Fordham University Press, 2003.

Koepgen, Georg, *Die Gnosis des Christentums*, Salzburg: Müller, 1939, ²1940, ³(Occidens, 4), Trier: Spee, 1978.

Küng, Hans, *Theologie im Aufbruch: Eine Ökumenische Grundlegung*,

Munich/Zurich: Piper, 1987. Published in English as *Theology for the Third Millennium: An Ecumenical View*, New York: Anchor, 1990.

—— *Das Christentum: Wesen und Geschichte*, Munich/Zurich: Piper, 1994. Published in English as *Christianity: Its Essence and History* (The Religious Situation of Our Time), London: SCM, 1995.

Labourdette, Marie-Michel, Marie-Joseph Nicolas and Raymond-Léopold Bruckberger, *Dialogue théologique: Pièces du débat entre 'La Revue Thomiste' d'une part et les R.R. P.P. de Lubac, Daniélou, Bouillard, Fessard, von Balthasar, S.J., d'autre part*, Toulouse: Saint-Maximin, 1947.

Laplanche, François, *La crise de l'origine: L'histoire et la science catholique des Évangiles au XXe siècle* (L'Évolution de l'humanité), Paris: Albin Michel, 2006.

Lebeau, Paul, *Jean Daniélou* (Théologiens et spirituels contemporains, 4), Paris: Fleurus, 1967.

Leinsle, Ulrich G., *Einführung in die scholastische Theologie* (UTB für Wissenschaft – Uni-Taschenbücher, 1865), Paderborn/Munich/Vienna/Zürich: Schöning, 1995.

Leprieur, François, *Quand Rome condamne: Dominicains et prêtres-ouvriers* (Terre humaine), Paris: Plon, 1989.

Le Roy, Édouard, *Dogme et critique* (Études de philosophie et de critique religieuse), Paris: Bloud, 1907.

Liberatore, Matteo, *Institutiones logicae et metaphysicae*, Mediolani: Rossi, 1846.

Livingston, James C., *Modern Christian Thought*, Vol. 1: *The Enlightenment and the Nineteenth Century*, Minneapolis, MN: Fortress Press, 1997, [2]2006.

Loisy, Alfred, *L'Évangile et l'Église*, Paris: Picard, 1902. Published in English as *The Gospel and the Church*, Philadelphia, PA: Fortress, 1976.

—— *Autour d'un petit livre*, Paris: Picard, 1903.

—— *Mémoires pour servir à l'histoire religieuse de notre temps*, 3 vols, Paris: Nourry, 1930–31.

Loome, Thomas Michael, *Liberal Catholicism – Reform Catholicism – Modernism: A Contribution to a New Orientation in Modernist Research* (Tübinger Theologische Studien, 14), Mainz: Matthias-Grünewald, 1979.

Maltha, Andreas H., *De Nieuwe Theologie: Informatie en Oriëntatie*, Bruges: Desclée de Brouwer, 1958.

Marín-Sola, Francisco, *La evolución homogénea del dogma católico* (Biblioteca de tomistas españoles, 1), Madrid: La Ciencia tomista, 1923, [3](Biblioteca de autores cristianos, 84; biblioteca de tomistas españoles, 14), Madrid: Biblioteca de autores cristianos, 1952.

Maritain, Jacques, *Primauté du spirituel* (Le roseau d'or : Œuvres et chroniques, 19), Paris: Plon, 1927.

—— *Humanisme intégral: problèmes temporels et spirituels d'une nouvelle chrétienté* (Bibliothèque philosophique), Paris: Aubier, 1936.

Marmion, Columba, *Le Christ, vie de l'âme*, Maredsous: Abbaye de Maredsous, 1914.

—— *Le Christ dans ses mystères*, Maredsous: Abbaye de Maredsous, 1919.

—— *Le Christ, idéal du moine: Conférences spirituelles sur la vie monastique et religieuse*, Maredsous: Abbaye de Maredsous, 1922.

Martin, Thomas F., *Our Restless Heart: The Augustinian Tradition* (Traditions of Christian Spirituality Series), Maryknoll, NY: Orbis, 2003.

McCarthy, John L., Martin D. O'Keefe and John W. Padberg (eds), *For Matters of Greater Moment: The First Thirty Jesuit General Congregations: A Brief History and A Translation of the Decrees* (Jesuit Primary Sources in English Translations, 12), Saint Louis, MO: Institute of Jesuit Sources, 1994.

McCool, Gerald A., *From Unity to Pluralism: The Internal Evolution of Thomism*, New York: Fordham University Press, 1989, ⁴2002.

—— *Nineteenth-Century Scholasticism: The Search for a Unitary Method*, New York: Fordham University Press, 1989, ³1999.

—— *The Neo-Thomists* (Marquette Studies in Philosophy, 3), Milwaukee, WI: Marquette University Press, 1994.

McInerny, Ralph, *Praeambula Fidei: Thomism and the God of the Philosophers*, Washington, DC: University of America, 2006.

McKim, Donald K., *Westminster Dictionary of Theological Terms*, Louisville, KY: Westminster John Knox, 1996.

Mersch, Émile, *Le Corps mystique du Christ: Étude de théologie historique* (Museum Lessianum: Section théologique, 28–29), 2 vols, Louvain: Museum Lessianum, 1933.

—— *Morale et Corps mystique* (Museum Lessianum: Section théologique, 34), Brussels: Desclée De Brouwer, 1937, ²1941.

—— *La théologie du Corps mystique* (Museum Lessianum: Section théologique, 38–39), 2 vols, Paris: Desclée De Brouwer, 1944.

Milbank, John, *The Suspended Middle: Henri de Lubac and the Debate concerning the Supernatural*, Grand Rapids, MI/Cambridge: Eerdmans, 2005.

Möhler, Johann Adam, *Die Einheit in der Kirche, oder das Prinzip des Katholizismus. Dargestellt im Geiste der Kirchenväter der drei ersten Jahrhunderte*, Tübingen: Laupp, 1825.

Montagnes, Bernard, *Marie-Joseph Lagrange: Une biographie critique* (Histoire – Biographie), Paris: Cerf, 2004.

Nédoncelle, Maurice, *La pensée religieuse de Friedrich von Hügel (1852–1925)* (Bibliothèque d'histoire de la philosophie), Paris: Vrin, 1935.

Newman, John Henry, *An Essay on the Development of Christian Doctrine*, London: Toovey, 1845; ⁶(Notre Dame Series in the Great Books), Notre Dame, IN: University of Notre Dame, 1989.

—— *The Church of the Fathers* (The Works of Cardinal John Henry Newman, Birmingham Oratory Millennium Edition, 5), Notre Dame: Gracewing/ University of Notre Dame, 2002.

—— *An Essay in Aid of a Grammar of Assent*, London: Burns and Oates, 1870; Notre Dame, IN: University of Notre Dame, 2001.

De Nieuwe Katechismus: Geloofsverkondiging voor volwassenen, Hilversum/ Antwerp: Paul Brand, 1966. Published in English as *A New Catechism: Catholic Faith for Adults*, London: Burns and Oates, 1967.

O'Meara, Thomas F., *Thomas Aquinas Theologian*, Notre Dame, IN/London: University of Notre Dame, 1997.

Oosterhuis, Huub and Piet Hoogeveen, *God is ieder ogenblik nieuw: Gesprekken met Edward Schillebeeckx*, Baarn: Ambo, 1982. Published in English as *God is New Each Moment*, Edinburgh: Clark, 1983.

Pauly, Wolfgang (ed.), *Geschichte der christlichen Theologie*, Darmstadt: Primus, 2008.

Peddicord, Richard, *The Sacred Monster of Thomism: An Introduction to the Life and Legacy of Reginald Garrigou-Lagrange, O.P.*, South Bend, IN: St. Augustine's Press, 2004.

Les Pères de l'Église au XXe siècle: Histoire, littérature, théologie: L'aventure des Sources chrétiennes (Patrimoines: Christianisme), Paris: Cerf, 1997.

Poels, Hendrik Andreas, *Examen critique de l'histoire du sanctuaire de l'Arche* (Universitas Catholica Lovaniensis. Dissertationes ad gradum doctoris in Facultate theologica consequendum conscriptae. Series 1, 47), Louvain: Vanlinthout, 1897.

Ponga, Silouane, *L'Écriture, âme de la théologie: Le problème de la suffisance matérielle des Écritures* (Théologies), Paris: Cerf, 2008.

Potworowski, Christophe F., *Contemplation and Incarnation: The Theology of Marie-Dominique Chenu* (McGill-Queen's Studies in the History of Ideas, 33), Montreal: McGill-Queen's University Press, 2001.

Poulat, Émile, *Histoire, dogme et critique dans la crise moderniste* (Religion et sociétés), Tournai: Casterman, 1962, ³(Bibliothèque de l'Évolution de l'Humanité), Paris: Albin Michel, ³1996.

—— *Les prêtres-ouvriers: Naissance et fin* (Religion et sociétés), Tournai: Casterman, 1965, ²(Histoire), Paris: Cerf, 1999.

Prévotat, Jacques, *Les catholiques et l'Action française: Histoire d'une condamnation 1899–1939* (Pour une histoire du XXe siècle), Paris: Fayard, 2001.

Prior, Joseph G., *The Historical Critical Method in Catholic Exegesis* (Tesi Gregoriana. Serie Teologia, 50), Rome: Pontificia Università Gregoriana, 1999.

Prouvost, Géry, *Thomas d'Aquin et les thomismes: Essai sur l'histoire des thomismes* (Cogitatio fidei, 195), Paris: Cerf, 1996.

Qatraya, Dadišo, *Commentaire du livre d'Abba Isaïe (logoi I–XV)* (Corpus scriptorium christianorum Orientalium, 326–27; Corpus scriptorium christianorum Orientalium. Scriptores Syri, 144–45), 2 vols, Louvain: Corpus scriptorium christianorum Orientalium, 1972.

Quisinsky, Michael, *Geschichtlicher Glaube in einer geschichtlichen Welt: Der Beitrag von M.-D. Chenu, Y. Congar und H.-M. Féret zum II. Vaticanum* (Dogma und Geschichte, 6), Berlin: LIT, 2007.

Rahner, Karl, *Maria, Mutter des Herrn: Mariologische Studien* (Sämtliche Werke, 9), Freiburg/Basel/Vienna: Herder, 2004.

Rogier, Ludovicus J. and Nicolaas De Rooij, *In vrijheid herboren: Katholiek Nederland 1853–1953*, The Hague: Pax, 1953.

Rondet, Henri, *Problèmes pour la réflexion chrétienne: Le Péché originel; L'Enfer et autres études*, Paris: Spes, 1945.

Russo, Antonio, *Henri de Lubac: Biographie*, Paris: Brepols, 1997.

Schatz, Klaus, *Vaticanum I* (Konziliengeschichte. A: Darstellungen), 3 vols, Paderborn: Schöningh, 1992–94.

Schillebeeckx, Edward, *De sacramentele heilseconomie*, Antwerp: 't Groeit, 1952.

—— *Openbaring en theologie* (Theologische Peilingen, 1), Bilthoven: Nelissen,

1964. Published in English as *Revelation and Theology* (Theological Soundings), 2 vols, London/Sydney: Sheed and Ward, 1967–68.

—— 'Op zoek naar de levende God', in Edward Schillebeeckx, *God en mens* (Theologische Peilingen, 2), Bilthoven: Nelissen, 1965. Published in English as 'The Search for the Living God', in Schillebeeckx, *God and Man* (Theological Soundings), London/Sydney: Sheed and Ward, 1969.

—— *Jezus, het verhaal van een levende*, Bloemendaal: Nelissen, 1974. Published in English as *Jesus: An Experiment in Christology*, London: Collins, 1979.

—— *Gerechtigheid en Liefde: Genade en Bevrijding*, Bloemendaal: Nelissen, 1977. Published in English as *Christ: The Christian Experience in the Modern World*, London: SCM, 1980.

—— *The Schillebeeckx Reader*, ed. Robert Schreiter, New York: Crossroad, 1984.

—— *Pleidooi voor mensen in de kerk: Christelijke identiteit en ambten in de kerk*, Baarn: Nelissen, 1985. Published in English as *The Church with a Human Face: A New and Expanded Theology of Ministry*, London: SCM, 1985.

—— *Mensen als verhaal van God*, Baarn: Nelissen, 1989. Published in English as *Church: The Human Story of God*, London: SCM, 1990.

—— *Theologisch testament: Notarieel nog niet verleden*, Baarn: Nelissen, 1994.

—— *I Am a Happy Theologian*, London: SCM, 1994.

Schmitz, Rudolf M., *Dogma und Praxis: Der Dogmenbegriff des Modernisten Édouard Le Roy kritisch dargestellt* (Studi tomistici, 51), Vatican: Libr. ed. Vaticana, 1993.

Schoof, Mark, *Breakthrough: Beginnings of the New Catholic Theology* (Logos Books), Dublin: Gill and MacMillan, 1970 (new edn: *A Survey of Catholic Theology, 1800–1970*, Eugene: Wipf and Stock, 2008).

Schoof, Ted, *De zaak Schillebeeckx: Officiële stukken*, Bloemendaal: Nelissen, 1980. Published in English as *The Schillebeeckx Case*, New York/Ramsey: Paulist Press, 1984.

Schoonenberg, Piet, *Het geloof van ons doopsel: Gesprekken over de Apostolische Geloofsbelijdenis*, Vol. 1: *God, Vader en Schepper: Het eerste geloofsartikel*, 's-Hertogenbosch: L.C.G. Malmberg, 1955. Published in English as *Covenant and Creation* (Stagbooks), London/Sydney: Sheed and Ward, 1968.

—— *Het geloof van ons doopsel: Gesprekken over de Apostolische Geloofsbelijdenis*, Vol. 2: *Jezus, de Christus, de Zoon Gods: Het tweede geloofsartikel*, 's-Hertogenbosch: L.C.G. Malmberg, 1956.

—— *Het geloof van ons doopsel: Gesprekken over de Apostolische Geloofsbelijdenis*, Vol. 3: *De Mensgeworden Zoon van God: Het derde geloofsartikel*, 's-Hertogenbosch: L.C.G. Malmberg, 1958.

—— *Het geloof van ons doopsel: Gesprekken over de Apostolische Geloofsbelijdenis*, Vol. 4: *De macht der zonde: Inleiding op de verlossingsleer*, 's-Hertogenbosch: L.C.G. Malmberg, 1962. Published in English as *Man and Sin: A Theological View*, London/Melbourne: Sheed and Ward, 1965.

—— *Gods wordende wereld: Vijf theologische essays* (Woord en Beleving, 13), Tielt/The Hague: Lannoo, 1962. Published in English as *God's World in*

the Making (Duquesne Studies: Theological series, 2), Duquesne University
    Press: Pittsburgh, PA; Louvain: Nauwelaerts, 1964.
—— *Hij is een God van mensen: Twee theologische studies*, 's-Hertogenbosch:
    L.C.G. Malmberg, 1969. Published in English as *The Christ: A Study of the
    God-Man Relationship in the Whole of Creation and in Jesus Christ*, New
    York: Herder and Herder, 1971.
—— *De Geest, het Woord en de Zoon: Theologische overdenkingen over Geest-
    christologie, Logos-christologie en drieëenheidsleer*, Averbode: Altiora;
    Kampen: Kok, 1991.
—— *Theologie als geloofsvertolking: Het proefschrift van 1948* (Documenta
    Libraria, 36), ed. L. Kenis and J. Mettepenningen, Louvain: Maurits
    Sabbebibliotheek/Faculteit Godgeleerdheid/Peeters, 2008.
Schultenover, David G., *George Tyrrell: In Search of Catholicism*,
    Shepherdstown: Patmos, 1981.
Scully, J. Eileen, *Grace and Human Freedom in the Theology of Henri Bouillard*,
    Bethesda, MD: Academica Press, 2007.
Serry, Hervé, *Naissance de l'intellectuel catholique* (L'espace de l'histoire),
    Paris: La Découverte, 2004.
Sesboüé, Bernard, *Karl Rahner* (Initiations aux théologiens), Paris: Cerf, 2001.
—— *Yves de Montcheuil (1900–1944): Précurseur en théologie* (Cogitatio fidei,
    255), Paris: Cerf, 2006.
—— *La théologie au XXe siècle et l'avenir de la foi: Entretiens avec Marc
    Leboucher*, Paris: Desclée de Brouwer, 2007.
Shanley, Brian J., *The Thomist Tradition* (Handbook of Contemporary
    Philosophy of Religion, 2), Dordrecht/Boston/London: Kluwer, 2002.
Six, Jean-François, *Cheminements de la Mission de France*, Paris: Seuil,
    1967.
Sperna Weiland, Jan, *Oriëntatie: Nieuwe wegen in de theologie* (Theologische
    Monografieën), Baarn: Het Wereldvenster, 1966; Published in French as
    *La nouvelle théologie: Tillich, Bultmann, Bonhoeffer, Fuchs, Ebeling,
    Robinson, Van Buren, Michalson, Winter, Cox, Hamilton, Altizer, Sölle*,
    Bruges: Desclée De Brouwer, 1969).
Teilhard de Chardin, Pierre, *Le phénomène humain* (Œuvres de Pierre Teilhard de
    Chardin, 1), Paris: Seuil, 1955.
—— *Le milieu divin: Essai de vie intérieure*, Paris: Seuil, 1957.
Thils, Gustave, *Théologie des réalités terrestres*, 2 vols, Bruges: Desclée De
    Brouwer, 1947–49.
—— *Orientations de la théologie* (Bibliotheca ephemeridum theologicarum
    Lovaniensium, 11), Louvain: Ceuterick, 1958.
Tshibangu, Tarcisus, *La théologie comme science au XXème siècle*, Kinshasa:
    Presses universitaires, 1980.
Truc, Gonzague, *Le retour à la scolastique* (Bibliothèque internationale de
    critique: Religion et philosophie, 20), Paris: La Renaissance du Livre, 1919.
Tyrrell, George, *Through Scylla and Charybdis or the Old Theology and the
    New*, London: Longmans, 1907.
Vangu Vangu, Emmanuel, *La théologie de Marie-Dominique Chenu: Réflexion
    sur une méthodologie théologique de l'intégration communautaire*, Paris:
    L'Harmattan, 2007.

Van Laarhoven, Jan, 'Thomas op Vaticanum II', in *De praktische Thomas: Thomas van Aquino: De consequenties van zijn theologie voor hedendaags gedrag* (Theologie en samenleving, 10), Hilversum: Gooi en Sticht, 1987, pp. 113–24.

Van Schaik, Ton H.M., *Alfrink: Een biografie*, Amsterdam: Anthos, 1997.

Vauchez, André (ed.), *Cardinal Yves Congar 1904–1995* (Histoire), Paris: Cerf, 1999.

Vilanova, Evangelista, *Histoire des théologies chrétiennes* (Initiations), Vol. 3: *XVIIIe-XXe siècle*, Paris: Cerf, 1997.

Voderholzer, Rudolf, *Henri de Lubac begegnen* (Zeugen des Glaubens), Augsburg: Sankt Ulrich, 1999. Published in English as *Meet Henri de Lubac: His Life and Work*, San Francisco: Ignatius, 2008.

Wagner, Jean-Pierre, *Henri de Lubac* (Initiations aux théologiens), Paris: Cerf, 2001.

Walgrave, Jan Hendrik, *Geloof en theologie in de crisis* (Bezinning en bezieling, 1), Kasterlee: De Vroente, 1966.

Weiss, Otto, *Der Modernismus in Deutschland: Ein Beitrag zur Theologiegeschichte*, Regensburg: Pustet, 1995.

Winling, Raymond, *La théologie contemporaine (1945–1980)*, Paris: Centurion, 1985.

Articles [in periodicals, journals and volumes]

Alberigo, Giuseppe, 'Christianisme en tant qu'histoire et "théologie confessante"', in G. Alberigo *et al.*, *Une école de théologie: le Saulchoir* (Théologies), Paris: Cerf, 1985, pp. 9–35.

—— '"Un concile à la dimension du monde": Marie-Dominique Chenu à Vatican II d'après son journal', in *Marie-Dominique Chenu, Moyen-Âge et modernité* (Les Cahiers du Centre d'études du Saulchoir, 5), Paris: Cerf, 1997, pp. 155–72.

Altera patris nostri adhortatio ad PP. Provinciarum Procuratores, 30 September 1950, in *Acta Romana Societatis Iesu* 11 (1946–50) 865–77.

Alvarez Alonso, F., 'La posizione del Laterano sui problemi ecclesiologici nella fase preparatoria del Concilio', in P. Chenaux (ed.), *L'Università del Laterano e la preparazione del Concilio Vaticano II: Atti del convegno internazionale di studi, Città del Vaticano, 27 gennaio 2000* (Studi e documenti sul Concilio Vaticano II, 1), Rome: Pontificia Università Lateranense, 2001, pp. 67–80.

'À propos de la conception médiévale de l'ordre surnaturel', in *Mélanges de science religieuse* 4 (1947) 365–79.

Arnold, Claus, 'Neuere Forschungen zur Modernismuskrise in der katholischen Kirche', in *Theologische Revue* 99 (2003) 91–104.

—— 'Alfred Loisy (1857–1940)', in F.W. Graf (ed.), *Klassiker der Theologie*, Vol. 2: *Von Richard Simon bis Karl Rahner*, Munchen: Beck, 2005, pp. 155–70.

Aubert, Roger, 'Discussions récentes autour de la Théologie de l'Histoire', in *Collectanea Mechliniensia* 33 (1948) 129–49.

—— 'L'intervention de Montalembert au Congrès de Malines en 1863', in *Collectanea Mechliniensia* 35 (1950) 525–51.

—— 'Die Enzyklika "Aeterni Patris" und die weiteren päpstlichen Stellungnahmen zur christlichen Philosophie', in E. Coreth, W. Neidl and R. Pfligersdorffer (eds), *Christliche Philosophie im katholischen Denken des 19. und 20. Jahrhunderts*, Vol. 2, Graz/Vienna/Cologne: Styria, 1988, pp. 310–32.

Avon, Dominique, 'Une école théologique à Fourvière?', in É. Fouilloux and B. Hours (eds), *Les jésuites à Lyon: XVIe-XXe siècle* (Sociétes, espaces, temps), Lyon: ENS, 2005, pp. 231–46.

Bakker, Leo, 'Schoonenberg's theologie: Spiegel van onze eigen ontwikkeling?', in *Tijdschrift voor Theologie* 11 (1971) 353–82.

Bauer, Christian, 'Marie-Dominique Chenu OP (1895–1990): Gottes messianisches Volk unter den Zeichen der Zeit', in T. Eggensperger and U. Engel (eds), *'Mutig in die Zukunft': Dominikanische Beiträge zum Vaticanum II* (Dominikanische Quellen und Zeugnisse, 10), Leipzig: Benno, 2007, pp. 105–46.

Beumer, Johannes, 'Konklusionstheologie?', in *Zeitschrift für katholische Theologie* 63 (1939) 260–365.

'Bibliographie des travaux du Cardinal J. Daniélou sur le Judéo-Christianisme', in *Recherches de science religieuse* 60 (1972) 11–18.

Boersma, Hans, '"Néoplatonisme belgo-français": "Nouvelle théologie" and the Search for a Sacramental Ontology', in *Louvain Studies* 32 (2007) 333–60.

—— 'A Sacramental Journey to the Beatific Vision: The Intellectualism of Pierre Rousselot', in *The Heythrop Journal* 49 (2008) 1015–34.

Bonino, Serge-Thomas, 'Le thomisme du père Labourdette', in *Revue thomiste* 92 (1992) 88–122.

—— 'Le fondement doctrinal du projet léonin: 'Aeterni Patris' et la restauration du thomisme', in P. Levillain and J.-M. Ticchi (eds), *Le pontificat de Léon XIII: Renaissances du Saint-Siège?* (Collection de l'École française de Rome, 368), Rome: École Française de Rome, 2006, pp. 267–74.

Bonnefoy, Jean-François, 'La théologie comme science et l'explication de la foi selon saint Thomas d'Aquin', in *Ephemerides theologicae Lovanienses* 14 (1937) 421–46, 600–31; 15 (1938) 491–516.

Bouillard, Henri, 'Notions conciliaires et analogie de la vérité', in *Recherches de science religieuse* 35 (1948) 251–71.

—— 'L'idée chrétienne du miracle', in *Cahiers Laënnec* 8 (1948), nr. 4, pp. 25–37.

—— 'L'intention fondamentale de Maurice Blondel et la théologie', in *Recherches de science religieuse* 36 (1949) 321–402.

Boulding, Mary Cecily, 'Yves Congar: Faithful Critic of the Church in "Mon Journal du Concile"', in *Louvain Studies* 29 (2004) 350–70.

Boyer, Charles, 'Qu'est-ce que la théologie: Réflexions sur une controverse', in *Gregorianum* 21 (1940) 255–66.

—— review [Bouillard, *Conversion et grace chez saint Thomas d'Aquin*], in *Gregorianum* 27 (1946) 157–60.

—— 'Nature pure et surnaturel dans le "Surnaturel" du Père de Lubac', in *Gregorianum* 28 (1947) 379–95.

—— 'Sur un article des Recherches de science religieuse', in *Gregorianum* 29 (1948) 152–4.

Brambilla, Franco Giulio, '"Theologia del Magistero" e fermenti di rinnovamento nella teologia cattolica', in G. Angelini and S. Macchi (eds), *La teologia del Novecento: Momenti maggiori e questioni aperte* (Lectio, 7), Milan: Glossa, 2008, pp. 189–236.

Bunnenberg, Johannes, 'Yves Congar OP (1904–1995): Mit dem Konzil über das Konzil hinaus', in T. Eggensperger and U. Engel (eds), *'Mutig in die Zukunft': Dominikanische Beiträge zum Vaticanum II* (Dominikanische Quellen und Zeugnisse, 10), Leipzig: Benno, 2007, pp. 39–63.

Cappuyns, Maïeul, review [Charlier, *Essai sur le problème théologique*], in *Recherches de théologie ancienne et médiévale* 11 (1939) [13]–[15].

Cardijn, Joseph, 'Théologie du travail, théologie pour l'homme', *in L'hommage différé au Père Chenu* (Théologies), Paris: Cerf, 1990, pp. 19–21.

Castro, Michel, 'Henri Bouillard (1908–1981): Éléments de biographie intellectuelle', in *Mélanges de science religieuse* 60 (2003) nr. 4, pp. 43–58; 63 (2006) nr. 2, pp. 47–59.

Chantraine, Georges, 'Henri de Lubac (1896–1991) : Une vue panoramique', in *Nouvelle revue théologique* 129 (2007) 212–34.

Charlier, Louis, 'Puissance passive et désir naturel selon saint Thomas', in *Ephemerides theologicae Lovanienses* 7 (1930) 5–28, 639–62.

—— 'Histoire des principales mises en ordre des données de la foi et des grandes synthèses théologiques: L'organisation des études sacrées au cours de l'histoire', in *Formation doctrinale des religieuses* (Problèmes de la religieuse aujourd'hui, 9), Paris: Cerf, 1954, pp. 231–70.

—— 'Les cinq voies de saint Thomas: Leur structure métaphysique', in *L'existence de Dieu* (Cahiers de l'actualité religieuse, 16), Tournai: Casterman, 1961, pp. 181–228.

—— 'Le Christ, Parole de Dieu: Réflexions théologiques', in *La Parole de Dieu en Jésus-Christ* (Cahiers de l'actualité religieuse, 15), Tournai: Casterman, 1961, pp. 121–39.

Chenaux, Philippe, 'La seconde vague thomiste', in Pierre Colin (ed.), *Intellectuels chrétiens et esprit des années 1920: Actes du colloque Institut catholique de Paris, 23–24 septembre 1993* (Sciences humaines et religions: nouvelle série), Paris: Cerf, 1997, pp. 139–67.

Chenu, Marie-Dominique, review [Maritain, *Primauté du Spirituel*], in *Revue des sciences philosophiques et théologiques* 16 (1927) 21*.

—— 'Position de la théologie', in *Revue des sciences philosophiques et théologiques* 24 (1935) 232–57.

—— 'Le sacerdoce des prêtres-ouvriers', in *Vie Intellectuelle* 1 (1954) nr. 2, pp. 175–81.

Comte, Bernard, 'Le Père de Lubac, un théologien dans l'Église de Lyon', in Jean-Dominique Durand (ed.), *Henri de Lubac: La rencontre au cœur de l'Église*, Paris: Cerf, 2006, pp. 35–89.

Congar, Yves-Marie-Joseph, 'Déficit de la théologie', in *Sept*, 18 January 1935.

—— 'Une conclusion théologique à l'enquête sur les raisons actuelles de l'incroyance', in *Vie Intellectuelle* 37 (1935) 214–49. Published in English as

'The Reasons for the Unbelief of Our Time: A Theological Conclusion', in *Integration*, August 1938, pp. 13–21 and December 1938, pp. 10–26.

—— review [Bonnefoy, *La théologie comme science et l'explication de la foi selon saint Thomas d'Aquin*; Charlier, *Essai sur le problem théologique*; Draguet, *Méthodes théologique d'hier et d'aujourd'hui*; Gagnebet, *La nature de la théologie spéculative*], in *Bulletin thomiste* 5 (1937–39) 490–505.

——, 'Théologie', in *Dictionnaire de théologie chrétienne* 15 (1946) 341–502. Published in English as *A History of Theology*, Garden City, NY: Doubleday, 1968.

Conticello, Carmelo G., '"De contemplatione" (Angelicum, 1920): La thèse inédite de doctorat du P. M.-D. Chenu', in *Revue des sciences philosophiques et théologiques* 75 (1991) 363–422.

Coppens, Joseph, 'In memoriam R. Draguet' *(1896–1980)*, in *Ephemerides theologicae Lovanienses* 57 (1981) 194–200.

Cordovani, Mariano, 'Per la vitalità della teologia cattolica', in *L'Osservatore Romano*, 22 March 1940, p. 3 (= *Angelicum* 17 [1940] 133–46).

—— 'Verità e novità in Teologia', in *L'Osservatore Romano*, 15–16 March 1948, pp. 1–2.

'Correspondance', in *Angelicum* 24 (1947) 210–14.

Corvez, Maurice, 'De la connaissance de Dieu', in *Revue thomiste* 48 (1948) 511–24.

—— 'Gratia Christi', in *Revue thomiste* 48 (1948) 525–37.

Cottiaux, Jean, review [Charlier, *Essai sur le problème théologique*], in *Revue d'histoire ecclésiastique* 36 (1940) 459–62.

Daley, Brian, 'The Nouvelle Théologie and the Patristic Revival: Sources, Symbols and the Science of Theology', in *International Journal of Systematic Theology* 7 (2005) 362–82.

Daniélou, Jean, 'L'Apocatastase chez Saint Grégoire de Nysse', in *Recherches de science religieuse* 30 (1940) 328–47.

—— 'Les orientations présentes de la pensée religieuse', in *Études*, Vol. 79, nr. 249, 1946, pp. 5–21.

—— 'Christianisme et histoire', in *Études*, Vol. 80, nr. 254, 1947, pp. 166–84.

—— 'Lettres au Père de Lubac', in *Bulletin des amis du Cardinal Daniélou*, nr. 2, June 1976, pp. 53–85; nr. 3, March 1977, pp. 23–41; nr. 8, March 1982, pp. 33–53; nr. 9, March 1983, pp. 28–62; nr. 21, November 1995, pp. 15–44; nr. 22, October 1996, pp. 1–50; nr. 23, September 1997, pp. 2–43; nr. 24, October 1998, pp. 1–24; nr. 25, December 1999, pp. 1–35; nr. 26–27, 2000–2001, pp. 3–52; nr. 28, 2002, pp. 3–34; nr. 29, 2009, pp. 1–22.

Darlapp, Adolf, 'Nouvelle théologie', in *Lexikon für Theologie und Kirche* 7 (1962) 1060–61.

De Blic, Jacques, 'Quelques vieux textes sur la notion de l'ordre surnaturel', in *Mélanges de science religieuse* 3 (1946) 359–62.

De Lubac, Henri, 'Deux augustiniens fourvoyés', in *Recherches de science religieuse* 21 (1931) 422–43, 513–40.

—— 'Le problème du développement du dogme', in *Recherches de science religieuse* 35 (1938) 130–60.

—— 'Le mystère du surnaturel', in *Recherches de science religieuse* 36 (1949) 80–121.

—— 'Un homme libre et évangélique', in *Cahiers de l'actualité religieuse et sociale* 81 (1974) 413–16.

Demoment, Auguste, 'Bouillard, Henri', in C.E. O'Neill and J.M. Domínguez (eds), *Diccionario histórico de la Compañia de Jesus: Biográfico-temático*, Madrid: Universidad Ponticia Comillas; Rome: Institutum historicum, 2001, pp. 506–7.

De Montclos, Xavier, 'Bouillard Henri', in Xavier de Montclos (ed.), *Lyon: Le Lyonnais – Le Beaujolais* (Dictionnaire du monde religieux dans la France contemporaine, 6), Paris: Beauchesne, 1994, pp. 74–75.

—— 'Lubac Henri Sonier de', in Xavier de Montclos (ed.), *Lyon: Le Lyonnais – Le Beaujolais* (Dictionnaire du monde religieux dans la France contemporaine, 6), Paris: Beauchesne, 1994, pp. 279–81.

De Munnynck, Mary, 'Notes on Intuition', in *The Thomist* 1 (1939) 143–68.

De Petter, Dominicus-Maria, 'Impliciete intuïtie', in *Tijdschrift voor Philosophie* 1 (1939) 84–105.

Desmazières, Agnès, 'La "nouvelle théologie", prémisse d'une théologie herméneutique? La controverse sur l'analogie de la vérité (1946–1949)', in *Revue thomiste* 104 (2004) 241–72.

De Solages, Bruno, 'Pour l'honneur de la théologie: Les contre-sens du R. P. Garrigou-Lagrange', in *Bulletin de littérature ecclésiastique* 48 (1947) 65–84, repr. in *Bulletin de Littérature ecclésiastique* 99 (1998) 257–72.

De Solages, Bruno and Marie-Joseph Nicolas, 'Autour d'une controverse', in *Bulletin de littérature ecclésiastique* 48 (1947) 3–17.

D'Hulst, Maurice, 'La question biblique', in *Le Correspondant* 50 (1893) 201–51.

Donneaud, Henri, 'Histoire d'une histoire: M.-D. Chenu et "La Théologie comme science au XIIIᵉ siècle"', in *Les Dominicains en Europe* (Mémoire Dominicaine, 9), Paris: Cerf, 1996, pp. 41–50.

Donnelly, Philip J., 'On the Development of Dogma and the Supernatural', in *Theological Studies* 8 (1947) 471–91.

—— 'Theological Opinion on the Development of Dogma', in *Theological Studies* 8 (1947) 668–99.

Doré, Joseph, 'Un itinéraire-témoin: Marie-Dominique Chenu', in P. Colin (ed.), *Les catholiques français et l'héritage de 1789: D'un centenaire à l'autre* (Bibliothèque Beauchesne: Religions, société, politique, 17), Paris: Beauchesne, 1989, pp. 313–39.

—— 'Henri de Lubac (1896–1991): La vie et l'œuvre d'un théologien exemplaire', in *Bulletin de littérature ecclésiastique* 94 (1993) 39–46.

—— 'Henri Bouillard: Un grand théologien jésuite à l'Institut Catholique de Paris', in *Transversalités*, nr. 109, January–March 2009, pp. 141–48.

D'Ouince, René, 'Quelques commentaires de l'encyclique "Humani generis"', in *Études*, Vol. 83, nr. 267, pp. 353–73.

Draguet, René, 'Méthodes théologiques d'hier et d'aujourd'hui', in *Revue catholique des idées et des faits* 15/42 (10 January 1936) 1–7; 15/46 (7 February 1936) 4–7; 15/47 (14 February 1936) 13–17.

—— 'L'évolution des dogmes', in M. Brillant and M. Nédoncelle (eds), *Apologétique: Nos raisons de croire, réponses aux objections*, Paris: Bloud & Gay, 1937, ²1939, ³1948, pp. 1166–92.

—— review [Charlier, *Essai sur le problem théologique*], in *Ephemerides theologicae Lovanienses* 16 (1939) 143–45.

—— 'Pièces de polémique antijulianiste: Le Pacte d'Union de 797 entre les jacobites et les julianistes du patriarcat d'Antioche', in *Le Muséon* 54 (1941) 59–106.

Duclos, Paul, 'Daniélou', in O'Neill and Domínguez (eds), *Diccionario histórico de la Compañia de Jesus: Biográfico-temático*, Madrid: Universidad Ponticia Comillas; Rome: Institutum historicum, 2001, pp. 1044–46.

Dumont, Camille, 'L'enseignement théologique au Collège jésuite de Louvain: Louvain 1838 – Bruxelles 1988', in *Nouvelle revue théologique* 111 (1989) 556–76.

Dupleix, André, '"Pour l'honneur de la théologie": Bruno de Solages le défenseur de Teilhard', in *Bulletin de littérature ecclésiastique* 99 (1998) 167–79.

Eicher, Peter, 'Von den Schwierigkeiten bürgerlicher Theologie mit den katholischen Kirchenstrukturen', in K. Rahner and H. Fries (eds), *Theologie in Freiheit und Verantwortung*, Munich: Kösel, 1981, pp. 96–137, p. 101, reissued in W. Kern (ed.), *Die Theologie und das Lehramt* (Quaestiones Disputatae, 91), Freiburg/Basel/Vienna: Herder, 1982, pp. 116–51.

Féret, Henri-Marie, 'La théologie concrète et historique et son importance pastorale présente', in *Théologie: Le service théologique dans l'Église: Mélanges offerts à Yves Congar pour ses soixante-dix ans*, Paris: Cerf, 1974, pp. 193–247.

—— 'Dans les cheminements de la sagesse de Dieu', in *L'hommage différé au Père Chenu* (Théologies), Paris: Cerf, 1990, pp. 208–38.

Fontaine, Jacques, 'Préface', in J. Fontaine (ed.), *Actualité de Jean Daniélou* (Paris: Cerf), 2006, pp. 7–8.

Forte, Bruno, 'Le prospettive della ricera teologica', in R. Fisichella (ed.), *Il Concilio Vaticano II: Recezione e attualità alla luce del Giubileo*, Milan: San Paolo, 2000, pp. 419–29.

Fouilloux, Étienne, 'Recherche théologique et magistère romain en 1952: Une "affaire" parmi d'autres', in *Recherches de science religieuse* 71 (1983) 269–86.

—— 'Le Saulchoir en process (1937–1942)', in G. Alberigo, *et al.*, *Une école de théologie: le Saulchoir* (Théologies), Paris: Cerf, 1985, pp. 37–59.

—— 'Comment devient-on expert au Vatican II? Le cas du Père Yves Congar', in *Le deuxième concile du Vatican (1959–1965)* (Collection de l'École Française de Rome), Rome: École française de Rome, 1989, pp. 307–31.

—— 'Courants de pensée, piété, apostolat, II.: Le catholicisme', in J.-M. Mayeur (ed.), *Guerres mondiales et totalitarismes (1914–1958)* (Histoire du christianisme des origines à nos jours, 12), Paris: Desclée, 1990, pp. 116–86.

—— 'Dialogue théologique? (1946–1948)', in S.-T. Bonino (ed.), *Saint Thomas au XXe siècle: Colloque du centenaire de la 'Revue thomiste' (1893–1992), Toulouse, 25–28 mars 1993*, Paris: Saint-Paul, 1995, pp. 153–95.

—— 'Autour d'une mise à l'Index', in *Marie-Dominique Chenu, Moyen-Âge et modernité* (Les Cahiers du Centre d'études du Saulchoir, 5), Paris: Cerf, 1997, pp. 25–56.

—— 'Frère Yves, Cardinal Congar, dominicain: Itinéraire d'un théologien', in *Revue des sciences philosophiques et théologiques* 79 (1995) 379–404.

Published in English as 'Friar Yves, Cardinal Congar, Dominican: Itinerary of a Theologian', in *US Catholic Historian* 17 (1999) 63–90.

—— 'Présentation générale', in Yves Congar, *Journal d'un théologien 1946–1956*, Paris: Cerf, 2000, pp. 9–18.

—— 'H. de Lubac au moment de la publication de "Surnaturel"', in *Revue thomiste* 101 (2001) 13–30.

—— 'Le "dialogue théologique" selon Marie-Joseph Nicolas, in *Bulletin de littérature ecclésiastique* 103 (2002) 19–32.

—— 'Une "école de Fourvière"?', in *Gregorianum* 83 (2002) 451–59.

—— '"Nouvelle théologie" et théologie nouvelle (1930–1960)', in B. Pellistrandi (ed.), *L'histoire religieuse en France et Espagne* (Collection de la Casa Velázquez, 87), Madrid: Casa de Velázquez, 2004, pp. 411–25.

—— *'La "nouvelle théologie" française vue d'Espagne (1948–1951)'*, in *Revue d'histoire de l'Église de France* 90 (2004) 279–93.

—— 'Pierre Ganne et l'affaire de Fourvière', in *Pierre Ganne: La liberté d'un prophète* (Cahiers de Meylan), Meylan: Centre Théologique de Meylan-Grenoble, 2005, pp. 29–54.

—— *'La seconde "École de Lyon" (1919–1939)'*, in E. Gabellieri and P. de Cointet (eds), *Blondel et la philosophie française*, Paris: Parole et Silence, 2007, pp. 263–73.

—— 'Itinéraire d'un théologien contrarié (1904–1979)', in M. Fédou (ed.), *Pierre Ganne (1904–1979): La théologie chrétienne pédagogie de la liberté: Colloque janvier 2009, Centre Sèvres – Facultés des Jésuites de Paris* (Théologie, 149), Paris: Médiasèvres, 2009, pp. 13–22.

—— 'Henri Bouillard et Saint Thomas d'Aquin (1941–1951)', in *Recherches de science religieuse* 97 (2009) 173–83.

Gagnebet, Marie-Rosaire, 'La nature de la théologie spéculative', in *Revue thomiste* 44 (1938) 1–39, 213–55, 645–74.

—— 'Un essai sur le problème théologique', in *Revue thomiste* 45 (1939) 108–45.

—— 'Le problème actuel de la théologie et la science aristotélicienne d'après un ouvrage récent', in *Divus Thomas* 43 (1943) 237–70.

—— 'L'amour naturel de Dieu chez saint Thomas et ses contemporains', in *Revue thomiste* 48 (1948) 394–446; 49 (1949) 31–102.

—— 'L'origine de la Jurisdiction collégiale du corps épiscopal au Concile selon Bolegni', in *Divinitas* 5 (1961) 431–93.

—— 'L'œuvre du P. Garrigou-Lagrange: itinéraire intellectuel et spirituel vers Dieu', in *Angelicum* 17 (1965) 7–31.

Garrigou-Lagrange, Réginald, 'La nouvelle théologie où va-t-elle?', in *Angelicum* 23 (1946) 126–45.

—— 'Vérité et immutabilité du dogme', in *Angelicum* 24 (1947) 124–39.

—— 'Les notions consacrées par les conciles', in *Angelicum* 25 (1948) 217–30.

—— 'Nécessité de revenir à la définition traditionnelle de la vérité', in *Angelicum* 25 (1948) 145–98.

Geerlings, Wilhelm, 'Sources chrétiennes', in *Lexikon für Theologie und Kirche*, Vol. 9, ³2000, c. 747.

Geffré, Claude, 'Recent Developments in Fundamental Theology: An Interpretation', in J.B. Metz (ed.), *The Development of Fundamental Theology* (Concilium, 46), New York/ Paramus, NJ: Paulist Press, 1969, pp. 5–27.

—— 'Théologie de l'incarnation et théologie des signes des temps chez le Père Chenu', in *Marie-Dominique Chenu, Moyen-Âge et modernité* (Les Cahiers du Centre d'études du Saulchoir, 5), Paris: Cerf, 1997, pp. 131–53.

Gevers, Lieve, 'Belgium and the Modernist Crisis: Main Trends in the Historiography', in A. Botti and R. Cerrato (eds), *Il modernismo tra cristianità e secolarizzazione: Atti del Convegno Internazionale di Urbino, 1–4 ottobre 1997* (Studi e testi, 2), Urbino: Quattro Venti, 2000, pp. 285–94.

Glé, Jean-Marie, '"Pour l'honneur de la théologie": Bruno de Solages le défenseur de Henri Bouillard', in *Bulletin de litérature ecclésiastique* 99 (1998) 157–65.

Goossens, Werner, 'Notion et méthodes de la théologie: "L'Essai" du P. L. Charlier, in *Collationes Gandavenses* 26 (1939) 115–34.

Guarino, Thomas G., 'Henri Bouillard and the Truth-Status of Dogmatic Statements', in *Science et Esprit* 39 (1987) 331–43.

Guelluy, Robert, 'Les antécédents de l'encyclique "Humani generis" dans les sanctions romaines de 1942: Chenu, Charlier, Draguet', in *Revue d'histoire ecclésiastique* 81 (1986) 421–97.

Guérard des Lauriers, Louis-Bertrand, 'La théologie de Saint Thomas et la grâce actuelle', in *L'Année théologique* 6 (1945) 276–325.

—— 'La théologie historique et le développement de la théologie', in *L'Année théologique* 7 (1946) 15–55.

Guggenheim, Antoine, 'La théologie de l'accomplissement de Jean Daniélou', in *Nouvelle revue théologique* 128 (2006) 240–57, repr.: *La théologie de l'accomplissement*, in J. Fontaine (ed.), *Actualité de Jean Daniélou*, Paris: Cerf, 2006, pp. 165–87.

Guillet, Jacques, 'Lubac, Henri de', in O'Neill and Domínguez (eds), *Diccionario histórico de la Compañia de Jesus: Biográfico-temático*, Madrid: Universidad Ponticia Comillas; Rome: Institutum historicum, 2001, pp. 2430–32.

Harinck, George and Lodewijk Winkeler, 'De Twintigste Eeuw', in Herman J. Selderhuis (ed.), *Handboek Nederlandse Kerkgeschiedenis*, Kampen: Kok, 2006, pp. 723–912.

Harl, Marguerite, 'In memoriam: Jean Daniélou', in *Bulletin des amis du Cardinal Daniélou*, nr. 10, April 1984, pp. 54–62.

Hofmann, Johannes, 'Daniélou', in *Biographisch-Bibliographisches Kirchenlexikon*, Vol. 15, 1999, pp. 453–61.

Jacobs, Jan Y.H.A., 'Dr. Klaas Steur (1905–1985): Geloofsdenker in dienst van verkondiging en toerusting', in *Trajecta* 6 (1997) 53–73.

Jossua, Jean-Pierre, 'Le Saulchoir: une formation théologique replacée dans son histoire', in *Cristianesimo nella storia* 14 (1993) 99–124.

—— 'In Hope of Unity', in Flynn (ed.), *Yves Congar: Theologian of the Church* (Louvain Theological Pastoral Monographs, 32), Louvain/Paris/Dudley, MA: Peeters, 2005, pp. 167–81.

'Judéo-christianisme: Recherches historiques et théologiques offertes en hommage au Cardinal Jean Daniélou', in *Recherches de science religieuse* 60 (1972) 5–323.

Kelly, James J., 'Modernism: A Unique Perspective: Friedrich von Hügel', in *The Downside Review* 122 (2004) 94–112.

Kenis, Leo and Jürgen Mettepenningen, 'Inleiding', in Schoonenberg, *Theologie als geloofsvertolking: Het proefschrift van 1948* (Documenta Libraria, 36), ed. by L. Kenis and J. Mettepenningen, Louvain: Maurits Sabbebibliotheek/ Faculteit Godgeleerdheid/Peeters, 2008, pp. 7*–22*.

Kerr, Fergus, 'Yves Congar and Thomism', in Flynn (ed.), *Yves Congar: Theologian of the Church* (Louvain Theological Pastoral Monographs, 32), Louvain/Paris/Dudley, MA: Peeters, 2005, pp. 67–97.

Klausnitzer, Wolfgang, 'Döllingers Theologierede vom 28. September 1863 in ihrem theologiegeschichtlichen Kontext', in G. Denzler and E.L. Grasmück (eds), *Geschichtlichkeit und Glaube: Zum 100. Todestag Johann Joseph Ignaz von Döllingers (1799–1890)*, Munchen: Wewel, 1990, pp. 417–45.

Komonchak, Joseph A., 'Theology at Mid-Century: The Example of Henri de Lubac', in *Theological Studies* 51 (1990) 579–602.

Koster, Mannus D., review [Charlier, *Essai sur le problème théologique*], in *Theologische Revue* 38 (1939) 41–48.

Laberthonnière, Lucien, 'Dogme et théologie', in *Annales de philosophie chrétienne* 69 (1908) 479–521.

Labourdette, Marie-Michel, 'La théologie, intelligence de la foi', in *Revue thomiste* 46 (1946) 5–44.

—— 'La théologie et ses sources', in *Revue thomiste* 46 (1946) 353–71.

—— 'Fermes propos', in *Revue thomiste* 47 (1947) 5–19.

Labourdette, Marie-Michel and Marie-Joseph Nicolas, 'L'analogie de la vérité et l'unité de la science théologique', in *Revue thomiste* 47 (1947) 417–66.

—— 'Autour du "Dialogue théologique"', in *Revue thomiste* 47 (1947) 577–85.

Le Blond, Jean-Marie, 'L'analogie de la vérité: Réflexion d'un philosophe sur une controverse théologique', in *Recherches de science religieuse* 34 (1947) 129–41.

Le Guillou, Marie-Joseph, 'P. Yves M.-J. Congar O.P.', in H. Vorgrimler and R. Vander Gucht (eds), *Bilanz der Theologie im 20. Jahrhundert: Bahnbrechende Theologen*, Freiburg/Basel/Vienna: Herder, 1970, pp. 99–199.

Lehmann, Karl, 'Karl Rahner', in H. Vorgrimler and R. Vander Gucht (eds), *Bilanz der Theologie im 20. Jahrhundert: Bahnbrechende Theologen*, Freiburg/Basel/Vienna: Herder, 1970, pp. 143–81.

Lobato, Abelardo, 'León XIII y el Neotomismo', in Á.G. García and J.B. Barquilla (eds), *León XIII y su tiempo* (Bibliotheca Salmanticensis: Estudios, 264), Salamanca: Universidad Pontificia, 2004, pp. 397–417.

Malanowski, Gregory E., 'Émile Mersch, S.J. (1890–1940): Un christocentrisme unifié', in *Nouvelle revue théologique* 112 (1990) 44–66.

Melloni, Alberto, 'The System and the Truth in the Diaries of Yves Congar', in Flynn (ed.), *Yves Congar: Theologian of the Church* (Louvain Theological Pastoral Monographs, 32), Louvain/Paris/Dudley, MA: Peeters, 2005, pp. 278–302.

Mettepenningen, Jürgen, 'Malheur devenu bénédiction: Un siècle de modernisme', in *Revue d'histoire ecclésiastique* 101 (2006) 1039–70.

—— review [Laplanche, *La crise de l'origine*], in *Revue d'histoire ecclésiastique* 101 (2006) 1294–302.

—— 'Truth as Issue in a Second Modernist Crisis? The Clash between Recontextualization and Retrocontextualization in the French-Speaking Polemic of 1946–47', in M. Lamberigts, L. Boeve and T. Merrigan (eds),

Theology and the Quest for Truth: Historical- and Systematic-Theological Studies (Bibliotheca ephemeridum theologicarum Lovaniensium, 202), Louvain: Peeters, 2006, pp. 119–41.

—— 'L'Essai de Louis Charlier (1938): Une contribution à la nouvelle théologie', in *Revue théologique de Louvain* 39 (2008) 211–32.

—— Edward Schillebeeckx: Herodero y promotor de la "nouvelle théologie"', in *Mayeuticá* 78 (2008) 285–302.

—— 'Schoonenberg', in *Biographisch-Bibliographisches Kirchenlexikon* 30 (2009) 1297–1300.

—— 'De "nouvelle théologie": Een scharniergeneratie van theologen tussen modernisme en Vaticanum II', in *Collationes* 39 (2009) 183–206.

Mettepenningen, Jürgen and Karim Schelkens, '"Quod immutabile est, nemo turbet et moveat". Les rapports entre H. de Lubac et le P. Général J.-B. Janssens dans les années 1946–1948: À propos de documents inédits', in *Cristianesimo nella storia* 29 (2008) 139–72.

Michiels, Robrecht, 'Het nieuwe christologische dossier', in *Collationes* 6 (1976) 480–512, esp. p. 485.

Milbank, John, 'Henri de Lubac', in David F. Ford and R. Muers (eds), *The Modern Theologians: An Introduction to Christian Theology Since 1918*, Malden, MA/Oxford/Victoria: Blackwell, ³2005, pp. 76–91.

Mühlen, Heribert, 'Gnadenlehre', in H. Vorgrimler and R. Vander Gucht (eds), *Bilanz der Theologie im 20. Jahrhundert: Perspektiven, Strömungen, Motive in der christlichen und nichtchristlichen Welt*, Vol. 3, Freiburg/Basel/Vienna: Herder, 1970, pp. 148–92.

Müller, Wolfgang W., 'Was kann an der Theologie neu sein? Der Beitrag der Dominikaner zur "nouvelle théologie"', in *Zeitschrift für Kirchengeschichte* 110 (1999) 86–104.

Murphy, Francesca A., 'Correspondance entre É. Gilson et M.-D. Chenu: Un choix de lettres (1923–1969)', in *Revue thomiste* 112 (2005) 25–87.

Murray, Paul D., 'Roman Catholic Theology after Vatican II', in D.F. Ford and R. Muers (eds), *The Modern Theologians: An Introduction to Christian Theology Since 1918*, Malden, MA/Oxford/Victoria: Blackwell, 2005, pp. 265–86.

Neufeld, Karl-Heinz, 'Fundamentaltheologie in gewandelter Welt: H. Bouillards theologischer Beitrag: Zur Vollendung seines 70. Lebensjahres', in *Zeitschrift für katholische Theologie* 100 (1978) 417–40.

—— 'Le paysage théologique des années 1930–1960 et deux itinéraires', in H.-J. Gagey and V. Holzer (eds), *Balthasar, Rahner: Deux pensées en contraste* (Theologia, 218), Paris: Bayard, 2005, pp. 31–46.

—— 'Daniélou', in *Lexikon für Theologie und Kirche*, Vol. 3, ³2006, pp. 16–17.

Nichols, Aidan, 'Thomism and the Nouvelle Théologie', in *The Thomist* 64 (2000) 1–19.

'La nouvelle théologie', in *Katholiek Archief* 2 (1947–48) 941–44.

O'Sullivan, Noel, 'Henri de Lubac's "Surnaturel": An Emerging Christology', in *Irish Theological Quarterly* 72 (2007) 3–31.

Parente, Pietro, 'Nuove tendenze teologiche', in *L'Osservatore Romano*, 9–10 February 1942, p. 1.

Petit, Jean-Claude, 'La compréhension de la théologie dans la théologie française

au XXe siècle: La hantise du savoir et de l'objectivité: l'exemple d'Ambroise Gardeil', in *Laval théologique et philosophique* 45 (1989) 379–91.
—— 'La compréhension de la théologie dans la théologie française au XXe siècle: Vers une nouvelle conscience historique: G. Rabeau, M.-D. Chenu, L. Charlier', in *Laval théologique et philosophique* 47 (1991) 215–29.
—— 'La compréhension de la théologie dans la théologie française au XXe siècle: Pour une théologie qui réponde à nos nécessités: la nouvelle théologie', in *Laval théologique et philosophique* 48 (1992) 415–31.
Pinggéra, Karl, 'Dadischo Qatraya', in *Biographisches-Bibliographisches Kirchenlexikon* 23 (2004) 249–52.
Poulat, Émile, 'Préface', in L. Courtois, *et al.* (eds), *Écrire l'histoire du catholicisme des 19ᵉ et 20ᵉ siècles: Bilan, tendances récentes et perspectives (1975–2005): Hommage au professeur Roger Aubert à l'occasion de ses 90 ans*, Louvain-la-Neuve: ARCA, 2005, pp. 11–16.
Quisinsky, Michael, 'Henri-Marie Féret OP (1904–1992): Auf dem Weg zu einer "konkreten und geschichtlichen Theologie"', in T. Eggensperger and U. Engel (eds), *'Mutig in die Zukunft'. Dominikanische Beiträge zum Vaticanum II* (Dominikanische Quellen und Zeugnisse, 10), Leipzig: St. Benno, 2007, pp. 65–103.
Raffelt, Albert, 'Nouvelle théologie', in *Lexikon für Theologie und Kirche* 7 (1998, ³2006) 935–37.
Rahner, Hugo, 'Wege zu einer "neuen" Theologie?', in *Orientierung* 11 (1947) 213–17.
Rahner, Karl, 'Chalkedon: Ende oder Anfang?', in A. Grillmeyer and H. Bacht (eds), *Das Konzil von Chalkedon: Geschichte und Gegenwart*, Vol. 3: *Chalkedon heute*, Wurzburg: Echter Verlag, 1954, pp. 3–49.
Reher, Margaret M., 'Americanism and Modernism: Continuity or Discontinuity?', in *US Catholic Historian* 1 (1981) 87–103.
Rikhof, Herwi, 'Uit oud en nieuw de schatten: P. Schoonenberg', in J. Beumer (ed.), *Zo de ouden zongen . . . Leraar en leerling zijn in de theologie-beoefening (tussen 1945 en 2000)*, Baarn: Ten Have, 1996, pp. 199–220.
—— 'Schoonenberg, Piet', in *Christelijke Encyclopedie*, ed. G. Harinck, 3 vols, Kampen: Kok, 2005, pp. 1612–13.
Rolland, Claude, 'Le Père Chenu, théologien au Concile', in *L'hommage différé au Père Chenu* (Théologies), Paris: Cerf, 1990, pp. 249–56.
Romero, Avelino Esteban, 'Nota bibliográfica sobre la llamada "Teología Nueva"', in *Revista Española de teología* 9 (1949) 303–18, 527–46.
Rondeau, Marie-Josèphe, 'Le Père de Lubac et le Père Daniélou', in *Bulletin des amis du Cardinal Daniélou*, nr. 19, October 1993, pp. 49–65.
—— 'Quatre lettres du Père de Lubac au Père d'Ouince 1948–1950', in *Bulletin des amis du Cardinal Daniélou*, nr. 26–27, 2000–1, pp. 53–96.
Rondet, Henri, 'Nouvelle théologie', in *Sacramentum Mundi* 3 (1969) 816–20.
Rouquette, Robert, 'L'encyclique "Humani generis"', in *Études*, Vol. 83, nr. 267, October 1950, pp. 108–16.
Rousselot, Pierre, 'Les yeux de la foi', in *Recherches de science religieuse* 1 (1910) 241–59, 444–75. Published in English as *The Eyes of Faith*, New York: Fordham University Press, 1990.

Sauser, Ekkart, 'Lubac, Henri Marie Joseph Sonnier de', in *Biographisch-Bibliographisches Kirchenlexikon* 5 (1993) 282–86.

Schaeffler, 'Modernismus', in *Historisches Wörterbuch der Philosophie* 6 (1984) 64.

Scheffczyk, Leo, 'Grundzüge der Entwicklung der Theologie zwischen dem Ersten Weltkrieg und dem Zweiten Vatikanischen Konzil', in *Die Weltkirche im 20. Jahrhundert* (Handbuch der Kirchengeschichte, 7), Fribourg/Basel/Vienna: Herder, pp. 263–301.

Schillebeeckx, Henricus, 'Dogma-ontwikkeling: A. Historisch overzicht van het vraagstuk, B. Perspectieven op een synthese', in *Theologisch Woordenboek*, Roermond/Maaseik: Romen & Zonen, 1952, c. 1087–106.

—— 'Nouvelle théologie', in *Theologisch Woordenboek*, Roermond/Maaseik: Romen & Zonen, 1954, c. 3519–20.

—— 'Geschiedenis', in *Theologisch Woordenboek*, Roermond/Maaseik: Romen & Zonen, 1957, c. 1838–40.

—— '"Humani generis"', in *Theologisch Woordenboek*, Roermond/Maaseik: Romen & Zonen, 1957, c. 2300–2

—— 'Theologie', in *Theologisch Woordenboek*, Roermond/Maaseik: Romen & Zonen, 1958, c. 4485–542.

—— '"Nieuwe theologie"?', in *Kultuurleven* 26 (1959) 122–25.

—— 'Het waarheidsbegrip en aanverwante problemen', in *Katholiek Archief* 17 (1962) 1169–80. Published in English as *The Concept of Truth and Theological Renewal*, New York: Sheed and Ward, 1968, pp. 5–29.

—— 'In memoriam M.-D. Chenu (1895–1990)', in *Tijdschrift voor Theologie* 30 (1990) 184–85.

—— 'In memoriam Yves Congar, 1904–1995', in *Tijdschrift voor Theologie* 35 (1995) 271–73.

Schlagenhaufen, Florian, review [Charlier, *Essai sur le problème théologique*], in *Zeitschrift für katholische Theologie* 63 (1939) 366–71.

Schoonenberg, Piet, 'Een Theoloog van Christus' Mystiek Lichaam: Emile Mersch S.J. en zijn laatste boek', in *Katholiek Cultureel Tijdschrift* 2 (1946, part 1) 93–96.

—— 'Theologie in zelfbezinning', in *Annalen van het Thijmgenootschap* 44 (1956) 225–36.

—— 'De menswording', in *Verbum* 27 (1960) 453–66.

—— 'Der Mensch in der Sünde', in J. Feiner and M. Löhrer (eds), *Mysterium Salutis: Grundriß heilsgeschichtlicher Dogmatik*, Vol. 2: *Die Heilsgeschichte vor Christus*, Einsiedeln/Zurich/Cologne: Benziger, 1967, pp. 845–941.

—— 'Roeping, vrijheid en onvrijheid van de theoloog', in *Bijdragen* 43 (1982) 2–29. Published in English as 'The Theologian's Calling, Freedom and Constraint', in *Journal of Ecumenical Studies* 19 (1982) 92–118.

Schreiter, Robert, 'Edward Schillebeeckx: An Orientation to His Thought', in Schillebeeckx, *The Schillebeeckx Reader*, ed. by Robert Schreiter, New York: Crossroad, 1984, pp. 1–24.

Schüssler Fiorenza, Francis, 'The New Theology and Transcendental Thomism', in J.C. Livingston and F. Schüssler Fiorenza (eds), *Modern Christian Thought: The Twentieth Century*, Minneapolis, MN: Fortress, 2006, pp. 197–232.

Sesboüé, Bernard, 'Le surnaturel chez Henri de Lubac: Un conflit autour d'une théologie', in *Recherches de science religieuse* 80 (1992) 373–408.

——— 'Le drame de la théologie au XXe siècle: A propos du "Journal d'un théologien (1946–1956)" du P. Yves Congar', in *Recherches de science religieuse* 89 (2001) 271–87.

——— 'Surnaturel et "Surnaturel"', in *Recherches de science religieuse* 90 (2002) 179–86.

——— 'La genèse d'une œuvre ou comment sortir de la "néoscolastique"?', in H.-J. Gagey and V. Holzer (eds), *Balthasar, Rahner: Deux pensées en contraste* (Theologia, 218), Paris: Bayard, 2005, pp. 47–67.

Sheehan, Thomas, 'Pierre Rousselot and the Dynamism of Human Spirit', in *Gregorianum* 66 (1985) 241–67.

Simonin, Henri-Dominique, 'De la nécessité de certaines conclusions théologiques', in *Angelicum* 16 (1939) 72–83.

Stegmüller, Franz, review [Chenu, *Une école de théologie*], in *Theologische Revue* 38 (1939) 48–51.

Suhard, Emmanuel, 'Essor ou déclin de l'Église', in *La semaine religieuse de Paris*, 15 and 22 March 1947, repr.: *Essor ou déclin de l'Église: Lettre pastorale, Carême de l'an de grâce 1947* (Livre de vie, 32), Paris: Lahure, 1962.

Talar, Charles J.T., 'The French Connection: The Church's "Eldest Daughter" and the Condemnation of Modernism', in *US Catholic Historian* 25 (2007) 55–69.

'La théologie et ses sources: Réponse', in *Recherches de science religieuse* 33 (1946) 385–401.

Trethowan, Illtyd, review [De Lubac, *Surnaturel*], in *The Downside Review* 65 (1947) 70–72.

Turbanti, Giovanni, 'Il ruolo del P. D. Chenu nell'elaborazione della constituzione "Gaudium et spes"', in *Marie-Dominique Chenu, Moyen-Âge et modernité* (Les Cahiers du Centre d'études du Saulchoir, 5), Paris: Cerf, 1997, pp. 173–212.

Van de Walle, Ambroos Remi, 'Theologie over de werkelijkheid: Een betekenis van het werk van Edward Schillebeeckx', in *Tijdschrift voor Theologie* 14 (1974) 463–90.

Van Rijen, Aloïs, 'Een nieuwe stroming in de Theologie', in *Nederlandse Katholieke Stemmen* 44 (1948) 177–88.

——— '"Nieuwe" en "katholiek-oecumenische" theologie', in *Studia Catholica* 24 (1949) 209–37.

Voderholzer, Rudolf, Die Bedeutung der sogenannten "Nouvelle Théologie" (insbesondere Henri de Lubacs) für die Theologie Hans Urs von Balthasars', in Kasper (ed.), *Logik der Liebe und Herrlichkeit Gottes: Hans Urs von Balthasar im Gespräch*, Ostfildern: Matthias Grünewald, 2006, pp. 204–28.

Vorgrimler, Herbert, 'Henri de Lubac', in H. Vorgrimler and R. Vander Gucht (eds), *Bilanz der Theologie im 20. Jahrhundert: Bahnbrechende Theologen*, Freiburg/Basel/Vienna: Herder, 1970, pp. 199–214.

Weiss, Otto, 'Alfred Firmin Loisy (1857–1940)', in *Theologische Revue* 103 (2007) 17–28.

Williams, A.N., 'The Future of the Past: The Contemporary Significance of the Nouvelle Théologie', in *International Journal of Systematic Theology* 7 (2005) 347–61.

Winkeler, Lodewijk, 'Het onderwijs op Warmond, 1799–1967', in *Trajecta* 9 (2000) 134–63.

Winling, Raymond, 'Nouvelle Théologie', in *Theologische Realenzyklopädie* 24 (1994) 668–75.

Wynants, Paul and Fernand Vanneste, 'Jeunesse ouvrière chrétienne', in *Dictionnaire de l'histoire et de géographie ecclésiastique* 27 (2000) 1254–80.

Zapelena, Timoteo, 'Problema theologicum', in *Gregorianum* 24 (1943) 23–47, 287–326; 25 (1944) 38–73, 247–82.

Zauner, Wilhelm, 'Schoonenberg, Piet', in *Lexikon für Theologie und Kirche* 9 (2000, 2006) 214.

Zimara, Coelestin, 'Theologie: Eine Denkaufgabe', in *Divus Thomas* 18 (1940) 89–112.

Index

Page numbers in **bold** refer to chapters or paragraphs dedicated to the person/subject.